the delicious. cookbook

the delicious.
cookbook

EDITOR **Matthew Drennan**

LONDON, NEW YORK,
MUNICH, MELBOURNE, DELHI

Editor	Daniel Mills
Art Editor	Saskia Janssen
Executive Managing Editor	Adèle Hayward
Managing Art Editor	Kat Mead
Senior Production Editor	Jennifer Murray
Senior Production Controller	Man Fai Lau
Creative Technical Support	Sonia Charbonnier
Art Director	Peter Luff
Publisher	Stephanie Jackson

Produced for Dorling Kindersley by

cobaltid

The Stables, Wood Farm, Deopham Road,
Attleborough, Norfolk NR17 1AJ
www.cobaltid.co.uk

Editors

Marek Walisiewicz, Kati Dye, Louise Abbott,
Robin Sampson, Sarah Tomley

Art Editors

Paul Reid, Darren Bland,
Claire Dale, Lloyd Tilbury

First published in Great Britain in 2009
by Dorling Kindersley Limited
80 Strand, London WC2R 0RL

Penguin Group (UK)

2 4 6 8 10 9 7 5 3 1

A CIP catalogue record for this book
is available from the British Library

ISBN 978-1-4053-5135-5

Colour reproduction by Colourscan, Singapore
Printed and bound in Germany by Mohn Media

Discover more at www.dk.com

contents

foreword

Welcome to our first big family cookery book, which features the very best of **delicious.** When we launched the magazine in 2003, our aim was to produce a glorious celebration of food, offering readers **brilliant but effortless** recipes. We create dishes for people who are passionate about the food they cook and eat, and about produce in season and the provenance of their ingredients. Every month our team of talented food writers produces food designed to fit into our busy modern lives with a **simple, relaxed** approach to cooking, emphasising fresh seasonal ingredients, simple-as-can-be preparation and, of course, great-tasting results.

This book is a wonderful reflection of the magazine, with **recipes for all occasions,** from simple light bites to clever solutions for everyday cooking, meals the kids will love and brilliant ideas for entertaining, whether you're catering for a couple or a crowd. We've included all the old favourites and family classics, but we

also pride ourselves on never being predictable or mundane. As a result, every chapter contains exciting original ideas and clever new takes on traditional favourites.

In the **soup** section, for example – a subject that could just round up all the usual suspects – you will find innovative recipes such as Summer Spanish-style Soup, Potato, Leek and Stilton Soup and Sweet Potato, Apple and Ginger Soup. Boring green **salads**? Not here. Check out Fresh Guacamole Salad, Italian Bean Salad and Seafood with Lime and Chilli Salad for some fantastic, fresh ideas that you may never have tried before.

When it comes to the end of the working day and there's a family to be fed or friends to be **entertained**, we all want the same thing: easy inspiration, and this book offers that in spades. Of course, you'll find all the **timeless classics** that are the backbone of every good kitchen repertoire, from Lasagne al Forno to Moussaka and Meatloaf. But we also offer a brilliant choice

of **everyday real food** solutions for your weekly menu that I hope that you'll agree are something special, whether it's the merest twist on **familiar recipes**, such as Meatballs with Tomato Pesto Tagliatelle or a Salmon and Potato Curry, or **brand new ideas** like Hot Poached Chicken and Coronation Sauce or Baked Sausages with Leeks, Apples and Cider. This clever chapter is also in touch with what's happening in kitchens today, with sections dedicated to **frugal food,** fast cooking and dishes for the freezer.

Our chapter on **occasion cooking** takes the hassle out of entertaining. Cooking for a crowd, whether it's a family Sunday lunch, a special dinner party for friends or a child's birthday party, is often a daunting prospect, but the recipes in this chapter are designed to **impress with minimal stress**. Whatever the occasion, you'll find down-to-earth suggestions, and great ideas for something a little bit different when you are in the mood to show off.

Home baking is back with a bang, and we have embraced this revival with a chapter dedicated to making bread, cakes and buns. And our **desserts** come in all shapes and sizes, from sweet and simple Chocolate Sponge Pudding and Marmalade Bread-and-Butter Pudding, to luxuriously indulgent concoctions such as White Chocolate Raspberry Trifle, Coffee and Rum Tiramisu, and Apple Crumble Ice Cream.

It's a joy for us to see these **delicious.** recipes, all rigorously tested in our very own kitchen, culminate in this beautiful cookery book. I hope it will become an indispensable kitchen resource for you and your family.

Enjoy!

Matthew Drennan

1

light
bites

- soups
- salads
- snacks

soups

Summery Spanish-style soup
SERVES 4 TAKES **30 MINUTES TO MAKE**

1 tbsp olive oil
1 medium onion, chopped
2 medium carrots, sliced
400g can chopped tomatoes
1.5 litres hot fresh vegetable stock
410g can mixed pulses, drained and rinsed
75g small soup pasta shapes
2 savoy cabbage leaves, shredded
Handful of flatleaf parsley, roughly chopped
Parmesan, freshly grated, to serve

1 Pour the oil into a large saucepan over a medium heat, then add the onion and carrot. Cook, stirring, for 5 minutes. Add the tomatoes, stock and pulses. Bring to the boil, reduce the heat and simmer for 5 minutes.
2 Stir in the pasta and simmer for another 5 minutes. Add the cabbage, season and cook for a further 2–3 minutes until the pasta is al dente.
3 Stir in the parsley and divide between 4 warmed bowls. Serve with Parmesan and crusty bread.

Small pasta shapes are perfect for this soup – if you can't find them, break up some spaghetti.

Fennel soup with winter greens and bacon
SERVES 4 TAKES **1 HOUR 15 MINUTES TO MAKE**

100g butter
2 large leeks, sliced and washed thoroughly
1 tsp fennel seeds, crushed
3 fennel bulbs, roughly chopped
900g potatoes, roughly chopped
1.2 litres hot fresh chicken stock
150ml whipping cream

For the winter greens and bacon
1 small or $\frac{1}{2}$ large savoy cabbage, or other winter greens
50g butter
175g pancetta or smoked streaky bacon, diced
Handful of thyme leaves, roughly chopped

1 Melt the butter in a large saucepan over a medium–low heat. Add the leeks and cook gently for 10 minutes, stirring occasionally, until very soft. Add the fennel seeds and cook for 2–3 minutes, then stir in the fennel and potatoes.
2 Cover the vegetables with a sheet of wet baking paper and put a lid on the pan. Cook gently for 10–12 minutes. Remove and discard the paper.
3 Pour in the stock, bring to the boil, cover and simmer for 30 minutes, until very tender. Leave to cool slightly, then pour half into a blender and whizz until smooth. Press it through a sieve then pour it back into the unblended soup in the pan.
4 While the soup cooks, discard the tough outer leaves from the cabbage and roughly tear the other leaves, discarding any hard stalks. Blanch them in rapidly boiling salted water for 2–3 minutes. Refresh under cold running water and drain. Melt the butter in a large frying pan over a medium heat. Add the pancetta or bacon and cook for 3–4 minutes, until golden. Add the cabbage and thyme and stir-fry for about 5 minutes, until tender. Season well.
5 Stir the cream into the soup and season to taste. Gently reheat, making sure it doesn't boil or it will curdle.
6 Ladle into 4 deep warmed bowls and spoon the winter greens and bacon into each.

Roasted vegetable soup with walnut and sage pesto

SERVES 6 TAKES **1 HOUR 10 MINUTES TO MAKE**

750g mixed butternut squash,
  parsnips and carrots
1 medium onion, cut into thin wedges
2 tbsp extra-virgin olive oil

For the walnut and sage pesto
2 walnut halves
1 tbsp pine nuts
1 small garlic clove, crushed
12 large sage leaves
15g flatleaf parsley leaves
2 tbsp extra-virgin olive oil
1 tbsp fresh white breadcrumbs
2 tbsp Parmesan, finely grated

1 Preheat the oven to 200°C/fan 180°C/gas 6.
Prepare the squash, parsnips and carrots by
peeling and cutting them into 2cm chunks.
Put them into a large, non-stick roasting tin
with the onion and olive oil, sprinkle with freshly
ground black pepper, toss well so that all the
vegetables are coated in oil, then roast in
the hot oven for 45 minutes.
2 Meanwhile, make the pesto. Put the nuts,
garlic, sage and parsley into a mini food
processor and blend until finely chopped. Scrape
into a bowl with a spatula and stir in the oil,
3 tbsp hot water, the breadcrumbs and
Parmesan until you have an evenly blended
paste. Cover and set aside.
3 Take the vegetables from the oven and tip them
into a large saucepan. Add 1.5 litres cold water
and bring to a simmer over a medium heat.
Cover and cook gently for 20 minutes until all
the flavours are amalgamated.
4 Leave the soup to cool slightly then whizz in
a food processor (you may need to do this in
2 batches) or with a stick blender, until fairly
smooth and a gorgeous warm colour.
5 Return to the pan and reheat gently over a low
heat. Season to taste, ladle into warmed bowls,
swirl a little pesto into each with a spoon and
serve immediately.

Fennel soup with winter
greens and bacon

Roasted vegetable
soup with walnut
and sage pesto

11

Roasted tomato soup
SERVES 4 TAKES **1 HOUR TO MAKE**

1kg ripe tomatoes, quartered
250g red onions, cut into thick wedges
4 garlic cloves
3 rosemary sprigs
2 red peppers, quartered and deseeded
4 tbsp olive oil
300ml hot fresh vegetable stock
1 tbsp red wine vinegar
2 dashes of Tabasco
4 dashes of Worcestershire sauce
Sprigs of parsley, to garnish

1 Preheat the oven to 220°C/fan 200°C/gas 7.
Put the tomatoes, onions, garlic, rosemary and
peppers into a large roasting tin. Drizzle with the
oil, tossing the vegetables so all are coated and
roast in the hot oven for 45 minutes, until tender
and beginning to char at the edges. Watch them
carefully so they don't burn.
2 Briefly blend the vegetables in a food processor,
aiming for a chunky texture.You may need to do
this in 2 batches.
3 Tip into a large saucepan, then add the stock,
vinegar and the Tabasco and Worcestershire
sauces. Stir until well blended and heat gently.
4 Divide among 4 warmed bowls, grind over some
black pepper and add a few sprigs of parsley.
Serve with slices of crusty French bread.

Potato, leek and Stilton soup
SERVES 4–6 TAKES **40 MINUTES TO MAKE**

25g butter
2 medium leeks (about 400g), thinly sliced
  and washed thoroughly
250g floury potatoes, such as maris piper
1.2 litres hot fresh vegetable stock
2 bay leaves
100ml single cream
125g Stilton, rind removed, crumbled,
  plus extra to serve

1 Melt the butter in a large saucepan over a
medium–low heat. Add the leeks and cook for
5 minutes, stirring now and then, until softened
but not browned.
2 Cut the potatoes into thick slices and add to
the pan with the stock and bay leaves. Season to
taste with salt and freshly ground white pepper.
3 Cover with a lid, bring to the boil, then reduce
the heat and simmer for 15 minutes or until the
potatoes are very soft. Remove from the heat.
4 Stir in the cream and Stilton, then pick out and
discard the bay leaves. Working quickly so the
soup does not lose too much of its heat, blitz with
a stick blender (or whizz in 2 batches in a food
processor), until smooth. Taste and adjust the
seasoning; you may not need any more salt.
5 Divide between warmed soup bowls, sprinkle
with Stilton and grind over black pepper to serve.

PEELING GARLIC

1. Put each garlic clove on a
cutting board. Place the flat
blade of a large, heavy knife
on top of the clove and pound
it with the palm of your hand.

2. Lift the skin away from the
garlic and discard it. Use a
small sharp knife to cut away
the ends of each clove, so the
garlic is ready for chopping.

Rich, crumbly
Stilton can turn
the humblest soup
into something
really special.

Potato, leek and
Stilton soup

Sweet potato, apple and ginger soup
SERVES 4 TAKES **40 MINUTES TO MAKE**

3 tbsp olive oil or butter
1 large onion, chopped
3 tsp finely chopped fresh ginger
450g sweet potato, peeled and cut into chunks
1 large bramley apple, peeled, cored and chopped
900ml hot fresh vegetable stock, plus a little extra as necessary
Small bunch of coriander, chopped, plus 4 sprigs to garnish
Lemon juice, to taste
2 pinches of caster sugar
1 large dessert apple, cored and chopped, to garnish
4 tbsp yogurt or soured cream

1 Put 2 tbsp of the oil or butter in a medium saucepan, place over a low heat and cook the onion very gently, covered, for 5 minutes. Add 2 tsp of the ginger and the sweet potato, cover again and continue to cook for 6–8 minutes. (The vegetables should gently sweat rather than fry.) Add the chopped apple, stir, and cook for another 2–3 minutes. Pour in the stock, add the chopped coriander and season. Bring to a simmer and cook, half-covered, for 15–20 minutes or until the sweet potato and apple are tender.
2 Blend with a stick blender – or whizz in 2 batches in a food processor – to form a smooth soup, thinning out with a little more stock if you like. Add some lemon juice and sugar to taste, depending on how sweet or tart the apple is. Reheat gently, but do not boil.
3 Fry the dessert apple and remaining ginger gently in a small pan in the remaining oil or butter until golden brown and just tender. Add a good pinch of sugar and cook for 1–2 minutes more, stirring, until all is well blended.
4 Ladle the soup into 4 warmed bowls. Drizzle a spoonful of yogurt or soured cream over each, then place a spoonful of the fried apple and a sprig of coriander at the centre of the bowls. Grind over some black pepper and serve.

Spicy spinach dhal with yogurt
SERVES 4 TAKES **30 MINUTES TO MAKE**

225g dried red lentils
3 tbsp sunflower oil
1 large onion, finely chopped
2 garlic cloves, crushed
2.5cm piece fresh ginger, grated
1 medium-hot red chilli, deseeded and chopped, plus extra to garnish (optional)
1 medium-hot green chilli, deseeded and chopped
1 tsp turmeric
1 tsp ground cumin
1 tsp ground coriander
Good pinch of cayenne pepper
300ml hot fresh vegetable stock
200g can chopped tomatoes
100ml coconut cream
100g baby leaf spinach
20g coriander leaves
4 tbsp natural yogurt, to serve

1 Put the lentils into a medium saucepan and cover with 900ml of cold water. Bring to the boil, skimming off any scum as it rises to the surface, and leave to simmer for 10 minutes, until the lentils are tender and just falling apart. Remove from the heat, cover, and set aside.
2 Meanwhile, heat the oil in a large saucepan, add the onion and fry gently for 15 minutes until browned. Reduce the heat, add the garlic, ginger and chillies and fry for 2 minutes.

Creamy coconut and fresh coriander make a delicious contrast to the fiery Indian spices.

3 Stir in the spices, season well with black pepper and cook for a further 2 minutes. Add the stock, the lentils and their liquid and the tomatoes then season with salt to taste. Cover and simmer for just 5 minutes.

4 Remove from the heat, cool slightly, then add the coconut cream. Blend, either in 2 batches in a food processor or using a stick blender, until the soup is almost smooth.

5 Reheat the soup gently over a moderate heat. Bring to a simmer, cook for 5 minutes, then add the spinach and most of the coriander and cook for 1 minute. Using a stick blender, blend briefly until the spinach is no more t han roughly chopped.

6 Ladle the soup into 4 warmed bowls and garnish each with a spoonful of yogurt, the remaining coriander leaves, and some finely chopped red chilli, if you like.

Winter minestrone
SERVES 8 TAKES **1 HOUR TO MAKE**

....

2 tbsp olive oil
1 small onion, finely chopped
1 leek, halved lengthways, washed and chopped
1 celery stick, halved lengthways and sliced
2 garlic cloves, finely chopped
400g piece beef brisket, diced
1 large carrot, diced
2 medium potatoes, diced
Sprig of rosemary
1 bay leaf
600ml hot fresh vegetable stock
400g can chopped tomatoes
100g savoy cabbage or Brussels sprouts, finely shredded
400g can cannellini or haricot beans, drained
100g small pasta shells
8 tbsp Parmesan or Grana Padano cheese, finely grated, to serve

....

1 Heat the oil in a large saucepan over a medium heat. Add the onion, leek, celery and garlic and cook for a few minutes, until softened. Add the brisket, carrot, potatoes and herbs.

2 Pour in the stock and tomatoes, and add 750ml cold water, or just enough to cover the meat and vegetables. Bring to a simmer, reduce the heat and cook for 45 minutes. Stir in the cabbage or sprouts, beans and pasta and simmer for a further 5 minutes.

3 If you want to freeze this soup (see below), allow it to cool at this point. (The pasta will be slightly undercooked but don't worry – it will be perfect after reheating.) Otherwise cook for a further 2 minutes until the pasta is ready.

4 Serve with the grated Parmesan or Grana Padano and griddled ciabatta.

delicious.**tip**

FREEZING SOUP FOR LATER
Soups freeze very well, so it is always worth making a large batch. To freeze, leave your soup to cool completely, transfer to a rigid plastic container, then freeze for up to 3 months. Defrost at room temperature, then reheat in a saucepan over moderate heat until piping hot.

Winter minestrone

Smoked haddock and sweetcorn chowder
SERVES 4 TAKES **35 MINUTES TO MAKE**

Small knob of butter
1 large onion, finely chopped
1 celery stick, finely chopped
1 leek, washed and finely chopped
3 medium potatoes, diced
600ml milk
200ml fresh chicken or fish stock
500g skinless smoked haddock,
  cut into 4cm pieces
326g can sweetcorn, drained
2 tbsp finely chopped flatleaf parsley

1 Melt the butter in a large saucepan over a gentle heat. Add the onion, celery and leek. Cook for 8–10 minutes or until just softened but without any colour.
2 Stir in the potatoes and toss with all the other vegetables. Pour over 400ml of the milk and the stock. Bring to the boil, then reduce the heat and simmer for 15 minutes, until the potatoes are completely tender.
3 Meanwhile, put the fish and remaining milk in a separate pan over medium heat and bring to the boil. Remove from the heat, strain the milk into the chowder and set the fish aside.
4 Stir the sweetcorn into the soup and heat for 1 minute. Remove from the heat, ladle half the mixture into a food processor and whizz until smooth. Return it to the pan and place over a gentle heat. Flake in the fish.
5 When the chowder is hot, ladle it into 4 warmed bowls. Sprinkle it with the finely chopped parsley and serve immediately.

delicious.tip

USING OTHER TYPES OF FISH
For a more exotic soup, replace the haddock with 1kg cleaned live mussels. Cook during step 3 for 4–5 minutes, remove from the shells, and return to the chowder at the end of step 4. Discard any mussels that open during cleaning (see p.180), or that stay closed after cooking.

Crab bisque
SERVES 4 TAKES **3 HOURS TO MAKE**

2 tbsp light olive oil
2 medium onions, chopped
3 garlic cloves, chopped
2 carrots, chopped
2 celery sticks, chopped
$1/2$ tsp fennel seeds
Remains of a picked cooked crab (dead men's fingers and stomach sac discarded, and shell broken up)
4 tbsp aniseed spirit, such as Pernod
2 tomatoes, chopped, or 1 tbsp tomato purée
Pinch of saffron threads
Juice of 1 orange, plus a couple of strips of zest
4 tbsp double cream or crème fraîche (optional)

To serve
Croûtons, aïoli (see p.32) and cayenne pepper

1 Heat the olive oil in a very large, high-sided pan and add the onions, garlic, carrots and celery. Season very well, add the fennel seeds, then reduce the heat. Cover and allow the vegetables to sweat for 10–15 minutes.
2 When the vegetables are becoming tender, add the broken crab shell and any remaining meat and turn up the heat. Add the Pernod and carefully ignite, standing well back. When the flames die down, add the tomatoes or tomato puree, saffron, orange juice and zest and 1.5 litres cold water. Bring to a simmer, reduce the heat and cook for 2 hours.
3 Strain the soup (now a stock) into a large heatproof container, discarding any really hard, big bits of shell from the colander. Put what's left back into the pan and, using the end of a rolling pin, smash the remaining meat and shell up until it is as small as you can get it. Using a ladleful of the stock, pass the smashed shell and bits of vegetable through a sieve to remove any sharp bits. Add the murky purée that's left to the stock.
4 Reheat gently in a clean pan and season to taste. Stir in the double cream or crème fraîche, if using. Serve with croûtons, aïoli, and a sprinkle of cayenne pepper.

Chicken noodle soup

SERVES 6 TAKES **2 HOURS TO MAKE**

4 carrots
3 celery sticks
3 onions
1.5kg whole chicken
2 bay leaves
1 tbsp vegetable oil
1 leek, sliced
1 garlic clove, chopped
100g dried egg noodles
2cm piece fresh ginger, grated
Parsley leaves, chopped, and spring onions,
  sliced, to garnish

1 Roughly chop 2 carrots and 2 celery sticks, and quarter 2 of the onions. Put them in a very large pan and add the chicken and bay leaves. Pour in about 2.5 litres cold water, or enough to cover the chicken and vegetables. Bring to the boil over a gentle heat, skim off any fat that rises to the top and simmer for 1 hour. Carefully remove the chicken and set aside. Strain the stock into a large bowl, discarding the solids.
2 Dice the remaining carrots and finely chop the remaining celery stick and onion. Heat the oil in a large pan over a medium heat and cook the chopped carrots, celery, onion, leek and garlic. Fry for 5 minutes, stirring, until tender. Add 2 litres of the strained stock (freeze any remainder) and bring to the boil, then reduce the heat to low and simmer gently for 10 minutes.
3 Meanwhile, remove and discard the skin and strip the meat from the chicken. Tear the meat into bite-size pieces and add to the soup. (The soup can be cooled and frozen at this point if desired. Simply ladle the cool soup into a rigid plastic container, and freeze for up to 2 months. Defrost completely before gently reheating.)
4 Add the noodles and ginger and simmer for 4–5 minutes, until the noodles are tender. Season and garnish with the parsley and spring onions.
5 Ladle into 6 warmed bowls and serve immediately. This soup makes an excellent winter warmer and is a great comfort when suffering from colds and flu.

Smoked haddock and
sweetcorn chowder

Chicken
noodle soup

Creamy bacon, potato and sweetcorn soup

Creamy bacon, potato and sweetcorn soup

SERVES 8 TAKES **40 MINUTES TO MAKE**

200g smoked lardons, or 6 rashers smoked
  bacon, roughly chopped
1 tbsp vegetable oil
1 onion, finely chopped
2 celery sticks, finely sliced
2 large potatoes, peeled and cut into bite-size
  pieces
1.2 litres hot fresh vegetable stock
198g can sweetcorn, drained and rinsed
142ml pot single cream
Handful of parsley, chopped

1 Place a large non-stick saucepan over a high
heat. When hot, add the lardons or bacon and
cook, stirring, for 5 minutes until golden.
Remove, tip on to kitchen paper to absorb the
excess fat and set aside.
2 Add the oil to the pan and reduce the heat to
medium, then add the chopped onion and celery.
Cook, stirring occasionally, for 5 minutes
until softened.
3 Add the potato and stock, bring to the boil,
then reduce the heat and simmer for around
10 minutes, until the potato is tender but still
holding its shape.
4 Add the sweetcorn, cream and bacon and
simmer for 2–3 minutes to heat through. Stir
in the parsley and season to taste.

Winter pea and watercress soup with crispy pancetta

SERVES 6 TAKES **25 MINUTES TO MAKE**

2 tbsp olive oil
15g butter
1 large onion, chopped
1 garlic clove, finely chopped
1 large floury potato, cubed
1.5 litres fresh chicken stock
900g frozen peas
100g watercress
70g finely sliced pancetta or thin rashers
  smoked streaky bacon

1 Heat the oil and butter in a large pan, add the
onion and garlic and cook gently for 5 minutes
until beginning to soften.
2 Add the potato and toss with the onion and
garlic, then pour in the stock. Bring to the boil
and simmer for 15 minutes, until the potato is
just tender.
3 Add the peas and simmer for 3 minutes. Tip in
the watercress and stir until wilted.
4 Remove from the heat, cool for a few minutes
then blitz until smooth (either with a stick blender
in the pan, or in 2 batches in a food processor).
5 Return the soup to the pan, season to taste and
keep warm over a gentle heat.
6 Meanwhile, preheat the grill to high. Grill the
pancetta or streaky bacon strips for 2–3 minutes
on each side, until crisp. Remove and drain on
kitchen paper, then break up into pieces.
7 Ladle the soup into 6 warmed bowls and top
each with a few shards of crispy pancetta or
streaky bacon.

Potato soup with chorizo and parsley pesto

SERVES 4 TAKES **30 MINUTES TO MAKE**

25g butter
500g floury potatoes such as maris piper,
  cut into small cubes
1 onion, chopped
850ml fresh chicken or vegetable stock
125ml milk
1 tbsp olive oil
50g chorizo, thinly sliced

For the parsley pesto
25g parsley, chopped
25g Parmesan or Grana Padano cheese, grated
25g pine nuts
2 garlic cloves, crushed
75ml extra-virgin olive oil, plus extra for covering

1 Melt the butter in a pan and add the potatoes and onion. Season, stir well, cover with a lid, and sweat over a gentle heat for 10 minutes.
2 Pour in the chicken or vegetable stock, bring to the boil, cover again and simmer for another 10 minutes, until the vegetables are soft. Add the milk, then blitz with a stick blender until the soup is smooth.
3 Make the parsley pesto. Put all the ingredients except the oil into a food processor and whizz to a textured purée. Add the oil and a good pinch of salt, and blend briefly to a coarse paste. (This will make more pesto than you need, so spoon the leftovers into a sterilised jar, and cover with a 1cm layer of oil. It can then be stored in the fridge for up to 2 weeks – just cover the pesto with more oil after each use to preserve it.)
4 Return to the soup: heat the olive oil in a large frying pan. Add the chorizo slices and fry for 30 seconds each side, until they are crisp and the oil has run out into the pan. Lift the chorizo on to kitchen paper to drain briefly, reserving the amber-coloured oil.
5 Divide the hot soup between 4 warmed bowls, and swirl 1 tsp pesto into each bowl. Top each bowl with some slices of chorizo and a few drops of its reserved oil.

Winter pea and watercress soup with crispy pancetta

Potato soup with chorizo and parsley pesto

salads

Country-style potato salad
SERVES 6 TAKES **30 MINUTES TO MAKE**

550g waxy potatoes, such as pink fir apple
  or charlotte
1 tbsp lemon juice
4 tbsp extra-virgin olive oil
2 tbsp oregano, chopped
1 small red onion, finely chopped
12 green olives, pitted
4 plum tomatoes, deseeded
  and roughly chopped
2 tbsp capers, rinsed
4 eggs, hard-boiled

1 Cook the potatoes in boiling salted water for
12–15 minutes until just tender. Drain well and
cut each in half. Put into a large serving bowl.
2 In a small bowl, whisk together the lemon juice,
oil, oregano and plenty of seasoning. Pour over
the warm potatoes and set aside.
3 When the potato salad has cooled, add the
chopped onion, olives, tomatoes and capers
and toss well. Roughly chop the boiled eggs and
scatter over the salad. Just before serving, gently
toss the salad once more.

This salad sings with the warm flavours of the Italian countryside.

Caesar salad
SERVES 6 TAKES **25 MINUTES TO MAKE**

3 slices German rye bread
1 garlic clove, crushed
3 tbsp olive oil
4 little gem lettuces, leaves separated
50g Parmesan

For the dressing
1 fat garlic clove
1 anchovy fillet
1 egg yolk
$1/4$ tsp Dijon mustard
1 tbsp lemon juice
100ml mild olive oil
2 tbsp grated Parmesan
$1/2$ tbsp double cream

1 First make the croûtons. Preheat the oven to
200°C/fan 180°C/gas 6. Cut the crusts off the
bread, then cut the bread into squares. Put into a
roasting tin, sprinkle with the garlic, olive oil and
a little salt and mix together. Bake for 10 minutes.
Cool and set aside.
2 Put the lettuce into a colander and rinse under
cold running water. Shake very well then blot with
a tea towel, or spin in a salad spinner. The leaves
should be completely dry.
3 Take a large salad bowl and put in the lettuce
leaves, tearing any large leaves so all the pieces
are bite-sized. Sprinkle with the croûtons.
4 Drag a vegetable peeler over the Parmesan
and let the shavings fall into the salad.
5 Make the classic Caesar salad dressing.
First, crush the garlic clove under the blade of
a large knife. Rub the crushed garlic around the
inside of a bowl, then discard. Mash the anchovy
fillet on a board with the blade of a knife and
add to the bowl.
6 Add the egg yolk, mustard and lemon juice
to the bowl. Mix all together then slowly whisk in
the olive oil, until the dressing is creamy. Stir
in the Parmesan and double cream and grind in
a little black pepper.
7 Drizzle the dressing liberally over the
salad, toss and serve.

Salad Niçoise
SERVES 4 TAKES **25 MINUTES TO MAKE**

75ml extra-virgin olive oil
Juice of $\frac{1}{2}$ lemon
300g small new potatoes
100g green beans or shelled broad beans
4 eggs
6 ripe tomatoes, each cut into eight
1 cos or 2 little gem lettuce, leaves
  separated
225g can tuna in olive oil
2 tbsp capers, rinsed
Generous handful of good olives, pitted
8 anchovy fillets

1 Mix the oil and lemon juice together to make a dressing and season very well.
2 Boil the potatoes until tender and drain. Unless they are really tiny, break them or cut them in half. Toss with about 1 tbsp of the dressing while still warm. Set aside.
3 Boil the green or broad beans over a high heat for 2–3 minutes, plunge them into a bowl of iced water to stop the cooking and set the colour, then drain and set aside.
4 Boil the eggs until the yolks are barely set. A foolproof way to do this is to bring the water to a rolling boil, add the eggs and cook for 6 minutes exactly. When done, plunge them in cold water for a minute and peel off the shells (this is much easier if you do it before the eggs have totally cooled).
5 Now build the salad. Toss the tomato, potato, lettuce, beans, tuna, capers and olives in the remaining dressing, and either serve in a large salad bowl or in 4 smaller shallow dishes.
6 Finish the top of the salad with the anchovies and quartered eggs.

delicious.**tip**
USING CAPERS
Capers (the flower buds of the caper bush) can be found in most supermarkets, pickled in either salt or vinegar. Use the large ones in mezze, and choose the smaller, finer-flavoured ones for this salad.

Country-style
potato salad

Caesar salad

Warm potato salad with red peppers and Parma ham

Beetroot, anchovy and watercress salad

SERVES 4 TAKES **1 HOUR 15 MINUTES TO MAKE**

600g small beetroot
3 shallots, very thinly sliced
1 tbsp capers, rinsed
2 tbsp balsamic vinegar
3 tbsp olive oil
1 tsp Dijon mustard
4 eggs
Bunch of watercress, thoroughly washed
12 anchovy fillets in olive oil, drained
Horseradish cream, to serve (optional)

1 Preheat the oven to 220°C/fan 200°C/gas 7. Wrap each beetroot in foil and bake until tender; about 30 minutes depending on the size. Cool in the foil, then push off the skins. Cut into bite-size wedges and set aside.
2 Mix the shallots, capers, vinegar, oil and mustard in a bowl. Season, add the beetroot, toss and leave to marinate for 30 minutes.

3 Meanwhile, put the eggs into a pan of boiling water and cook for 6 minutes, for soft yolks. Cool under cold running water, peel, and halve.
4 Lay the watercress on 4 serving plates and top with the marinated beetroot, halved eggs and the anchovy fillets. A dollop of horseradish cream, if liked, makes a delicious addition.

Warm potato salad with red peppers and Parma ham

SERVES 6 TAKES **55 MINUTES TO MAKE**

2 large red peppers
600g Jersey Royals (or other new potatoes), scrubbed
4 tsp extra-virgin olive oil, plus extra for drizzling
1 tbsp chopped flatleaf parsley
12 thin slices Parma ham
50g baby salad leaves
$^1/_2$ tsp white wine vinegar

1 Preheat the oven to 220°C/fan 200°C/gas 7. Put the peppers in a roasting dish and place in the hot oven for 20–25 minutes, until lightly charred. Seal in a plastic bag and leave to cool. Remove and discard the stalks, seeds and skin – the skin should slip off easily – reserving any delicious juices. Cut the flesh into strips.
2 Cook the potatoes in a large pan of boiling salted water for 10–12 minutes or until tender. Drain. When cool enough to handle, thickly slice into a large bowl. Fold in the oil and parsley.
3 Ruffle 2 slices of Parma ham on to each of 6 plates, then pile on some salad leaves.
4 Stir the vinegar into the potatoes, season to taste and arrange on top of the salad with the pepper strips and their juices. Drizzle over a little more extra-virgin olive oil and serve.

delicious.**tip**

ADVANCE PREPARATION

If you want to get ahead with this recipe, prepare the peppers the day before, cover and chill overnight. Bring to room temperature before using.

Beetroot, anchovy
and watercress salad

Italian bean
salad

3 Sprinkle each salad with a pinch of chilli flakes and season. Scatter with the sunblush tomatoes, drizzling over about 1 tsp of the reserved tomato oil. Serve with wholemeal bread.

Italian bean salad

SERVES 4 TAKES **30 MINUTES TO MAKE**

7 tbsp extra-virgin olive oil
1 small onion, finely chopped
2 plump garlic cloves, crushed
1 stick celery, finely chopped
2 red chillies, deseeded and chopped
2 tsp oregano, chopped
410g can cannellini beans, drained and rinsed
410g can borlotti beans, drained and rinsed
6 plump tomatoes, deseeded and chopped
Handful of parsley, chopped
2 tbsp lemon juice

1 Heat 3 tbsp of olive oil in a large saucepan and gently cook the onion, garlic, celery and chilli for 6–8 minutes until softened. Stir in the oregano and beans and continue to cook for 5–6 minutes, stirring occasionally. Remove from the heat and allow to cool to room temperature.
2 Stir in the tomatoes and parsley. Whisk the remaining olive oil with the lemon juice and season well. Just before serving, pour this dressing over the bean mixture and toss well.

Guacamole salad

SERVES 4 TAKES **15 MINUTES TO MAKE**

4 little gem lettuces, washed
3 ripe beef tomatoes, sliced
$1/2$ small onion, finely chopped
1 garlic clove, crushed
1 tbsp coriander leaves
4 ripe avocados
Juice of 1 lime
4 pinches of chilli flakes
100g sunblush tomatoes in oil,
  drained and oil reserved

1 Separate the lettuce leaves and arrange on 4 serving plates. Divide the tomato slices among the plates, then scatter over the onion, garlic and coriander leaves.
2 Halve and stone the avocados, then cut each half in quarters. Slip a knife under the pointed end of each quarter and pull away the skin. Slice the avocado lengthways and arrange on the plates. Squeeze over the lime juice.

delicious.**technique**
DESEEDING AND CHOPPING CHILLIES

1. *Halve the chilli lengthways. Working from the bottom up, scrape out and discard the seeds and ribs of white pith.*

2. *Chop the chilli finely, then immediately wash your hands very thoroughly to remove the juices before continuing.*

Russian salad
SERVES 4 TAKES **1 HOUR TO MAKE**

2 medium or 4 small beetroot
2–3 waxy potatoes
100g fresh shelled peas
100g green beans, sliced
100g baby carrots
$1/2$ small cauliflower, cut into florets
3 large eggs
2 dill-pickled gherkins or a handful of
  cornichons, diced
3 heaped tbsp mayonnaise (see p.32,
  or use a good bought one)
Small bunch of fresh dill (optional)

1 Boil the beetroot in a pan of salted water over medium-high heat for 20–30 minutes, until tender. Cool, then push the skins off and dice.
2 Meanwhile, peel and dice the potatoes to the same size as the beetroot. Boil them in a pan of lightly salted water until tender, then allow both potatoes and beetroots to cool completely.

3 Now blanch the peas, beans, carrots and cauliflower. Use the same pan in succession rather than several (it saves on washing up!) but blanch the cauliflower last, as it will flavour the water. The peas and beans will take 2–3 minutes and the carrots and cauliflower 4–5 minutes. They should remain a little crisp. Drain and cool.
4 Finally, cook the eggs in boiling salted water for 6–7 minutes. Plunge them into a bowl of cold water, then peel and halve.
5 Mix the gherkins or cornichons with all the vegetables and fold them into the mayonnaise in a bowl. Season, top with dill sprigs and the eggs.

A truly golden feast and a family favourite in Russia, where it is known as Salat Olivier.

Russian
salad

Seafood salad with lime and chilli salsa

SERVES 6 TAKES **40 MINUTES TO MAKE**

Large handful of parsley
1kg live mussels, cleaned and debearded
  (discard open mussels that do not close
  when tapped against the sink, and any
  with cracked shells)
500g raw tiger prawns, peeled and deveined,
  with tail-shells on
300g fresh squid, cleaned and sliced into rings
2 tbsp avocado oil (or olive oil)
Juice of 1 lime
1 small shallot, finely chopped
100g rocket

For the lime and chilli salsa
Finely grated zest of 1 lime
1 garlic clove
1 small red chilli, halved and deseeded
Large handful of mint

1 Pour 100ml water into a large pan. Tear the stalks from the parsley (reserve the leaves for the salsa) and add to the pan with a couple of whole black peppercorns. Bring to the boil over a high heat, add the mussels, cover, and cook for 5 minutes, shaking the pan until the shells have opened. Remove the mussels with a slotted spoon, discarding any that haven't opened. Add the prawns and squid to the pan for 2 minutes or so, tossing, until both are cooked. Remove with a slotted spoon. Shell the mussels, and mix with the prawns and squid. Cover and chill.
2 Boil the liquor in the pan until reduced by half, then strain about 3 tbsp of it into a bowl and allow to cool. Whisk in the avocado oil and lime juice. Season, and stir in the shallot.
3 To make the salsa, put the lime zest, garlic and chilli in a blender and whizz until chopped. Add the mint and reserved parsley leaves and process again to make a fine mixture.
4 Toss together the seafood and shallot dressing, then gently fold in the rocket. Divide between serving bowls and spoon over the salsa.

Seafood salad with lime and chilli salsa

Tuna and pesto pasta salad
SERVES 4 TAKES **20 MINUTES TO MAKE**

225g dried pasta shapes of your choice
$^1/_3$ cucumber
100g cherry tomatoes
2 tsp green pesto
185g can tuna steak in olive oil, drained
4 tbsp Classic Vinaigrette (see p.33), or a good
  bottled French dressing

1 Fill a large saucepan with water, add a generous pinch of salt, and place over a high heat. Bring the water to a rolling boil, add the pasta and stir it once to prevent the pieces sticking together. Keep the heat high so the water stays boiling, but be careful it does not boil over. Cook for 10 minutes, or according to the packet instructions. To test when the pasta is cooked, fish out a piece and take a bite: it should be soft, but still al dente.
2 Meanwhile, chop the cucumber into chunky pieces. Cut each cherry tomato in half.
3 Drain the pasta, transfer to a large bowl and leave to cool slightly. Stir in the pesto (its oil will stop the pasta sticking together).
4 Roughly flake the tuna and stir into the pasta along with the chopped cucumber and tomatoes. Season and add the Classic Vinaigrette or French dressing, then stir it all together.
5 You can eat this salad immediately, or cover and chill in the fridge for up to 2 days.

> Choose a good quality line-caught tuna, vine-ripened cherry tomatoes and fresh pesto.

Hot-smoked trout with cucumber and dill salad

Hot-smoked trout with cucumber and dill salad
SERVES 4 TAKES **5 MINUTES TO MAKE**

1 cucumber
$^1/_2$ small bunch of dill, chopped
$^1/_2$ tsp caster sugar
1 tbsp rice wine vinegar
4 hot-smoked trout fillets
Boiled new potatoes and a dollop of mayonnaise,
  to serve

1 Halve the cucumber lengthways, and deseed it by drawing a teaspoon firmly down the centre of each half. Thinly slice into half-moons.
2 In a large bowl, toss the cucumber slices very well together with the dill, caster sugar and rice wine vinegar. The sugar should dissolve into the sweet-and-sour dressing.
3 Divide the salad between 4 plates. Flake a trout fillet into pieces and scatter over each serving.
4 Serve with hot buttered new potatoes and a dollop of mayonnaise.

Shredded chicken noodle salad with ginger and peanut dressing
SERVES 2 TAKES **1 HOUR 30 MINUTES TO MAKE**

2 chicken breasts, skin on
3 tsp fresh ginger, grated
Zest of 1 lime, grated
2 tbsp groundnut or sunflower oil
2 garlic cloves, finely chopped
1 green chilli, deseeded and finely chopped
3 tbsp crunchy peanut butter
2 tsp Thai fish sauce or light soy sauce
1 kaffir lime leaf, finely shredded (optional)
2 globes of preserved stem ginger in syrup,
  drained and chopped
Lime juice, to taste
Brown sugar, to taste
Small handful of coriander
100–120g thin or thick rice noodles
225g carrots, cut into long, thin shreds
1 small green or red pepper, cut into long,
  thin shreds
10cm piece cucumber, deseeded
  and cut into long, thin shreds
2–3 tbsp roasted peanuts, roughly chopped

1 Slash the skin of the chicken a few times with a sharp knife. Mix together half the grated ginger, the lime zest and 1 tbsp of the oil and rub into the chicken. Cover and marinate in the fridge for at least an hour. Meanwhile, preheat the oven to 180°C/fan 160°C/gas 4. Roast the chicken for 20–25 minutes, until cooked. Allow to cool a little, then slice or shred into bite-size pieces.
2 While the chicken is cooking, make the dressing. In a small pan, heat the remaining oil and gently cook the remaining grated ginger with the garlic and chilli for a few minutes; don't let it brown. Remove from the heat, stir in the peanut butter and let it melt. Stir in 4–6 tbsp water to make a thick, creamy dressing. Place back over a low heat and add the Thai fish sauce or soy sauce, kaffir lime leaf (if liked), chopped stem ginger and lime juice. Add sugar to taste. Let it bubble gently for a few more minutes. Then thin down with 2–3 tbsp water to make a spoonable dressing. Chop the coriander stalks and stir in.

3 Cook the noodles according to packet instructions (the easiest way is to put them in a bowl, pour over boiling water, and leave for 4–5 minutes until tender). Drain, rinse and leave in a bowl of iced water until ready to serve.
4 Drain the noodles well and divide between 2 shallow bowls. Place the shredded vegetables and most of the coriander leaves on top, followed by the still-warm shredded chicken. Spoon the dressing over and scatter with more coriander and the peanuts.

Warm chicken and fennel salad with a sweet-and-sour dressing
SERVES 4 TAKES **50 MINUTES TO MAKE**

2 large fennel bulbs
4 tbsp olive oil
3 fat garlic cloves, halved lengthways
3 sprigs of rosemary, halved
4 boneless chicken breasts, skin on
150g watercress, washed, with thick stalks
  removed

For the sweet-and-sour dressing
2 tbsp olive oil
1 small red onion, chopped
4 tsp light muscovado sugar
3 tbsp red wine vinegar
2 tsp toasted sesame oil
2$\frac{1}{2}$ tsp dark soy sauce

1 To cook the fennel, remove the outer layer of each bulb, if woody, then cut lengthways through the root into slices. The root will hold the layers together at the base of each slice.
2 Heat a cast-iron griddle pan over a high heat until smoking hot, then reduce the heat to medium. Brush the fennel slices with half the olive oil, season and place them on the griddle, in batches if necessary, with the garlic cloves and half the rosemary pieces. Cook for 5 minutes on each side, until the fennel is golden brown and nicely marked with lines from the griddle pan. Sprinkle with a couple of tablespoons of water and continue to cook for another 3–5 minutes,

Warm chicken and fennel
salad with a sweet-and-
sour dressing

adding more water every now and then to help speed up the cooking. When tender, set the fennel aside on a plate and keep warm. Discard the garlic and rosemary.

3 Make the sweet-and-sour red onion dressing. Heat the olive oil in a non-stick frying pan over a medium heat. Add the red onion and cook for 5 minutes, stirring, until soft and just beginning to brown. Add the sugar and continue to cook, stirring, for 1–2 minutes, until the sugar has dissolved and the onion is golden-brown. Reduce the heat, add the vinegar, and allow it to bubble gently for a few seconds, then add the sesame oil and soy sauce and grind over some black pepper. Keep the dressing warm.

4 Heat the remaining olive oil in a large frying pan over a medium heat. Season the chicken, then add to the pan, skin-side down, with the remaining rosemary. Cook for about 6 minutes or until golden-brown. Turn over and cook for a further 6–7 minutes or until cooked through and tender. (You can add a little water to the pan after turning the chicken to speed up the process.)

5 Discard the rosemary and lift the chicken on to a plate, cover with foil and a clean tea towel to insulate and leave to rest for 5 minutes in a warm place. This resting will render the meat far more juicy and succulent, as the fibres will relax after tensing up in the hot pan and the juices flow back throughout. If the meat is not rested, it will lose all its juices once cut. Place the chicken breasts on to a chopping board and slice each slightly on the diagonal into thickish slices.

6 Put the chicken pieces, fennel slices and watercress into a large bowl and spoon over the dressing. Toss everything together very well so all the elements are coated in dressing, then divide between 4 plates. Serve immediately.

delicious.**tip**

THINNING THE DRESSING
If the dressing has become too thick, add any chicken juices from the plate or a tablespoon of warm water to loosen it a little before tossing it through the salad.

Warm Sunday roast salad

2 Meanwhile, cook the potatoes in boiling salted water for 10–15 minutes until tender. Drain and tip into a roasting tin, drizzle with 2 tbsp of the oil and season. Roast in the hot oven for 30 minutes.
3 Cook the beans in boiling salted water, drain and refresh under cold running water. Set aside.
4 Make the dressing: whisk together the remaining oil with the vinegar, sugar and mint. Season well.
5 Take the lamb and potatoes out of the oven. Leave the lamb to rest for 15 minutes and the potatoes to cool. Slice the lamb and put on to a plate. Put the tomatoes, salad leaves, beans and warm potatoes into a large bowl and toss well. Drizzle with enough dressing to coat and toss again. Add the lamb to serve. Put the rest of the dressing into a jug, to pour over if desired.

Tuna, cannellini bean and red onion salad on griddled tomato bread
SERVES 4 TAKES **25 MINUTES TO MAKE**

400g can cannellini beans, drained and rinsed
300g tuna in olive oil, drained and flaked
  into large chunks
1 small red onion, finely sliced
12 cherry tomatoes, halved
Large handful of flatleaf parsley, roughly chopped
3 tbsp olive oil
2 small lemons
1 tsp Dijon mustard
1 garlic clove, crushed or grated
4 thick slices sourdough or rye bread
3 tbsp sun-dried tomato paste

1 In a large bowl, mix together the beans, tuna, red onion, tomatoes and parsley.
2 In another small bowl, whisk together 2 tbsp of the oil, the juice of 1 lemon and the mustard and garlic. Season, pour over the tuna and beans and toss together well.
3 Heat a griddle pan until very hot. Brush the bread on both sides with the remaining oil and griddle until golden with charred lines.
4 Spread each slice with the tomato paste. Pile on the beans and tuna and serve with the remaining lemon cut into wedges, to squeeze over.

Warm Sunday roast salad
SERVES 6 TAKES **2 HOURS 15 MINUTES TO MAKE**

2–2.5kg leg of lamb
4 garlic cloves, cut into slivers
Few sprigs rosemary
450g baby new potatoes
175ml olive oil
200g French beans
4 tbsp red wine vinegar
Generous pinch of sugar
Handful of mint, chopped
600g cherry tomatoes, halved
350g baby spinach leaves, rocket, or watercress

1 Preheat the oven to 220°C/fan 200°C/gas 7. With the tip of a small, sharp knife make slits all over the lamb. Insert a sliver of garlic and a sprig of rosemary into each slit. Roast the lamb for 20 minutes, then reduce the oven temperature to 190°C/fan 170°C/gas 5 and roast for a further 20 minutes per 450g for pink lamb; add 20 minutes more if you like it medium.

Tuna, cannellini bean and red onion salad on griddled tomato bread

Mayonnaise

SERVES 4–6 TAKES **15 MINUTES TO MAKE**

2 egg yolks, at room temperature
1 tsp Dijon mustard
300ml light olive oil
Good squeeze of fresh lemon juice

1 Stand a large bowl on a cloth to stop it moving. Put the egg yolks into the bowl with the mustard and a little seasoning and whisk until smooth.
2 Gradually add the olive oil in a slow, steady stream, whisking all the time. Do not hurry this step or the mixture will not form an emulsion. The end result should be a smooth, quite thick mayonnaise that stands in peaks.
3 Add lemon juice to taste and briefly whisk. If it's too thick, whisk in a few drops of warm water to give a good consistency.

delicious.**technique**

MAKING MAYONNAISE

1. *For the best results, start with the egg yolks at room temperature. Whisk together with the mustard, salt, and freshly ground black pepper.*

2. *With a very steady hand, begin to add the oil drop by drop, whisking all the time, and gradually increase to a thin stream of oil.*

3. *Continue to add the oil in a thin stream, whisking all the time to keep the emulsion stable, and the mixture will start to thicken noticeably.*

4. *Add the lemon juice only when all the oil has been incorporated, and whisk in briefly. Check and adjust the seasoning if necessary.*

Aïoli

SERVES 6–8 TAKES **10 MINUTES TO MAKE**

6 garlic cloves, crushed
3 egg yolks
3 tbsp white breadcrumbs
4 tbsp white wine vinegar
300ml good olive oil

1 Put the garlic, egg yolks, breadcrumbs, vinegar and a little seasoning into a bowl and whisk well (or whizz in a food processor) until everything is thoroughly amalgamated.
2 Gradually whisk in the olive oil in a slow, steady trickle (or pour through the food processor's funnel with the motor running). Do not hurry this step or the mixture will not form an emulsion.
3 Whisk in 1 tbsp warm water and adjust the seasoning to taste.

Blue cheese dressing

SERVES 4 TAKES **10 MINUTES TO MAKE**

50g blue cheese (Gorgonzola is good)
2 tbsp milk
1 tbsp white wine vinegar
6 tbsp olive oil

1 Put the cheese in a food processor with the other ingredients. Season and blend until smooth.
2 Add a few drops of warm water if it's a little too thick until you have a consistency you like.

Olive oil, balsamic vinegar and miso dressing

SERVES 10 TAKES **10 MINUTES TO MAKE**

100ml extra-virgin olive oil
300ml water
50ml balsamic vinegar
3 tbsp barley miso paste

1 Put the olive oil, water and balsamic vinegar into a screw-top jar. Mixing any dressing in a jar is hassle-free, saves on washing up and allows you easily to store any leftovers in the fridge.

2 Add the miso paste and season with a pinch of salt, and freshly ground black pepper. Seal the jar and shake to mix very well, so that the liquids emulsify together.

3 Serve immediately, drizzled over salads – it's especially good with Asian dishes – or store in the sealed jar in the fridge for up to 1 month. Shake very well before each use.

Blue cheese dressing

Classic vinaigrette

SERVES 4 TAKES **5 MINUTES TO MAKE**

1 tbsp white wine vinegar
1 tsp mild mustard (such as wholegrain or Dijon)
Small pinch of sugar
3 tbsp extra-virgin olive oil

1 Put the vinegar, mustard and sugar into a large bowl and season to taste. Whisk until very well blended together.

2 Add the oil in a slow stream, whisking all the time, until cloudy and slightly thickened.

Herb leaf salad

SERVES 4–6 TAKES **10 MINUTES TO MAKE**

50g flatleaf parsley,
  all stems removed
50g chives, snipped into lengths
50g tarragon leaves,
  all stems removed
50g basil, all stems removed
2 tsp red wine vinegar
1–2 tbsp extra-virgin olive oil

1 Wash all the herbs and carefully dry them in a salad spinner or on kitchen paper. Put into a large serving bowl.

2 Whisk the vinegar into the olive oil and season with sea salt. Taste and adjust the seasoning, remembering that it should not overpower the delicate flavour of the herbs. Just before serving, drizzle the dressing over the leaves and toss everything together.

Classic vinaigrette

snacks

Houmous and carrot bap
SERVES 1 TAKES **5 MINUTES TO MAKE**

1 granary bap
2 tbsp plain or roasted pepper houmous
1 medium carrot, peeled
$1/4$ punnet mustard and cress

1 Use a serrated knife to cut the bap in half through the middle. Spread both of the cut sides with houmous, being quite generous with it and making sure it covers the whole surface.
2 Grate the carrot (for a crunchier texture, use the coarse side of the grater). Sprinkle the grated carrot over the houmous. Snip the mustard and cress from the punnet and scatter over the carrot. Sandwich both halves together.

Tuna guacamole bagel
SERVES 1 TAKES **5 MINUTES TO MAKE**

1 bagel
70g can tuna in olive oil
2 tbsp guacamole
2 little gem lettuce leaves

1 Cut the bagel in half through the middle. Open the can of tuna, drain, and put into a bowl. Add the guacamole and mix together until it is very well blended.
2 Spread the tuna mixture over half of the bagel, top with the lettuce leaves and sandwich the bagel together, pressing well.

Cauliflower cheese on toast
SERVES 4 TAKES **35 MINUTES TO MAKE**

500g cauliflower (about 1 small or $1/2$ large), cut into bite-size florets
30g butter, plus extra for spreading
2 tbsp plain flour
400ml milk
200g mature, crumbly cheese, diced
$1/4$ nutmeg, freshly grated
1 egg yolk
4 slices dark rye bread

1 Cook the cauliflower florets in boiling water for 8-10 minutes, until just tender with a little crunch left. Drain thoroughly and set aside.
2 Heat the butter in a small pan and add the flour. Cook, stirring, for 2–3 minutes then remove from the heat. Add the milk, a little at a time, stirring after each addition. Return to the heat and cook gently for 8–10 minutes, or until thickened.
3 Stir in the diced cheese and nutmeg, then the cauliflower, and season to your liking. Remove the pan from the heat and fold in the egg yolk.
4 Preheat the grill to high and toast the rye bread. Allow it to cool then butter lightly. Top each slice with the cauliflower, then pop under the grill and cook until the topping has browned nicely.

Smoked salmon toasties
SERVES 4 TAKES **20 MINUTES TO MAKE**

2 tbsp butter, softened
8 slices good-quality bread
300g smoked salmon, sliced
4 tbsp sauerkraut, drained
150g Gruyère, grated

1 Butter each slice of bread on both sides and season well with black pepper. Divide the salmon, sauerkraut, and cheese between the sandwiches and gently press the top slices down.
2 Heat a frying pan and fry the sandwiches lightly on both sides until the cheese begins to melt. Keep the heat low to avoid burning the bread.
3 Serve immediately with very cold beer or cider.

Chicken and mushrooms on bruschetta
SERVES 4 TAKES **25 MINUTES TO MAKE**

2 chicken breasts
2 tbsp olive oil
Leaves from 2 fresh thyme sprigs
50g pine nuts
8 medium button mushrooms
Juice of $1/2$ lemon
Extra-virgin olive oil or salad oil
4 generous slices ciabatta
1 clove garlic, halved
2 large handfuls of lamb's lettuce,
  washed and dried

1 Preheat the oven to its highest setting. Rub the chicken breasts with half the oil and the thyme and season very well. Place in a small roasting tray and cook for 15 minutes, or until cooked through and beginning to turn golden brown. Set aside and allow to cool a little.
2 Meanwhile, place the pine nuts on a baking sheet and roast at the same temperature for 2-3 minutes, until golden brown. Watch carefully and shake the sheet once or twice. Remove from the oven as soon as they take on a golden colour and give off their resinous aroma. Set aside.
3 Slice the mushrooms into fine slivers, lay them on a plate and squeeze over the lemon juice to lift the flavour. Drizzle with a little extra-virgin olive oil (or a salad oil of your choice) and toss so they are very well coated.
4 Put the ciabatta slices on a baking sheet and drizzle with the remaining oil. Bake in the hot oven for 5 minutes, turning once, until crisp, watching to make sure they don't burn. Remove from the oven and rub each slice with the cut side of the garlic clove; the toasted bread will act as a "grater" for the garlic. Put each slice on a plate.
5 Slice the chicken breasts as finely as you can, reserving any juices that run out. Toss the chicken, mushrooms and lettuce with the juices, then taste and adjust the seasoning.
6 Divide the mixed salad between the rounds of bruschetta and scatter each with pine nuts. Drizzle with a little extra-virgin olive oil. For extra decadence, finish with shaved Parmesan.

Smoked salmon toasties

Houmous and carrot bap

Hot cheesy brunch croissant
SERVES 1 TAKES **15 MINUTES TO MAKE**

1 croissant (pick a long, straightish pastry
   rather than crescent-shaped)
Fresh 4-cheese sauce (a 300g tub will fill
   8 croissants in all)
Few tomato slices
Slice of good ham
Handful of grated extra-mature Cheddar
Snipped fresh chives, to garnish

1 Preheat the oven to 180°C/fan 160°C/gas 4.
2 Split the croissant lengthways along the top,
so that the "pocket" for the filling is at right
angles to the base. Fill with a couple of spoonfuls
of the 4-cheese sauce. Add the tomato slices,
ham and, finally, the Cheddar, being quite
generous. Season well with freshly ground
black pepper.
3 Pop on to a baking sheet and bake in the
hot oven for 10–12 minutes until piping hot.
4 Sprinkle with the chives to serve.

Falafel and herb yogurt pittas
SERVES 4–6 TAKES **25 MINUTES TO MAKE**

2 tsp each cumin and coriander seeds
2 x 400g cans chickpeas, rinsed, drained
   and patted dry
1¹/₂ tsp baking powder
2 tbsp plain flour
1 red chilli, deseeded and chopped
1 garlic clove, crushed
3 tbsp chopped flatleaf parsley
Zest of 1 small lemon, grated
Vegetable oil, for shallow-frying
Pitta bread, griddled, to serve
Lime wedges, to serve

For the herb yogurt
100ml Greek yogurt
1 tbsp chopped coriander
1 tbsp chopped mint, plus fresh mint sprigs,
   to serve
Juice of 1 lime

Falafel and herb
yogurt pittas

Perfect
pancakes

1 Dry-fry the cumin and coriander seeds in a frying pan over a medium heat until fragrant. Grind in a pestle and mortar, then add them to a food processor with the chickpeas, baking powder, flour, chilli, garlic, parsley and lemon zest, season, then pulse to combine. Mould the mixture into about 24 walnut-size balls.
2 Heat some oil in a griddle or frying pan and fry the falafels in batches, turning once, for about 3 minutes or until golden. Drain on kitchen paper.
3 Blend the yogurt with the herbs and lime juice and serve with the warm falafels, griddled pittas and lime wedges. Garnish with mint sprigs.

Perfect pancakes
SERVES 4 TAKES **30 MINUTES TO MAKE**

125g plain flour
1 egg, beaten
275–300ml semi-skimmed milk
Vegetable or sunflower oil, for frying

1 To make the batter, sift the flour with a pinch of salt into a large bowl. Make a well in the centre, pour in the egg, and slowly whisk in the milk until the mixture becomes a smooth batter; it needs to be the consistency of pouring cream. Cover with a clean tea towel and rest for at least 20 minutes.
2 Heat a 28cm crêpe pan or a smaller heavy-based frying pan over a medium heat. When hot, dip some kitchen paper in the oil and wipe it across the surface of the pan. Add a small ladleful of batter and tilt the pan to swirl the batter evenly and thinly. Cook for 1–2 minutes, until the pancake is golden underneath.
3 Loosen all around the pancake with a spatula or palette knife. Flip it over and cook for a further minute, until golden. (Be prepared for the first pancake you cook to break up – it usually does!) Slide out on to a plate and repeat, oiling the pan between each pancake. As you cook, pile them up, placing baking paper between each pancake to prevent them sticking.
4 Serve the pancakes with lemon wedges to squeeze over and sprinkle with caster sugar.

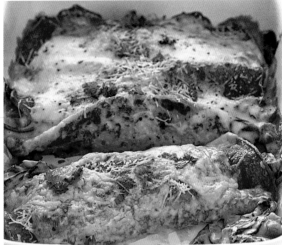

Cheesy mushroom, pancetta
and spinach pancakes

Chicken and
chorizo wraps

Cheesy mushroom, pancetta and spinach pancakes

SERVES 2 TAKES **30 MINUTES TO MAKE**

75g pancetta, cubed
150g baby chestnut mushrooms, sliced
2 garlic cloves, crushed
500g carton fresh 4-cheese sauce
Large handful of baby spinach leaves
4 thin savoury pancakes (buy ready-made,
  or make: see p.37)
25g Parmesan, grated
Small handful of fresh parsley, roughly chopped

1 Preheat the oven to 200°C/fan 180°C/gas 6.
2 In a medium frying pan, dry-fry the pancetta for
5 minutes until golden. Add the mushrooms and
garlic, and cook for a further 3 minutes. Stir in
$^3/_4$ of the cheese sauce and heat until bubbling.
Add the spinach and cook for 1 minute or until
just wilted. Set aside.
3 Take 1 pancake and spoon $^1/_4$ of the filling
down the centre. Carefully roll up the pancake
to encase the filling and put it into a baking
dish. Repeat with the remaining pancakes.
4 Drizzle the remaining cheese sauce over the
pancakes, sprinkle with the Parmesan and
season to taste. Bake for 15 minutes, until
piping hot and turning golden.
5 Scatter with parsley and serve with plenty
of green salad.

These soft pancakes
go down well any
time of year with
children and
adults alike.

Chicken and chorizo wraps
SERVES 4 TAKES **25 MINUTES TO MAKE** PLUS **MARINATING**

2 large, skinless chicken breasts
$^1/_2$ tsp smoked hot paprika
1 garlic clove, crushed
Grated zest and juice of 1 lemon
1 tbsp olive oil
Warmed tortilla wraps, to serve
142ml pot soured cream, to serve

For the sauce
280g jar roasted red peppers in oil
1 small onion, thinly sliced
75g piece chorizo, skinned and diced

1 Cut the chicken into large chunks and put into a non-metallic bowl with the paprika, garlic, lemon zest and juice and oil. Season, toss, cover and put in the fridge for 30 minutes or up to 3 hours.
2 Meanwhile, make the sauce. Drain and roughly chop the peppers, reserving 2 tbsp of their oil. Heat this oil in a frying pan over a medium heat. Add the sliced onion and cook for 5 minutes, until softened. Add the peppers, chorizo and a splash of water. Cover and simmer for 5 minutes, until thickened. Season, cover and keep warm.
3 Preheat the grill to medium-high. Thread the chicken on to metal skewers. Grill for 5 minutes each side or until cooked through.
4 Remove from the skewers and serve in wraps with the sauce and soured cream.

Mediterranean vegetable and ricotta pasties
SERVES 4 TAKES **30 MINUTES TO MAKE**

375g puff pastry sheet
100g young leaf spinach
150g ricotta
1 large egg, beaten,
   plus extra for brushing
20g Parmesan or Grana Padano cheese, grated
390g can ratatouille, drained
Dressed lettuce, to serve

1 Preheat the oven to 220°C/fan 200°C/gas 7. Cut the puff pastry sheet evenly into 4 rectangles.
2 Put the spinach in a colander and pour over boiling water to wilt. Cool under cold running water then squeeze really well. Tip into a bowl and add the ricotta, egg and grated cheese. Gently fold in the ratatouille and season.
3 Spoon this filling on to 1 half of each pastry rectangle and brush the edges with egg. Fold the pastry over the filling, seal by pressing with a fork and put on a baking sheet. Brush with egg and bake for 15–20 minutes until risen and golden.

Chicken and mozzarella quesadillas
SERVES 4 TAKES **20 MINUTES TO MAKE**

2 cooked chicken breasts, finely diced
$^1/_2$ small red pepper, deseeded and finely diced
4 spring onions, trimmed and finely chopped
200g smoked mozzarella, finely diced
Small handful of sage leaves, finely chopped
8 soft flour tortillas
Olive oil, for greasing
Watercress, to serve
Cherry tomatoes on the vine, to serve

1 Put the chicken, pepper, spring onions, mozzarella and sage into a bowl. Season and mix.
2 Lay a tortilla flat. Scatter $^1/_4$ of the chicken mix over it, top with another tortilla, and press together. Repeat, making 3 more quesadillas.
3 Grease 2 large frying pans with a little olive oil and place over a medium heat. Put 1 quesadilla into each and cook for 2 minutes until golden. Invert on to a plate, slide back into the pan and cook for 2 minutes, until the cheese is just melting. Repeat for the other 2 quesadillas.
4 Cut each into 4 and serve with watercress and cherry tomatoes.

delicious.**tip**
BUYING MOZZARELLA
Smoked mozzarella has a smoky, almost nutty flavour. It's often found in Italian delis, but if you have trouble finding it, use regular mozzarella.

Naan bread pizzas

SERVES 2 TAKES **15 MINUTES TO MAKE**

4 beef sausages
Pinch of dried chilli flakes
2 garlic and coriander mini naan breads
4 tbsp crème fraîche
1/2 red onion, thinly sliced
Small handful of mint leaves, roughly chopped
Handful of rocket leaves
Olive oil to drizzle over

1 Preheat the grill to medium. Slit and remove the sausage skins. Put a frying pan over a medium heat and add the sausagemeat with the chilli flakes. Roughly break up the meat with a wooden spoon and cook until brown and tender.
2 Place the naan breads on a baking sheet and divide the sausagemeat and crème fraîche evenly between them. Scatter over the onion and mint leaves. Grill for 3–4 minutes.
3 Remove from the grill and top each with a handful of rocket leaves and a drizzle of olive oil.

Spinach and goat's cheese muffins

MAKES 9 TAKES **45 MINUTES TO MAKE**

25g butter, plus extra for greasing
200ml milk
100g spinach
250g plain flour
1 tbsp baking powder
1 tsp bicarbonate of soda
Good pinch of cayenne pepper
50g Parmesan, finely grated
1 egg, lightly beaten
200g rindless goat's cheese, crumbled

1 Preheat the oven to 190°C/fan 170°C/gas 5. Grease 9 holes of a deep muffin tin with butter.
2 Place the milk and butter in a large pan over a high heat. When the butter has melted, stir in the spinach and bring just to the boil. Remove from the heat and pour into a blender or food processor. Whizz until the spinach is finely chopped. Allow to cool for 5 minutes.

3 Sift the flour, baking powder and bicarbonate of soda into a large bowl. Add the cayenne and some pepper. Stir in the Parmesan. Add the egg and the spinach mixture, then beat with a wooden spoon until just mixed. Divide half the batter between the 9 muffin holes.
4 Sprinkle half the goat's cheese evenly over the muffins. Top with the remaining batter, followed by the rest of the cheese, pushing it down into the mixture. Bake for 20–25 minutes, until risen and firm to the touch. Leave to cool for 5 minutes, then turn out on to a wire rack. Serve hot or cold.

Ham, cheese and mustard mini muffins

MAKES 40–45 TAKES **25 MINUTES TO MAKE**

225g self-raising flour
1 tsp baking powder
3 slices oak-smoked ham, chopped
6 fresh sage leaves, finely chopped
75g mature Cheddar, chopped
50g unsalted butter, melted and cooled slightly
1 egg, lightly beaten
1 1/2 tbsp wholegrain mustard
150ml semi-skimmed milk

1 Preheat the oven to 200°C/fan 180°C/gas 6. Sift the flour and baking powder into a large bowl and add a generous pinch of salt.
2 Stir the ham, sage and Cheddar into the flour. Make a well in the centre, then add the butter, egg, mustard and milk. Mix together briefly, until just combined. It doesn't need to be beaten smooth, but all the dry flour should have been amalgamated into the batter.
3 Put teaspoonfuls of the mixture into petits fours cases, so that each is about 3/4 full. Place on 2 large baking sheets and bake in the hot oven for 8–10 minutes, until risen and golden. Watch carefully as they can quickly catch and burn. Transfer to wire racks to cool a little.
4 Peel off the petits fours cases, and eat the muffins warm or at room temperature. They're delicious dunked into your favourite chutney. Store any uneaten muffins in an airtight tin – but don't expect them to be around for long!

Sweetcorn fritters
SERVES 5 TAKES **15–20 MINUTES TO MAKE**

40g polenta or rice flour
30g plain flour, sifted
$1/2$ tsp baking powder
3 large eggs, beaten
100ml crème fraîche
Kernels cut from 2 sweetcorn cobs
 (or 200g can sweetcorn, drained)
Bunch of spring onions, finely sliced
Small bunch of chives, snipped
2 red chillies, deseeded and finely diced
1–2 tbsp olive oil

1 Put the polenta or rice flour, plain flour, and baking powder in a bowl, then make a well in the centre. Gradually add the eggs and mix to a smooth batter.
2 Stir in the crème fraîche, sweetcorn kernels, spring onions, chives and chillies, and season.
3 Pour the oil into a large frying pan over a medium-high heat. When the oil is hot, drop in spoonfuls of the fritter mixture, spacing them out well. Flatten each to make little cakes. Cook for 2–3 minutes each side, until crisp and golden. Serve with some chutney.

Microwaved jacket sweet potato
SERVES 1 TAKES **10 MINUTES TO MAKE**

1 sweet potato, about 175g
Olive oil for rubbing

1 Wash the sweet potato then prick the skin several times with a fork. Do not skip this step, as if you don't prick the skin the potato may explode in the microwave.
2 Rub a little olive oil over the potato, to crisp the skin, and stand it on some kitchen paper on the microwave turntable.
3 The potato will take 4–5 minutes to cook on high (in a 900W oven) until tender. You can cook more: 2 x 175g sweet potatoes will take a little longer, about 6–7 minutes; 3 x 175g sweet potatoes could take as long as 12–14 minutes.

Vegetable chilli jackets
SERVES 2 TAKES **45 MINUTES TO MAKE**

2 large baking potatoes
1 tbsp olive oil, plus extra for rubbing
1 onion, finely diced
1 red pepper, diced
1 courgette, diced
1 tsp chilli powder
$1/2$ tsp paprika
600ml pot fresh chilli bean soup
Handful coriander leaves, roughly chopped
2 tbsp crème fraîche

1 Preheat the oven to 200°C/fan 180°C/gas 6. Rub a little olive oil over each potato, prick well with a fork, then rub with salt.
2 Place on kitchen paper and cook in the microwave for 10 minutes on high, then bake in the oven for 20 minutes, until crispy and tender.
3 Meanwhile, heat the olive oil in a sauté or frying pan. Add the onion and cook over a low heat for 5 minutes until softened but without any colour, then add the red pepper and courgette. Stir through the chilli powder and paprika until all the vegetables are coated with the spices.
4 Cook for 8 minutes more or until everything has softened, stirring so the vegetables do not catch on the bottom of the pan. Pour in the soup and bring to a simmer. Bubble for about 3 minutes, until thickened. Remove the potatoes from the oven, place each on a warmed plate and carefully split them open to form pockets for the chilli.
5 Spoon the chilli into the jackets, scatter with coriander and top each with a spoon of crème fraîche. Serve with dressed salad.

Few things are more satisfying on a cold winter's day than a hearty jacket potato lunch.

Spiced prawns
SERVES 2 TAKES **20 MINUTES TO MAKE**

For the tomato sauce
1 tbsp olive oil
1 onion, finely chopped
1 garlic clove, finely chopped
400g can chopped tomatoes
Pinch of sugar

For the prawns
1 onion, sliced
1 tbsp olive oil
2 tsp fresh ginger, grated
$1/2$ tsp cumin seeds, roughly crushed
$1/2$ tsp coriander seeds, roughly crushed
$1/2$ tsp ground turmeric
Pinch of crushed dried chillies
250g raw, peeled large prawns
Small handful of coriander, chopped

1 Start the sauce. Heat the oil in a large frying pan over a medium heat, add the onion and garlic and cook for 3–4 minutes until softened.
2 Add the tomatoes to the pan (swish out the can with a little water and pour that in, too). Add the sugar, season, then leave to cook gently for 6–8 minutes, until thickened.
3 Meanwhile, in a separate frying pan, fry the sliced onion in the olive oil for 5 minutes over a medium heat, until golden.
4 Stir in the ginger, cumin and coriander. After 1–2 minutes, add the turmeric, chillies and prawns. Stir for 2–3 minutes until they turn pink.
5 Pour the sauce over the prawns. Sprinkle with coriander and serve with flatbread or rice.

delicious.**tip**

SLOW-ROASTED TOMATO SAUCE
Spiced prawns can make a wonderful starter too, especially if you use a slow-roasted tomato sauce instead of the quick recipe given above. Simply put 150g cherry tomatoes and some chopped garlic into a roasting tray, drizzle with olive oil and bake at 190°C/fan 170°C/gas 5 for an hour, then mash roughly into a delicious sauce.

Vegetable chilli jackets

Spiced prawns

everyday
eating

- weekday suppers
- family stews and casseroles
- vegetable mains and sides
- frugal food
- fast cooking
- freeze-ahead cooking

2

weekday suppers

Risotto alla Milanese

SERVES 4 TAKES **30 MINUTES TO MAKE**

1 tbsp olive oil
50g butter
1 onion, finely chopped
$1/2$ tsp saffron threads
300g arborio or carnaroli risotto rice
150ml dry white wine
1 litre fresh vegetable or chicken stock
75g Parmesan, grated, plus extra Parmesan
  shavings to serve
Good handful of parsley, chopped

1 Get all your ingredients ready. Heat the olive oil and half the butter in a wide, non-stick pan over a medium heat. Add the onion and cook, stirring, for 5 minutes until softened. Stir in the saffron until it begins to release its colour, then add the rice. Stir for 1 minute to coat in the butter, then pour in the wine and bubble until absorbed.
2 Meanwhile, heat the vegetable or chicken stock in a small saucepan and keep at a low simmer. Add a ladleful to the rice, stirring until absorbed. Continue adding the stock – 1 ladleful at a time, stirring frequently and making sure it is absorbed before adding the next ladleful – until the rice is al dente. This will take about 20 minutes. You might not need all the stock.
3 Stir in the remaining butter, cover with the lid and set aside for 2 minutes.
4 Stir in the grated Parmesan and parsley, and season. Divide the risotto between shallow bowls, top with Parmesan shavings and serve.

Lemon risotto with garlic prawns

SERVES 4 TAKES **35 MINUTES TO MAKE**

20 large peeled raw prawns, tail-shells on
1 tsp finely grated fresh ginger
3 garlic cloves, crushed
4 tbsp sweet chilli dipping sauce
Finely grated zest and juice of 1 large lemon
1.2 litres fresh vegetable stock, hot
Pinch of saffron threads
1 tbsp low-fat spread
1 bunch spring onions, finely chopped
300g arborio rice
Small handful flatleaf parsley, to serve

1 Put the raw peeled prawns in a bowl with the ginger, 1 crushed garlic clove, the chilli sauce and 1 tablespoon of lemon juice. Mix together, then set aside while you make the risotto.
2 Pour the stock into a saucepan, add the saffron and simmer over a low heat. Melt the spread in a heavy-based pan and sauté the onions and

delicious.**technique**
MAKING RISOTTO

1. *Soften an onion in oil, add the arborio rice and stir to coat each grain with oil.*

2. *Add a ladleful of stock at a time, stirring constantly as the rice absorbs the stock.*

3. *As the risotto thickens, stir very gently, just lifting the rice from the bottom of the pan.*

4. *The finished risotto should be creamy, but with the grains of rice still distinguishable.*

remaining crushed garlic for 2 minutes. Stir in the rice and zest and cook for 1 minute. Add a ladleful of the stock and cook, stirring occasionally, until it has been absorbed. Keep adding the stock, a ladleful at a time, and cook for about 20 minutes, or until the rice is just cooked. Remove from the heat, stir in the remaining lemon juice and set aside.

3 Heat a wok or large frying pan over a very high heat. When really hot, tip in the prawn mixture and cook, stirring, for 2–3 minutes, until the prawns turn pink and the sauce is bubbling and thick.

4 Spoon the risotto into warm bowls, top with the prawns and scatter over the parsley to serve.

Risotto alla Milanese

Spaghetti with prawns, lemon, chilli, garlic and rocket

SERVES 4 TAKES **20 MINUTES TO MAKE**

400g dried spaghetti
6 tbsp olive oil
3 garlic cloves, crushed
2 medium-hot red chillies, deseeded
  and finely chopped
150g vine-ripened tomatoes,
  skinned and chopped
Finely grated zest of $^1/_2$ lemon,
  plus 2 tbsp lemon juice
300–400g cooked and peeled tiger prawns
150g rocket leaves

1 Bring a large saucepan of water to the boil. Add the spaghetti and cook according to pack instructions or until the pasta is al dente.

2 Shortly before the spaghetti is ready, put the oil and garlic into a large deep frying pan or shallow saucepan over a medium-high heat. As soon as the garlic starts to sizzle, add the chillies and fry for 1 minute. Add the tomatoes and fry for a further minute. Then add the lemon zest, lemon juice, prawns and seasoning, and cook for $1^1/_2$–2 minutes, until the prawns are heated through.

3 Drain the spaghetti and add to the pan of prawns with the rocket; toss it all together well. Divide between 4 warmed pasta bowls and serve.

Spaghetti with prawns, lemon, chilli, garlic and rocket

Chicken and lemon spaghetti carbonara
SERVES 4 TAKES **25 MINUTES TO MAKE**

2 tbsp extra-virgin olive oil
2 boneless chicken breasts, skin on
450g dried spaghetti
175g piece smoked pancetta, cut into lardons
4 fresh sage leaves, chopped
2 large eggs, plus 2 large egg yolks
100ml double cream
Finely grated zest of 1 lemon
100g Parmesan, finely grated
50g butter

1 Slowly bring a pan of well-salted water to the boil. Meanwhile, heat half the oil in a small frying pan over a medium heat. Season the chicken and add to the pan skin-side down. Cook for 6 minutes each side or until cooked through. Transfer to a plate and leave to cool slightly.
2 Cook the spaghetti in the boiling water for 12 minutes or until al dente. Meanwhile, remove the skin from the chicken and cut the meat into small pieces. Put the remaining oil into the pan over a medium-high heat, add the pancetta and cook for 3–4 minutes, until lightly golden. Stir in the sage, then remove from the heat.
3 Lightly beat the eggs and egg yolks, the cream and the lemon zest together in a small bowl. Drain the spaghetti, tip back into the pan and add the pancetta, the chicken, the egg and cream mixture, two-thirds of the grated Parmesan, the butter and some freshly ground black pepper. Toss together well but do not return to the heat; the residual heat from the spaghetti will be sufficient to cook the eggs but still keep them smooth and creamy. Serve with the remaining grated cheese sprinkled on top.

Chicken and lemon
spaghetti carbonara

Meatballs with tomato pesto tagliatelle
SERVES 4–6 TAKES **35 MINUTES TO MAKE**

50g pine nuts
500g lean beef steak mince
2 garlic cloves, crushed
2 shallots, finely chopped
Good handful of fresh basil leaves, chopped
500g dried tagliatelle
5 tbsp sun-dried tomato pesto

1 Preheat the oven to 200°C/fan 180°C/gas 6. Line a large baking tray with baking paper.
2 Put the pine nuts into a dry, non-stick pan and toast over a high heat for 1–2 minutes, tossing continuously, until golden brown. Spill onto a chopping board and leave to cool slightly. Chop roughly and set aside.
3 Put the mince in a large bowl and season it well. Add the pine nuts, garlic, shallots and basil. Use your hands to squeeze the mixture together, then roll into about 24 walnut-sized balls. Place on the lined tray and bake for 15 minutes, until cooked through.
4 Meanwhile, bring a large pan of salted water to the boil, add the pasta, and cook according to packet instructions. Drain, reserving some of its liquid. Return the pasta to the pan and stir in the pesto and a little of the reserved liquid. Season, toss the meatballs into the pasta, and serve.

Creamy mushroom, pancetta and chilli penne

SERVES 2 TAKES **15 MINUTES TO MAKE**

200g dried penne
125g pancetta or bacon lardons
4 sliced flat or portabella mushrooms
1 red chilli, deseeded and sliced
Generous splash of olive oil
150g garlic & herbs Boursin
3 handfuls of fresh basil leaves
  (save some for decoration)

1 Cook the penne according to pack instructions, then drain.
2 Meanwhile, heat a frying pan over a high heat. Add the pancetta or bacon lardons and fry them for 5 minutes, stirring, until golden. Add the mushrooms and red chilli. Add the oil and cook for 4–5 minutes, then reduce the heat slightly.
3 Add the cheese and a splash of water. Stir until melted, then bring to a simmer. Cook for 1 minute to thicken, and season to taste.
4 Stir in the cooked pasta with torn basil leaves. Serve scattered with whole basil leaves.

Spaghetti with pancetta, butter beans and rosemary

SERVES 2 TAKES **20 MINUTES TO MAKE**

200g dried spaghetti
75g cubed pancetta or 4 rashers streaky
  bacon, diced
6 tbsp olive oil
1 small onion, chopped
1 garlic clove, crushed
1 tsp chopped fresh rosemary
400g can butter beans, drained and rinsed
Grated zest and juice of $1/2$ small lemon
Handful of parsley, chopped
Fresh Parmesan shavings, to serve

1 Bring a large saucepan of water to the boil and cook the spaghetti according to the packet instructions or until al dente.
2 Meanwhile, heat a non-stick pan and cook

Spaghetti with pancetta, butter beans and rosemary

the pancetta or bacon for 3–4 minutes until golden and crisp. Add the olive oil, onion, garlic and rosemary and cook for 6–7 minutes until softened. Add the beans and warm through. Stir in the lemon zest and juice, and the chopped fresh parsley. Season well with salt and freshly ground black pepper.
3 Drain the spaghetti well and return to the saucepan. Toss in the pancetta and butter bean mixture. Divide between two plates, and serve with several shavings of fresh Parmesan.

A simple dish using storecupboard staples – just what you need after a busy day.

Pesto, bacon and pine nut gnocchi
SERVES 2 TAKES 12 MINUTES TO MAKE

6 rashers streaky bacon
25g pine nuts
500g gnocchi
3 tbsp fresh green pesto
100ml half-fat crème fraîche

1 Heat a non-stick frying pan until hot. Add the bacon and cook for 5 minutes, turning, until golden and crisp. Remove, allow to cool, then break into pieces.
2 Add the pine nuts to the hot pan and cook, stirring, for 1 minute until golden. Set aside.
3 Cook the gnocchi according to the pack instructions, drain and return to the pan. Stir in the pesto and crème fraîche, season and gently heat through.
4 Mix in half the bacon and nuts, then divide between bowls. Scatter with the remaining bacon and nuts to serve.

Lasagne al forno
SERVES 6 TAKES 3 HOURS 30 MINUTES TO MAKE

750g rump or chuck steak
2 tbsp olive oil
1 large carrot, finely diced
1 celery stick, finely diced
1 onion, finely diced
2 garlic cloves, crushed
1 tbsp tomato purée
50g butter
50g plain flour
600ml full-fat milk
100g Parmesan, coarsely grated
9 dried plain lasagne sheets
Good bunch of basil leaves

1 Trim and discard any fat from the steak, then cut the meat into very small dice and set aside. Heat the oil in a large saucepan. Add the carrot, celery, onion and garlic and cook over a medium heat for 5 minutes, until the onion becomes translucent. Add the beef and cook for 5 minutes, stirring, until coloured all over. Stir in the tomato purée and cook for 1 minute. Add enough cold water (about 350ml) to just cover the meat and bring to a simmer. Cover and cook for $1\frac{1}{2}$ hours. Top up with water occasionally, if necessary. Uncover and simmer for 25–30 minutes, until you have a rich bolognese sauce.
2 When the bolognese is nearly ready, make a béchamel sauce. Melt the butter in a pan over a medium heat. Stir in the flour and cook for 1 minute. Remove from the heat and gradually whisk in the milk. Return to the heat and bring to the boil, stirring constantly. Reduce the heat slightly and simmer for 5 minutes, stirring until thickened. Stir in 2 tablespoons of the Parmesan, season and set aside.
3 If you are using lasagne sheets that don't need pre-cooking, go to step 4. If using sheets that need blanching, bring a large pan of water to a rolling boil. Drop a few sheets at a time into the water and cook for a few minutes. Remove with a slotted spoon and drop into iced water.
4 Preheat the oven to 200°C/fan 180°C/gas 6. Layer the lasagne. Spread a little of the béchamel sauce in the base of a deep, 2.25-litre ovenproof dish. Add 3 lasagne sheets in 1 layer, cutting them to fit your dish, if necessary. Add a third of the béchamel sauce, then top with half the meat. Scatter with torn basil and a little Parmesan. Make another layer of 3 lasagne sheets, then spread with a third of the béchamel. Add the rest of the meat and a little more basil and Parmesan. Add a final layer of 3 lasagne sheets and spread the rest of the béchamel on top. Sprinkle with the remaining Parmesan. Cover with foil (don't let it touch the Parmesan, or it will stick and pull it away) and bake for 40 minutes, then uncover and bake for 8-10 minutes until deep golden.
WINE NOTE Try a fruity Italian red, such as Barbera or Dolcetto, or a French Côtes-du-Rhône.

delicious.tip
BRINGING OUT THE FLAVOUR
If you have a bottle of red wine open, add a splash after you add the tomato purée in step 1 to give a little more depth to the flavour of the dish.

Classic prawn pad Thai

SERVES 4 TAKES **35 MINUTES TO MAKE**

300g wide rice stick noodles
2–3 tbsp dried shrimp
3 tbsp tamarind paste
3 tbsp *nam pla* (Thai fish sauce)
3 tbsp palm sugar
2 tbsp vegetable or groundnut oil
3 garlic cloves, finely chopped
2 Thai or regular shallots, finely chopped
1–2 tsp chilli flakes
2 large eggs, beaten
500g small cooked and peeled prawns
2 handfuls of beansprouts
Bunch of spring onions, shredded
Handful of unsalted roasted peanuts, chopped
Bunch of coriander, leaves roughly chopped
2 limes, cut into wedges

1 Place the rice noodles in a large bowl and pour over warm water to cover. Put the dried shrimp in another bowl and add warm water to cover. Leave both to soak for 20 minutes or until soft, then drain well.

2 Meanwhile, make the sweet-and-sour paste. Mix the tamarind paste with a splash of hot water to loosen. Add the fish sauce and palm sugar; mix, taste, and adjust to give a nice combination of sweet, salty, and sour.

3 Heat the oil in a wok or frying pan. When it's good and hot, fry the garlic and shallots for 30 seconds. Add the drained dried shrimp and the chilli flakes and toss together. Add the drained noodles to the wok and stir-fry for a couple of minutes, then push to one side. Add the eggs and allow to set, then scramble them and mix into the noodles.

4 Add the sweet-and-sour paste and stir well. Add the prawns, the beansprouts, the spring onions and half the peanuts. Toss well and cook for a few minutes.

5 Divide the pad Thai among 4 serving bowls, sprinkle with the coriander and remaining peanuts, and serve with the lime wedges, to squeeze over.

Classic prawn
pad Thai

Salmon and potato curry

SERVES 3 TAKES **30 MINUTES TO MAKE**

2 medium potatoes, cut into bite-size pieces
1 tbsp vegetable oil
1 onion, sliced
425g rogan josh curry sauce
2 skinless salmon fillets, cut into large chunks
2 good handfuls of cherry tomatoes, halved
Coriander leaves, to garnish

1 Cook the potato in boiling water for 8 minutes, until almost tender. Drain.
2 Heat 1 tablespoon of vegetable oil in a large, deep frying pan over a medium heat. Add the onion and cook, stirring, for 3–4 minutes.
3 Add the curry sauce, then put a good splash of water into the jar and swish out into the pan. Stir in the potatoes, then gently stir the fish into the sauce. Simmer for 5 minutes.
4 Add the cherry tomatoes and cook for a further 5 minutes, until the tomatoes have softened and the salmon is cooked through. Season to taste, divide between bowls and garnish with the coriander. Serve with boiled basmati rice, poppadoms and lime pickle.

Salmon steaks with basil, lemon and olive butter

SERVES 4 TAKES **20 MINUTES TO MAKE**

Large handful of basil
1 large lemon
4 pitted black olives, roughly chopped
50g butter, softened
4 salmon steaks, about 175g each

1 Preheat the oven to 200°C/fan 180°C/gas 6. Roughly chop the basil and put into a large bowl. Grate the zest of $^1/_2$ lemon and add to the bowl with the black olives. Add the butter and beat well with a wooden spoon until blended. Put aside.
2 Put the salmon steaks into an ovenproof dish large enough to fit the salmon in a single layer. Score the zest of the remaining $^1/_2$ lemon with a canelle knife if you have one (you don't have to do

Salmon and
potato curry

this, but it looks pretty). Cut 4 slices from the half of lemon you have just "canelled" and place one on top of each steak. Divide the olive butter into 4 and spoon on top of each lemon slice. Cover the dish with foil and bake in the oven for 12 minutes until just tender.
3 Divide the salmon between plates and spoon over the melted butter. Season and serve with cooked new potatoes and steamed and sliced baby leeks.

Lemon and herb butters are an easy way to add interest to grilled or baked fish.

Plaice with lemon parsley butter and crushed potatoes

Plaice with lemon parsley butter and crushed potatoes

SERVES 2 TAKES **15 MINUTES TO MAKE**

300g small new potatoes, halved
3 tbsp olive oil
2 handfuls of flatleaf parsley, chopped
2 plaice fillets with skin,
  about 150g each
2 tbsp plain flour
25g butter
1 lemon

1 Boil the potatoes in salted water for about
10 minutes or until tender. Drain, return to the
pan, and roughly crush with a fork. Season and
stir in 2 tablespoons of olive oil and a handful of
chopped fresh flatleaf parsley.
2 Meanwhile, season the plaice fillets and dust
them with a little plain flour. Heat 1 tablespoon
of olive oil in a large frying pan over a high heat.
Add the fish, with the skin side down, and cook
for 2 minutes. Carefully turn the fish over and

cook for a further 2 minutes, or until cooked
through. Transfer the plaice to 2 serving plates.
3 Melt the butter in the hot pan, stir in the juice
of $^1/_2$ lemon, a handful of parsley and some
seasoning. Drizzle the hot butter over the plaice
and spoon the potatoes alongside. Serve with the
remaining $^1/_2$ lemon, cut into wedges.

Thai fishcakes

SERVES 4 TAKES **25 MINUTES TO MAKE**

500g frozen white fish (pollack or cod),
  defrosted and finely chopped
1 lemongrass stick, outer layers discarded
  and finely chopped
2.5cm piece fresh ginger, grated
2 garlic cloves, crushed
Handful fresh coriander, finely chopped
Finely grated zest of 1 lime,
  plus extra wedges to serve (optional)
$^1/_2$ red pepper, finely chopped
1 red chilli, deseeded and finely chopped
2 tbsp plain flour
2 tbsp soy sauce
1 large free-range egg white
3 tbsp groundnut oil
400g steamed rice, to serve

1 In a food processor, whizz the fish, lemongrass,
ginger and garlic to a paste. Put this into a bowl
and mix in the coriander, lime zest, red pepper
and chilli, flour, soy sauce and egg white.
2 Heat the oil in a frying pan and fry dollops of
the mixture, in batches, for 2–3 minutes each
side until golden.
3 Serve the fishcakes with steamed rice, and with
lime wedges to squeeze over and sweet chilli
dipping sauce, if you like.

Zingy lime juice brings out all the flavour of the Thai spices.

Fish pie

SERVES 4 TAKES **1 HOUR 10 MINUTES TO MAKE**

1.25kg potatoes, cut into even-sized pieces
50g butter
225g baby spinach leaves
2 shallots, very finely chopped
2 bay leaves
Splash of extra-virgin olive oil
284ml carton double cream
125g Parmesan, grated
Juice of $\frac{1}{2}$ lemon
1 handful of flatleaf parsley, roughly chopped
450g cod or haddock fillet, skinned and boned
250g large shelled tiger prawns

1 Preheat the oven to 200°C/fan 180°C/gas 6. Cook the potatoes in boiling, salted water for 10–12 minutes until tender. Drain well and return to the pan over the heat and dry out for about 1 minute, shaking the pan well. Mash with plenty of seasoning and half the butter, then put aside.
2 Meanwhile, wash the spinach and put it in a clean pan with just the water that clings to the leaves; cook until just wilted. Then drain well and squeeze out any excess moisture.
3 In a separate pan, gently cook the shallots and bay leaves in the oil for 6–8 minutes until softened. Add the cream and bring just to the boil. Remove from the heat. Stir in the cheese, lemon juice and parsley.
4 Cut the fish into bite-size pieces and put into a buttered 1.8-litre ovenproof dish with the prawns. Break up the spinach with a knife and toss together with the fish. Remove the bay leaves from the sauce and pour into the dish, shaking it so it all distributes evenly. Spoon over the mash and dot with the remaining butter. Put on a tray and bake for 25–30 minutes, until golden and bubbling.

delicious.tip

ADDING FLAVOUR

You can use any firm white fish, unsmoked or smoked, for this pie. A handful of shelled mussels adds interest and makes a tasty addition.

Thai fishcakes

Fish pie

Grilled mackerel with potato and chorizo hash

SERVES 2 TAKES **35 MINUTES TO MAKE**

450g potatoes
2 whole mackerel, filleted into 4
  (ask your fishmonger to do this)
2 tbsp olive oil
Juice of 1 small lemon
1 garlic clove, crushed
Small handful of flatleaf parsley, chopped
100g piece chorizo, roughly chopped
Wild rocket, to serve

1 Parboil the potatoes (in their skins) in salted water until just tender to the centre. Drain and cool slightly.
2 Put the mackerel in a shallow dish. Mix together the oil, lemon juice, garlic and parsley, and pour over the fish. Season and toss together. Peel and discard the skin from the potatoes, then chop into bite-sized pieces.
3 Preheat the grill. Heat a large frying pan and

Grilled mackerel with potato and chorizo hash

cook the chorizo over a high heat for 2 minutes until the oil starts to run. Stir in the potatoes and cook for 8–10 minutes, stirring, until golden.
4 When the potato hash is nearly cooked, lift the fish from the marinade onto a grill rack and season. Grill for 5–8 minutes, until the skin is golden and the flesh is cooked through.

Baked fish with a herb and lemon crust

SERVES 4 TAKES **25 MINUTES TO MAKE**

1 tbsp extra-virgin olive oil,
  plus extra for greasing
4 thick white fish fillets, about 175g each, skinned
  (try hake, haddock or sustainably-caught cod)
4 slices white bread, toasted and crusts removed
1 garlic clove, crushed
1 small lemon, for zest and juice
15g tarragon
15g chives
15g flatleaf parsley

For the tartare sauce
4 tbsp mayonnaise
3 tbsp natural yogurt
$1/2$ tsp Dijon mustard
4 cocktail gherkins, finely chopped
1 tbsp capers, drained and finely chopped

1 Preheat the oven to 230°C/fan 210°C/gas 8. Line a baking sheet with baking paper and lightly grease with oil. Season the fish all over and put it skinned-side down on the paper.
2 Break the toast into a food processor, add the garlic and lemon zest, and whizz into fine crumbs. Set aside a few chives, then mix the rest with the tarragon and parsley. Add 25g of the mixture to the processor and whizz again until the herbs are finely chopped. Add oil, seasoning and 1 tsp of lemon juice, then briefly whizz again to mix.
3 Carefully press the breadcrumb mixture onto each piece of fish. Slide the baking sheet onto the top shelf of the oven and bake for 10–12 minutes or until the topping is golden and the fish is opaque and cooked through.

Salmon bake

4 Meanwhile, make the tartare sauce. Chop the remaining herbs (except a few chives) and mix with the mayonnaise, yogurt, mustard, gherkins, capers and a little salt. Serve the fish on warmed plates with the tartare sauce, garnished with chives.

Salmon bake

SERVES 2 TAKES **30 MINUTES TO MAKE**

··

250g salmon fillet, skinned and cut into chunks
100g baby spinach leaves
200g ricotta
20g Parmesan, grated
1 small lemon, for juice and zest
50ml vegetable stock
1 tbsp dill, chopped
2 large, ready-made potato rosti

··

1 Preheat the oven to 200°C/fan 180°C/gas 6. Scatter the salmon over the base of 2 ovenproof pie dishes (around 500ml each).
2 Pour boiling water over the spinach leaves, to

wilt, then refresh under cold water, squeeze dry, and roughly chop. Put the spinach in a bowl with the ricotta, Parmesan or Grana Padano, the zest and juice of the lemon, vegetable stock and dill. Mix, season well and divide evenly between the 2 ovenproof dishes.
3 Gently stir the fish and mixture together, then top each dish with a large, ready-made potato rosti. Place in the oven for 15–20 minutes, covering with foil after 10 minutes, and bake until the salmon is cooked through.

delicious.**technique**
SKINNING FISH

1. *At the tail end or one corner of the piece of fillet, make a nick between the flesh and skin so that you have a flap of skin you can pinch between finger and thumb. Grasping the skin tightly, slide the knife away from your fingers to separate the flesh from the skin.*

One-pan roast fish

2 minutes. When the potatoes are done, pile the onions and garlic on top of them, then top with the sliced tomatoes, parsley and tarragon. Arrange the fish fillets on top, and drizzle with olive oil and the juice of 1 lemon. Season well, top with lemon slices and bake for 10–12 minutes until the fish is pearly white and cooked through.

Tarragon chicken
SERVES 2 TAKES **25 MINUTES TO MAKE**

2 chicken breasts
Splash of olive oil
Knob of butter
1 shallot, chopped
1 garlic clove, chopped
Handful of tarragon, chopped,
  plus extra leaves to garnish
3 tbsp crème fraîche
Sautéed new potatoes, to serve

1 Heat a splash of olive oil and a knob of butter in a frying pan and pan-fry the chicken breasts until golden. Cover the pan, lower the heat and cook for 8–10 minutes.
2 Push the chicken aside and add the shallot and garlic. Cook for 1–2 minutes, until soft. Add the tarragon and crème fraîche and cook for 1 minute.
3 Season, garnish with fresh tarragon sprigs, and serve with sautéed new potatoes.

One-pan roast fish
SERVES 4 TAKES **40 MINUTES TO MAKE**

450g waxy potatoes
Olive oil, to drizzle
Knob of butter
2 red onions, cut into wedges
2 garlic cloves, sliced
4 tomatoes, sliced
1 tbsp chopped fresh flatleaf parsley
2 fresh tarragon sprigs,
  leaves stripped from stalks
4 skinless white fish fillets,
  such as haddock or pollack
2 lemons

1 Preheat the oven to 180°C/fan 160°C/gas 4. Peel and slice the potatoes and layer them in a roasting tin. Drizzle with olive oil, dot with butter and season. Roast for 25 minutes.
2 Meanwhile, heat 1 tablespoon of olive oil in a pan over a low heat and fry the onions for 5 minutes. Add the garlic and cook for a further

Poached chicken and coronation sauce
SERVES 4 TAKES **1 HOUR TO MAKE**

1 chicken, about 1.8kg
30g butter
1 tbsp olive oil
6 banana shallots or regular shallots,
  finely diced
3 tsp mild curry powder
250ml dry white wine
1 tbsp tomato purée
1/2 cinnamon stick
1 bay leaf
1 litre chicken stock

2 large egg yolks
Juice of $^1/_2$ lemon
200ml cold-pressed rapeseed oil or other
  mild vegetable oil
Coriander leaves, to garnish (optional)

1 Joint the chicken (see p.204) or ask your butcher to do this for you. Season the chicken pieces generously with salt and freshly ground black pepper.
2 Heat the butter and oil in a casserole over a high heat. Add the chicken, in batches, and gently brown all over – this will take around 10 minutes. Remove the chicken. Now fry the shallots in the same butter with the curry powder. As soon as the shallots start to soften, add the wine and let it simmer until it totally evaporates. Remove 3 tablespoons of the shallot mix and set aside.
3 Add the tomato purée, cinnamon and bay leaf to the casserole. Return the chicken and just cover with the stock. Bring the stock to a simmer, cover with a lid and poach the chicken for about 40 minutes, until tender and cooked through.

4 Meanwhile, make the coronation sauce. Put the egg yolks, the reserved shallot mix and the lemon juice into a food processor. Start the processor and pour the olive oil through the funnel in a very thin stream until you have a thick, glossy and slightly curried sauce.
5 Ladle the warm chicken into bowls, with plenty of the cooking liquor and a dollop of coronation sauce. Garnish with coriander leaves, if you wish.

Poaching is a gentle cooking technique that allows the chicken to remain tender and moist.

Tarragon
chicken

Sticky lemon chicken
SERVES 2 TAKES **25 MINUTES TO MAKE**

1 tbsp groundnut oil
2 skinless chicken breasts
2 pak choi
Handful of roasted cashew nuts
120g lemon stir-fry sauce
1 tbsp runny honey
250g pack ready-cooked basmati rice
  (or cook from dried before starting recipe)
1 large egg, whisked
Handful of coriander leaves, chopped
Juice and zest of $\frac{1}{2}$ lemon

1 Slice the chicken breasts into strips. Heat the oil in a wok or large frying pan, then season and stir-fry the chicken until browned.
2 Quarter the pak choi and stir-fry with the chicken until wilted. Add the cashew nuts, pour over the lemon stir-fry sauce and runny honey, and stir-fry until the chicken is cooked.
3 Meanwhile, heat a separate frying pan, add the cooked basmati rice and fry until warmed through. Make a well in the centre and pour in the whisked egg. Cook a little, then scramble through the rice. Stir through the coriander leaves and a squeeze of lemon juice.
4 Divide the rice between 2 plates, top with the chicken, and sprinkle with lemon zest.

Sticky lemon chicken

Chicken laksa
SERVES 4 TAKES **25 MINUTES TO MAKE**

2 shallots, finely sliced
2 red chillies, finely sliced
5cm piece stem ginger, sliced
1 tsp vegetable oil
2 lemongrass stalks, finely chopped
2–3 chicken breasts, sliced
600ml chicken stock
2 tbsp *nam pla* (Thai fish sauce)
1 tbsp soft brown sugar
Several handfuls of baby leaf spinach
200ml coconut milk
3 limes
2 bundles of thin rice noodles
Small bunch of coriander leaves

1 In a pan, gently fry the shallots, chillies and ginger in vegetable oil for 2 minutes.
2 Add the lemongrass, chicken and chicken stock, and bring to a simmer. Stir in the fish sauce and brown sugar, and simmer for 10 minutes until the chicken is cooked. Add the spinach, coconut milk and the juice of 2 limes, and then warm through until the spinach wilts.
3 Boil the rice noodles in plenty of water until soft (around 3–4 minutes). Stir the cooked noodles into the laksa. Divide between bowls and garnish each with coriander sprigs and lime wedges.

delicious.**tip**
RINGING THE CHANGES
To turn this into a tasty Thai curry, stir in 2–3 tbsp red or green Thai curry paste when frying the chicken, then use 300ml chicken stock and 400ml coconut milk instead of 600ml chicken stock.

Chicken and sweetcorn pie
SERVES 6 TAKES **1 HOUR 30 MINUTES TO MAKE**

3 chicken breasts
1 onion, halved
2 carrots, halved
50g leeks, washed, trimmed and halved
50g broccoli, broken into florets
2 bay leaves
400g potatoes, quartered
300g parsnips, quartered
300g sweet potatoes, quartered
400ml milk
40g butter
25g plain flour
198g can sweetcorn, drained

1 Put the chicken breasts into a large saucepan with the onion, carrots, leeks, broccoli and bay leaves and cover with 750ml cold water. Bring to the boil, cover, then put over a low heat to simmer for 15 minutes until the chicken and vegetables are tender.
2 Meanwhile, put the potatoes, parsnips and sweet potatoes into a second saucepan of water and bring to the boil. Simmer for 20 minutes until tender, then drain well. Mash with 100ml milk and a knob of butter.
3 Remove the chicken from the pan and slice. Drain off 300ml liquid (this is now chicken stock) and reserve or freeze for another recipe. Whizz the vegetables and the rest of the liquid in a food processor until really smooth.
4 Heat the remaining butter in a pan, add the flour, and cook for 1 minute, then gradually whisk in the rest of the milk until the sauce is thick and smooth. (If any lumps form while cooking, simply beat them out.) Gradually stir in the thickened vegetable liquid, then add the sliced chicken and sweetcorn.
5 Preheat the oven to 200°C/fan 180°C/gas 6. Put all the chicken filling into one large ovenproof dish or divide it between 6 individual ones. Top with the potato and vegetable mash and smooth with a fork. Bake individual pies for 20 minutes or a large one for around 30 minutes, until bubbling.

Chicken, pea and bacon pies
SERVES 4 TAKES **35 MINUTES TO MAKE**

6 rashers streaky bacon
1 quantity defrosted Creamy Chicken in a White Sauce (see p.162)
4 tbsp crème fraîche
A good handful of frozen peas
375g ready-rolled puff pastry
A little beaten egg or milk

1 Preheat the oven to 200°C/fan 180°C/gas 6. Chop the bacon and dry-fry in a hot pan, until golden and crisp. Drain and set aside.
2 Tip the creamy chicken mixture into a bowl and stir in crème fraîche, frozen peas (no need to defrost) and the bacon. Spoon into 4 individual (300ml) dishes or a large 1-litre ovenproof dish.
3 Unroll the puff pastry and cut to fit the dish/es, (you can use the trimmings, if you have any, to line the inner edge of the dish/es). Brush with a little beaten egg or milk and bake for 25 minutes. Serve with green vegetables or a salad.

Chicken curry
SERVES 6 TAKES **55 MINUTES TO MAKE**

4 tbsp vegetable oil
2 onions, halved and sliced
4 garlic cloves, crushed
3cm piece fresh ginger, grated
150g rogan josh curry paste
8 fresh or 4 dried curry leaves (optional)
12 boneless, skinless chicken thigh fillets
500g potatoes, peeled and cut into
  large chunks
2 small aubergines, cut into large chunks
400g can chopped tomatoes
750ml chicken stock, hot
200g French beans, trimmed

1 Heat the oil in a heavy-based pan, add the onions and fry for 5 minutes. Add the garlic and ginger and cook for 30 seconds. Stir in the curry paste and curry leaves, and fry for 1 minute. Add the chicken and cook for 10 minutes, stirring occasionally.

2 Add the potatoes and aubergines, then pour in the tomatoes and stock. Add the salt and some black pepper. Cover and cook for 15 minutes.
3 Uncover and cook for another 10 minutes. To serve, add the beans and cook for 3–4 minutes. Serve with Pilau Rice (see below).

Pilau rice

SERVES 4 TAKES **25 MINUTES TO MAKE**

1 tbsp groundnut oil
1 small onion, finely chopped
1 cinnamon stick, split lengthways
³/₄ tsp cumin seeds
2 cardamom pods
6 cloves
2 tsp ground turmeric
Few sprigs of fresh thyme
2 bay leaves
300ml long grain rice, measured out in a
    measuring jug

1 Heat the oil in a large pan with a tight-fitting lid. Add the onion and gently cook until softened.
2 Dry-toast the cumin seeds in a dry skillet or frying pan over a medium heat for around 30 seconds, then crush in a bowl or with a mortar and pestle. Stir in the spices and herbs and cook for 1 minute. Add the rice and stir until coated.
3 Add 600ml boiling water and bring to the boil. Cover, then simmer on the lowest setting for 12–15 minutes until tender. Let the steam dry off, then fluff up with a fork.

The wonderful fragrance of pilau spices lifts any curry dish, making it feel truly exotic.

Chicken, pea and bacon pies

Pilau rice

Chicken noodles

Chicken noodles
SERVES 2 TAKES **15 MINUTES TO MAKE**

100g dried thin egg noodles
200g ready-cooked red Thai chicken mini fillets
2 spring onions, finely sliced
2 sachets instant miso soup
2 tbsp soy sauce

1 Cook the noodles in plenty of boiling water until soft (around 3–4 minutes), then drain and set them aside in a bowl.
2 Cut the chicken mini fillets into thin strips.
3 Make up the miso soup according to pack instructions, add the soy sauce, and stir to mix.
4 Return the noodles to the pan and gently separate them with a fork. Add the chicken and spring onions, pour in the miso soup and cook for 2 minutes.
5 Divide the chicken noodles between 2 bowls and eat immediately.

Chicken and cashew nut stir-fry

Chicken and cashew nut stir-fry
SERVES 4 TAKES **30 MINUTES TO MAKE**

1 tbsp groundnut oil
450g skinless chicken breasts, diced
1 large carrot, quartered and cut into matchsticks
2 celery sticks, finely sliced
1 red pepper, deseeded and sliced
1 red chilli, deseeded and sliced
Thumb-size piece fresh root ginger, grated
1 large garlic clove, finely chopped
2 pak choi, stems sliced and leaves torn
Bunch of spring onions,
  trimmed and sliced
300g beansprouts
100g cashew nuts, toasted
200g dried egg noodles, to serve

For the sauce
1 tbsp cornflour
3 tbsp soy sauce
3 tbsp Chinese rice wine or dry sherry
1 tbsp toasted sesame oil

1 Mix all the ingredients for the sauce, season with black pepper, and set aside.

2 Put the wok over a high heat for 1 minute. Add the groundnut oil and chicken, and cook for 4–5 minutes, stirring, until nearly cooked. Remove with a slotted spoon and set aside.

3 Cook the egg noodles in plenty of boiling water until soft (around 3–4 minutes), then drain and set aside.

4 Meanwhile, add the carrot, celery, pepper and chilli to the wok and stir-fry for 3–4 minutes. Add the ginger, garlic and pak choi stems, and stir-fry for another 2–3 minutes. Add the onions and beansprouts and stir-fry for a further 2 minutes.

5 Return the chicken to the pan, along with the pak choi leaves. Stir-fry for 1 minute, add the sauce and stir-fry for 1–2 minutes, until the sauce has thickened. Stir in the cashews and serve with the cooked noodles.

Chicken and leek pie
SERVES 4 TAKES **1 HOUR 15 MINUTES TO MAKE**

2 tbsp vegetable oil
1 onion, finely chopped
2 medium leeks, washed, trimmed and thickly sliced
4 skinless chicken breasts, cut into bite-size pieces
1 garlic clove, crushed
150ml white wine
150ml chicken stock, hot
142ml double cream
Several sprigs of fresh tarragon, leaves picked and roughly chopped
375g pack ready-rolled puff pastry
1 egg

1 Heat the oil in a large frying pan over a medium heat. Add the onion and leeks and cook for 4–5 minutes until softened.

2 Add the chicken pieces and cook, stirring, for another 4–5 minutes. Stir in the garlic, add the wine, and let it all bubble away until reduced by two-thirds.

3 Pour in the stock and simmer until reduced by half. Add the cream and tarragon leaves, bring to the boil, then simmer for 5–6 minutes until thickened. Season, then spoon into one large (2.5-litre) pie dish or 4 individual ovenproof dishes (about 300ml each). Set aside to cool.

4 Brush a little water along the edge of the pie dish or dishes. Unroll the pastry and cut out a piece large enough to cover the dish or dishes. Press down the edges and trim off the excess. (You can do this very neatly by laying the rolled pastry over each dish, and then rolling over the pastry in place – the pressure from the rolling pin seals the pastry gently into place and cuts off any excess.) Snip a small hole in the centre of the pastry to let the steam escape. Put on a baking tray and chill for 15 minutes. Meanwhile, preheat the oven to 220°C/fan 200°C/gas 7.

5 Beat the egg with a little salt, then brush over the pastry. Bake for 40–45 minutes (20–25 minutes if you are making individual pies) until the pastry is golden.

WINE NOTE Cut through the richness with a good-quality dry white such as Riesling or Vouvray.

Chicken and leek pie

Tandoori chicken with mango raita
SERVES 4 TAKES **1 HOUR TO MAKE**

4 tbsp tandoori paste
250ml low-fat natural yogurt
Juice of $1/2$ lemon
4 boneless, skinless chicken breasts,
  cut into strips
2 tbsp groundnut oil

For the mango raita
1 small unripe mango, peeled, pitted and
  chopped
2 tbsp coriander leaves
1 tsp ground coriander
1 green chilli, deseeded and chopped
$1/2$ tsp mint sauce
250ml low-fat natural yogurt
$1/2$ cucumber, peeled and diced

1 Put the tandoori paste, yogurt and lemon juice
in a dish and stir in the chicken. Cover and chill
for at least 30 minutes.

Sausage and
potato bake

2 Meanwhile, make the raita. Put the mango,
fresh and ground coriander, chilli and mint sauce
in a food processor. Blend until smooth, then add
the yogurt and whizz for a few seconds. Put into a
bowl and stir in the cucumber. Cover and chill.
3 Preheat the oven to 220°C/fan 200°C/gas 7. Put
the chicken into a roasting tin and drizzle with oil.
Roast for 20 minutes until cooked. Serve with the
raita, with lime wedges to squeeze over, if you like.

Chicken with fennel and thyme
SERVES 6 TAKES **40 MINUTES TO MAKE**

4 tbsp olive oil
4 garlic cloves, finely sliced
20g thyme, leaves picked from stalks
6 boneless, skinless chicken breasts
200g smoked bacon lardons or pancetta pieces
2 fennel bulbs, each cut into 12 wedges
1 red onion, sliced into 12 wedges
300ml dry white wine

1 Preheat the oven to 200°C/fan 180°C/gas 6. Put
2 tablespoons of the oil into a non-stick roasting
tin. Add the garlic, thyme, 1 tbsp of sea salt and
2 tsp of ground black pepper and mix. Add the
chicken and turn to coat. Scatter with the lardons
or pancetta, add the fennel and onion, and drizzle
with the remaining oil. Cook for 15 minutes, then
increase the oven temperature to 230°C/fan
210°C/gas 8.
2 Pour the wine into the tin and cook for another
10 minutes, or until the chicken is golden and the
vegetables tender.

The deep saltiness of the pancetta gives a real kick of flavour to this subtle dish.

Baked sausages
with leeks, apples
and cider

Baked sausages with leeks, apples and cider

SERVES 4 TAKES **1 HOUR 15 MINUTES TO MAKE**

....

3 leeks, washed and cut into
   2.5cm lengths
2 apples, cored and cut into wedges
8 pork sausages
3 tbsp olive oil
25g butter
250ml medium cider
2 tbsp wholegrain mustard

....

1 Preheat the oven to 190°C/ fan 170°C/gas 5.
Put the leeks and apples into a roasting tin that
will hold the sausages in a single layer. Put the
sausages on top of the leeks and apples, and
drizzle over the oil. Season and toss together.
Dot with the butter and pour over the cider.
Bake for 50 minutes.
2 Take the sausages from the oven and spread
them with mustard. Return to the oven and cook
for a further 15 minutes.

3 Serve the sausages and leeks with the pan
juices spooned over, accompanied with mash
or rosemary roasted potatoes.
WINE NOTE A good-quality apple or pear cider
is the perfect complement to this dish.

Sausage and potato bake

SERVES 4 TAKES **45 MINUTES TO MAKE**

....

8 sausages
500g baby new potatoes, halved
3 red onions, cut into wedges
12 fresh sage leaves
Green salad, to serve

....

1 Preheat the oven to 200°C/fan 180°C/gas 6.
Place the sausages in a roasting tin with a drizzle
of oil, and brown in a hot oven for 10 minutes.
2 Add the potatoes, onions and sage leaves.
Season well and bake for 25–30 minutes until
everything is cooked. Serve while piping hot with
a green salad.

Bubble and squeak cakes with ham and avocado

sausages to the edge of the pan and add the apple wedges. Cook for about 2 minutes on each side, until turning golden. Remove the apple with a slotted spoon and drain on kitchen paper.

4 Add the onion to the pan and cook, stirring, for 6–8 minutes, until softened. Stir in the flour and cook for 1 minute, then gradually add the wine, mustard and Worcestershire sauce. Pour in 120ml hot water and allow to bubble for a few minutes to thicken the gravy. Return the apple to the pan and season.

5 Drain the potatoes, then put them back in their pan and return to the heat for about 30 seconds to drive off any excess moisture. Mash well with the butter and milk, and season.

6 Divide the mash between 4 plates and top with the bangers. Spoon over the apple and gravy.

Bubble and squeak cakes with ham and avocado
SERVES 4 TAKES **20 MINUTES TO MAKE**

3 cooked medium potatoes (about 325g)
325g cooked vegetables (such as parsnips, Brussels sprouts and carrots)
200g chopped cooked ham
2 eggs, beaten
Olive oil, for frying and drizzling
Knob of butter
Bag of wild rocket
2 avocados, sliced
Lemon juice, to serve

1 Put the cooked potatoes on a chopping board and break them up. Add the other cooked vegetables and chop it all up into a rough mixture. Put into a bowl and add the ham, eggs and seasoning, and mix well. Divide into 4 and roughly shape into 4 cakes.

2 Heat a splash of oil and the butter in a frying pan and fry the cakes for about 8–10 minutes, turning once, until golden and crispy.

3 Divide a bag of rocket between 4 plates. Top each with a bubble and squeak cake and half an avocado. Drizzle with good olive oil and squeeze over some lemon juice to serve.

Bangers and mash, mustard gravy and apple wedges
SERVES 4 TAKES **50 MINUTES TO MAKE**

1 tbsp vegetable oil
8 pork and herb sausages
700g floury potatoes
2 cox's apples
1 red onion, sliced
2 tsp plain flour
150ml red wine
1 tsp wholegrain mustard
1 tbsp Worcestershire sauce
50g butter
50ml milk

1 Heat the oil in a large frying pan over a high heat and add the sausages. Cook for 15 minutes, turning to brown all over.

2 Meanwhile, cut the potatoes into even chunks and put into a pan of cold salted water. Bring to the boil and simmer for 15 minutes, until tender.

3 Core the apples and cut into wedges. Push the

Bangers and mash,
mustard gravy and
apple wedges

Sesame and ginger pork stir-fry

Sesame and ginger pork stir-fry

SERVES 4 TAKES **20 MINUTES TO MAKE**

4 tbsp dark soy sauce, plus extra to serve
1 tbsp toasted sesame oil
5cm fresh ginger, peeled and thinly sliced
500g pork tenderloin fillet, trimmed of fat
1 tbsp sesame seeds
300g mixed Chinese stir-fry vegetables
Medium egg noodles, to serve

1 Mix together the soy sauce, the sesame oil and the ginger in a shallow dish. Thinly slice the pork, add to the marinade and season with black pepper. Toss together and set aside for 5 minutes.
2 Heat a wok and toast the sesame seeds (there's no need for oil) for 2–3 minutes until coloured and fragrant. Remove from the wok and set aside.
3 Lift the pork from the marinade. Sear the pork in batches in the wok until browned all over. Remove and set aside.
4 Add all the vegetables to the wok, pour over the marinade and stir-fry for 3 minutes. Toss in the pork and stir-fry for a further 2–3 minutes.
5 Cook the egg noodles in boiling water for about 2 minutes, until tender (see below). Divide the noodles between 4 warmed plates and top with the pork and stir-fried vegetables. Serve sprinkled with the sesame seeds and with soy sauce to drizzle.

delicious.**technique**
BOILING EGG NOODLES

1. Bring a large pan of boiling water to the boil. Add the noodles, allow the water to return to the boil, and cook until softened and tender.

2. Drain in a colander or sieve, then rinse under cold, running water. Return them to the still-hot pan, tossing in a little oil to rewarm without sticking.

Pan-fried pork noisettes with green peppercorn sauce
SERVES 4 TAKES **20 MINUTES TO MAKE**

2 pork tenderloins (fillets),
  about 450g each
50g butter
25g plain flour
150ml dry white wine
150ml chicken stock
300ml whipping cream
1 tsp Dijon mustard
Squeeze of lemon juice
2–3 tsp green peppercorns in brine,
  drained and rinsed

1 Trim the pork tenderloins of any excess fat and membrane (otherwise this will cause the meat to twist as it shrinks during cooking) then slice them across, very slightly on the diagonal, into slices ("noisettes") about 2cm thick.
2 Melt the butter in either 1 large or 2 small heavy-based pans. Season the noisettes with salt and freshly ground pepper, then coat them lightly in the flour, patting off the excess. As soon as the butter is foaming, add the noisettes to the pan(s) and cook over a medium-high heat for about 3–4 minutes on each side, until nicely browned and cooked through. The juices should run clear, not pink. Remove the pork noisettes from the pan(s) and arrange on a warmed serving dish. Set aside in a warm place.
3 Pour any excess fat away from the pan or pans, set one of them over a high heat and add the wine and stock. Allow it to boil rapidly, scraping up all the caramelized juices from the base of the pan with a wooden spoon, until it has reduced by three-quarters (to about 75ml). Add the cream and mustard and continue to boil for 3–4 minutes until reduced to a light sauce consistency. Keep tasting it, as you don't want to cook it any longer than necessary. Add a squeeze of lemon juice and the green peppercorns, and adjust the seasoning if necessary.
4 Return the pork noisettes to the pan to just warm through. Spoon the sauce over the pork and serve, with boiled or mashed potatoes.

Liver and bacon with celeriac mash
SERVES 4 TAKES **30 MINUTES TO MAKE**

8 rashers dry-cured streaky bacon
350g calf's liver, thinly sliced
Large pinch of caster sugar
1 tbsp plain flour, for dusting
1 tbsp sunflower oil
1 tbsp balsamic vinegar

For the celeriac mash
2 large potatoes (about 450g), diced
450g celeriac, diced
3 tbsp skimmed milk
Bunch of spring onions, trimmed and chopped

1 Make the celeriac mash. Simmer the potatoes and celeriac in a large pan of boiling salted water for about 15 minutes or until tender. Drain and return to the pan, covered, to dry out.
2 In a small pan, gently heat the milk. Add the spring onions and cook for 2–3 minutes, until the onions have softened. Add to the potatoes and celeriac, then mash and season. Set aside, covered, to keep hot.
3 Meanwhile, grill the bacon until beginning to crisp at the edges.
4 Season the liver on both sides with salt, pepper and the sugar, then coat lightly in the flour. Heat a large frying pan over a high heat. When hot, add the oil, then the liver, and cook for 2 minutes each side, until nicely browned but still pink and juicy on the inside. Add the balsamic vinegar to the pan. Serve the liver and pan juices immediately with the celeriac mash and crispy bacon.
WINE NOTE Go for a rich, hearty red from France's Rhône region or, from further south, a Vin de Pays d'Oc based on the Syrah (Shiraz) grape.

delicious.**tip**
PREPARING IN ADVANCE
It's important to cook calf's liver right at the last minute so it's eaten while tender and juicy. If you're worried about keeping your eye on different pans at the same time, make the mash ahead and reheat in the microwave to serve.

Roots, ham and caramelised onion pie

SERVES 6 TAKES **1 HOUR 25 MINUTES TO MAKE**

....

12 whole pickling onions or small shallots
90g butter
1 sprig of fresh thyme, leaves picked
2 tsp caster sugar
225g carrots, cut into small chunks
225g swede, cut into chunks
225g celeriac, cut into chunks
225g piece cooked ham, cut into chunks
30g plain flour, plus extra for dusting
600ml full-fat milk
50g fresh Parmesan, grated
Good handful of chopped fresh parsley
375g ready-rolled shortcrust pastry
1 egg, beaten

....

1 Put the onions into a bowl, pour over a kettle of boiling water, and soak for 5 minutes. Drain, halve and peel. Melt 50g of the butter in a large pan over a very low heat, then add the onions and cook, covered, for 15–20 minutes, stirring occasionally, until tender. Increase the heat to medium, add the thyme and sugar and cook, uncovered, for 5–6 minutes, until caramelised. Allow to cool.
2 Meanwhile, put the rest of the vegetables into a steamer or colander over a pan of boiling water, cover, and steam for 10–12 minutes, until tender. Drain well and toss together with the onions and the ham.
3 Preheat the oven to 200°C/fan 180°C/gas 6. Make the sauce. Melt the remaining butter in a pan over a medium heat. Add the flour and cook, stirring, for 1 minute. Gradually stir in the milk and cook, stirring, until smooth and thickened. Simmer for 2 minutes, stirring continuously. Remove from the heat and stir in the cheese and parsley. Season.
4 Pour the sauce over the vegetables and ham, and stir well. Spoon into a 2-litre pie dish. Unroll the pastry on a lightly floured surface and cut out a shape about 2cm bigger than the dish. Cover the dish with the pastry, trim the edges and use the trimmings to decorate the top of the pie.

5 Brush the pastry with the egg and make a snip in the top for the steam to escape. Sit on a baking sheet and bake for 40 minutes, until golden.
WINE NOTE Try an aromatic, off-dry Riesling or Pinot Blanc from the Alsace region of France, where white wines are often matched with local ham and onion dishes.

Creamy black pepper and spinach pork

SERVES 2 TAKES **25 MINUTES TO MAKE**

....

Vegetable oil for frying
2 good-quality pork loin chops
1 small onion, sliced
80g peppered Boursin
150ml hot chicken stock
Grated zest of $\frac{1}{2}$ lemon
Handful of baby spinach leaves

....

1 Heat a little vegetable oil in a frying pan. Season the chops, add to the pan and sear on both sides. Remove and set aside.
2 Add the onion to the pan and cook for 5 minutes to soften. Crumble in the pack of peppered cheese, add the chicken stock and stir until combined. Add the chops and simmer for 8 minutes, turning over in the sauce halfway, or until cooked through.
3 Transfer the chops to 2 plates. Stir the lemon zest into the sauce, then simmer for a few minutes to thicken. Add spinach and cook until just wilted. Spoon over the chops and serve with boiled new potatoes.

delicious.**technique**
ZESTING A LEMON

1. To zest a lemon without clogging the grater, lay a sheet of baking paper over the zesting surface of the grater. Rub the lemon over this, and the grated zest will fall away instead of becoming trapped between the teeth of the grater.

Roots, ham and
caramelised
onion pie

Creamy mustard pork

Creamy mustard pork
SERVES 4 TAKES **25 MINUTES TO MAKE**

1 tbsp olive oil
4 pork chops
2 garlic cloves, peeled but unsliced
2 leeks, washed and sliced
Glass of white wine (or extra 250ml
   chicken stock, if preferred)
1 tbsp wholegrain mustard
100ml chicken stock
50ml double cream
2 tbsp chopped flatleaf parsley,
   plus extra parsley leaves to garnish
A good squeeze of lemon juice
Mashed potato and green beans, to serve

1 Heat the olive oil in a large frying pan and fry
the pork chops with the garlic over a medium
heat for 5 minutes each side, so the chops are
lightly browned. Discard the garlic and set the
chops aside, covered with foil to keep warm.
2 Add the leeks to the pan and cook for another
6 minutes. Add the white wine to the pan and
cook to reduce the liquor by two-thirds, then stir
in the mustard, chicken stock, double cream and
some seasoning.
3 Bubble for a couple of minutes, then add the
chopped parsley and a squeeze of lemon juice.
4 Serve the chops on 4 plates, covered with the
creamy sauce and sprinkled with parsley leaves.
This dish works well with mashed potato and
slightly crunchy green beans.
WINE NOTE As the recipe uses wine, select one that
you can drink with the meal – perhaps an off-dry
white, such as French Vouvray.

delicious.**tip**
RINGING THE CHANGES
With a few simple changes, this recipe can be used
to make a quick version of pork stroganoff. Cut the
pork into strips, and fry it with the garlic and
150g chestnut mushrooms, thickly sliced. Continue
to follow the recipe just as given here, but use
1 tbsp smoked paprika instead of mustard.

Pea, ham and Taleggio tart
SERVES 8 TAKES **1 HOUR 10 MINUTES TO MAKE**

4 eggs, beaten
150g freshly shelled or frozen peas
4 slices smoked ham, about 25g each, roughly
  torn into large pieces
50g Gruyère, coarsely grated
100g Taleggio cheese or mozzarella, cut
  into cubes
1/2 bunch of fresh chives, chopped
140ml double cream

For the pastry
200g plain flour, plus extra for dusting
1/4 tsp salt
100g unsalted butter, diced
1 egg, lightly beaten

1 Make the pastry. Put the flour, salt and butter into a food processor and whizz to fine crumbs. Then, with the machine running, add the egg and continue to whizz until it starts to stick together (add a teaspoon or two of water if it's too dry). Take it out of the processor and knead briefly until smooth. Roll it out on a lightly floured surface and use it to line a 23cm round fluted loose-bottomed tart tin. Chill for 20 minutes.
2 Preheat the oven to 200°C/fan 180°C/gas 6. Prick the pastry base with a fork and line with baking paper and beans. Place on a baking tray and bake for 10 minutes, then remove the paper and beans and bake for another 10 minutes.
3 Brush the pastry with the beaten egg and bake for a further 5 minutes until pale golden. Remove and reduce the oven temperature to 180°C/fan 160°C/gas 4.
4 Cook the peas in a pan of lightly salted water for 2–3 minutes. Drain, refresh in cold water, then drain again. Sprinkle the ham, cheeses, peas and chives in the pastry case. Beat the eggs with the cream and some seasoning (you can add any egg left over from brushing the pastry to the mix), pour into the pastry case and bake for 25–30 minutes, until the filling is just set and pale golden in places.

Pea, ham and
Taleggio tart

Pork chops with apple, red onion and walnut sauce

Pork chops with apple, red onion and walnut sauce

SERVES 4 TAKES **30 MINUTES TO MAKE**

1 tsp cumin seeds
Pinch of dried chilli flakes
2 tbsp olive oil
4 bone-in pork chops

For the apple, red onion and walnut sauce
1 tbsp olive oil
25g butter
2 red-skinned apples,
  cored and cut into wedges
2 red onions, cut into wedges
50g walnut pieces
2 rosemary sprigs, leaves picked and chopped
2 tbsp cider vinegar

1 Dry-fry the cumin seeds in a pan over a medium heat for 30 seconds or until fragrant. Tip into a pestle and mortar, add the chilli flakes and some seasoning, and roughly crush. Stir in the olive oil.
2 Preheat the grill to high. Using scissors, snip sideways through the layer of fat on each pork chop, at intervals – this stops them curling up. Arrange on a grill rack over a foil-lined tray. Brush with half the spiced oil and grill for 4–5 minutes. Turn and brush with the remaining spiced oil. Grill for a further 4–5 minutes or until golden and just cooked through. Set aside, loosely covered with foil.
3 While the pork is resting, heat the oil and butter in a large frying pan over a medium heat. Add the apple wedges and onions to the hot pan and cook, stirring occasionally, for 5 minutes or

Szechuan pork

Chunky apples and walnuts give a warm, autumnal feel to sweet, juicy pork chops.

until beginning to soften. Add the walnuts and rosemary, cook for 2 more minutes, then add the vinegar and let it bubble away. Season to taste.

4 Divide the pork chops between 4 serving plates, spoon the hot apple, onion and walnut sauce alongside, and serve.

WINE NOTE A bright New World Pinot Noir has the perfect crisp freshness for this dish.

Mexican-style pork with sweet potatoes and lime yogurt

SERVES 4 TAKES **1 HOUR TO MAKE**

4 sweet potatoes, about 180–200g each
150g natural yogurt
1 red chilli, deseeded and finely chopped
Small bunch of coriander, chopped
Finely grated zest of 1 lime, plus extra lime
  halves to serve
1 tsp cumin seeds
$^1/_2$ tsp paprika
$^1/_2$ tsp mild chilli powder
2 garlic cloves, crushed
1 tbsp brown sugar
1 tbsp mild olive oil
4 boneless pork loin steaks

1 Preheat the oven to 180°C/fan160°C/gas 4. Put the sweet potatoes on a baking tray and cook for 45 minutes until soft. Cover with foil and keep warm. While they're cooking, mix the yogurt with the chilli, coriander, and lime zest in a bowl.

2 Preheat the grill to medium. Mix the cumin, paprika, chilli powder, garlic, sugar and oil together in a large bowl. Add the pork steaks and turn until they are completely coated with sauce. Place the pork steaks on a foil-lined baking tray, spaced apart, and grill for about 6 minutes, turning halfway, until cooked but still juicy.

3 Cut the sweet potatoes into wedges and serve with the grilled pork steaks, a lime half, and the yogurt on the side. Add a mixed salad, if you like.

WINE NOTE Partner this with a white wine – a fairly rich, fruity Chardonnay from South Africa or California will hold its own against the spice and the tang of the lime and yogurt flavours.

Szechuan pork

SERVES 4 TAKES **25 MINUTES TO MAKE**

1 tbsp groundnut oil
2 shallots, finely sliced
2.5cm piece root ginger
1 red chilli, deseeded and finely chopped
500g pork mince
2 tsp Szechuan peppercorns, crushed
1 tsp Chinese five-spice
2 tbsp soy sauce
1 tbsp honey
Juice of 1 lime
350g basmati rice
165ml coconut milk
2 tbsp coriander, chopped
4 spring onions, finely sliced, to garnish

1 Heat the groundnut oil in a pan or wok. Reserve a little of the ginger and chilli for garnish, and fry the rest with the shallots for a couple of minutes.

2 Add the mince and quickly brown, then stir in the peppercorns and five-spice, and cook for a couple more minutes. Add the soy sauce, honey and lime juice, and cook for a further 5 minutes.

3 Meanwhile, cook the basmati rice in boiling salted water for 10 minutes. Drain and return to the pan over a low heat with the coconut milk until it is absorbed. Stir the coriander into the mince and serve on a bed of coconut rice. Garnish with the spring onions, ginger and chilli.

delicious.technique
CHOPPING HERBS

1. *Use a large, sharp knife to slice through the herbs. Hold the bunch of herbs with your other hand, keeping your fingers well tucked in.*

2. *Hold the knife handle with one hand, and rest the fingers of your other hand on top of the end of the blade. Chop the herbs using a rocking motion.*

Courgette and ham gratin
SERVES 4 TAKES **40 MINUTES TO MAKE**

750g courgettes, roughly grated
2 leeks, thinly sliced
1 garlic clove, finely chopped
10 slices ham
200ml crème fraîche
Large handful of baby spinach leaves
Butter, for greasing
100g fresh white breadcrumbs
1 tbsp olive oil
50g Parmesan, coarsely grated

1 Preheat the oven to 180°C/fan 160°C/gas 4.
Put the courgette, leek, garlic and plenty of salt
and freshly ground pepper into a saucepan. Add
enough water to just cover the base of the pan.
Cover and cook for 10 minutes until softened.
Drain well, squeeze out the excess water and
return to the saucepan.
2 Tear the ham into pieces and add to the pan.
Stir in the crème fraîche and spinach, and season

well with salt and freshly ground black pepper.
3 Grease an ovenproof dish with butter. Spoon
in the courgette and ham mixture. Combine the
breadcrumbs, olive oil and Parmesan. Sprinkle
over the courgette mixture to cover completely.
Bake for 25 minutes.
WINE NOTE The best wine for this is a lightly oaked
Chardonnay from New Zealand. A delicately
sweet Riesling with lots of underlying acidity
would also cut through the richness of the ham
and balance out its saltiness.

One-pot spiced lamb with chickpeas
SERVES 4 TAKES **40 MINUTES TO MAKE**

1 tbsp vegetable oil
650g lamb neck fillet, trimmed of
    excess fat and cut into cubes
    (or use lamb leg steaks)
2 small red onions, sliced
1¹/₂ tsp ground cumin
1¹/₂ tsp ground coriander
820g canned chickpeas, drained and rinsed
Juice of 1 lemon
300ml fresh vegetable stock, hot
Small handful of fresh mint leaves, chopped,
    plus few extra to garnish

1 Heat the oil in a casserole or large, deep
saucepan with a lid over a high heat. When hot,
add half the lamb and cook for 3–4 minutes,
turning gently, until browned all over. Remove
the meat with a slotted spoon and set aside.
Brown the rest of the lamb in the pan, then
remove and set aside.
2 Reduce the heat to medium. Add the onions
to the pan and cook, stirring, for 5 minutes, until
softened. Stir in the spices and cook for 1 minute.
Add the chickpeas, lemon juice and stock, plus
the lamb and any lamb juices. Mix, cover and
bring to the boil, then reduce to a simmer,
covered, for 15 minutes.
3 Uncover the casserole and simmer for a further
5 minutes to reduce the sauce slightly. Stir in the
mint and season to taste. Divide between 4 shallow
bowls and garnish with a few mint leaves.

Courgette and
ham gratin

Moussaka

Moussaka

SERVES 4 TAKES **1 HOUR 25 MINUTES TO MAKE**

1 tbsp olive oil, plus extra for
  brushing
1 large onion, finely chopped
2 garlic cloves, crushed
500g lamb mince
1 tbsp tomato purée
$^1/_2$ tsp ground cinnamon
400g can chopped tomatoes
2 tsp dried oregano
2 medium aubergines, about 300g each,
  for the topping
150ml Greek yogurt
1 egg, beaten
25g freshly grated Parmesan
50g feta

1 Heat the oil in a large frying pan over a medium heat. Add the onion and garlic and cook, stirring, for 5 minutes until soft. Increase the heat, add the minced lamb and cook, stirring, for another 5 minutes until browned. Drain off the fat in a sieve, then return the meat to the pan.
2 Add the tomato purée and cinnamon and cook, stirring, for 1 minute. Add the tomatoes, then half-fill the empty can with water and pour into the pan. Add the oregano, season, and bring to the boil. Reduce the heat and simmer, stirring occasionally, for 20 minutes.
3 Meanwhile, preheat the grill to medium-high. Cut each aubergine diagonally into 5mm-thick slices. Brush with oil, put half of the aubergines on a baking sheet and grill for 5 minutes, turning halfway, until pale golden. Drain on kitchen paper while grilling the remainder.
4 Preheat the oven to 200°C/fan 180°C/gas 6. For the topping, mix the yogurt, egg and half the cheeses. Season with pepper.
5 Spread half the lamb mixture in a deep, 1.2-litre ovenproof dish. Layer half the aubergines on top, then the rest of the lamb. Top with the rest of the aubergine, spoon over the yogurt mixture and scatter with the remaining cheeses. Bake for 35 minutes or until golden and bubbling.

Greek lamb kebabs

Greek lamb kebabs

SERVES 4 TAKES **20 MINUTES TO MAKE**

400g lean lamb, cubed
1 lemon, cut into wedges
12 bay leaves
1 large courgette, sliced
1 red pepper, cut into chunks
2 tbsp olive oil
2 tsp dried oregano
Squeeze of lemon
Potato wedges, to serve

1 Thread the lamb onto skewers, alternating meat chunks with pieces of lemon, bay leaves, sliced courgette and red pepper.
2 Mix together the olive oil, oregano and lemon juice. Brush this over the kebabs, then cook them on a hot griddle, or under a hot grill, for 6–8 minutes until the lamb is cooked but still a little pink. Serve with potato wedges.
WINE NOTE New Zealand Pinot Noir is incredibly good with these kebabs.

Lamb rogan josh

SERVES 4 TAKES **25 MINUTES TO MAKE**

2 tbsp groundnut oil
8 lamb leg steaks, cut into 2.5cm cubes
1 tsp cayenne pepper
1 tbsp hot paprika
1 tsp garam masala
1 portion Basic Curry Sauce,
  defrosted (see p.167)
Handful of coriander leaves, chopped

1 Heat the groundnut oil in a large saucepan and fry the cubed lamb, in batches, until browned all over. Return all of the lamb to the pan and stir in the cayenne pepper, paprika and garam masala, tossing well to coat the cubes of lamb. Pour in the curry sauce and 100ml water, and simmer for 10 minutes until the sauce is reduced, thickened, and coats the meat well. Garnish with coriander.
2 Serve with steamed basmati rice or Pilau Rice (see p.63), chutneys and yogurt.

Lamb rogan josh

Cornish pie
SERVES 4–6 TAKES **2 HOURS 45 MINUTES TO MAKE**

750g lamb neck fillet, cubed
2 baking potatoes, cubed
1 swede, about 500g, diced
1 large onion, roughly chopped
750ml lamb stock, hot
1 tbsp thyme leaves, stripped from stalk
2 tbsp Worcestershire sauce
500g fresh ready-made puff pastry
Plain flour, for dusting
1 egg, beaten

1 Put the lamb, vegetables (including the potatoes), stock, thyme and Worcestershire sauce into a large pan. Bring to the boil on the hob, skimming off any foam that rises to the surface. Reduce the heat, cover and simmer for 1 hour.
2 Remove the lid and simmer for a further hour, until the cooking liquid has reduced slightly and the potatoes have partially dissolved, thickening the sauce into a gravy.

3 Preheat the oven to 200°C/fan 180°C/gas 6. Tip the filling into a 2-litre pie dish. Roll out the pastry on a floured surface until 3–4cm bigger than the pie dish, then lay on top of the filling. Crimp the edges inside the dish with your fingers, so it looks like the crust of a Cornish pasty.
4 Brush the top of the pie with egg, make a few air holes in the centre of the pastry, and bake for 30 minutes until golden.

WINE NOTE A good French Vin de Pays d'Oc Cabernet works well with this heart-warming pie.

delicious.**technique**
TOPPING A PIE WITH PASTRY

1. *Place the rolled pastry over the pie dish, and roll over it again in place to seal the edges and cut off the excess pastry. Crimp the edges with your fingers. Make a few slits to let steam escape, then brush over the entire pastry top with beaten egg.*

Cornish pie

Stir-fried beef with noodles and oyster sauce

the cut side all over the lamb chops, then brush each chop with a little mint jelly. Season well. Grill for 3 minutes each side for pink lamb, or 4 minutes each side if you like it cooked a little more. Set the meat aside to rest for a couple of minutes.

3 Divide the chops and boulangère potatoes between 4 warm serving plates, garnish with rosemary sprigs and serve with some seasonal vegetables and mint jelly.

Stir-fried beef with noodles and oyster sauce

SERVES 2 TAKES **25 MINUTES TO MAKE**

225g lean beef steak (sirloin or rump),
  cut into strips
2 tsp light soy sauce
2 tsp sesame oil, plus a splash
  to dress the noodles
2 tsp dry sherry
1 tsp cornflour
1 red pepper
Small bunch of spring onions
150g medium or thin dried egg noodles
3 tbsp oyster sauce

1 Put the beef in a bowl with the soy sauce, sesame oil, sherry and cornflour, mix well and set aside for 10 minutes.
2 Meanwhile, deseed the pepper, cut into thin strips and set aside. Finely shred the spring onions and set aside.
3 Cook the egg noodles in boiling water for 3–4 minutes, or according to any packet instructions. Drain, refresh and toss with a splash of sesame oil.
4 Heat a wok until very hot and stir-fry the beef for 5 minutes until seared all over. Tip into a sieve to drain away the oil and set aside. Put the wok back onto the heat, add the pepper and stir-fry for 1–2 minutes. Remove and set aside.
5 Add the oyster sauce to the wok and bring to a simmer, then add the beef and noodles and toss together. Add the pepper and onions, toss through and serve.

Minty lamb chops with quick boulangère potatoes

SERVES 4 TAKES **25 MINUTES TO MAKE**

750g waxy potatoes, thinly sliced
1 large onion, thinly sliced
500ml fresh vegetable stock, hot
2 sprigs fresh rosemary or 2 bay leaves,
  plus rosemary sprigs to garnish
1 garlic clove
8 small lamb chops
2–3 tbsp mint jelly, plus extra to serve

1 Preheat the grill to medium-high. Put the potatoes, onion, stock and rosemary sprigs or bay leaves in a wide saucepan over a high heat. Cover, bring to the boil, then reduce the heat and simmer, partially covered, for 15 minutes until the potatoes are tender but not breaking up. Drain off some of the thickened cooking liquid, and remove and discard the rosemary or bay. Season, then cover.
2 Meanwhile, cut the garlic clove in half and rub

Cottage pie with Cheddar
and parsnip mash

Cottage pie with Cheddar and parsnip mash

SERVES 4 TAKES **1 HOUR 30 MINUTES TO MAKE**

1 onion, finely chopped
1 large carrot, diced
500g lean beef mince
1 tbsp tomato purée
300ml beef stock, hot
1$^1/_2$ tbsp Worcestershire sauce
Few fresh thyme leaves

For the Cheddar and parsnip mash
350g floury potatoes
350g parsnips
3 tbsp semi-skimmed milk
$^1/_4$ tsp nutmeg, freshly grated
50g extra-mature Cheddar, roughly grated

1 Heat 2 tablespoons of the vegetable oil in a large pan over a medium heat. Add the chopped onion and diced carrot and cook, stirring, for 5 minutes. Add the mince, turn up the heat and cook for 5 minutes, stirring until browned.
2 Add the tomato purée, cook for 1 minute, then pour in the stock, Worcestershire sauce and thyme. Bring to the boil, then cover and reduce to a simmer for 20 minutes. Uncover and cook for 5–10 minutes, until most of the liquid is absorbed. Season, then spoon into a 2- or 2.5-litre ovenproof dish.
3 For the mash, cut the potatoes and parsnips into medium-sized chunks and put into a large pan of cold salted water. Bring to the boil and simmer for 15 minutes, or until tender. Drain and return to the pan to heat for 30 seconds to drive off excess moisture. Mash with the milk and nutmeg. Season with salt and freshly ground black pepper and set aside.
4 Preheat the oven to 180°C/fan 160°C/gas 4. Spoon the mash onto the mince. Fluff it up with a fork and sprinkle with the cheese. Bake for 25 minutes, until the mash is golden and crisp in places.
WINE NOTE Choose a big, ripe red such as an Australian Shiraz or Merlot.

Steak pie
SERVES 4 TAKES **4 HOURS TO MAKE**

1 piece (flute) of marrowbone,
  about 2cm long (optional)
2 tbsp plain flour
$1/4$ tsp ground mace (optional)
800g diced braising beef
  (a mixture of shin and brisket is best)
4 level tbsp dripping (such as lard or duck fat),
  plus extra for greasing
3 onions, roughly chopped
300ml stout or dark real ale
1 tbsp Worcestershire sauce
750ml–1 litre beef or chicken stock

For the pastry
200g self-raising flour, plus extra for dusting
100g suet
$1/2$ tsp salt
1 egg, beaten

1 First, make the pastry: combine the flour, suet and salt in a large bowl. Add 120ml cold water and work by hand until you have a cohesive but non-sticky dough. If it seems dry, add 10–15ml more water. Wrap in cling film and chill for 1 hour. (You can make the pastry up to a day ahead.)
2 If you're using a marrowbone, soak it in cold water for 1–2 hours to remove any blood, then roast at 180°C/fan 160°C/gas 4 on a tray lined with baking paper for 20 minutes, until slightly browned. Remove and cool completely.
3 Season the flour with salt and pepper, and the mace (if using). Toss the beef in the flour. Heat half the fat in a wide frying pan or casserole and when it is starting to smoke, brown the meat in batches. Remove with a slotted spoon. Add the remaining fat to the pan with the onions and a

pinch of salt and fry over a low heat for 20 minutes, until the onions are soft and sweet but not brown. Add the stout or beer and the Worcestershire sauce and bring to a simmer.
4 Return the meat to the pan and cover with stock, then bring to a simmer. Lower the heat and braise, stirring occasionally, until the meat is really tender – this should take $2^1/2$ hours. Top up with more stock if it looks really dry. Once cooked, check the seasoning, then cool completely. (You could also cook up to this step the day before, chilling the meat overnight.)
5 Grease a 1-litre pie dish and spoon in the pie filling. Plant the flute of marrowbone, cut-side up, in the middle. If it sits proud of the meat, it can act as a natural support for the pastry lid.
6 Preheat the oven to 240°C/fan 220°C/ gas 9. Lightly flour a work surface and roll out the pastry until it is 5mm thick. Drape it over the dish allowing it to overhang slightly. Eggwash the pastry and cook the pie for 30 minutes, covering with foil for the last 10 minutes if it's browning too much. Serve immediately.
WINE NOTE You can't beat a sturdy, spicy French red with this hearty pie – Châteauneuf-du-Pape or Minervois are both great.

Beef cannelloni
SERVES 4 TAKES **30 MINUTES TO MAKE**

100g baby spinach
8 fresh-pasta lasagne sheets
1 portion Beef Ragù, defrosted and reheated
  (see p.168)
300g fresh ready-made cheese sauce
40g Parmesan, grated

1 Put a few tablespoons of water in a pan with the spinach and heat, shaking gently, until the spinach has wilted. Squeeze out the liquid then finely whizz in a food processor.
2 Line each lasagne sheet with hot ragù and spinach, roll up and put in an ovenproof dish.
3 Top with the cheese sauce and Parmesan. Bake at 190°C/fan 170°C/gas 5 for 25 minutes, until golden. Garnish with fresh oregano.

---

delicious.**tip**

IMPROVISING A PIE FUNNEL
Using a flute of marrowbone to support a pastry crust is a great way of keeping the pastry just clear of the filling. It acts as a pie funnel, allowing steam to escape from the pie and enriching the flavour.

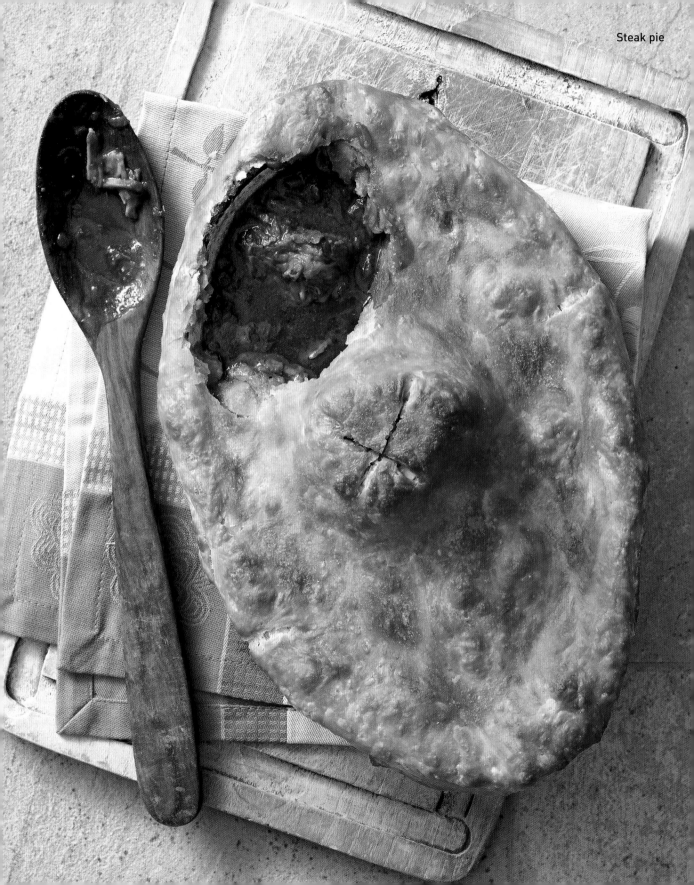

Steak pie

Meatloaf

Meatloaf

SERVES 4 TAKES **1 HOUR 50 MINUTES TO MAKE**

Vegetable oil, for greasing
700g minced beef, or 500g minced beef
 and 200g minced pork
2 onions, finely chopped
2 garlic cloves, crushed
1 large carrot, grated
2 tsp dried thyme
1 egg, lightly beaten
250g fresh breadcrumbs
50ml milk
2 tbsp Worcestershire sauce
2 tsp Dijon mustard

1 Preheat the oven to 160°C/fan 140°C/ gas 3. Grease a 1kg loaf tin. In a bowl, mix the mince, onions, garlic, carrot, thyme and egg.
2 In a separate bowl, mix the breadcrumbs with the milk, then add to the meat mixture. Stir in the Worcestershire sauce and mustard and season well with salt and freshly ground black pepper.

3 Fill the loaf tin with the mixture. Cover with foil. Put in a deep roasting tin and pour in boiling water until it reaches a third of the way up the loaf tin's sides. Bake for 1 hour 30–40 minutes, until cooked through. Cool for 15 minutes in the tin, then remove carefully to a serving dish. Slice and serve with mashed potato, gravy and mixed vegetables.

Meatballs with soupy tomato and herb risotto

SERVES 4 TAKES **30 MINUTES TO MAKE**

1 tbsp olive oil
12 (about 430g) best-quality beef
 meatballs
1 large onion, diced
250g risotto rice
1.2 litres chicken or vegetable stock
400g can chopped tomatoes with herbs
50g grated Parmesan, plus extra to serve

1 In a large frying pan, heat the olive oil and quickly brown the meatballs all over (about 2 minutes). Remove from the pan with a slotted spoon and set aside.
2 Add the onion to the pan and cook, stirring, for 5 minutes or until softened.
3 Add the risotto rice and cook for a further minute. Pour in the stock and tomatoes. Bring to the boil, then cover, reduce the heat and simmer gently for 15 minutes.
4 Add the meatballs and simmer for another 5 minutes, adding a little more stock or boiling water if the rice isn't soupy enough.
5 Stir in the cheese and serve in warmed bowls, with soup spoons and some extra grated cheese to sprinkle over.

Tex Mex beef

SERVES 4 TAKES **50 MINUTES TO MAKE**

2 tbsp vegetable oil
500g topside or rump steak, cut into pieces
1 tbsp vegetable oil
1 red onion, cut into wedges
2 tsp ground cumin
1 tsp sweet smoked paprika
1 tsp cocoa powder
2 tbsp tomato purée
1 tbsp chipotle paste
175ml chicken stock
1 green chilli, thinly sliced
Nachos, guacamole, soured cream
  and grated Cheddar, to serve

1 Heat 1 tablespoon of vegetable oil in a pan and brown the meat, then set aside. Heat another tablespoon of vegetable oil and fry the onion for 5 minutes, until tender.
2 Add the cumin, paprika and cocoa powder and cook for a further minute, then stir in the tomato purée, chipotle paste and chicken stock. Season well and simmer for 30 minutes, until the beef is sticky but still tender.
3 Put in a serving dish, garnish with the chilli, and serve with nachos, guacamole, soured cream and grated cheese to sprinkle over.

Meatballs with soupy tomato and herb risotto

Tex Mex beef

Family stews and casseroles

Vegetable stew with herb dumplings
SERVES 4 TAKES **1 HOUR TO MAKE**

25g butter
1 onion, chopped
1 leek, thickly sliced and washed
3 carrots, roughly chopped
2 celery sticks, roughly chopped
3 tbsp plain flour
600ml vegetable stock or water, hot

Vegetable stew with
herb dumplings

400g can mixed pulses, drained and rinsed
Few sprigs of fresh thyme

For the herb dumplings
225g self-raising flour
110g vegetable suet
2 tbsp fresh thyme leaves

1 Melt the butter in a large saucepan over a medium heat. Add the onion and cook for 5 minutes, until softened. Add the leek, carrots and celery and continue cooking for a further 10 minutes, stirring occasionally, until softened. Stir in the flour, then gradually stir in the stock or water. Add the drained pulses and thyme, cover and simmer for 20 minutes.
2 Meanwhile, make the dumplings. Mix together the flour, suet and thyme, and season to taste. Add about 125ml cold water to form a soft, slightly sticky dough – add a touch more water if it seems a little dry.
3 Drop large spoonfuls of the dough into the simmering stew, pushing them in so they're just poking out – aim to end up with 12 dumplings. Cover again and simmer for a further 20 minutes, until the dumplings are risen and no longer sticky. Serve with seasonal greens.

Saffron, paprika and garlic seafood stew
SERVES 4–6 TAKES **35 MINUTES TO MAKE**

3 tbsp extra-virgin olive oil
1 large onion, chopped
4 garlic cloves, crushed
2 medium-hot red chillies, halved,
  deseeded and finely chopped
2 tsp sweet paprika
Good pinch of saffron strands
2 strips pared orange zest
4 fresh bay leaves
Leaves from 2 large sprigs of fresh lemon thyme
2 x 400g cans chopped tomatoes
300ml dry white wine
50ml well-flavoured chicken or
  vegetable stock

Saffron, paprika and garlic seafood stew

1 tsp salt
600g cleaned mussels in their shells
225g cooked and peeled tiger prawns
400g mixed seafood such as prawns, mussels,
  squid and scallops, thawed if frozen

For the garlic bread
2 plain part-baked ciabattas
100g butter, softened
2 fat garlic cloves, crushed
1 tsp chopped fresh lemon thyme leaves
2 tbsp chopped fresh parsley leaves

1 Preheat the oven to 200°C/fan 180°C/gas 6. Heat the olive oil in a casserole or wide shallow saucepan. Add the chopped onion and cook over a low heat for 10 minutes, stirring occasionally, until very soft but not browned. Add the crushed garlic and chillies and cook for 1 minute. Stir in the paprika, saffron, orange zest, bay leaves and lemon thyme, and cook for 1 minute more.
2 Add the tomatoes, wine, stock and salt, bring to the boil, then cover and simmer for 15 minutes.

3 Meanwhile, make the garlic bread. Bake the ciabattas in the oven according to the packet instructions. Remove the bread but leave the oven on. Mix the butter with the garlic, thyme leaves, parsley and a little salt. Cut the ciabattas into 2cm slices but don't cut all the way through to the base. Spread each slice with the garlic butter. Wrap up securely in 2 pieces of foil and bake for a further 8–10 minutes.
4 After 5 minutes, uncover the stew and stir in the mussels, prawns and mixed seafood. Simmer gently, stirring occasionally, for 5 minutes, until the seafood is heated through – don't cook it for too long or the seafood will become tough.
5 Ladle the stew into deep bowls and serve with the garlic bread.

delicious.**tip**
USING SAFFRON
Saffron is expensive, but you only need a pinch to give a dish its distinctive fragrance. Buy in small quantities, so that you use it as fresh as possible.

Butter bean and chorizo stew

Cassoulet

Butter bean and chorizo stew

SERVES 4 TAKES **2 HOURS 45 MINUTES TO MAKE**, PLUS **OVERNIGHT SOAKING**

180g dried butter beans
1 tbsp extra-virgin olive oil
250g piece of raw chorizo sausage,
 cut into 5mm-thick diagonal slices
1 onion, roughly chopped
3 garlic cloves, roughly chopped
1 red chilli, halved,
 deseeded and finely chopped
400g can chopped tomatoes
500ml chicken stock, hot
Few sprigs of fresh thyme
Grated zest of 1 lemon

1 The day before serving, put the butter beans in a bowl of water and soak overnight.
2 The next day, place the beans in a large saucepan and cover with plenty of fresh water. Bring to the boil and simmer rapidly for 1 hour until just tender. Drain.
3 Meanwhile, heat the olive oil in an ovenproof casserole and fry the chorizo for 2–3 minutes, until starting to brown. Remove from the pan with a slotted spoon and set aside. Add the onion, garlic and chilli to the casserole and cook for 5 minutes, stirring, until the onion is beginning to soften and become translucent.
4 Add the chopped tomatoes, stock, thyme and lemon zest to the casserole, mix all together well, then add the chorizo and beans, stirring in gently so as not to break up the beans too much. Bring to the boil and simmer, partially covered, for 1¼ hours or until the sauce is thick and the beans are meltingly tender. Check the seasoning and discard the thyme sprigs.
5 Serve in warmed bowls, with crusty bread to mop up the juices and a crunchy leaf salad.

> delicious.**tip**
> ### SOURCING INGREDIENTS
> Raw chorizo is stocked by many delicatessens, but if you can't find it, used cooked, sliced chorizo, adding it only for the last 15 minutes of cooking.

Cassoulet

SERVES 8 TAKES **5 HOURS 30 MINUTES TO MAKE**,
PLUS **2 DAYS OVERNIGHT SOAKING AND CHILLING**

1kg dried haricot beans
4 onions
8 cloves
2 carrots, cut in half
8 bay leaves
4 good sprigs of fresh thyme
8 garlic cloves
900g pork belly, skin removed
$1/2$ large or 1 small shoulder of lamb
2 large duck breasts, skin removed
8 Toulouse sausages
3 tbsp olive oil,
   plus extra for drizzling
2 celery sticks,
   washed and chopped
2 tbsp sun-dried tomato purée
10 tomatoes, skinned,
   deseeded and roughly chopped
300ml dry white wine
100g fresh white breadcrumbs

1 Two days before serving, put the haricot beans into a large bowl and cover with plenty of cold water to soak. The next day, drain the beans and put in a large saucepan so that the beans come no more than halfway up the side.
2 The day before serving, cut 2 of the onions in half, stud each half with 2 cloves and add to the pan. Add the carrots, 4 bay leaves, 2 thyme sprigs and 4 whole garlic cloves. Cut the pork belly into generous bite-size pieces and add to the pan. Cover everything with plenty of cold water and bring to the boil. Skim off any white scum, reduce the heat, cover and cook for 1 hour 20 minutes. Drain the cooking liquid, reserving 300ml. Cool, then cover and chill. Discard the studded onion, carrot, bay leaves, thyme and garlic. Put the cooked beans and pork into a bowl. Leave to cool, then cover and chill in the fridge overnight.
3 While the beans are cooking, preheat the oven to 160°C/fan 140°C/gas 3. Trim off any excess fat from the lamb and cut into generous bite-size pieces. Cut each duck breast into 4 pieces. Cut

each sausage into 3 or 4 pieces. Finely chop the remaining onions and crush the remaining garlic. Heat the olive oil in a large roasting tin on the hob, add the lamb, duck, and sausage and brown all over (cook in batches). Add the chopped onion, garlic and celery to the browned meat in the roasting tin and cook for 8–10 minutes, stirring occasionally, until softened. Add the tomato purée and stir well. Add the tomatoes, the wine and the remaining thyme and bay leaves. Season and bring to the boil. Cover with foil and braise in the oven for $1^1/2$ hours until tender. Remove and leave to cool. Cover and chill overnight.
4 On the day of serving, take all the ingredients out of the fridge and preheat the oven to 180°C/ fan 160°C/ gas 4. Take a 7-litre ovenproof dish and put a layer of beans and pork in the bottom, then follow with a layer of the braised meat and tomato mixture. Repeat until both mixtures are used up. Pour the reserved bean water over, cover with foil and cook for $1^1/2$ hours in the oven.
5 Top with the breadcrumbs, drizzle with a little olive oil and bake for a further 45 minutes. Alternatively, for individual servings, take 8 x 15cm clean terracotta flower pots (if they have a drainage hole at the bottom, line them with foil). After cooking the cassoulet for $1^1/2$ hours, spoon into the pots, top with breadcrumbs, drizzle with oil and bake for 30–35 minutes. Serve in the pots.
WINE NOTE A fairly young, rich red such as a southern French Syrah would enhance the comforting qualities of this warming stew.

The signature dish of southern France, made in the classic way for a deep, rich mix of flavours.

Sausage, haricot bean and red wine casserole
SERVES 4 TAKES **40 MINUTES TO MAKE**

1 tbsp sunflower oil
8 good pork and herb sausages
1 onion, sliced
2 celery sticks, sliced
2 fresh thyme sprigs, plus extra to serve
2 tbsp tomato purée
1 tbsp flour
150ml red wine
600ml fresh chicken or vegetable stock, hot
410g canned haricot or cannellini beans, drained
  and rinsed
Chopped fresh flatleaf parsley, to serve

1 Heat the oil in a casserole or large frying pan over a medium heat. Add the sausages and brown until golden all over. Remove them with a slotted spoon and set aside. Add the onion, celery and thyme sprigs to the pan and cook, stirring, for 5 minutes. Add the tomato purée and flour and cook for 1 minute. Pour in the red wine, bring to the boil and bubble until reduced by two-thirds. Add the stock, bring back to the boil and reduce the heat to a fast simmer.
2 Halve each sausage diagonally and return to the pan, then simmer for 15 minutes until the sausages are cooked through and the sauce has thickened slightly.
3 Stir the beans into the casserole and cook for a further 5 minutes to heat through. Season to taste, then divide between 4 warm plates. Garnish with the extra thyme leaves and the parsley. Serve with mash and vegetables.
WINE NOTE This sturdy, cold-weather casserole cries out for a glass of rich, spicy Rhône red.

Grown-up bangers and beans for a hearty, satisfying supper.

Easy sausage casserole
SERVES 4 TAKES **1 HOUR 15 MINUTES TO MAKE**

4 large potatoes
4 carrots
8 good-quality sausages
2 tbsp olive oil
1 onion, chopped
1 garlic clove, crushed
1 tsp paprika
400g can chopped tomatoes
400ml vegetable stock
1–2 bay leaves

1 Preheat the oven to 180°C/fan 160°C/gas 4. Peel the potatoes and cut them in half, then into quarters. Peel the carrots and cut each carrot into about 4 or 5 even pieces.
2 Prick the sausages all over with a fork – this helps the fat to run out of the sausages so that they don't split open as they cook. Heat the olive oil in a heavy-based casserole and fry the sausages, turning often, until lightly golden all over – this should take about 10 minutes. Remove the sausages from the pan and put them on a plate. Set aside.
3 Add the chopped onion to the casserole (there will still be enough oil left in the pan from cooking the sausages) and continue to cook over a low heat for 5–10 minutes, until the onion is slightly soft. Add the garlic and paprika and cook for another 2 minutes.
4 Add the chopped potatoes and carrots and mix in well to coat the vegetables with the oil.
5 Add the tomatoes and stock and the bay leaves. Bring to a simmer so it's just bubbling gently. Return the sausages to the casserole.
6 Put the casserole into the oven. Cook for 45 minutes, until the potatoes are cooked through, and serve.

delicious.**tip**
MEASURING STOCK
To measure the vegetable stock for this recipe, you can use the empty tomato can – filled up, it will hold 400ml of stock.

Easy sausage casserole

Coq au vin
SERVES 4 TAKES **1 HOUR 40 MINUTES TO MAKE**

2kg whole chicken, cut into 8 pieces (see p.204)
2 tbsp plain flour
1 tbsp olive oil
Large knob of butter
125g piece smoked bacon, cut into short fat strips
12 baby onions or shallots,
    peeled and halved if large
1 large carrot, diced
1 celery stick, diced
200g small chestnut mushrooms, halved
4 garlic cloves, finely chopped
60ml brandy
750ml red wine
400ml chicken stock
1 bay leaf
Bunch of fresh flatleaf parsley,
    finely chopped, to serve

1 Place the chicken pieces in a large bowl and season well with salt and freshly ground black pepper. Toss with the flour until well coated.
2 Heat the oil and butter in a large, wide ovenproof pan over a medium heat and brown the chicken pieces well all over – do this in batches. Remove and set aside.
3 Add the bacon to the pan and cook for a few minutes until lightly browned. Remove with a slotted spoon and set aside with the chicken.
4 Add the onions, carrot and celery and cook for 5 minutes, until softened and lightly browned. Set aside.
5 Add the mushrooms to the pan with the garlic and cook for 2–3 minutes. Add the brandy and wine and stir well to remove any cooked-on bits stuck to the pan. Add the stock and bay leaf, and return the vegetables, chicken and bacon to the pan. Bring just to the boil, then reduce the heat to low and simmer for 25–30 minutes, until the chicken is cooked through.
6 Remove the chicken pieces, increase the heat and simmer the sauce for about 25 minutes, until reduced, thickened and glossy.
7 Return the chicken to the pan and reheat until piping hot to serve. Garnish with finely chopped parsley and serve with creamy mash.
WINE NOTE Lots of red wines are great with this classic dish, including red Burgundy and New World Pinot Noir, but best of all is premium red Bordeaux, preferably an older vintage.

Normandy chicken
SERVES 4 TAKES **35 MINUTES TO MAKE**

75g butter
8 skinless chicken thighs
6 shallots, halved
4 celery sticks, chopped
300ml apple juice (or cider)
300ml fresh chicken stock, hot
200ml crème fraîche
4 eating apples, such as cox's or braeburn,
    cored and cut into wedges
3 tbsp chopped fresh chives, to serve

1 Heat 50g of the butter in a roasting tin on the hob and brown the chicken thighs all over, turning as needed. Add the shallots and celery and cook for a few minutes. Pour over the apple juice or cider and stock, and season to taste. Bring to the boil, then cover tightly with foil and cook for 20 minutes, or until the juices run clear when the chicken is pierced. Stir in the crème fraîche and bring just to the boil, then simmer for 1 minute.
2 Heat the rest of the butter in a large frying pan over a medium heat. Add the apple wedges and fry for 5 minutes until lightly coloured. Stir the apples into the chicken. Sprinkle with some chopped chives and serve. This is great with French beans, broccoli and mashed potato.

Classic French country stews ask only for good red wine and long, lazy cooking times.

Coq au vin

Spanish chicken and potato stew

SERVES 4 TAKES **45 MINUTES TO MAKE**

2 tbsp olive oil
Pack of 8 chicken pieces
1 onion, chopped
2 garlic cloves, crushed
110g chorizo, cut into small dice
100ml white wine
800g canned chopped tomatoes
Few fresh thyme sprigs,
  plus extra leaves to garnish
2 bay leaves
100ml fresh chicken stock
Good pinch of sugar
650g potatoes, cut into rough chunks
Handful of black olives (optional)

1 Heat the olive oil in a large saucepan over a medium heat, then brown the chicken pieces all over – in batches if necessary. Remove from the pan with a slotted spoon and set aside. Add the onion and garlic to the pan and cook for 3–4 minutes, stirring frequently, until softened, translucent and lightly browned.

2 Add the chorizo and cook for 3–4 minutes, stirring occasionally. Add the wine and reduce by half. Stir in the tomatoes, thyme, bay leaves, stock and sugar. Return the chicken to the pan and push the pieces down so that they are under the sauce. Cover and cook for 20 minutes.

3 Stir in the potatoes and olives, if using, and cook for another 35 minutes. Taste the sauce and add more seasoning if necessary. Garnish with thyme leaves, and serve.

delicious.**tip**

PREPARING IN ADVANCE

To freeze this dish, at step 3 cook for only 5 minutes instead of 35. Remove from the heat and season. Spoon into a freezer-proof container and cool, then freeze. The day before you want to eat the dish, thaw in a cool place overnight (it takes longer in the fridge). Then spoon into a saucepan, cover and simmer for 35–40 minutes until cooked through.

Fragrant chicken stew
SERVES 4 TAKES **1 HOUR TO MAKE**

3 tbsp olive oil
1 chicken, 1.5–1.75kg, jointed into 8 pieces
  (see p.204)
Good pinch of saffron strands
2 fennel bulbs
12–16 shallots, peeled
125g pancetta or bacon lardons
2 garlic cloves, finely chopped
1 tsp fennel seeds, lightly crushed
1 tbsp Pernod (optional)
250ml dry white wine
350ml chicken stock, hot
3 sprigs of fresh thyme, leaves picked off
2 fresh bay leaves
2 tbsp butter, softened
2 tbsp plain flour
4 tbsp crème fraîche
2 tbsp chopped fresh parsley, to serve

1 Heat the oil in a large flameproof casserole.
Season the chicken pieces with salt and freshly
ground black pepper, and fry, in batches, over a
medium-high heat until browned.
2 Put the saffron into a bowl, cover with
1 tablespoon of hot water and leave to soak.
Slice the fennel lengthways through the root,
so that the layers stay together in 1 piece.
3 Lift the chicken pieces onto a plate and set
aside. Add the shallots to the casserole and fry
until lightly browned. Set aside with the chicken.
Add the fennel slices to the pan and fry until very
lightly golden. Set aside on a second plate.
4 Pour all but 1 teaspoon of the oil from the
casserole, add the pancetta and fry until golden.
Add the garlic and fennel seeds and fry for a few
seconds. Add the Pernod and wine, bubble for a
few seconds, then add the stock, the herbs and
the saffron with its soaking water.
5 Return the chicken and shallots to the
casserole, cover and simmer gently for 5 minutes.
Stir in the fennel slices, and cover and simmer for
30–35 minutes, until the chicken is almost tender.
With a slotted spoon, lift the vegetables and
chicken into a large bowl, and set aside.

6 Mix the butter and flour together into a smooth
paste. Bring the cooking liquor back to a simmer
and whisk in the flour paste, a little at a time (you
might not need to use it all), until the sauce has
thickened. Simmer for a further 2–3 minutes. Stir
in the crème fraîche and adjust the seasoning.
7 Return the chicken and vegetables to the
casserole, cover and place over a medium heat.
Bring to a simmer and cook, stirring, for 15–20
minutes, or until piping hot. Scatter with the
chopped parsley to serve.
WINE NOTE Try a fruity, full-bodied white like a
Viognier, which is perfumed and peachy.

Lambs' liver with sticky onions, port and raisins
SERVES 2 TAKES **2 HOURS 40 MINUTES TO MAKE**

25g raisins
2 tbsp ruby port
30g sunflower margarine
$1/2$ tbsp olive oil
1 onion, cut into thin wedges
1 tsp redcurrant jelly
300g thinly sliced lambs' liver

1 Put the raisins and port in a small bowl and
leave to soak for 2 hours.
2 Heat half the margarine and the oil in a small
frying pan. Add the onion and cook over a
medium heat for 30 minutes, stirring occasionally,
or until soft, brown and caramelised. Add the
raisins and port and the redcurrant jelly and
simmer for 2 minutes, or until the mixture is
"sticky". Season and keep warm.
3 Season the liver slices on both sides. Melt the
rest of the margarine in a large non-stick frying
pan, until nutty brown in colour. Add the liver
slices in 1 layer and cook over a high heat,
without moving them, for 30–40 seconds on each
side, until nicely browned but still pink in the
centre. This will depend on how thinly the liver
has been sliced and how pink you like it.
4 Lift onto warmed plates and spoon some of
the onions on top. Serve with green cabbage
and mashed potatoes.

Lambs' liver with
sticky onions, port
and raisins

Curried lamb mince cobbler
SERVES 4 TAKES **1 HOUR 10 MINUTES TO MAKE**

1 tbsp olive oil
1 large onion, finely chopped
1 tbsp mild or medium curry powder
500g lamb mince
450g swede, cubed
3 tbsp mango chutney
400ml fresh lamb stock, hot

For the cobbler
225g self-raising flour
60g butter, cut into cubes
1 tsp cumin seeds
1 egg
125ml milk

1 Heat the oil in a large, deep frying pan over a medium heat. Add the onion and cook for 5 minutes, until soft. Stir in the curry powder and cook for 1 minute. Increase the heat, add the mince and cook for 5 minutes, breaking it up with the spoon, until browned.
2 Stir in the swede, chutney and stock and bring to a simmer. Cook for 20 minutes, stirring, until the swede is tender. Season and tip into 4 (about 500ml each) dishes.
3 Preheat the oven to 190°C/fan 170°C/gas 5. Make the cobbler. Sift the flour and a good pinch of salt into a bowl. Add the butter and rub in with your fingertips to coarse crumbs. Stir in the cumin. Beat the egg with the milk, add to the flour mixture and mix to a firm dough. Dot clumps of it on top of the mince, spaced apart.
4 Bake for 15–20 minutes, then serve.

Curried lamb mince cobbler

Lancashire hotpot

SERVES 4 TAKES **1 HOUR 15 MINUTES TO MAKE**

1 tbsp olive oil
500g lamb leg steaks, cubed
2 tbsp plain flour, seasoned
1 large onion, sliced
2 small carrots, sliced
300ml hot chicken stock
1 tbsp Worcestershire sauce
Few sprigs of fresh thyme
600g waxy potatoes
Knob of butter

1 Preheat the oven to 190°C/fan 170°C/gas 5. Heat the oil in a large, wide pan over a medium heat. Dust the cubed lamb in the flour and fry, in batches, until browned. Set aside.
2 Add the sliced onion and carrots to the pan, and cook for 5 minutes. Return the lamb to the pan with the stock, Worcestershire sauce and thyme. Season and remove from the heat.
3 Thinly slice the potatoes and place half in an overlapping layer in a shallow ovenproof pan with a lid. Top with the meat mixture, then layer over the remaining potato and dot with butter. Cover and cook in the oven for 30 minutes, then remove the lid and cook for a further 20 minutes, until the potatoes are golden brown.

Lamb stew

SERVES 6 TAKES **2 HOURS 45 MINUTES TO MAKE**

1.3kg stewing lamb on the bone (ask the butcher
  to cut it into large chunks)
2 tbsp plain flour
2 tbsp gravy powder
2 tbsp olive oil
2 large onions, sliced
2 garlic cloves, crushed
500g small carrots, scraped
1kg new potatoes, scrubbed
3 tbsp sun-dried tomato paste
Few sprigs of fresh thyme and fresh mint
1 chicken or pork stock cube

Lamb stew

1 Put the lamb onto a tray and season generously with salt and freshly ground black pepper. Mix together the flour and gravy powder and sprinkle over the lamb.
2 Heat the oil in a large deep pan. Add the lamb and cook over a high heat for 10 minutes or until browned all over (do it in batches, if necessary). Reduce the heat to medium and add the onions and garlic. Cook for 5 minutes until softened.
3 Add the carrots, potatoes, sun-dried tomato paste and herbs. Crumble in the stock cube, add 1 litre water and mix together. Bring to the boil, then cover and simmer for 2¼ hours, until the meat and vegetables are tender. Gently stir every 30 minutes, to stop anything catching on the base of the pan. Serve in soup plates or bowls, with plenty of the gravy.

delicious.**tip**
OVEN-COOKING
You can oven-cook this at 180°C/fan 160°C/gas 4 for the same time. If you do use an oven, only use 600ml of stock, because it won't bubble away and evaporate as it does on a hob.

Braised lamb shanks with lemon, garlic and parsley

SERVES 4 TAKES **3 HOURS 30 MINUTES TO MAKE**

2 tbsp olive oil
4 lamb shanks (about 400g each)
1 small onion, chopped
1 small fennel bulb, chopped
3 fresh bay leaves, torn
2 fresh rosemary sprigs
5 garlic cloves – 4 chopped, 1 whole
8 fresh thyme sprigs
700ml lamb, chicken or beef stock
150ml white wine
Zest of 1 lemon, finely grated
2 tbsp finely chopped fresh parsley
2 tbsp extra-virgin olive oil

1 Preheat the oven to 140°C/fan 120°C/gas 1. Heat the olive oil in a large, wide pan with a lid over a medium heat. Season the shanks generously with salt and freshly ground black pepper, and brown them all over in the pan for 8–10 minutes. Remove to a plate. Add the onion and fennel to the pan and cook for 8 minutes, stirring, until turning golden.
2 Add the bay leaves, the rosemary, the chopped garlic and half the thyme, and return the lamb shanks to the pan.
3 Pour in the stock and wine and heat until just bubbling. Cover with a tight-fitting lid and bake for 2½–3 hours, until the meat is completely tender and almost falling from the bone.
4 Meanwhile, crush the remaining garlic with a pinch of salt and finely chop the remaining thyme. Put in a bowl with the lemon zest, parsley and extra-virgin olive oil and mix together well. Season with black pepper only. This classic lemony accompaniment is called gremolata.
5 Transfer the shanks to a dish and cover loosely with foil. Skim off and discard the fat from the surface of the sauce, then bring to the boil and simmer for a few minutes. Mix 2 tablespoons of sauce into the lemon, garlic and parsley mixture.
6 Divide the lamb shanks between plates, strain over the sauce and spoon over the gremolata. Serve with mashed potato.

Spiced lamb shanks with preserved lemon couscous

SERVES 4 TAKES **3 HOURS TO MAKE**

2 tsp cumin seeds
1 tbsp fennel seeds
3cm piece fresh ginger, chopped
4 garlic cloves, chopped
2 tbsp olive oil
4 lamb shanks, about 450g each
2 large onions, cut into wedges
2 tbsp rose harissa
400g can chopped tomatoes
500ml chicken or lamb stock, hot
1 cinnamon stick

For the couscous
250g couscous
300ml vegetable stock, hot
3 tbsp each finely chopped fresh mint and coriander
2 preserved lemons, halved, deseeded and finely chopped
15g butter

1 Preheat the oven to 160°C/ fan 140°C/gas 3. Crush the cumin and fennel spice seeds and a good pinch of salt in a pestle and mortar, add the ginger and garlic and work to a rough paste. Set aside.
2 Heat the oil in a large casserole over a high heat. Generously season the lamb shanks and add them to the pan, browning well all over. Remove and set aside.
3 Reduce the heat to medium. Add the onions and cook for 5 minutes. Stir in the spice paste and harissa, cook for 1 minute, then add the tomatoes and stock. Return the lamb shanks to the casserole and stir. Bring to the boil and add the cinnamon. Cover and bake in the oven for 2 hours, until the lamb is very tender.
4 Just before serving, put the couscous in a bowl and pour over the hot stock. Cover and stand for 5 minutes. Fluff up with a fork and stir in the herbs, lemon and butter. Season and serve with the lamb shanks and sauce.

Spiced lamb shanks
with preserved
lemon couscous

Slow-braised lamb, cheesy polenta and green beans

Slow-braised lamb, cheesy polenta and green beans
SERVES 6 TAKES **1 HOUR TO MAKE**

1 boned shoulder of lamb, about 1.6kg,
  trimmed of excess fat
25g plain flour, seasoned
25g butter
2 tbsp extra-virgin olive oil
4 garlic cloves, crushed
600ml dry white wine
300ml tomato passata
4 fresh bay leaves
300ml lamb or chicken stock, hot
2 large red peppers
2 large orange or yellow peppers
Sprigs of fresh flatleaf parsley,
  to garnish

For the cheesy polenta
200g quick-cook polenta
60g butter
125g fresh Parmesan, finely grated

For the mild garlic green beans
6 large unpeeled garlic cloves
4 tbsp extra-virgin olive oil
25g butter
4 shallots, finely chopped
700g fine green beans, trimmed

1 Trim any excess fat from the shoulder of
lamb, and discard. Cut the meat into 75g pieces
and toss, a few at a time, in the seasoned flour
until well coated. Shake off and reserve the
excess flour.
2 Heat the butter and oil in a flameproof
casserole and fry the lamb, in batches, until well
browned. Return the lamb to the pan, add the
garlic and cook for 1 minute. Stir in the reserved
flour and cook for 1 minute more.
3 Add the wine and cook over a high heat until it
has reduced by about a third. Stir in the passata,
bay leaves, hot stock and a little seasoning.
Part-cover the casserole and simmer for
40 minutes, or until the lamb is tender and
the sauce has reduced and thickened slightly.

4 Meanwhile, preheat the oven to 220°C/ fan 200°C/gas 7. Put the peppers onto a baking tray and roast for 25 minutes. Seal in a plastic food bag and leave to cool, then remove and discard the skin, stalks and seeds and cut the flesh into wide strips.

5 While the peppers are roasting, start preparing the green beans. First, cook the unpeeled garlic cloves in a pan of boiling water for 10–15 minutes or until very tender. Drain, cool slightly then peel and mash on a board with the blade of a large knife until smooth. Scoop it up with the blade of the knife, put in a small bowl and set aside.

6 For the polenta, bring 1.25 litres of water to the boil. Meanwhile, heat the olive oil and butter for the beans in a large pan over a gentle heat. Add the shallots and cook for 5 minutes until soft but not browned. Stir in the garlic paste.

7 Slowly pour the polenta into the boiling water, stirring all the time, and bring to a simmer. Leave to cook gently, stirring constantly for a few minutes, until very thick and less grainy. Meanwhile, cook the beans in another pan of boiling water for 4 minutes or until tender. Drain well, add to the pan with the shallots and garlic and toss together. Stir the butter, cheese and some salt into the polenta, then divide between 6 serving plates.

8 Uncover the lamb and remove the bay leaves. Stir in the pepper strips and season. Simmer briefly to heat through, then serve, garnished with parsley, with the polenta and the beans.

ROASTING AND PEELING PEPPERS

1. Roast the peppers in a hot oven until the skins have blackened, then pop them into a plastic bag and seal tightly. Put aside to cool.

2. Once cool, use your fingers to peel away the charred skin. Rinse under the cold tap to wash away small fragments. Don't worry if a few remain.

Pot-roasted brisket
SERVES 6 TAKES **2 HOURS 30 MINUTES TO MAKE**

2 tbsp olive oil
1.5kg piece boned and rolled beef brisket
100g thick-cut rindless bacon, cut across
  into strips
50g butter
2 parsnips, cut into long wedges
1 large fennel bulb, cut lengthways into
  8 wedges
2 small leeks (about 225g), cut into lengths
4 carrots, thickly sliced
2 celery sticks, sliced
2 bay leaves
2 sprigs fresh thyme
300ml chicken stock

1 Preheat the oven to 150°C/fan 130°C/gas 2. Heat the oil in a casserole large enough to snugly accommodate everything. Season the brisket all over, add to the casserole and brown on all sides. Lift out onto a plate. Add the bacon and fry briefly until golden brown. Set aside on another plate. Pour away any excess oil.

2 Melt the butter in the casserole over a medium heat. Add the vegetables and herbs. Season. Cook gently for a few minutes until lightly browned. Add the brisket, bacon and stock, then cover with foil and a tight-fitting lid and cook in the oven for 2–2½ hours.

3 Put the brisket on a board and carve thin slices. Skim excess oil from the casserole and boil for a couple of minutes. Serve with the juices, with mustard on the side.

WINE NOTE Don't overdo it with a heavy red – a good quality, juicy Beaujolais hits just the right note with this dish.

Slow cooking makes this economical cut of beef meltingly tender.

Braised beef stew

Braised beef stew
SERVES 4 TAKES **3 HOURS TO MAKE**

2 tbsp olive oil
1.6kg piece rolled and tied brisket,
  blade or braising steak
2 carrots, halved lengthways and
  cut into large chunks
2 celery sticks, chopped
2 onions, cut into small wedges
400g can chopped tomatoes
2 bay leaves
1 litre hot beef stock
250g dried country vegetable mixture,
  including split peas, lentils and pearl barley
Small handful of fresh flatleaf parsley,
  finely chopped

1 Heat the oil in a large casserole and sear the piece of beef all over until just browned. Add all of the prepared fresh vegetables, the can of tomatoes and the bay leaves to the pan, tumble together and cover with the beef stock. Bring to the boil, then cover the pan with its lid, reduce the heat and simmer gently for 1 hour.
2 Add the dried pulses and continue to cook for a further 1$\frac{1}{2}$ hours, until the stock has thickened and the pulses are cooked. Remove the beef onto a chopping board and cut into thick slices, discarding the string.
3 Ladle the stock and pulses into bowls and serve with the beef slices and a good sprinkling of chopped parsley.

This classic British stew is a treat to come home to after a bracing winter weekend walk.

Red beef stew

SERVES 8 TAKES **1 HOUR 30 MINUTES TO MAKE**

4 tbsp vegetable oil
900g lean stewing beef steak, diced
2 onions, chopped
2 tbsp paprika
1 garlic clove, crushed
1 jar tomato sauce for pasta
1 tsp concentrated beef stock
  or $\frac{1}{2}$ beef stock cube
2 red peppers, deseeded and cut into
  chunks
250g button mushrooms, halved
1 large sweet potato, cut into big chunks

1 Heat the vegetable oil in a large frying pan over a medium-high heat. Fry the beef in batches until just browned. Remove with a slotted spoon and put into a medium casserole.
2 Add the onions to the frying pan and cook for 5 minutes, stirring, until just transparent. Stir in the paprika and garlic, cook for 1 minute, then pour in the tomato sauce. Fill the empty jar with hot water and pour into the pan. Stir in the stock concentrate or cube, then add the peppers, mushrooms and sweet potato. Bring to the boil then add to the casserole. Simmer over a medium-low heat for 1 hour, or until the meat is tender.
3 Season to taste with salt and freshly ground black pepper, and serve with a dollop of soured cream and jacket potatoes.
WINE NOTE This deserves a good red wine – try a French Pinot Noir or Chilean Merlot.

delicious.tip

PREPARING IN ADVANCE

This hearty stew freezes well. After completing step 2, cool completely, then freeze (divided into portions, if you like) for up to 3 months. To reheat, thaw for 24 hours in the fridge, put the stew into a large pan over a medium heat and heat until piping hot – or, defrost and reheat in the microwave according to portion size.

Red beef stew

Beef goulash with tagiatelle

Yummy winter chilli

Provençal beef daube
SERVES 6 TAKES **3 HOURS TO MAKE**

1 large celery stick
2 bay leaves
4 sprigs fresh thyme
Handful of fresh parsley
1kg lean braising steak, such as chuck or blade
4 tbsp olive oil
225g thick-cut rindless streaky bacon,
  cut into strips
3 onions, halved and thinly sliced
6 fat garlic cloves, thinly sliced, plus 1 fat clove,
  sliced, to garnish
600ml red wine, such as Cabernet Sauvignon
200ml beef stock
350g carrots, cut into small chunky pieces
400g can chopped tomatoes
2 salted anchovies, rinsed and chopped
3 large strips pared orange zest
20g softened butter
20g plain flour
100g small black olives

1 Make a bouquet garni by cutting the celery in half and sandwiching the bay, thyme and all but 3 parsley sprigs in between. Tie everything into a tight bundle with some string.
2 Cut the steak into large chunky pieces. Heat 3 tablespoons of the olive oil in a large casserole over a high heat. Brown the beef in batches until well coloured all over. Season. Add the bacon to the pan and fry until golden brown. Set aside with the beef. Add the remaining oil and the onions to the casserole and fry for 10–12 minutes until richly browned. Add the garlic and fry for 1–2 minutes more. Add the wine and simmer vigorously, scraping the base of the casserole to release the caramelized juices, until the liquid has reduced by half.
3 Meanwhile, preheat the oven to 150°C/ fan 130°C/gas 2. Stir in the stock, then return the beef and bacon to the casserole with the carrots, tomatoes, anchovies, orange zest and bouquet garni, and season. Cover with foil and a tight-fitting lid and cook in the oven for 2 hours.
4 Shortly before it's ready, make the garnish by

chopping together the 3 remaining parsley sprigs and garlic. Mash the butter and flour together to make a thickening paste (*beurre manié*).

5 Remove the daube from the oven, uncover and skim off any excess oil. Discard the bouquet garni and orange and bring to a gentle simmer on the stove. Whisk in the *beurre manié* paste a little at a time until thickened. Stir in the olives. Simmer for 5 minutes, then sprinkle with the parsley and garlic. Serve with pasta or mashed potato.

WINE NOTE Try a soft but peppery French red – maybe a Bourgueil or Chinon from the Loire Valley.

Yummy winter chilli
SERVES 4 TAKES **1¼ HOURS TO MAKE**

1 tbsp sunflower oil
1 large red onion, chopped
1 celery stick, chopped
4 garlic cloves, chopped
1 tsp cayenne pepper
1 tsp cumin seeds
1 tbsp smoked paprika
1kg good minced beef
400g can aduki beans, drained
400g can pinto or borlotti beans, drained
400g can chopped tomatoes
600ml chicken or beef stock
2 squares plain chocolate
450g ready-cooked long grain rice
50g salted tortilla chips
Large handful of grated mature
 Cheddar, to serve

1 Heat the oil in a large pan and cook the onion, celery and garlic for 5 minutes, until softened. Add the cayenne, cumin seeds and paprika and cook for 1 minute more.

2 Stir in the beef, beans, tomatoes and stock. Bring to the boil, cover and simmer gently for 1 hour. Stir in the chocolate. Check the seasoning.

3 Shortly before the chilli is ready, reheat the rice in the microwave. Divide it between bowls and ladle on a generous helping of chilli. Sprinkle with grated cheese, and garnish with tortilla chips. Put more tortilla chips in a bowl for extra helpings.

Beef goulash with tagliatelle
SERVES 4 TAKES **2 HOURS TO MAKE**

500g beef stewing steak, cut into chunks
1 tbsp plain flour, seasoned
2 tbsp vegetable oil
2 onions, roughly chopped
1 garlic clove, crushed
3 tbsp paprika, plus extra to sprinkle
400g can plum tomatoes
300ml fresh beef stock, hot
142ml soured cream
Handful of chopped fresh curly parsley
300g dried tagliatelle
15g butter

1 Preheat the oven to 160°C/fan 140°C/gas 3. Toss the beef in the seasoned flour. Heat the vegetable oil in a large casserole over a high heat. Add half the beef and brown for 4–5 minutes. Remove and set aside. Repeat with the remaining beef.

2 Add the onions and cook, stirring, for 5 minutes. Stir in the garlic and paprika for 1 minute, then add the tomatoes, breaking them up with the spoon. Add the stock and cooked beef, bring to the boil and season.

3 Cover and bake for 1 hour. Stir then bake, uncovered, for a further 30 minutes, until the beef is tender. Stir in 100ml cream and the parsley.

4 Cook the tagliatelle according to the packet instructions. Drain and toss with the butter.

5 To serve, divide the pasta between bowls. Spoon the goulash on top, garnish with the remaining soured cream and sprinkle with paprika.

Buttery noodles and rich slow-cooked beef make a mouth-watering combination.

Vegetable mains and sides

Cheddar, mushroom and leek tortilla

SERVES 4 TAKES **35 MINUTES TO MAKE**

2 tbsp vegetable oil
2 medium potatoes, cut into small dice
1 leek, trimmed, washed and sliced
250g mushrooms, sliced
6 large eggs
Handful of fresh chives, snipped
150g mature Cheddar, diced

1 Heat the oil in a deep, non-stick frying pan over a medium-low heat. Tip in the potato and cook, stirring, for 5 minutes until turning golden.
2 Add the leek and mushrooms and cook for a further 5 minutes, stirring, until both are softened and wilted and any juices have evaporated.
3 Meanwhile, beat the eggs with 2 tbsp cold water in a bowl. Add the chives, stir in the cheese and season. Pour into the pan, cover (use a large plate or baking sheet) and reduce the heat to low. Cook for 15 minutes, tilting the pan now and then so any remaining raw egg runs to the edges and cooks. The tortilla should be just set throughout and golden underneath.
4 If you like, you can pop the tortilla (still in the pan) under the grill for a few minutes to lightly brown the top (if you choose to do this, make sure you use an ovenproof frying pan).
5 Divide the tortilla into 4 and serve hot or warm, with chunks of bread and a green salad.
WINE NOTE A rich, young rosé from California or a good English ale works well here.

Pumpkin, spinach, ricotta and sage tortilla

SERVES 6 TAKES **1 HOUR TO MAKE**

1 mini pumpkin or small squash, about 750g
1½ tbsp extra-virgin olive oil
1 red onion, cut into thin wedges
1 tbsp chopped sage
225g spinach, stalks removed
Good pinch of saffron
2 extra-large whole eggs
  and 8 extra-large egg whites
25g Parmesan, finely grated
150g ricotta, drained

1 Preheat the oven to 200°C/fan 180°C/gas 6. Cut the pumpkin into 8 wedges and scoop out the fibres and seeds. Cut each wedge into 3 thinner wedges, peel and put into a roasting tin with half the oil and plenty of black pepper. Toss, then arrange so the tips point upwards. Roast for 25 minutes, then remove and lower the oven temperature to 190°C/fan 170°C/gas 5.
2 Meanwhile, heat the remaining oil in a 23cm non-stick ovenproof frying pan over a medium heat, add the onion and cook for 6–7 minutes, until soft and lightly golden. Add the sage and cook for 1 minute. Set aside. Wilt the spinach in a pan over a medium heat for 4 minutes, drain and press out the excess liquid. Set aside.
3 Grind the saffron into a powder in a mortar and pestle. Add 1 tsp hot water and mix well. Put the eggs into a bowl with the saffron water, season and beat with a fork. Stir in half the Parmesan.
4 Arrange the pumpkin, spinach and spoonfuls of ricotta between the onion wedges, pour over the egg and sprinkle over the rest of the Parmesan. Transfer to the middle shelf of the oven and cook for 20–25 minutes, until set, puffed up and lightly golden. Cut into wedges and serve hot.

---

delicious.**tip**

GETTING THEIR GREENS

Tortillas can be a great way to get your kids to eat vegetables. Serve up plain tortilla a few times, then get them to try these veggie versions.

Pumpkin, spinach, ricotta
and sage tortilla

Tagliatelle with field mushrooms, lemon and tarragon

Tagliatelle with field mushrooms, lemon and tarragon
SERVES 4 TAKES **30 MINUTES TO MAKE**

2 tbsp olive oil
8–10 large black field, parasol or portabella
  mushrooms, very finely sliced
2 garlic cloves, finely sliced
500g fresh egg tagliatelle
Finely grated zest and juice of 1 unwaxed lemon
2 tbsp butter
50g grated Parmesan
Tarragon leaves, to garnish

1 Heat the oil in a large saucepan over a medium-low heat. Add the garlic and fry gently. When it starts to become transparent – about 1 minute – add the mushrooms and $1/2$ tsp salt. Stir gently, cover and cook for 10–15 minutes, then season.
2 Meanwhile, cook the pasta in boiling water for 2–3 minutes or until al dente. Drain briefly and quickly return to the saucepan. Fold the lemon zest and juice into the pasta with the butter and the mushrooms and their juices. Check the seasoning and adjust as necessary. Gently fold in the Parmesan, garnish with the tarragon leaves and serve immediately.
WINE NOTE All you need here is a simple, fresh Italian white, such as Soave or Frascati.

Wild mushroom and walnut pasta
SERVES 2 TAKES **20 MINUTES TO MAKE**

200g dried pasta shapes (such as conchiglie)
270g jar marinated mixed wild mushrooms in oil
25g walnut pieces, plus extra to serve
4 tbsp grated Parmesan, plus extra to serve
2 tbsp half-fat crème fraîche
2 tbsp chopped flatleaf parsley

1 Cook the pasta in a large saucepan of lightly salted boiling water until al dente. Drain well and return to the pan.
2 Meanwhile, drain the mushrooms, chop roughly and mix them in a bowl with the walnuts. Add the Parmesan, crème fraîche and parsley. Season.
3 Toss the mix through the pasta and heat gently for 1–2 minutes. Serve piping hot scattered with more walnuts and plenty of Parmesan.

Roasted Mediterranean vegetable lasagne
SERVES 6–8 TAKES **1 HOUR 30 MINUTES TO MAKE**

2 small aubergines, cut into 2.5cm chunks
2 red onions, cut into wedges
2 red peppers, deseeded and cut into strips
4 garlic cloves, finely chopped
5 tbsp olive oil
450g courgettes, sliced
225g fresh lasagne sheets
50g Parmesan, finely grated

For the sauce
900ml semi-skimmed milk
60g sunflower margarine
70g plain flour
125g mature Cheddar, grated

1 Preheat the oven to 220°C/fan 200°C/gas 7. Mix the aubergines, onions, peppers, garlic and 3 tbsp of the oil in a large roasting tin and cook in the hot oven, tossing once halfway through, for 30 minutes or until soft.

2 Meanwhile, pour the rest of the oil into a large frying pan and place over a high heat. Fry the courgettes for 4 minutes until browned. Tip on to a plate lined with kitchen paper and set aside. Remove the vegetables from the oven and stir in the courgettes. Set aside. Lower the oven temperature to 200°C/fan 180°C/gas 6.

3 Make the sauce. Bring the milk to the boil in a pan, then set aside. Melt the margarine in another pan, add the flour and cook for 1 minute; this will take away the raw flour taste. Remove from the heat and gradually stir in the milk until there are no remaining lumps. You may need to use a whisk to help achieve a smooth sauce. Bring to the boil, stirring, then simmer gently for 10 minutes, stirring occasionally. Stir in the Cheddar, season and remove from the heat.

4 Cook the lasagne according to the packet instructions, separating the sheets and draining on a clean tea towel.

5 Spoon a thin layer of sauce over the base of an oiled 2.4-litre ovenproof dish. Cover with lasagne sheets, overlapping them slightly. Top with half the vegetables, then one-third of the remaining sauce and another layer of lasagne. Repeat once more. Spread over the remaining sauce, sprinkle with Parmesan and bake in the hot oven for 40 minutes, until piping hot and bubbling. Serve with a dressed green salad.

The sweetness of roasted veg with a smooth cheese sauce makes this a favourite.

Wild mushroom and walnut pasta

Roasted Mediterranean vegetable lasagne

Zesty bulgur wheat tabouleh
SERVES 6 TAKES **20 MINUTES TO MAKE**

200g bulgur wheat
Juice of 1 large lemon
1 garlic clove, finely chopped
3 tbsp olive oil
1 cucumber, peeled, deseeded and diced
6 medium tomatoes, diced
Bunch of spring onions or 1 small red onion,
  finely chopped
Large bunch of flatleaf parsley, finely chopped
Large bunch of mint, finely chopped

1 Place the bulgur wheat in a large bowl and pour over boiling water until just covered. Place a clean tea towel over the bowl and leave it to stand for 15–20 minutes, or until the wheat has absorbed all the water and the grains have swollen. Drain the bulgur wheat well through a sieve. Squeeze out the excess water using the back of a spoon or tip on to a scrupulously clean tea towel and pat dry.

2 Transfer the wheat to a large serving bowl and add the lemon juice, garlic and olive oil. Season well. Just before serving, add the cucumber, tomatoes, onions, parsley and mint and toss together well. Serve with grilled fish or chicken.
WINE NOTE This calls for a crisp, fresh Sauvignon Blanc. Pick one from France's Loire Valley.

delicious.**technique**
MAKING TABOULEH

1. *Soak the bulgur wheat for 15–20 minutes then drain well. Squeeze out excess water with a spoon or pat the grains dry for a fluffier final texture.*

2. *Add the lemon juice, garlic and oil and stir through. The vegetables will dampen the mixture over time, so add them just before serving.*

Zesty bulgur wheat tabouleh

Veggie pilau

SERVES 2 TAKES **40 MINUTES TO MAKE**

550g pack ready-prepared British
    roasting vegetables
2 tbsp olive oil
2 tsp baharat or ras el hanout spice mix
2 large shallots, sliced
280g pack ready-cooked pilau rice
Handful of mixed dried fruit and nuts
Juice of ½ lemon
Handful of coriander leaves

1 Preheat the oven to 220°C/fan 200°C/gas 7. Put
the vegetables, cut into smaller chunks if large,
on a baking tray and toss with half the olive oil
and the baharat or ras el hanout spices. Cook in
the oven for 30 minutes, turning occasionally so
they cook evenly, until browned and tender.
2 Meanwhile, heat the remaining olive oil in a
large sauté pan. Tip in the shallots and fry for
10 minutes until softened and lightly coloured.
Stir through the ready-cooked pilau rice and the
mixed dried fruit and nuts. Cook for 5 minutes
until thoroughly warmed through.
3 Squeeze over the lemon juice and stir it well
through the warm roasted vegetable pilau. Serve
sprinkled with the coriander leaves.

Summer vegetable risotto

Summer vegetable risotto

SERVES 4 TAKES **45 MINUTES TO MAKE**

300g risotto rice
700ml hot fresh vegetable stock
Knob of butter, plus extra for greasing
3 tbsp grated Parmesan
300g mixed summer vegetables (such as broad
    beans, runner beans, asparagus), blanched
1 tbsp snipped chives
Parmesan shavings, to serve

1 Preheat the oven to 180°C/fan 160°C/gas 4.
Put the risotto rice and hot vegetable stock
into a lightly buttered baking dish and stir well
together. Cover with foil or a lid and bake in the
hot oven for 25 minutes.

> Few things are
> more relaxing than
> gently stirring a
> risotto as it bubbles
> away on the stove.

2 Stir in the Parmesan, butter and the summer
vegetables. Re-cover the dish and leave to stand
for about 5 minutes, until all the flavours are
very well infused together.
3 Stir in the chives. To serve, sprinkle with
Parmesan shavings and season to taste.
WINE NOTE Match this light risotto with a grassy
Sauvignon Blanc, ideally from Chile.

Risotto with mushrooms and radicchio

SERVES 4 TAKES **40 MINUTES TO MAKE**

3 tbsp olive oil
200g oyster mushrooms, shredded
  (but not too finely)
30g cold unsalted butter
1 red onion, finely chopped
2 garlic cloves, roughly chopped
6 fresh sage leaves, roughly chopped
300g risotto rice
125ml white wine
1 litre hot fresh vegetable stock
1 large or 2 small radicchio, finely shredded
100g vegetarian Parmesan, freshly grated

1 Heat the oil in a wide, deep-sided pan over a medium-high heat. Add the mushrooms and stir-fry until golden. Remove and set aside.
2 Lower the heat to medium-low and add half the butter to the pan. Add the onion, garlic and sage and cook, stirring occasionally, for 6–8 minutes.

3 Add the rice and stir a few times until it is coated with the buttery mix and pearly-white; this may take a couple of minutes. Pour in the wine and stir until it has almost been absorbed. Add just enough of the stock to cover the rice and cook gently, stirring frequently, until the stock has been absorbed.
4 Continue gradually adding and stirring in the stock for about 20 minutes or until the rice is just al dente. If it isn't ready, add a little more stock and continue to cook until it is.
5 Fold in the mushrooms and most of the radicchio. Season to taste and stir in the remaining butter.
6 Set aside, covered, for 5 minutes; this enables the rice to settle and come together with a gorgeous, silky texture. Fold in two-thirds of the Parmesan, mixing very well. Serve with the remaining radicchio on top and the remaining cheese on the side.
WINE NOTE This would be best with a very soft, mellow red wine. Try a French Pinot Noir, a Beaujolais or even a mature Italian Barolo.

Risotto with mushrooms and radicchio

Squash risotto

Squash risotto

SERVES 2 TAKES **30 MINUTES TO MAKE**

180g squash
180g sweet potato
Olive oil
1/2 tsp chilli flakes
2 knobs of butter
2 shallots, diced
200g risotto rice
600ml hot fresh vegetable stock
1 heaped tbsp vegetarian Parmesan, grated
Baby spinach leaves

1 Preheat the oven to 190°C/fan 170°C/gas 5. Peel and dice the squash, and dice the sweet potato (no need to peel it). Tip the squash and sweet potato into a roasting tin, drizzle with olive oil and toss with chilli flakes and seasoning. Roast for 20 minutes, until golden and tender.
2 Meanwhile, heat 1 tbsp of olive oil and 1 knob of butter in a large pan and gently fry the shallots for 4–5 minutes, until softened.

3 Stir the risotto rice through the mixture and combine well with the shallots and butter. Cook for 2–3 minutes, until the rice becomes pearly white. (This stage of cooking quickly heats up the exterior of the rice grains, preventing them from breaking and sealing in the starch.) Gradually add the vegetable stock, a ladleful at a time, stirring well with each addition and waiting until the stock is absorbed by the rice grains before adding more, for 20 minutes or until the rice is tender but still al dente.
4 Stir in the remaining butter and the Parmesan. Season, then stir through the warm roasted squash and some baby spinach leaves to wilt. Serve immediately.

delicious.**tip**
ADDING COLOUR
For a more colourful variation, you could also use red onion wedges and red pepper quarters in this dish, instead of the squash. Roast the onions and peppers to bring out their sweetness.

Pearl barley risotto with roasted squash, red peppers and rocket

SERVES 4 TAKES **1 HOUR TO MAKE**

450g butternut squash,
  peeled and cut into 2cm chunks
2 red peppers, halved,
  deseeded and cut into chunky pieces
2 tbsp extra-virgin olive oil
1 onion, finely chopped
2 garlic cloves, finely chopped
Leaves from 3 large thyme sprigs
350g pearl barley
1.5 litres hot fresh vegetable stock
3 tbsp chopped flatleaf parsley
4 small handfuls wild rocket
Parmesan shavings, to serve

1 Preheat the oven to 200°C/fan 180°C/gas 6. Put the butternut squash and the peppers into a small roasting tin, drizzle with 1 tbsp of the oil, season and toss so everything is well coated with oil. Roast for 35 minutes or until tender, turning halfway through cooking, then remove from the oven and set aside.
2 Meanwhile, start the risotto. Heat the remaining oil in a medium pan over a medium-low heat. Add the onion, garlic and thyme leaves and cook gently, stirring occasionally, for 6–8 minutes, until softened. Add the pearl barley and cook for another minute.
3 Add a quarter of the vegetable stock to the pan and simmer, stirring occasionally, until all the stock has been absorbed. Add another quarter of the stock and continue in this way until all the stock is absorbed – it should take about 40 minutes in total for the barley to become tender but still al dente.
4 Gently stir in the parsley followed by the squash and peppers, trying not to break up the squash chunks as you do so. Season and spoon into warmed bowls. Serve topped with the rocket and some Parmesan shavings.
WINE NOTE Look for some sweet notes and a few herby ones too – go for a soft, ripe Mediterranean red such as a southern French Grenache or an Italian Nero d'Avola.

Baked stuffed tomatoes filled with lemon, basil and Parmesan rice

SERVES 4 TAKES **1 HOUR 10 MINUTES TO MAKE**

8 large beef tomatoes, each about 200g
1 tbsp olive oil, plus extra for oiling the dish
1 small onion, finely chopped
2 garlic cloves, crushed
150g long grain rice
30g mi-cuit or sun-dried tomatoes, chopped
300ml hot fresh vegetable stock
15g basil leaves, finely shredded,
  plus extra leaves to garnish
Finely grated zest of $1/2$ lemon
25g Parmesan, finely grated

1 Cut a 2cm thick slice from the top of each beef tomato and set aside. Scoop out the pulp with a melon baller or teaspoon into a bowl. Set aside.
2 Heat the olive oil in a medium pan. Add the onion and garlic and cook over a medium heat until soft but not browned. Add the tomato pulp to the pan, increase the heat slightly, and simmer vigorously for about 10 minutes, stirring now and then, until the mixture is well-reduced and thickened. Stir in the rice, mi-cuit or sun-dried tomatoes and the vegetable stock, cover and leave to cook over a low heat for 10 minutes, until the rice is half-cooked. Stir in the basil, lemon zest and Parmesan and season to taste.
3 Preheat the oven to 190°C/fan170°C/gas 5. Put the hollowed out tomatoes into a lightly oiled baking dish and fill with the rice mixture. Replace the tops to act as lids and bake in the oven for 35–40 minutes, until the tomatoes are completely tender and the rice is thoroughly cooked through. Garnish with the extra basil leaves and serve with a crisp mixed salad.

Enjoy plump beef tomatoes filled with some of Italy's finest things.

Pearl barley risotto with roasted squash, red peppers and rocket

Couscous with broad
beans, peas, mint and feta

Couscous with broad beans, peas, mint and feta

SERVES 4–6 TAKES **30 MINUTES TO MAKE**

225g couscous
4–5 tbsp extra-virgin olive oil
225g fresh or frozen broad beans
225g fresh or frozen peas
4 plum tomatoes, deseeded and finely chopped
4 tbsp chopped mint
150g feta

1 Put the couscous into a large bowl and gradually stir in 300ml of warm water until it is all absorbed. Leave to stand for 10–15 minutes until the grains are tender and plump. Stir in 1 tbsp olive oil and rub the grains gently between your fingers to break up any lumps.
2 Cook the broad beans and peas in boiling salted water over a high heat for 4–5 minutes until just tender. Refresh under cold running water. Drain well. Nick the tough outer white skin on each broad bean with a fingernail and peel it off.

3 Stir the beans and peas into the couscous, then add the chopped tomatoes and mint. Season the rest of the olive oil well and stir it in, then gently mix in the feta. Spoon the mixture into bowls or on to a platter and serve.
WINE NOTE Some gently sweet flavours would go well here, so opt for a ripe, unoaked Chardonnay.

Mushroom, red wine and thyme ragù

SERVES 2 TAKES **20 MINUTES TO MAKE**

1 tbsp olive oil
1 onion, chopped
200g large, flat mushrooms, halved and thickly sliced
1 tbsp tomato purée
100ml red wine
100ml hot fresh vegetable stock
Few fresh thyme leaves, plus extra to serve
Mashed potato and broccoli, to serve

1 Heat the oil in a wide saucepan over a medium heat. Add the onion and cook for 5 minutes until softened. Stir in the mushrooms. Cover and cook for 5 minutes, until the mushrooms have released some of their juices.
2 Uncover the saucepan and cook for a few more minutes until all the juices have evaporated, then stir in the tomato purée. Cook for 30 seconds, then stir in the red wine. Allow to bubble for a few minutes until the mixture has reduced by half.
3 Stir in the hot stock with a few fresh thyme leaves. Bubble for a few minutes, until reduced a little, then season. Spoon over some mashed potato, sprinkle with more fresh thyme and serve with steamed broccoli.

delicious.**tip**

STEAMED TO PERFECTION
For the perfect steamed broccoli, use a stove-top steamer over plenty of rapidly boiling water. Usually 3–5 minutes is long enough. Your florets should remain crisp, but with a bright green colour and stalks that are easy to cut.

Baked mushrooms with polenta and cheese sauce

SERVES 4 TAKES **30 MINUTES TO MAKE**

1 litre fresh vegetable stock
250g instant polenta
50g butter
25g Parmesan, grated
8 portabella mushrooms
2 tbsp olive oil, plus extra for drizzling
2 shallots, finely chopped
2 garlic cloves, chopped
150ml white wine
150g garlic and herb soft cheese
2 tbsp milk

1 Bring the vegetable stock to the boil in a pan. Tip in the instant polenta and simmer gently, stirring constantly, until thick and creamy. Make sure it does not catch on the bottom of the pan as it cooks. Remove the pan from the heat and stir in the butter and Parmesan to make a smooth paste. Cover and set aside.

2 Preheat the grill, then place the portabella mushrooms on a baking sheet, rounded side up. Drizzle with olive oil and grill for 5 minutes. Turn over and grill for a further minute.
3 Heat 2 tbsp olive oil in a frying pan over a low heat and cook the shallots and garlic, stirring, until softened. Add the white wine, increase the heat and simmer rapidly until reduced by half.
4 Add the soft cheese and melt to form a creamy sauce. Thin the sauce with the milk.
5 Spoon the polenta into shallow bowls and top with mushrooms and sauce. Serve immediately.

The humble but extraordinarily versatile polenta is the staple food of northern Italy.

Baked mushrooms with polenta and cheese sauce

Portabella mushroom burgers

SERVES 4 TAKES **25 MINUTES TO MAKE**

4 large, open-cup mushrooms
Olive oil
4 seeded buns
4 slices of Taleggio cheese
Chilli jelly, to serve
Rocket leaves, to serve

1 Drizzle the open-cup mushrooms with olive oil and season. Grill until tender, turning once.
2 Split open the seeded buns, top the base of each with a slice of Taleggio and grill until melted. Serve the mushrooms in the grilled cheese buns with a dollop of chilli jelly and some rocket leaves.
WINE NOTE Pour a glass of soft, smooth, easy Beaujolais-Villages.

Gratin of winter squash with tomatoes, cream and Gruyère

SERVES 4–6 TAKES **1 HOUR 15 MINUTES TO MAKE**

1.25kg winter squash (the crown prince variety is ideal, but if you can't find it, use a butternut squash)
4 tbsp olive oil
1 small onion, finely chopped
2 garlic cloves, crushed
120ml dry white wine
$^1/_2$ tsp caster sugar
2–3 fresh thyme sprigs, leaves picked, plus extra to garnish (optional)
1 bay leaf
Good pinch of dried chilli flakes
450g vine-ripened tomatoes, peeled, deseeded and chopped
142ml double cream
Grated nutmeg
100g Gruyère, finely grated

1 Cut the squash into quarters and remove the seeds, fibre and peel (see right). Cut into small, chunky pieces. You should have around 750g of prepared squash, but don't worry if you have a little more or less. Set aside.

2 Heat 2 tbsp of the olive oil in a medium-sized pan, then add the onion and garlic and cook gently, stirring occasionally, until the onion has become soft and transparent but without taking on any colour.
3 Add the wine and sugar and simmer over a medium heat until reduced by half. Add the thyme, bay leaf, chilli flakes and tomatoes and leave to simmer gently for 15 minutes, stirring from time to time, until the sauce has reduced and thickened. Fish out and discard the bay leaf and spoon the tomato sauce evenly on to the base of a shallow ovenproof dish.
4 Preheat the oven to 200°C/fan 180°C/gas 6. Pour the rest of the oil into a large pan over a medium heat, then add the squash and sauté gently for 3–4 minutes, tossing, until lightly golden on all sides. Scatter the squash over the tomato sauce in the dish.
5 In a small pan, bring the cream and a little grated nutmeg just to the boil, then immediately remove from the heat.
6 Evenly sprinkle the Gruyère over the top of the squash. Pour over the cream and nutmeg and bake the gratin in the hot oven for 30 minutes, until the squash is tender and the cheese is golden and bubbling. Sprinkle with thyme leaves to garnish, if you like. This is a fantastic, comforting autumnal meal.
WINE NOTE Try a ripe, buttery white, such as a rich Chardonnay.

delicious.technique

PEELING A SQUASH

1. Cut the squash lengthways in half, working from the stalk end downwards. Use a spoon to remove the seeds and fibres from each squash half.

2. Use a vegetable peeler or knife to remove the skin, working upwards from the base towards the stalk end. Cut into shapes as required.

Creamy leek, courgette and Brie bake with soufflé topping

SERVES 4–6 TAKES **45 MINUTES TO MAKE**

2 tbsp olive oil
200g butternut squash, peeled and diced
100g sweet potato, peeled and diced
20g butter
1 onion, finely chopped
4 leeks, washed and sliced
4 courgettes, sliced
2 garlic cloves, crushed
200g ricotta
1 large egg, lightly beaten
2 tsp Dijon mustard
240g ripe Brie, torn
1 heaped tbsp plain flour
2 heaped tbsp pine nuts, toasted
Bunch of fresh mint, roughly chopped
Bunch of parsley leaves, roughly chopped
4 large egg whites
25g Parmesan, finely grated

1 Preheat the oven to 200°C/fan 180°C/gas 6. Heat 1 tbsp of the oil and gently fry the squash and sweet potato for 5 minutes. Put into a large ovenproof dish.
2 Heat the butter and remaining oil in a large pan. Add the onion and cook over a low heat for 5 minutes until soft and transparent. Turn up the heat, add the leeks, courgettes and garlic and cook for a further 10–15 minutes, until the vegetables are golden and tender. Remove from the pan and set aside in a bowl.
3 Mix the ricotta, egg, mustard, Brie, flour, pine nuts and herbs into the courgette and leek mix. Season well, then spoon on to the squash and sweet potato.
4 In a very clean, grease-free bowl, use a balloon whisk or hand-held electric whisk to whisk the egg whites to stiff peaks. Fold in the grated Parmesan. Carefully spoon the mixture on to the vegetables. Cook in the oven for 15 minutes, until puffed up and golden brown.
WINE NOTE This rich, creamy dish suits a ripe, rounded white, such as a white Burgundy made from the Chardonnay grape.

Portabella mushroom burgers

Gratin of winter squash with tomatoes, cream and Gruyère

Spinach and feta filo pie

Spinach and feta filo pie
SERVES 4 TAKES **45 MINUTES TO MAKE**

500g spinach
Knob of butter, plus melted butter for brushing
1 large onion, finely chopped
2 garlic cloves, finely chopped
200g feta, crumbled
4 tbsp pine nuts, toasted
3 large eggs, beaten
4–6 filo pastry sheets
$1/2$ tsp caraway seeds
Tomato and red onion salad, to serve

1 Preheat the oven to 180°C/fan 160°C/gas 4. Wash the spinach well, removing all grit, and place it in a large pan with the water that clings to the leaves. Wilt it over a low heat. Allow to cool, then drain well, squeezing out excess liquid.
2 Melt the butter in a frying pan over a low heat and add the onion. Cook for 5 minutes, until soft and transparent. Stir in the garlic and cook for a further minute until softened.

3 Remove from the heat and put in a bowl together with the spinach, feta, pine nuts and eggs. Mix together and season well. Spoon into the base of a 1-litre baking dish.
4 Brush each filo pastry sheet with melted butter to lubricate and help it to crisp up in the oven. Lightly scrunch up the sheets and lay them over the spinach mixture, making sure the filling is covered. Sprinkle evenly with the caraway seeds and bake in the hot oven for 25–30 minutes, until crisp and golden.
5 Serve with a juicy tomato and red onion salad.

delicious.**tip**
BUYING WISELY
Filo pastry comes in large packs, though often you only need a few sheets, so buy it fresh, wrap it in cling film and freeze in about 10- or 20-sheet sections, to be thawed as needed. For this recipe, don't always go for baby spinach, as it can be expensive. Trim the tougher stems from larger spinach leaves and roughly chop before blanching.

Summer vegetable tagine
SERVES 4–6 TAKES **40 MINUTES TO MAKE**

2 tbsp olive oil
12 shallots, peeled and halved if large
2 garlic cloves, finely chopped
4cm piece fresh ginger, finely chopped
150g brown or green lentils
2 tsp ras el hanout spice mix
$\frac{1}{2}$ tsp cumin seeds
800ml hot fresh vegetable stock
100g dried ready-to-eat apricots
150g baby carrots, scrubbed
3 small fennel bulbs, each cut in 6 wedges,
   fronds chopped and reserved
2 courgettes, halved lengthways and cut into
   4cm wedges
200g fresh or frozen peas
Grated zest of 2 lemons, plus the juice of 1
100g blanched almonds, toasted and chopped
Handful fresh flatleaf parsley, chopped

1 Heat the oil in a large tagine base, casserole or saucepan. Add the shallots and cook, stirring, for 3 minutes. Add the garlic, ginger, lentils, ras el hanout and cumin, and cook for a further minute. Pour in the stock, stir it through and bring to the boil. Reduce the heat, cover and simmer for 15 minutes.
2 Add the apricots, carrots, fennel and courgettes and simmer, covered once more, for 5 minutes. Add the peas and half the lemon zest and continue to cook for 5 more minutes. Stir in the lemon juice and season to taste.
3 Scatter with the remaining lemon zest, toasted almonds, fennel tops and parsley.

Spiced vegetable curry
SERVES 4 TAKES **30 MINUTES TO MAKE**

1 tbsp vegetable oil
1 onion, thinly sliced
1 garlic clove, crushed
5 tbsp mild curry paste
400ml can coconut milk
150ml vegetable stock
125g fine green beans, trimmed
1 large sweet potato, cut into chunks
175g baby corn, halved lengthways
$\frac{1}{2}$ small cauliflower, about 375g,
   broken into small florets
100g ground almonds
410g can green lentils, drained

1 Pour the oil into a large saucepan and place over a medium-low heat. Add the the onion and garlic and sauté for 5–6 minutes until softened, being careful not to let them burn as this will make them taste bitter. Stir in the curry paste and allow to fry for 2 minutes to cook out its spices, so it becomes aromatic.
2 Add the coconut milk, stock, green beans, sweet potato, corn and cauliflower florets. Bring to the boil, cover and simmer for 10 minutes, until the vegetables are just tender.
3 Season to taste, then stir in the ground almonds and lentils. Simmer for a few minutes more until warmed through. Serve with plain boiled rice.

Summer vegetable tagine

Fried potatoes with savoy cabbage, garlic and juniper

Oven-roasted chips

Jacket potatoes with soured cream and chives

SERVES 4 TAKES **1 HOUR 30 MINUTES TO MAKE**

4 large baking potatoes, such as cara,
  maris piper or king edward
Olive oil
40g butter
150g soured cream
Handful of snipped chives

1 Preheat the oven to 220°C/fan 200°C/gas 7. Scrub the potatoes then dry with a clean tea towel. Prick them all over with a fork (so they don't split in the oven), then rub with a little oil and sea salt – this will make them golden and crispy. Put them directly on the top shelf of the oven and cook for $1\frac{1}{4}$ hours, or until crisp and tender. Remove and place on a board.
2 Make a cross in each potato and ease open. Put in a serving dish and top each with butter and soured cream.
3 Season and serve sprinkled with chives. Or try one of these variations: Cheese and mustard (mix 200g grated Cheddar with 1 tbsp Dijon mustard); Spicy coleslaw and prawns (mix 200g coleslaw with 100g cooked peeled prawns and 1 deseeded and chopped chilli); Mushroom, crème fraîche and spinach (200g fried, sliced mushrooms simmered in 200ml crème fraîche for 10 minutes, mixed with wilted spinach and a pinch of paprika).

A jacket potato never fails to hit the spot, especially when you need some comfort food.

Fried potatoes with savoy cabbage, garlic and juniper
SERVES 8 TAKES **50 MINUTES TO MAKE**

750g medium waxy potatoes
2 tbsp olive oil
70g unsalted butter
2 garlic cloves, crushed
8 juniper berries, crushed
1 medium-large savoy cabbage, about 500g,
  discoloured outer leaves discarded, halved,
  cored and cut into 2cm strips

1 Put the potatoes in a large saucepan of salted water, cover and place over a high heat. Bring to the boil, then uncover and simmer for 12–15 minutes or until just tender. Drain, cool until just warm, then halve or cut into chunks, if large.
2 Heat the olive oil and 45g of the butter in a large frying pan over a medium-low heat. Add the potatoes, season well and cook for about 20 minutes, gently shaking them occasionally, until golden and crumbly – be careful that you don't break them up too much.
3 When the potatoes are nearly ready, melt the rest of the butter in another large saucepan over a low heat. Add the garlic, juniper berries, cabbage, 2 tbsp cold water and season well. Cover and cook for about 4 minutes, shaking the pan vigorously every so often to cover everything in butter and to prevent any cabbage catching and burning on the bottom of the pan. Uncover, increase the heat slightly and let the juice boil off, again shaking the pan gently, until the cabbage is just tender and glossy with butter.
4 Carefully toss the potatoes with the cabbage, tip everything into a warm serving dish and serve immediately. This dish is excellent with sausages and Braised Puy Lentils (p.127).

delicious.**tip**
PREPARING IN ADVANCE
Make the cabbage, then cool and freeze for up to 1 month. Defrost thoroughly in the fridge overnight then reheat gently over a low heat, stirring all the time, until piping hot throughout.

Oven-roasted chips
SERVES 6 TAKES **1 HOUR TO MAKE**

4 large baking potatoes
Vegetable oil, for coating
Few sprigs of fresh thyme, leaves picked

1 Preheat the oven to 200°C/fan 180°C/gas 6. Cut the unpeeled potatoes into chunky slices, then cut each slice into medium chips. Pile into a large non-stick roasting tin and drizzle with plenty of vegetable oil. Sprinkle with some sea salt and thyme. Using both hands, toss everything together very well to coat in the oil. Spread out in an even layer in the tin, making sure that the potatoes have room to lie in a single layer.
2 Put the chips in the hot oven for about 45–50 minutes, tossing them halfway through, until golden brown and tender.

Perfect roast potatoes
SERVES 4 TAKES **1 HOUR 15 MINUTES TO MAKE**

50g goose fat, olive oil or beef dripping
700g large floury potatoes, peeled and quartered
Handful of fresh rosemary sprigs

1 Preheat the oven to 220°C/fan 200°C/gas 7.
2 Put the fat, olive oil or dripping in a large roasting tin and pop in the oven to get really hot.
3 Meanwhile, place the peeled potatoes in a pan of cold, salted water, bring to the boil then cook for 6 minutes. Drain very well, then return to the pan and shake gently in the pan so that the edges of the potatoes are slightly roughened up – this will help the outsides to become nice and crisp as they roast in the oven.
4 Carefully tip the potatoes into the roasting tin, coat in the hot fat and sprinkle with a little sea salt. Roast in the oven for 1 hour, turning each potato over halfway through cooking, until crisp and golden all over. About 15 minutes before the end of the cooking time, scatter the rosemary sprigs over the roasted potatoes.
5 Serve immediately, sprinkled with a little extra sea salt if you like.

Celeriac and potato dauphinoise
SERVES 6 TAKES **1 HOUR 20 MINUTES TO MAKE**

25g butter, plus extra for greasing
500g floury potatoes, such as maris piper or
  king edward, peeled and finely sliced
500g celeriac, peeled, quartered and sliced
1 garlic clove, crushed
568ml tub double cream
200ml pot half-fat crème fraîche

1 Preheat the oven to 180°C/fan 160°C/gas 4.
Lightly butter a large ovenproof dish. Layer the
potatoes and celeriac randomly in the dish.
2 Put the remaining ingredients into a large pan,
bring just to the boil, then season. Pour into the
dish, cover with foil and bake in the hot oven for
40 minutes. Check halfway through, and pat down
with a spatula.
3 Uncover and bake the dauphinoise for a further
10–15 minutes, until golden and bubbling. Stand
for 10 minutes to cool slightly and meld together
before serving.

Celeriac and potato
dauphinoise

Roast carrots and parsnips with walnut sauce
SERVES 6 TAKES **50 MINUTES TO MAKE**

500g small carrots
500g small parsnips
3–4 tbsp olive oil

For the walnut sauce
1–2 slices stale white bread (sourdough is best)
2 tbsp red wine vinegar
100ml olive or walnut oil
100g walnut pieces
Generous handful of fresh flatleaf parsley
1 garlic clove

1 Preheat the oven to 200°C/fan 180°C/gas 6.
Wash the carrots and parsnips (don't peel them
– scrub with a vegetable brush). Put into 2 large
roasting trays so they sit in a single layer. Drizzle
with the oil, sprinkle with sea salt and toss. Roast
for 40 minutes, turning them over once for even
colour. The oil will be slightly infused with the
carrot colour and sweetness – drizzle it over the
vegetables when you serve them.
2 Meanwhile, make the walnut sauce. In a large
bowl, mix the bread, vinegar, about half the oil
and 50ml cold water. As soon as the bread is soft,
squash it into a loose paste. Set aside.
3 Roast the walnuts on a baking tray in the oven
for 10 minutes. Remove from the oven and while
still warm shake off as many of the skins as you
can by tossing them gently in a colander; the
skins will start to fall through the holes. Roughly
crush the nuts with a pestle and mortar or rolling
pin – a processor will make them too fine.
4 Roughly chop the parsley and garlic and toss it
with the bread, nuts and remaining oil. Season,
pour over the roasted carrots and parsnips and
serve immediately.

delicious.**tip**
TASTE OR TEXTURE?
Small carrots and parsnips tend to have a better
texture for roasting. Set aside the bigger ones to
use in mash or soups.

Roasted garlic and thyme beetroot

SERVES 4 TAKES **45 MINUTES TO MAKE**

400g peeled fresh beetroot, cut into wedges
1 garlic bulb, cloves separated but unpeeled
Leaves from 5 thyme sprigs
4 tbsp olive oil

1 Preheat the oven to 190°C/fan 170°C/gas 5. Put the beetroot, garlic, thyme leaves and olive oil into a small roasting tin, toss together and season well.
2 Roast for 40 minutes in the hot oven until the beetroot is tender. Serve with the whole roasted garlic cloves, which will be sweet and mild.

Carrots with thyme and chilli

SERVES 6 TAKES **15 MINUTES TO MAKE**

500g carrots, sliced lengthways
Knob of butter
Few fresh thyme leaves
Pinch of dried chilli flakes

1 Cook the carrots in boiling water for around 4 minutes, then drain well.
2 Melt a little butter in a pan over a medium heat, add the carrots, thyme leaves and a small pinch of dried chilli flakes to taste.
3 Toss for a few minutes until heated through.

Braised Puy lentils

SERVES 8 TAKES **30 MINUTES TO MAKE**

5 tbsp olive oil
1 small onion, finely chopped
2 celery sticks, finely diced
1 carrot, finely diced
300g Puy or Castelluccio lentils, rinsed
3 fresh thyme sprigs
750ml hot vegetable stock (fresh or made from
  a good-quality stock cube)
Squeeze of lemon juice
Extra-virgin olive oil, to taste

Roasted garlic and thyme beetroot

1 Heat 3 tbsp of olive oil in a wide saucepan over medium heat. Add the chopped onion, celery and carrot and cook, stirring occasionally, for about 5 minutes, until the onion is beginning to soften.
2 Stir in the lentils, then add the thyme and hot stock. Season with freshly ground black pepper. Bring to the boil, then reduce the heat and simmer for 15–20 minutes or until the lentils are tender but holding their shape and the stock is absorbed. Add a dash of boiling water if they look a little dry during cooking. Discard the thyme.
3 Stir the lemon juice and a splash of extra-virgin olive oil into the lentils and adjust the seasoning. These are excellent eaten hot, warm or at room temperature, served with sausages.

These lentils are versatile, healthy and very tasty.

Brussels sprouts with
spiced breadcrumbs

Brussels sprouts with spiced breadcrumbs

SERVES 6 TAKES **30 MINUTES TO MAKE**

1kg Brussels sprouts
4 slices stale white bread or $1/2$ small
  ciabatta loaf
1 tbsp butter
2 tbsp light olive oil
3 garlic cloves, finely chopped
1 red chilli, deseeded and finely chopped
1 tbsp capers, rinsed, drained and
  roughly chopped

1 Preheat the oven to 190°C/fan 170°C/gas 5. Wash the Brussels sprouts in salty water – this is a good way of getting rid of little bugs that can hide in their tiny creases. Set aside to drain.
2 Tear the bread into chunks and bake in the oven for 10–15 minutes until dry and crispy. Transfer to a food processor and pulse it into fairly rough crumbs, or firmly rub it into crumbs with your fingers. Set aside.
3 The best way to cook sprouts is to boil them briefly. Contrary to popular belief, there is no need to mark the hard, stalky ends with a cross; they cook just as well left whole. Trim their bases and remove any dirty outer leaves. Bring a saucepan of water to a rolling boil over high heat and blanch the sprouts for no longer then 5 minutes – any longer and they risk becoming waterlogged and colourless. Drain thoroughly.
4 In a wide-based frying pan, heat the butter and oil, then fry the garlic, chilli and capers until the garlic is golden brown. Quickly toss the sprouts in the pan. Season to your liking and scatter with the crumbs. Serve immediately. (For a real treat toss more butter through than is necessary.)

This dish has been known to convert the most fervent sprout-haters.

Red cabbage and preserved lemon tagine

SERVES 6 TAKES **1 HOUR 10 MINUTES TO MAKE**
PLUS **30 MINUTES RESTING**

2 tbsp olive oil
4 garlic cloves, peeled
2 cloves
1 cinnamon stick
$1/2$ tsp cumin seeds
1 onion, sliced
1 red cabbage, about 800g, cored and chopped
1 large or 2 small preserved lemons
2 tbsp sultanas
2 tbsp wine vinegar or verjuice
1 tbsp brown sugar
125ml fresh vegetable stock or water

1 Preheat the oven to 180°C/fan 160°C/gas 4. Heat the olive oil in a flameproof casserole with a lid over a medium heat. Fry the garlic, cloves and cinnamon quite briskly, until the garlic starts to brown. Add the cumin and onion and stir to coat in the spicy oil. Add the cabbage and stir again.
2 Halve the lemons, then discard all the flesh and pips inside. Slice the skin thinly and add to the cabbage. Add the sultanas, vinegar or verjuice, sugar and stock or water and stir well again. Cover and put in the oven for 50 minutes. Remove from the oven, cover and rest for another 30 minutes. Discard the cinnamon and serve sprinkled with chopped fresh coriander, if you like.

delicious.**technique**
CORE AND SHRED CABBAGE

1. *Hold the head of cabbage firmly on the cutting board and use a sharp knife to cut it in half through the core.*

2. *Cut the halves through the stalk lengthways, slice out and discard the core from each quarter, then shred.*

Roast asparagus with lemon, feta, mint and capers

SERVES 4 TAKES **25 MINUTES TO MAKE**

24 spears asparagus, washed and trimmed
2 tbsp olive oil
Generous fistful of mint, roughly chopped, plus small leaves to garnish
2 tbsp capers, washed and squeezed dry
Extra-virgin olive oil
Juice of 1 lemon
200g feta, crumbled

1 Preheat the oven to its highest setting. Toss the asparagus, oil and some sea salt in a mixing bowl and spread the asparagus out on a baking tray in a single layer, making sure the spears do not overlap. Roast for 10–15 minutes, depending on how you like it. The softer and wrinklier, the sweeter. Cool or dress it immediately.
2 In a large mixing bowl, gently combine the mint, capers and black pepper with just enough extra-virgin olive oil to make a rough sauce.

3 Place the asparagus in a bowl and scatter spoonfuls of the sauce over the top. Squeeze on the lemon juice and garnish with the extra mint leaves, then scatter with crumbled feta. Serve immediately. For a more substantial snack, serve on slices of toast or bruschetta.
WINE NOTE Pick an easy-going Pinot Blanc.

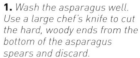

delicious.technique
PREPARING ASPARAGUS

1. *Wash the asparagus well. Use a large chef's knife to cut the hard, woody ends from the bottom of the asparagus spears and discard.*

2. *Holding the tip of a spear gently, use a vegetable peeler to peel off a thin layer of skin from the base of each stalk, rotating to peel all sides.*

Braised peas with leeks, little gem lettuces and mint

Sautéed broccoli with garlic
SERVES 6 TAKES **15 MINUTES TO MAKE**

2 broccoli heads (about 750g), cut into florets
6 tbsp good olive oil
2 garlic cloves, thinly sliced

1 Drop the broccoli into a pan of boiling salted water and cook over high heat for 4 minutes, until al dente. Drain very well.
2 Put the olive oil and garlic into a frying pan over a medium heat. As soon as the garlic begins to sizzle and colour, add the broccoli and toss around for 1–2 minutes to coat. Check the seasoning and serve straightaway.

Steamed spinach with shallots
SERVES 6 TAKES **15 MINUTES TO MAKE**

2 tbsp olive oil
4 shallots, thinly sliced
750g spinach, washed, large stalks removed
25g butter
Freshly grated nutmeg, to taste

1 Heat the olive oil in a wide shallow pan. Add the shallots and cook gently for about 5 minutes, until soft and translucent but not browned. Add the spinach, increase the heat and cook for 2–3 minutes until the spinach has wilted.
2 Tip the spinach and shallots into a colander and use your hands to firmly press and squeeze out the excess liquid from the spinach; you will be surprised by how much there is. Return the pan to the heat and add the butter, spinach, shallots and the nutmeg. Season to taste. Turn over briefly until the butter has melted and all the flavourings are very well combined.

delicious.**tip**
PEELING SHALLOTS
To make peeling shallots easier, drop them into boiling water, leave for 1 minute, then refresh in cold water and drain. You should find that outer skin now pulls away far more easily.

Sautéed broccoli with garlic

Braised peas with leeks, little gem lettuces and mint
SERVES 6 TAKES **20 MINUTES TO MAKE**

3 little gem lettuces or 5 little gem hearts
75g butter
2 small (about 150g) leeks, trimmed, washed and thinly sliced
750g frozen or freshly shelled peas
1 tbsp chopped mint leaves

1 Trim the lettuces and cut each into 6 wedges.
2 Melt half the butter in a deep sauté pan over a medium-low heat. Add the leeks and sauté gently for 2 minutes or until softened. Add the lettuces and cook for 1–2 minutes or until they begin to wilt. Add the peas and 100ml cold water. Season. Simmer for 3–4 minutes, stirring, until the peas are softened and about half the liquid has evaporated from the pan.
3 Dot over the remaining butter, sprinkle with the mint and shake the pan briefly until all the elements are very well mixed.

Frugal food

Perfect egg and chips
SERVES 2 TAKES **55 MINUTES TO MAKE**

600g maris piper potatoes
3 tbsp vegetable oil
2 eggs

1 Preheat the oven to 200°C/fan 180°C/gas 6.
Cut the potatoes into medium-thick chips. Drop
into boiling water, bring back to the boil and cook
for 5 minutes. Drain well, and spread out to cool
and dry fully (this is vital!).
2 Heat the oil in a large, deep baking tray in
the oven for 10 minutes. Add a chip – if it fizzes,
your fat is hot enough; if not, heat for another
5 minutes. Add the chips in a single layer and
give them all a good basting. Cook for 35 minutes,
until really golden. Lift from the fat with a slotted
spoon and drain on kitchen paper. Sprinkle them
with coarse sea salt.
3 Fry the eggs to your liking. Serve with the chips.

A piping hot chip
dipped into a
perfectly fried egg
is one of life's
little pleasures.

Bean and potato hash with fried egg
SERVES 4 TAKES **35 MINUTES TO MAKE**

450g floury potatoes, cubed
400g can butter beans, drained and
  rinsed
400g can lentils, drained and rinsed
1 small red onion, very finely chopped
1 tsp ground cumin
1 tsp ground coriander
5 eggs
50g Cheddar, grated
Flour, for dusting
2 tbsp olive oil

1 Put the potatoes in a saucepan, cover with
water and bring to the boil. Simmer for
10 minutes until just cooked through. Drain
well and set aside.
2 In a bowl, roughly mash the butter beans with
the back of a fork. Tip in the cooked potato,
lentils, onion and spices and roughly mash
together. Add 1 beaten egg and the cheese.
Season. Mix together using lightly floured hands,
and shape into 4 large patties.
3 Heat half the oil in a large non-stick frying pan
over a medium heat. Add the patties to the pan
and cook for 5 minutes until the underside is set
and golden. Carefully flip over and cook for
another 5 minutes until golden. Transfer to
4 plates and keep warm.
4 Heat the remaining olive oil in the pan. Crack in
the remaining eggs and fry until the white is set
and the yolk is hot but still runny. Top each patty
with a fried egg and season. Serve with wild
rocket leaves. This dish is fantastic with a splash
of Tabasco sauce.

Tomato calzone
SERVES 2 TAKES **30 MINUTES TO MAKE**

200g white bread mix
1 tbsp tomato chutney
1 tbsp caramelised onions
60g cherry tomatoes, halved
60g baby plum tomatoes, halved

A few semi-dried tomatoes in oil, drained
100g creamy goat's cheese, crumbled
A little milk
Green salad, to serve

1 Preheat the oven to 220°C/fan 200°C/gas 7. Make the bread mix dough following the pack instructions, kneading until soft and smooth. Halve the dough, roll each half into an 18cm circle, and leave to rest for 10 minutes in a warm place.
2 Leaving a 2cm border, spread 1 tbsp tomato chutney and 1 tbsp caramelised onions over each base. Mix the cherry tomatoes with 60g baby plum tomatoes and a few semi-dried tomatoes. Season and spoon between the dough circles, then top with creamy goat's cheese.
3 Brush the borders with a little water and fold each into a semi-circle, pressing the edges together well to seal. Place on a baking tray, brush all over with a little milk and cook in the oven for 15–20 minutes, until golden and crisp.

Stuffed peppers

SERVES 4 TAKES **30 MINUTES TO MAKE**

4 red or green peppers
Oil, for brushing
150g rice
350ml vegetable stock
75g grated mixed Gruyère and Parmesan
  (plus a little extra Gruyère for the topping)
8 sun-dried tomatoes, chopped
A handful of pitted black olives, chopped
A handful of rocket

1 Preheat the oven to 200°C/fan 180°C/ gas 6. Cut the top off the peppers, deseed them, then brush with oil and bake, cut-side down, on a baking tray for 12–15 minutes.
2 Meanwhile, cook the rice in the vegetable stock until just tender, then stir in the mixed Gruyère and Parmesan, tomatoes, a handful of olives and a handful of rocket. Fill the peppers with the mixture and grate extra Gruyère on top.
3 Bake for 10–12 minutes until the cheese has melted and the peppers are tender.

Tomato calzone

delicious.**tip**

MAKING IT VEGETARIAN

This budget dish of stuffed peppers works just as well with vegetarian cheeses. Look online for British cheesemakers producing Parmesan-style and Gruyère vegetarian options.

delicious.**technique**

CORING AND STUFFING PEPPERS

1. *Cut around the stalk of each pepper and pull out the core. Rinse to remove any stray seeds, than pat dry with kitchen paper.*

2. *Take spoonfuls of the rice filling (this is a wild rice mixture) and push them in, tamping down each spoonful before adding the next.*

133

Cauliflower and lentil curry

Cauliflower and lentil curry
SERVES 2 TAKES **15 MINUTES TO MAKE**

1 small onion, sliced
Knob of butter
2 tbsp vegetable oil
300g pack Indian lentil tadka dhal
  (or tarka dhal) ready-meal
200g small cauliflower florets
2 sprigs fresh coriander, chopped,
  plus 2 sprigs to garnish
3 tbsp hot water

1 Put the onion, sliced, a knob of butter and a little vegetable oil into a bowl. Cover with cling film, pierce a few times, then microwave on high (900W) for 5 minutes.
2 Stir and microwave for a further 1–2 minutes, checking continuously, until golden brown. Set aside to cool.
3 Meanwhile, cook the pack of tadka dhal (which is a mix of lentils and spices that vary according to the brand), following the packet instructions.

Boil the cauliflower florets until tender, drain and tip into a bowl. Add the daal, the chopped fresh coriander and a splash of hot water. Gently mix, then season.
4 Divide between 2 plates and top with the onions and a torn sprig of fresh coriander. Serve with boiled basmati rice.

PREPARING CAULIFLOWER

1. *Place the head of cauliflower on a chopping board with the stalk facing up. Cut off the large stalk and remove any leaves.*

2. *Using a small paring knife, carefully cut the florets from the centre, and discard the stubby stem. Rinse the florets under cold water and drain.*

Cauliflower cheese-style gnocchi
SERVES 2 TAKES **30 MINUTES TO MAKE**

400g gnocchi
A handful each of cauliflower and broccoli
  florets
A handful of halved cherry tomatoes
350g tub fresh cheese sauce
Grated Pecorino cheese or Parmesan

1 Cook the gnocchi according to the packet
instructions. Meanwhile, preheat the grill to high.
2 Cook the cauliflower and broccoli florets in
boiling, salted water for 5 minutes. Drain the
gnocchi and vegetables, then mix together in a
shallow, heatproof dish. Scatter over a handful
of halved cherry tomatoes, then season to taste.
3 Heat the tub of fresh cheese sauce in the
microwave according to tub instructions.
Pour the sauce over the gnocchi and vegetables.
Scatter with grated Pecorino or Parmesan,
season with black pepper and pop under the hot
grill until golden.

Carbonara-style penne pasta
SERVES 2 TAKES **7 MINUTES TO MAKE**

4 smoked bacon rashers, sliced
350g tub fresh cheese sauce
250g fresh penne
Grated zest of 1 lemon
Handful of chopped fresh flatleaf
  parsley leaves
50g soft goat's cheese

1 Fry the bacon in a frying pan until crisp.
2 Meanwhile, warm the fresh cheese sauce in a
small pan and bring a large pan of salted water
to the boil.
3 Cook the penne in the water for 3–4 minutes,
until al dente.
4 Drain and return to the pan. Stir through the
cheese sauce, bacon, grated lemon zest and
most of the parsley.
5 Divide between 2 bowls. Scatter over the
soft goat's cheese and a sprinkle of parsley
to serve.

Carbonara-style
penne pasta

Macaroni cheese

Tomato and basil spaghetti

Macaroni cheese

SERVES 4 TAKES **30 MINUTES TO MAKE**

600ml white sauce
  (from a packet, or see p.160)
200g medium or mature Cheddar, grated
300g dried macaroni
2 tbsp Parmesan, freshly grated

1 Preheat the oven to 180°C/fan 160°/gas 4.
Lightly butter a large ovenproof dish. Heat the
white sauce, and stir in three-quarters of the
grated cheese. Season according to taste.
2 Bring a pan of water to the boil and tip in the
macaroni. Stir well and cook for 8–10 minutes
or according to pack instructions, keeping it at
a good rolling boil and stirring occasionally.
3 Once the macaroni is cooked al dente, drain
well, shaking the colander to remove any excess
water. Place the macaroni in an ovenproof dish
and spoon over the cheesy white sauce. Sprinkle
over the remaining Cheddar and Parmesan.
4 Put the dish onto a baking sheet and transfer
to the oven. Cook for 10–15 minutes until the
top is golden and the sauce is bubbling around
the edges.

Tomato and basil spaghetti

SERVES 2 TAKES **20 MINUTES TO MAKE**

2 tbsp olive oil
1 small onion, chopped
2 garlic cloves, crushed
400g can cherry tomatoes in juice
1 tsp sugar
Handful of fresh basil leaves
200g dried spaghetti
2 tbsp grated Parmesan

1 Fill a large saucepan with water, add a
good pinch of salt, cover with a lid and bring
to the boil.
2 Meanwhile, heat the oil in a frying pan. Add
the onion and cook for 5 minutes until soft,
stirring regularly. Add the garlic and cook for a
couple of minutes, then stir in the tomatoes and

their juice. Add some salt and pepper, the sugar and most of the basil. Simmer for 10 minutes.
3 Add the spaghetti to the pan of boiling water, and cook for 8–10 minutes or according to the pack instructions.
4 Drain the pasta then return it to the pan. Pour in the tomato sauce and toss together.
5 Divide the spaghetti between bowls. Sprinkle with Parmesan and fresh basil leaves.

Ham and leek stovetop pasta
SERVES 4 TAKES **25 MINUTES TO MAKE**

300g gammon steak, trimmed of fat
  and cubed
1 tbsp olive oil
30g butter
3 medium leeks, washed and sliced
2 garlic cloves, crushed
2 tsp shredded fresh sage
350g dried macaroni or other small pasta
  shapes
1.2 litres chicken or vegetable stock, hot

1 In a large frying pan, sauté the gammon in the oil and butter until golden. Reduce the heat slightly and add the leeks. Cook, stirring, for 2 minutes, then add the garlic and sage, and cook for 1 minute.
2 Add the pasta and keep stirring around for 1–2 minutes, then pour in enough stock to just cover the pasta. Cover and simmer gently for 8–10 minutes, stirring and adding more stock as the pasta absorbs it, until it's al dente. Season and serve.

Winter greens risotto with crunchy bacon
SERVES 4 TAKES **30 MINUTES TO MAKE**

Knob of butter
2 tbsp olive oil
2 large shallots, finely sliced
350g risotto rice
250ml white wine

Ham and leek stovetop pasta

750ml–1 litre hot chicken stock
150g streaky bacon
200g winter greens
35g Parmesan, grated

1 Heat the butter and 1 tbsp oil in a deep pan and gently fry the shallots for 5 minutes, until soft.
2 Add the rice and cook for a few minutes. Add the white wine and stir until absorbed. Gradually add the stock, a ladleful at a time, stirring until absorbed before adding another (see also p.46).
3 Meanwhile, heat the remaining olive oil in a frying pan and fry the bacon until just crisp. Add the greens and stir-fry for 5 minutes, until wilted.
4 When the risotto is done, stir in the bacon and greens, season and sprinkle over the Parmesan.

delicious.**tip**
CHOOSING YOUR GREENS
"Winter greens" refers to any green-leafed winter vegetables such as savoy cabbage, kale, cavolo nero or Swiss chard.

Smoked mackerel kedgeree

SERVES 2 TAKES **30 MINUTES TO MAKE**

1 tub of chilled pilau rice
200g smoked mackerel
50g butter
4 sliced spring onions
2 hard-boiled eggs, peeled and quartered
Coriander leaves

1 Heat up the tub of pilau rice in the microwave according to the label instructions.
2 Meanwhile, remove and discard the skin from the smoked mackerel, then flake the fish.
3 Melt the butter in a large pan, add the spring onions and cook for 2 minutes. Stir in the fish and rice, along with the peeled and quartered hard-boiled eggs. Season with salt and pepper.
4 When piping hot, stir in some coriander leaves and divide between 2 plates.

Tuna fishcakes

SERVES 4 TAKES **20 MINUTES TO MAKE**

Vegetable oil for frying
1 finely chopped onion
A few chopped chives
500g ready-made or leftover mashed potato
2 x 200g jars or cans of tuna steak in
  spring water
2 matzo crackers, crushed
4 tablespoons mayonnaise
4 tablespoons tartare sauce
1 lemon, to serve

1 Heat a little oil in a frying pan and fry the onion until softened.
2 Put into a large bowl and stir in a few chopped chives, the mashed potato and the drained jars or cans of tuna steak. Season well. Shape into 8 patties and press firmly into crushed matzo crackers until well-coated.
3 Shallow-fry on both sides until golden, then drain on kitchen paper.
4 Mix the mayonnaise with the tartare sauce and a few more chopped chives. Serve alongside the fishcakes with lemon wedges to squeeze over.

Tuna, parsley and lemon spaghetti

SERVES 2 TAKES **20 MINUTES TO MAKE**

250g spaghetti
9 tbsp extra-virgin olive oil
2 shallots, finely chopped
1 garlic clove, very thinly sliced
1 long red chilli, deseeded and
  finely chopped
185g can tuna steaks in brine, drained
Juice of 1 small lemon
Large handful fresh flatleaf parsley,
  chopped

1 Bring a large pan of salted water to the boil. Add the spaghetti and cook according to packet instructions. Drain, then return to the pan.
2 Meanwhile, make the sauce. Heat 4 tablespoons of the oil in a frying pan over a medium heat, add the shallots and garlic and cook for 2 minutes. Add the chilli and cook for a further 2 minutes, until everything is softened.
3 Add the tuna, lemon juice and parsley and mix together. Add the remaining oil (this will act as a dressing for the pasta), and stir over the heat for 1 minute to heat through. Toss through the cooked spaghetti and season to taste. Divide between 2 warm bowls and serve with grated Parmesan, if you like.
WINE NOTE This is just the kind of simple dish that goes so well with a fresh, easy-drinking, inexpensive Italian white, such as a Verdicchio or Soave.

> Homemade fishcakes are much tastier and more economical than shop-bought ones.

Smoked mackerel
kedgeree

Potted ham is comfort food – tasty on toast or with chunks of nubbly granary bread.

One-pot sausages with cannellini beans

SERVES 4 TAKES **20 MINUTES TO MAKE**

- 8 good-quality pork and herb sausages, cut into chunky pieces
- 350g smoky bacon pasta sauce
- 2 ripe tomatoes, quartered
- 410g can cannellini beans, drained
- Handful of fresh curly parsley, chopped

1 Heat a large, wide frying pan over a high heat. When hot, add the sausages and cook for 5 minutes, stirring, until evenly browned.

2 Reduce the heat slightly and add the pasta sauce. Half-fill the jar with water, rinse out into the pan and simmer for 5 minutes.

3 Stir in the tomatoes and cannellini beans and simmer for 3–4 minutes. Season to taste and stir through the parsley. Divide between bowls or soup plates, and serve with crusty bread or hot buttery jacket potatoes.

One-pot sausages with cannellini beans

Potted ham with mustard

SERVES 4 TAKES **15 MINUTES TO MAKE** PLUS **OVERNIGHT CHILLING (OPTIONAL)**

- 200g good unsalted butter
- 250g good cooked ham, all fat removed
- Up to 1 heaped tsp Dijon mustard or a smaller amount of English mustard
- Up to ¼ tsp ground mace or freshly grated nutmeg
- ½ tsp chopped fresh sage
- 4–8 small sage leaves (optional)

1 Place the butter in a small pan over a low heat and let it melt gently. Wet a clean muslin cloth and place it in a sieve over a bowl, then pour the butter through the cloth and sieve very gently, trying to keep as much of the cloudy milk solids in the pan as possible. You should be left with a clear, golden liquid in the bowl. Discard the milky solids left in the pan and the cloth.

2 Put the ham in a food processor and blend briefly. While blending, pour in about three-quarters of the cooled butter and blend to a paste. Season with mustard, mace or nutmeg, sage and black pepper. The mustard should give a warm background flavour and not dominate the ham. (For a more textured paste, blend half the ham in the processor and pull the rest into shreds with two forks, then mix it together.)

3 Pack into 4 small ramekins, pots or glasses. Put 1–2 sage leaves on each, if desired, then spoon over enough of the remaining butter to make a thin layer. Chill until the butter sets (about 30 minutes), then cover and chill for several hours. The flavour matures if this is made a day in advance.

Sticky spare ribs
and crunchy slaw

Sticky spare ribs and crunchy slaw

SERVES 6 TAKES 1 HOUR 20 MINUTES TO MAKE

1.5kg pork spare ribs
6 tbsp dark soy sauce
3 tbsp kecap manis (Indonesian sweet soy sauce)
4 tbsp honey
60g piece fresh ginger, sliced into thick rounds
4 spring onions
3 tbsp Chinese rice wine or sherry vinegar

For the crunchy slaw
6 spring onions, thinly sliced
1 large carrot, cut into short thin strips
1 small cucumber, cut into short thin strips
2 tbsp mayonnaise
3 tbsp olive oil
Juice of 1 lime, plus extra lime wedges, to serve

1 Put the spare ribs in a large non-stick roasting tin. Mix the soy sauce, kecap manis and honey in a bowl and pour over the ribs. Add the ginger, whole spring onions and rice wine.

2 Put the tin on the hob, pour over 1 litre water and bring to the boil. Cover with foil and simmer over a medium heat for 45 minutes, turning regularly to ensure the ribs cook evenly.

3 Put all the slaw ingredients in a serving bowl, season, and toss well.

4 Remove and discard the ginger and spring onions from the rib mixture. Increase the heat to high and cook, uncovered, for a further 30–40 minutes, until the sauce is thick and syrupy. Once cooked, the ribs should be evenly coated with a dark glaze and the meat very tender.

5 Pile the ribs and pan juices on a platter, put the bowl of slaw alongside and serve with the lime wedges to squeeze over.

delicious.tip

BUYING RIBS

You can buy pork spare ribs from Chinese stores or large supermarkets, or get racks of ribs from your butcher and ask him to halve the rack widthways to make "short ribs", about 7.5cm in length.

Toad-in-the-hole with red onions and quick gravy

SERVES 4 TAKES **45 MINUTES TO MAKE**

250g plain flour, plus extra 1 tbsp for the gravy

¹/₂ tsp salt

4 eggs, lightly beaten

300ml milk

4 tbsp sunflower or light olive oil

8 sausages

3 red onions, each cut into 8 wedges

2 tbsp fresh thyme leaves

100ml red wine

450ml chicken stock, hot

1 Preheat the oven to 220°C/fan 200°C/gas 7. Sift the 250g flour and the salt into a bowl. Make a well in the centre, add the eggs and milk, and whisk to a smooth batter.

2 Heat 1 tablespoon of the oil in a large frying pan over a medium heat and add the sausages. Cook for 5 minutes, turning regularly to brown them all over, then set aside. Add the onions to the pan

and cook for a further 8 minutes, adding the fresh thyme leaves halfway through. Set aside.

3 Pour the remaining oil into a medium ovenproof dish and heat in the oven for 5 minutes. Arrange the sausages and onions in the dish, then pour over the batter. Bake for 20–25 minutes, until puffed up and golden.

4 Meanwhile, put the frying pan back over a medium–high heat, sprinkle in the extra flour and stir for 30 seconds. Gradually whisk in the red wine, then the chicken stock. Bubble for about 5 minutes to reduce the gravy by half. Keep warm over a very low heat.

5 Serve the toad-in-the-hole with the hot gravy, a dollop of wholegrain mustard and some steamed greens, if you like.

delicious.tip

MAKING IT VEGETARIAN

For vegetarians, use veggie sausages – there's a wide range to choose from in major supermarkets. Use vegetable stock for the gravy.

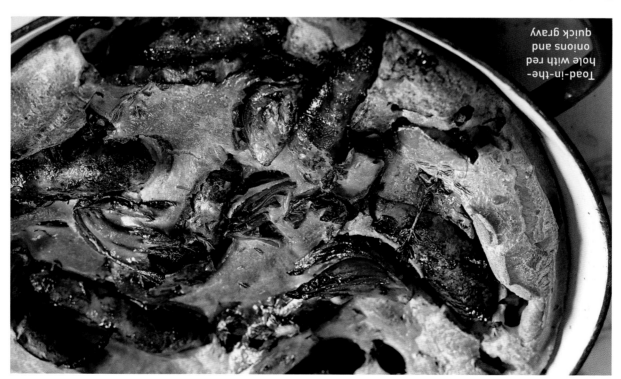

Toad-in-the-hole with red onions and quick gravy

Baked mushrooms with sausage, bacon and tomatoes

SERVES 6 TAKES **35 MINUTES TO MAKE**
PLUS **OVERNIGHT CHILLING**

6 very large field mushrooms
75g butter, at room temperature,
  plus extra for greasing
1 heaped tbsp chopped fresh thyme leaves
4 pork and herb sausages, skinned
100g smoked bacon lardons
1 beef tomato, cut into small dice
6 tbsp coarsely grated Cheddar

1 Preheat the oven to 190°C/fan 170°C/gas 5.
Remove the mushroom stalks and chop finely.
Clean the caps and place gill-side up in a lightly
greased roasting tin. Mix the butter, thyme and
some seasoning and spread over each one.
Scatter with the stalks.
2 Pull the sausagemeat into small pieces and pile
onto the mushrooms with the lardons and
tomato. Season lightly.

3 Bake for 15 minutes or until the bacon and
sausage are lightly golden and the mushrooms
have softened. Remove from the oven, sprinkle
each mushroom with the grated cheese, then
bake for a further 5 minutes.

delicious.**tip**
GETTING AHEAD
This makes a fabulous brunch dish. The evening
before, prepare the recipe up to step 2, then cover
the mushrooms and chill overnight. They'll be ready
and waiting to pop in the oven the next morning.

The chunky mushrooms soak up the meaty juices to become a luscious treat.

Baked mushrooms
with sausage, bacon
and tomatoes

Fast cooking

Egg-fried peanut rice
SERVES 4 TAKES **20 MINUTES TO MAKE**

2 eggs, beaten
1 red chilli, deseeded and chopped
2 tbsp vegetable oil
150g salted peanuts
Bunch of spring onions, sliced
225g long grain rice, cooked
100g frozen peas
2 tbsp light soy sauce, plus extra to serve

1 Mix the eggs and chilli, and season to taste. Heat half the oil in a wok or large frying pan over a medium heat. Add the egg and cook like a pancake, until set and pale golden. Slide out, roll up and finely shred. Set aside.
2 Add the remaining oil and peanuts to the wok and stir-fry for 2 minutes. Add the spring onions, cook for 1 minute, then add the cooked rice, peas and soy sauce. Stir-fry until the rice is hot. Serve topped with the egg and extra soy sauce to drizzle over.

Quick prawn laksa
SERVES 2 TAKES **15 MINUTES TO MAKE**

375g rice noodles
1 tsp vegetable oil
A handful of shiitake mushrooms, sliced
1½ tbsp red Thai curry paste
400ml coconut milk
A handful of sugar snap peas, halved
A handful of baby corn, halved
A handful of asparagus tips
2 tbsp *nam pla* (Thai fish sauce)
200g cooked peeled prawns
Fresh coriander leaves and lime wedges, to serve

1 Soak the rice noodles in hot water according to the pack instructions, then drain.
2 Meanwhile, heat the vegetable oil in a wok, stir-fry the shiitake mushrooms for 2 minutes, then stir in the red Thai curry paste.
3 Add the coconut milk and bring to a simmer. Add the sugar snap peas, baby corn, asparagus tips, fish sauce and cooked prawns.
4 Cook for a further 3 minutes, then stir in the noodles. Serve with fresh coriander and lime wedges to squeeze over.
WINE NOTE Go for an aromatic Alsace Riesling or Gewurztraminer.

Prawn noodle stir-fry
SERVES 2 TAKES **10 MINUTES TO MAKE**

2 tbsp vegetable oil
1 egg, lightly beaten
200g large, cooked and peeled prawns
120g sachet Kung Po sauce
40g dry-roasted peanuts, chopped
Bunch of spring onions, sliced
300g straight-to-wok rice noodles
Lime wedges, to serve

1 Heat 1 tablespoon of vegetable oil in a wok or large frying pan over a medium heat. Add the egg and stir gently until scrambled. Remove and set aside.
2 Heat another tablespoon of oil, then add the prawns and Kung Po sauce. Simmer for 1 minute then stir in the dry-roasted peanuts and three-quarters of the spring onions.
3 Return the egg to the pan, add the rice noodles and toss well for 1 minute. Divide the noodles between wide bowls and garnish with the remaining spring onions. Serve with lime wedges to squeeze over.

Prawn noodle
stir-fry

Crab and lemon farfalle

SERVES 2 TAKES **20 MINUTES TO MAKE**

150g frozen pea and bean mix
150g farfalle or other pasta shape
1 tbsp oil
3 tbsp frozen diced shallots or 3 shallots, diced
2 tbsp frozen snipped chives or a small bunch
  of fresh chives, snipped
2 tbsp crème fraîche
Zest and juice of 1 lemon
200g fresh or tinned white crab meat, shredded
Lemon wedges, to serve

1 Bring a small pan of salted water to the boil
and cook the frozen pea and bean mix for
3 minutes, then drain and refresh in cold water.
2 Bring a large pan of salted water to the boil and
cook the pasta according to pack instructions,
until al dente.
3 Meanwhile, heat 1 tbsp oil in a frying pan and
sweat the shallots for 5 minutes until softened.
Drain the pasta and add the chives along with the
beans, peas and softened shallots. Stir through
the crème fraîche, the lemon zest and juice and
the white crab meat.
4 Divide between shallow bowls and serve, with
extra lemon wedges to squeeze over.

Creamy salmon linguine

SERVES 2 TAKES **15 MINUTES TO MAKE**

180g linguine
1 tbsp olive oil
1 small onion, finely chopped
130ml crème fraîche
1 tbsp horseradish
Zest of 1 lemon
1 heaped tbsp capers, rinsed
140g smoked salmon
Handful of baby spinach leaves

1 Cook 180g linguine in a large pan of salted
boiling water for 8–10 minutes, until al dente.
2 Meanwhile, heat the olive oil in a frying pan and

Crab and lemon
farfalle

sweat the onion for 10 minutes until softened.
3 Add the crème fraîche, horseradish and lemon zest. Simmer for 3 minutes, adding a splash of water if you need to. Tear the smoked salmon into bite-size pieces and stir it through the creamy sauce with the capers and baby spinach leaves. Season with cracked black pepper.
4 Drain the pasta, then toss it through the sauce, pile onto plates and serve with lemon wedges to squeeze over.

Smoked salmon and beetroot carpaccio
SERVES 4 TAKES **15 MINUTES TO MAKE**

....

100g round or curly lettuce leaves,
  ripped into bite-size pieces
300g cooked beetroot, thinly sliced
125g smoked salmon, cut into ribbons
2 medium shallots, thinly sliced
100g caperberries
1 punnet salad cress, snipped
1¹/₂ tbsp runny honey
1 tbsp wholegrain mustard
1 tbsp cider vinegar
1 tbsp sunflower oil

....

1 Divide the lettuce and beetroot slices between 4 plates. Top with the salmon, the shallots, the caperberries and the cress.
2 Make the dressing. Put the honey, mustard, vinegar, oil and 2 tablespoons of water in a clean jam jar, put the lid on and shake together. Season to taste. Pour the dressing over the salad and serve immediately.

Salmon is incredibly nutritious – it's full of healthy omega 3 oils and packed with protein.

Creamy salmon linguine

Smoked salmon and beetroot carpaccio

Chicken and feta couscous

Cheat's prawn and salmon puff pie

SERVES 4 TAKES **30 MINUTES TO MAKE**

······································

600g salmon fillet, skinned
250g raw shelled tiger prawns
260g fresh lemon, caper and parsley sauce
Handful of frozen peas
2–3 large handfuls of baby spinach leaves,
  washed
185g chilled ready-to-roll puff pastry
1 egg, beaten

······································

1 Preheat the oven to 220°C/fan 200°C/gas 7.
Cut the salmon into bite-size pieces and put into
a large saucepan with the prawns. Gently mix in
the sauce, and season. Cook over a medium heat
until just bubbling, then reduce the heat and
simmer for 10 minutes, or until the fish is just
cooked through – only stir the sauce once or
twice, or the salmon will break up. Add the peas
and cook for 3 minutes, then add the spinach and
cook briefly until the leaves have just wilted.
Check the seasoning.

2 While the fish is simmering, bake the pastry.
Unroll the pastry and cut into 4 pieces. Put on a
baking sheet and use a sharp knife to score each
piece with a criss-cross pattern. Brush with a
little egg and bake for 10 minutes, or until well
risen and golden. Divide the fish between 4 warm
plates and serve each one topped with a piece of
puff pastry.

WINE NOTE Cold, salty fino or manzanilla sherries
– the driest styles of all – go well with this, or pick
a dry, succulent white, such as Spanish Rueda.

Almost anything
cooked in a sauce
can be gloriously
topped with a
puff of pastry.

Chicken and feta couscous
SERVES 2 TAKES **8 MINUTES TO MAKE**

100g couscous
50g feta, crumbled
Small handful of fresh mint leaves
2 ripe vine tomatoes
100g mixed marinated olives
200g pack roasted lemon and herb chicken
 fillets
Lemon wedges to squeeze over (optional)

1 Put the couscous in a large bowl. Pour over
175ml of boiling water, stir, cover with cling film
and leave to stand for 5 minutes.
2 Meanwhile, roughly chop the tomatoes and
shred the mint leaves. When the couscous has
soaked up all the water, fluff up the grains with
a fork and stir through the feta, mint leaves,
tomatoes and olives.
3 Tear the chicken into large pieces, and stir
through the couscous. Serve with lemon wedges
to squeeze over, if you like.

Quick Thai green chicken curry
SERVES 4 TAKES **30 MINUTES TO MAKE**

200ml coconut cream
3 tbsp Thai green curry paste
2 tbsp runny honey
Juice of 1 lime
450g mini chicken breast fillets
Handful of chopped fresh coriander,
 plus extra leaves to garnish
1 red chilli, thinly sliced, to garnish (optional)

1 Pour the coconut cream into a shallow
non-metallic dish. Add the curry paste, runny
honey and lime juice and mix together well.
Add the chicken, toss well and set aside for
15 minutes.
2 Transfer to a saucepan and gently simmer
for 12–15 minutes, until the chicken is cooked
through and the sauce has thickened slightly.
Add the coriander and stir through.
3 Garnish with coriander leaves and the chilli,
if you like, and serve with cooked basmati rice.

**Quick Thai green
chicken curry**

Creamy chicken korma

SERVES 4 TAKES **25 MINUTES TO MAKE**
PLUS **DEFROSTING OVERNIGHT**

1 portion Basic Curry Sauce (see p.167)
2 tbsp groundnut oil
4 large boneless, skinless chicken pieces,
  cubed
50g ground almonds
100ml double cream
25g flaked almonds, toasted

1 Defrost the curry sauce overnight in the fridge, until completely thawed. Heat the groundnut oil in a large saucepan and cook the chicken pieces until golden brown all over.
2 Stir in the curry sauce, ground almonds, double cream and 100ml water. Simmer for 15 minutes until the sauce is creamy and thickened.
3 Divide the curry between 4 bowls, garnish with toasted almonds and serve with naan bread sprinkled with chopped fresh coriander, or steamed basmati rice and wilted spinach, if you like.

Quick chicken
tikka masala

Quick chicken tikka masala

SERVES 4 TAKES **15 MINUTES TO MAKE**

500g tomato passata
2 tbsp tikka masala curry paste
400g cooked chicken tikka mini fillets
142ml single cream
Handful of chopped fresh coriander leaves

1 Heat the passata in a deep, wide frying pan over a medium heat until simmering. Stir in the curry paste and cook for 1 minute.
2 Add the chicken tikka mini fillets and cream. Allow the sauce to come up to a simmer again and cook for 4–5 minutes, stirring occasionally, until the chicken is hot throughout.
3 Stir in the coriander and serve with cooked basmati rice and warmed naan bread.

Quick lamb tagine

SERVES 4 TAKES **20 MINUTES TO MAKE**

1 tbsp olive oil
4 lamb leg steaks
1 large red onion, cut into wedges
400g jar of tagine sauce (preferably fennel and
  apricot tagine sauce)
200g canned chickpeas, drained and rinsed
100g marinated and grilled aubergines, sliced
Handful of dried apricots, roughly chopped
Fresh coriander leaves, roughly chopped
Zest of $1/2$ lemon
Couscous, to serve

1 Heat the olive oil in a pan, season the lamb steaks and cook for 4–5 minutes each side. Remove from the pan and set aside to rest somewhere warm.
2 Meanwhile, add the onion to the pan and gently fry for 5 minutes until softened. Pour over the tagine sauce, bring to a simmer, then stir through chickpeas and aubergines. Add a handful of dried apricots and bubble for 4 minutes.
3 Spoon the sauce over the lamb steaks and scatter with fresh coriander leaves and the lemon zest. Serve with warm couscous.

Creamy
chicken korma

Apricot and sage
pork chops

Quick cottage pie

Apricot and sage pork chops

SERVES 2 TAKES **15 MINUTES TO MAKE**

2 pork chops
1 tbsp olive oil
20g butter
2 shallots, chopped
Good handful of dried apricots,
  roughly chopped
1 tbsp chopped fresh sage leaves
100ml white wine
5 tbsp apricot compote
450g pack ready-made mashed potato

1 Preheat the grill to medium. Season the pork chops and grill for 4 minutes each side or until cooked through. Remove and rest for 2 minutes.
2 Meanwhile, in a frying pan, heat the olive oil and butter. Add the shallots and cook for 5 minutes, until softened. Stir in the dried apricots and the sage. Cook for 3 minutes.
3 Pour in the white wine and bubble until reduced by half. Stir through the apricot compote, add a splash of water and cook for 2 more minutes.
4 Heat the pack of ready-made mashed potato according to the pack instructions. Serve the pork chops with the mash and apricot sauce, with wilted spinach, if you like.

Quick cottage pie

SERVES 2 TAKES **15 MINUTES TO MAKE**

250g good-quality beef mince
1 small onion, chopped
415g can baked beans in tomato sauce
2 tbsp Worcestershire sauce
1 tbsp dried mixed herbs
450g pack ready-made mashed potato
Cooked peas, to serve

1 Heat a large, dry frying pan over a high heat. Add the beef mince and the chopped onion and cook, stirring to break up the meat, for 3–4 minutes.
2 Stir in the beans, sauce, mixed herbs, some seasoning and a good dash of water. Simmer

rapidly for 3–4 minutes, until the sauce has thickened. Tip into a deep, 1.2-litre baking dish.
3 Meanwhile, preheat the grill to high. Heat the ready-made mashed potato according to the pack instructions, spoon on top of the mince and rough up the surface. Pop under the hot grill for a few minutes, until golden.

Cheat's beef stroganoff

SERVES 4 TAKES **20 MINUTES TO MAKE**

225g long grain rice
500g quick-frying beef steaks,
  cut into thin strips
1 tsp mixed peppercorns, crushed
1 tbsp olive oil
1 onion, finely sliced
150g closed cup mushrooms,
  wiped and halved
284ml soured cream
2 tsp paprika

1 Cook the rice according to packet instructions. Meanwhile, toss the beef strips in the crushed peppercorns to coat. Set aside.
2 Heat the olive oil in a large frying pan over a medium heat and cook the sliced onion for 3–4 minutes or until soft but not coloured. Add the mushrooms and cook for a further 5 minutes.
3 Increase the heat, add the beef and fry for 4–5 minutes. Add 3 tablespoons of water and bubble to deglaze the pan.
4 Stir in most of the soured cream and half the paprika, and gently heat until warmed through. Check the seasoning. Spoon the beef stroganoff onto plates. Top with the remaining soured cream. Season with the remaining paprika and black pepper and serve with the rice.

delicious.**tip**
REPLACING SOUR CREAM
If you can't find soured cream, use crème fraîche in its place. This French product is very similar, and is also available in both full- and low-fat versions.

Cheat's beef stroganoff

153

Sticky stir-fried beef with broccoli and cashew nuts

Quick chilli with rice

SERVES 2 TAKES **20 MINUTES TO MAKE**

1 tbsp olive oil
1–2 leeks, washed and sliced
Pinch of chilli flakes
600g carton beef and vegetable soup
400g can red kidney beans
Handful chopped fresh flatleaf parsley
Long grain rice and soured cream, to serve

1 Heat the olive oil in a saucepan over a medium heat. Add the leeks and cook for about 5 minutes or until just soft.
2 Mix in a large pinch of dried chilli flakes, then add the beef and vegetable soup and continue to cook until just simmering.
3 Drain and rinse the beans. Roughly mash about a third of the beans with a fork. Add them to the pan with the whole beans and heat for about 5 minutes, or until thickened and simmering.
4 Garnish with parsley and serve with boiled rice and dollops of soured cream.

Sticky stir-fried beef with broccoli and cashew nuts

SERVES 4 TAKES **15 MINUTES TO MAKE**

2 tbsp vegetable oil
2 sirloin steaks, about 200g each, trimmed of fat and thinly sliced
2 garlic cloves, thinly sliced
2.5cm piece fresh ginger, finely sliced into strips
50g unsalted cashew nuts, chopped
3 tbsp sweet chilli sauce
1 tbsp tomato ketchup
3 tbsp light soy sauce
Pinch of chilli flakes
200g Chinese or tenderstem broccoli

1 Heat the oil in a wok or large frying pan over a high heat. Add the beef, in 2 batches, and stir-fry for 3 minutes. Remove the beef and set aside.
2 Add the garlic, ginger and cashews and stir-fry for just a minute, then add the sweet chilli sauce, ketchup, soy sauce, chilli flakes and 100ml water. Bring to the boil, then reduce the heat and

simmer for 2 minutes. Add the broccoli to the sauce and stir-fry for 2 minutes, then return the beef to the wok to heat through. Serve with plain rice or Egg-fried Peanut Rice (see p.144).

Teriyaki beef noodles
SERVES 2 TAKES **10 MINUTES TO MAKE**

2 tbsp toasted sesame oil
310g beef frying steak, sliced
100g baby corn
100g mangetout
1 carrot, cut into matchsticks
300g pack straight-to-wok egg noodles
220g can water chestnuts, drained
150ml teriyaki stir-fry sauce
Prawn crackers, to serve

1 Heat 1 tablespoon of the toasted sesame oil in a wok over a high heat. Add the beef and stir-fry for 2 minutes, until browned. Set aside.
2 Add another tablespoon of oil to the wok. Add the corn, carrot matchsticks and mangetout, and stir-fry for 2–3 minutes.
3 Add the egg noodles, separating them carefully with your fingers, then the water chestnuts, teriyaki sauce and a dash of water. Return the beef to the wok and stir-fry for 1–2 minutes or until piping hot. Divide between bowls and serve with prawn crackers.

delicious.**technique**
CUTTING CARROT MATCHSTICKS

1. Peel and cut each carrot into thirds, so they are more manageable. Cut each piece into slices lengthways, creating thin, flat "panels".

2. Stack the carrot panels into piles of two or three, then slice down through them several times, so the carrot pieces fall away as matchsticks.

Teriyaki beef noodles

Quick chilli with rice

freeze-ahead cooking

Honey butter carrots and parsnips
SERVES 6 TAKES **55 MINUTES TO MAKE**

600g carrots
600g parsnips
30g butter
3 tbsp runny honey

1 Peel the carrots and parsnips and cut each in half lengthways, then half again widthways, if large. Drop into a large pan of boiling salted water and cook for about 3–4 minutes. Drain well and lay out in a single layer on a baking tray to dry out and cool completely. Place in the freezer for a couple of hours, then put in freezer bags and freeze for up to 1 month.
2 To cook, preheat the oven to 190°C/fan 170°C/gas 5. Place the butter and honey on a large baking tray or in a roasting tin and heat in the oven for 5 minutes. Tip the frozen vegetables into the tray and turn in the honey and butter. Add a good pinch of salt and lots of black pepper. Roast for 30 minutes until golden and tender.

Rosemary roasted potatoes
SERVES 6 TAKES **1 HOUR 45 MINUTES TO MAKE**

1.5kg large floury potatoes, such as maris piper or king edward
4 tbsp sunflower oil or 4 tbsp goose fat
1 large sprig fresh rosemary, leaves picked, plus extra small sprigs, to garnish

1 Cut the potatoes in half or quarters, depending on their size. Parboil in a large pan of boiling, salted water for 7 minutes. Drain and return to the pan to dry out. Shake the potatoes to rough up the edges. Lay out on a baking tray and cool. Once cold, put the tray in the freezer for 2 hours, then transfer to freezer bags and freeze for up to 1 month.
2 To cook, preheat the oven to 200°C/fan 180°C/gas 6. Heat the oil or fat in a large roasting tin for 5 minutes until very hot. Tip in the frozen potatoes and the rosemary leaves, and toss to coat. Roast for 1 hour 10 minutes, turning halfway. Sprinkle with extra rosemary sprigs and sea salt to serve.

Ratatouille
SERVES 6 TAKES **45 MINUTES TO MAKE**

4 tbsp olive oil, plus extra for drizzling
3 garlic cloves, roughly chopped
1kg fresh tomatoes, roughly chopped
2 red onions, cut into about 3cm cubes
3 red peppers, deseeded and cut into about 3cm cubes
2 aubergines, cut into about 3cm cubes
4 courgettes, cut into about 3cm cubes
15g bunch of fresh oregano, leaves roughly chopped
Large bunch of fresh flatleaf parsley, leaves roughly chopped

1 Preheat the oven to 200°C/fan 180°C/gas 6. Put the oil, garlic, tomatoes and the vegetables in a single layer in 2 roasting tins. Toss together, season and roast for 45 minutes, until tender.
2 Mix the contents of both roasting tins together, finish with an extra drizzle of olive oil and stir in the fresh herbs.
3 To freeze: divide the mixture into 3 amounts, weighing about 600g each, and spoon into 3 individual 1-litre rigid freezer containers. Freeze for up to 1 month. Remove from the freezer and defrost for about 6 hours before using.

Creamy mushroom and chestnut filo pie

SERVES 4 TAKES **30 MINUTES TO MAKE**

100g butter, melted
2 leeks, trimmed, washed and sliced
2 garlic cloves, crushed
750g mixed mushrooms (such as girolle,
   chestnut and oyster), wiped clean and
   thickly sliced
150ml dry white wine
200g cooked chestnuts, roughly chopped
142ml double cream
Juice of $1/2$ small lemon
Leaves from a few sprigs of fresh thyme
8 fresh filo pastry sheets

1 Melt 40g of the butter in a large, deep frying pan over a medium heat. Add the leeks and garlic and cook for 3–4 minutes, stirring occasionally, until beginning to soften.
2 Add the mushrooms, increase the heat to high and stir-fry for 2–3 minutes, until wilted slightly. Add the wine to the pan and bubble until

nearly all of it has evaporated. Reduce the heat to medium-low and stir in the chestnuts, cream, lemon juice and half the thyme leaves. Simmer gently for a few minutes, until the sauce has reduced a little, then season to taste. Transfer to a deep, 1.5-litre freezerproof and ovenproof dish and cool completely.
3 Stir the remaining thyme into the remaining melted butter. Brush half the filo pastry sheets with some of the thyme butter, lay 1 unbuttered filo sheet on top of 1 buttered filo sheet, then brush again with thyme butter. Halve each of the 4 filo piles through the middle, so you have

Use wild mushrooms if you can, for their rich forest flavours.

Creamy mushroom and chestnut filo pie

8 smaller squares. Scrunch each square, then lay side by side on top of the filling, to give a ruffled filo topping.

4 Cover with cling film, label and freeze for up to 1 month.

5 When you want to eat the pie, defrost it at room temperature for 8 hours, or in the fridge for 24 hours. Bring up to room temperature. Cook at 190°C/fan 170°C/gas 5 for 25 minutes or until the filling is piping hot and the filo pastry is golden. Serve with some steamed spring greens.

WINE NOTE Match with a smooth and aromatic French Pinot Noir.

Fluffy topped cheese and onion tarts
SERVES 6 TAKES **1 HOUR 15 MINUTES TO MAKE**

Flour, for dusting
500g shortcrust pastry
Knob of butter, plus extra for baking
2 tbsp olive oil
3 large onions, halved and finely sliced
2 tbsp fresh thyme leaves
1 tbsp soft brown sugar
700g floury potatoes, such as maris piper,
   quartered
100g crème fraîche
6 tbsp cranberry sauce
400g Camembert, most of the rind removed,
   cut into chunks

1 Preheat the oven to 200°C/fan 180°C/gas 6. On a floured surface, roll out the pastry until 2mm thick. Use a saucer to cut out 6 pastry circles to line 6 individual 10cm-wide loose-bottomed, fluted tart tins. You will need to re-roll the trimmings. Chill while you prepare the filling.

2 Heat the butter and oil in a frying pan over a very gentle heat. Add the onions and cook for 15 minutes, until very soft. Add the thyme and sugar and cook for a further 5 minutes. Remove from the heat and cool.

3 Meanwhile, cook the potatoes in a pan of salted water for 12–15 minutes, until tender. Drain and return to the pan. Place over a low heat to dry

Fluffy topped cheese and onion tarts

out, then mash with the crème fraîche and plenty of salt and freshly ground pepper.

4 Prick the bases of the pastry cases and fill with crumpled-up foil or baking beans. Blind bake for 15 minutes, then remove the foil or beans and bake for a further 5 minutes. Remove from the oven and allow to cool a little. (Leave the oven on if you want to eat any of the tarts immediately.)

5 Spoon the softened onions into the pastry cases and top each with 1 tbsp cranberry sauce. Divide the Camembert between the tarts, spoon over the mash and dot with butter.

6 To eat any tarts immediately, bake them for 15–20 minutes. To freeze, put the tarts in a freezerproof container to freeze for up to 3 months. When you want to eat them, preheat the oven to 200°C/fan 180°C/gas 6. Put the tarts back in their tins and bake from frozen for 30 minutes, until the potato is golden and the filling is bubbling.

WINE NOTE Alsace makes terrific, unoaked whites that go really well with savoury pastries and tarts – try an Alsace Pinot Blanc or Riesling.

Swiss chard and Gruyère lasagne
SERVES 6–8 TAKES **1 HOUR TO MAKE**

750g Swiss chard or baby leaf spinach,
  washed and trimmed
250g fresh lasagne pasta sheets
25g butter
50g Parmesan, finely grated

For the sauce
1 small onion, halved
4 cloves
900ml milk
2 fresh bay leaves
4 gratings fresh nutmeg
2 sprigs fresh thyme
1 tsp black peppercorns
60g butter
60g plain flour
125g Gruyère cheese, grated

1 First, make the sauce (see Making a White Sauce, right). Stud the onion with the cloves and put into a pan with the milk, bay leaves, nutmeg, thyme and peppercorns. Bring just to the boil, then simmer for 5 minutes. Set aside for 20 minutes to allow the flavours to infuse.
2 In a separate pan, melt the butter, add the flour and cook gently for 2–3 minutes, stirring, to make a frothy, golden roux. This stage "cooks out" the raw, starchy flour taste, and binds together the starch and liquid. Remove from the heat and add the infused milk, pouring it through a sieve. Discard the solids left in the sieve. Stir in the milk and return to the heat. Bring to the boil, whisking constantly. Don't worry if the sauce seems slightly lumpy to begin with – just keep whisking out any lumps that form until you have a smooth, glossy sauce. Reduce the heat to a gentle simmer, and continue to stir for 4–5 minutes until thickened. Add the Gruyère to the sauce and stir it in. Remove from the heat and set aside.
3 Slice the Swiss chard's green leaves away from the stems, roll up into bunches and cut into thin strips. Slice the stems into 1cm pieces and spread out in a colander. Steam the stems for 5 minutes, stirring halfway, until almost tender.

Uncover, add the green leaves, cover and steam for 3 minutes until cooked. Set aside to drain and cool. Alternatively, if using spinach, steam until just wilted, squeeze dry and leave to cool.
4 Prepare the lasagne sheets according to the packet instructions. Set aside. Melt the butter in a pan, add the chard and toss together for 1 minute. Season. (There's no need to do this if using spinach.) Layer the lasagne sheets, chard or spinach and cheese sauce in a lightly buttered, shallow 2.5-litre ovenproof dish or deep foil tray with a lid, finishing with a layer of cheese sauce.
5 Sprinkle over the Parmesan and leave to cool. Cover with cling film, or a lid, put into a large plastic bag and seal. Label and freeze.
6 To eat, remove from the freezer and thaw in the fridge for 24 hours. The next day, preheat the oven to 200°C/fan 180°C/gas 6. Bake for 50 minutes, or until bubbling. Serve with a leafy salad.

delicious.technique
MAKING A WHITE SAUCE

1. Stud a halved onion with cloves. Place in a pan with milk and any herbs required. Bring to the boil, then simmer for 5 minutes. Set aside to cool.

2. In another pan, melt the butter over a low heat. Add the flour and cook for 2–3 minutes, stirring into a roux using a wooden spoon.

3. Remove the pan from the heat. Strain in the milk mixture and whisk until the mix is smooth. Return to the heat and whisk while heating.

4. Whisk as the sauce comes to the boil then reduce the heat to a gentle simmer for 5 minutes, stirring constantly. Season to taste.

Salmon filo parcels with Thai butter
SERVES 4 TAKES **35 MINUTES TO MAKE**

125g butter, softened
1 tbsp Thai red curry paste
Zest of 1 lime, finely grated
Handful of fresh coriander, chopped
12 sheets fresh filo pastry
4 skinless salmon fillets, about 125g each

1 In a small bowl, mix half the butter with the curry paste, lime zest and coriander. Season, wrap in cling film and shape into a log. Chill in the freezer for 20 minutes to firm up.
2 Melt the remaining butter in a small pan over a low heat. Trim the filo into 18 x 26cm rectangles. Brush 1 rectangle with a little butter. Top with another rectangle, brush again with butter and finish with a third filo rectangle. Repeat until you have 4 piles of filo pastry.
3 Place a salmon fillet, skinned-side down, in the centre of each filo pile. Cut the Thai butter into discs and put 2 along each fillet. Bring up 2 edges of pastry over the salmon to enclose. Brush the open ends with butter, and fold up and over to seal. Put on a baking sheet and brush with butter.
4 Open-freeze for 2 hours until solid, then store in a food bag, label and freeze for up to 2 months.
5 To cook, preheat the oven to 200°C/fan 180°C/gas 6 and put in a baking sheet to heat up. Once the oven is hot, put the frozen parcels on the sheet and cook for 25 minutes until the pastry is golden. Serve with stir-fried vegetables.

Honey-ginger chicken
SERVES 4 TAKES **1 HOUR 10 MINUTES TO MAKE**

Thumb-sized piece of fresh ginger, grated
3 garlic cloves, crushed
6 tbsp light soy sauce
6 tbsp runny honey
Juice of 1 lemon
8 chicken thighs
1 tbsp vegetable oil
700g Chinese stir-fry vegetables, to serve

1 In a large bowl, mix together the ginger, garlic, soy sauce, honey and lemon juice. Trim the chicken thighs neatly. Add them to the bowl with the remaining marinade and mix well. Set aside for 20 minutes, or overnight if you like.
2 Preheat the oven to 200°C/fan 180°C/gas 6. Lift the chicken from the marinade – leave the marinade in the bowl – and lay on a large lined baking sheet in a single layer. Cook for 20 minutes, then turn over and brush with the marinade from the bowl. Cook for a further 20 minutes, until cooked through and golden.
3 Allow to cool, then open-freeze (on uncovered trays) before transferring to a resealable plastic freezer bag.
4 Thaw as many chicken pieces as you need for a quick meal or snack, and reheat in the oven or microwave until piping hot. Serve with rice and stir-fried vegetables, such as baby corn and mangetout.
WINE NOTE Kids will like the sweetish flavours of a cloudy apple juice with this. Adults could open an off-dry white such as Chenin Blanc.

Salmon filo parcels
with Thai butter

Creamy chicken in
a white sauce

Creamy chicken in a white sauce
MAKES 3 MEALS EACH SERVING 4 TAKES **1 HOUR TO MAKE**

2 tbsp vegetable oil
Knob of butter, plus extra 3 tbsp,
  softened
16 boneless chicken thighs or
  8 chicken breasts, diced
1 large onion, finely chopped
2 garlic cloves, crushed
150ml dry white wine
4 fresh bay leaves
3 sprigs fresh thyme, leaves picked
3 tbsp plain flour
 700ml chicken stock, hot
 75ml double cream

1 Heat the vegetable oil and knob of butter in
a large, deep frying pan or flameproof casserole.
Season the chicken pieces with salt and freshly
ground pepper and fry, in batches, over a medium-
high heat, until lightly browned. Remove the
chicken to a large bowl and set aside.

2 Add the chopped onion to the pan and fry gently,
without colouring, until softened and translucent.
Add the garlic and cook for a further 30 seconds.
Add the wine and herbs, then cover and cook for
10 minutes.
3 Remove the lid and bubble over a high heat
until the liquid is reduced to about 1 tablespoon.
Add to the bowl with the cooked chicken.
4 Add the extra 3 tablespoons of butter to the pan
and melt. Add the flour and stir well to make a
paste. Cook for 5 minutes, until a pale golden
colour. Gradually add the hot stock, stirring
constantly, until smooth and thickened.
5 Return the chicken and onions to the pan.
Cover and simmer gently for 5 minutes, then
add the double cream. Check the seasoning.
Set aside to cool.
6 Once cool, divide the creamy chicken between
3 freezer bags or freezerproof containers, label
and freeze for up to 3 months. Each batch will
defrost in 8 hours, or overnight in the fridge.
Serve with rice and green vegetables, or use as
a base for Chicken, Pea and Bacon Pies (p.62).

Creamy pork with apples, celery and sage
MAKES 2 MEALS, EACH SERVING 4 TAKES **45 MINUTES TO MAKE**

4 tbsp vegetable oil
8 thick pork loin steaks
4 red dessert apples, each cored
  and cut into eighths
400g shallots, halved
4 celery sticks, sliced diagonally
500ml cider
200ml crème fraîche
10 fresh sage leaves, shredded

1 Divide half the oil between 2 deep, wide frying pans and put over a high heat. Season the pork with salt and freshly ground pepper, then add 4 steaks to each hot pan. Cook for 2 minutes each side to brown, remove and set aside in 2 separate bowls.
2 Divide the apples between the pans, reduce the heat and cook for 3–4 minutes, turning halfway, until golden. Set aside with the pork.
3 Divide the remaining oil, shallots and celery between the pans. Cook for 10 minutes, stirring occasionally, until the vegetables have softened. Slowly pour the cider between each pan and bring to the boil. Simmer rapidly for 5 minutes to reduce. Divide the pork and apples between the pans. Simmer gently for 5 minutes, turning over the pork halfway.
4 Remove both pans from the heat and divide the crème fraîche and sage between them. If you want to eat one meal now, return one pan to the heat and simmer for 3–4 minutes until the pork is cooked and the sauce has thickened. Divide between plates and serve with mashed potato and green beans.
5 To freeze, tip the contents of one or both pans into freezer-proof containers and allow to cool. Freeze for up to 1 month. Thaw in the fridge for 24 hours or until completely thawed, then reheat in a deep frying pan over a medium heat for 10 minutes, until piping hot throughout.
WINE NOTE A medium-sweet cider always makes a lovely match with appley pork dishes, or try an off-dry white wine, such as French Vouvray.

Creamy pork with apples, celery and sage

Sausage, mushroom and Guinness casserole

MAKES 2 MEALS, EACH SERVING 4
TAKES **40 MINUTES TO MAKE**

1 tbsp vegetable oil
16 pork and herb sausages
2 large onions, sliced
2 celery sticks, chopped
12 rashers smoked streaky bacon,
  chopped
2 tbsp plain flour
2 tbsp tomato purée
330ml bottle of Guinness
300ml beef stock, hot
250g chestnut mushrooms, halved
3 tbsp fresh parsley leaves,
  to garnish

1 Heat the oil in a large casserole or deep, wide frying pan over a medium-high heat. Add the sausages and cook for 6–8 minutes, turning, until browned all over. Remove and set aside.

2 Add the onions, celery and bacon to the casserole and cook, stirring, for 6–8 minutes until softened. Stir in the flour and tomato purée and cook for 1 minute. Pour in the Guinness, bring to the boil and cook for 2 minutes until reduced. Add the stock, bring back to the boil, then return the sausages to the casserole with the mushrooms. Simmer for 5 minutes, stirring occasionally, and season to taste.

3 To freeze: transfer the mixture to 2 freezer-proof containers. Cool, then label and freeze for up to 3 months. To eat half now: return half the remaining mixture to the heat and simmer for a further 10 minutes, until the sausages are cooked and the sauce has thickened. Garnish with parsley and serve with mashed potato and savoy cabbage.

4 To reheat, defrost in the fridge for 24 hours or until completely thawed. Transfer to a saucepan and simmer over a medium heat for 10 minutes, stirring occasionally, until piping hot.

WINE NOTE A velvety pint of Guinness would wash this down well, but so would a fruity Merlot from Chile or France.

Sausage, mushroom and
  Guinness casserole

Lamb moussaka with feta topping
MAKES 2 MEALS, EACH SERVING 4
TAKES **1 HOUR 35 MINUTES TO MAKE**

1.3kg aubergines (about 4 large)
Olive oil, for brushing
1kg lamb mince
2 large onions, chopped
4 garlic cloves, crushed
4 tbsp tomato purée
1 tsp ground cinnamon
1¹/₂ tbsp dried mixed herbs
800g chopped tomatoes

For the topping
2 large eggs
500g Greek yogurt
200g feta, crumbled
25g Parmesan, finely grated

1 Preheat the oven to 220°C/fan 200°C/gas 7.
Thinly slice half the aubergines diagonally, brush
on 1 side with a little oil and lay on 2 large
baking trays. Roast in the oven for 20 minutes,
turning halfway and brushing with more oil,
until tender and turning golden. Set aside in
a bowl and repeat with the remaining
aubergines. Reduce the oven temperature
to 200°C/fan 180°C/gas 6.
2 Meanwhile, heat a large casserole or deep,
wide frying pan over a high heat. When hot, add
the mince and cook, breaking up with a spoon,
for 5 minutes. Stir in the onions and garlic and
cook for a further 5 minutes, until the meat has
browned and the onions have softened. Tip into
a colander to drain off the excess fat, then
return to the pan.
3 Add the tomato purée, cinnamon and mixed
herbs to the mince and cook, stirring, for
1 minute. Stir in the chopped tomatoes, half-
filling 1 of the empty cans with water and
rinsing out into the pan. Season and simmer
rapidly for 15 minutes, stirring occasionally,
until most of the liquid has evaporated.
4 Meanwhile, make the topping. Mix the eggs
into the yogurt until combined. Stir in the feta
and season well with black pepper.

Lamb moussaka
with feta topping

5 Layer up the moussaka. Divide half the mince
mixture between 2 deep (about 1.75 litre)
oven- and freezer-proof dishes. Divide half the
aubergines between them, in a layer on top of
the mince. Season, then top each with the
remaining mince, then the remaining
aubergines. Divide the yogurt mixture between
them, spreading evenly on top of the aubergines.
Sprinkle each with the Parmesan.
6 To freeze: set aside one or both of the
moussaka dishes to cool, then freeze for up to
1 month. If you want to eat one moussaka now,
put it back in the oven on a baking tray and cook
for 35–40 minutes, until piping hot and golden –
cover with foil halfway through cooking if the top
gets too brown. Once cooked, divide between
plates and serve with cooked peas or a salad.
7 To reheat: defrost in the fridge for 24 hours or
until completely thawed, then bring up to room
temperature. Cook at 200°C/fan 180°C/gas 6
for 45 minutes or until piping hot throughout.
WINE NOTE A modern, juicy Greek red would make
a good match.

Keema lamb mince
MAKES 2 MEALS, EACH SERVING 4
TAKES **45 MINUTES TO MAKE**

1kg pack lamb mince
2 onions, finely chopped
4 garlic cloves, finely chopped
8 tomatoes, finely chopped
4 tbsp curry paste
400ml coconut milk

1 Heat a deep, wide frying pan. Add the mince, onion and garlic and fry for 5 minutes.
2 Stir in the tomatoes, curry paste and coconut milk. Simmer for 30 minutes.
3 To eat now: serve half (one meal) with steamed rice, garnished with fresh coriander. To freeze: allow the mince to cool, then transfer it to a large freezer-proof container. Cover and freeze for up to 3 months. Defrost at room temperature. Tip into a saucepan, add a splash of water and reheat for 5–10 minutes until piping hot.

Lamb kofta curry
SERVES 4–6 TAKES **1 HOUR 30 MINUTES TO MAKE**

2 tbsp coriander seeds
1 tbsp cumin seeds
2 tsp ground turmeric
2 tsp garam masala
$1/2$ tsp cayenne pepper
6 tbsp sunflower oil
4 medium onions, finely chopped
4 garlic cloves, crushed
2 red chillies, deseeded and finely chopped
2.5cm fresh root ginger, finely grated
2 tbsp tomato purée
600ml lamb stock, hot
7.5cm piece cinnamon stick
6 cloves
8 green cardamom pods, cracked open
25g creamed coconut
700g lean lamb mince
3 tbsp fresh coriander, chopped,
   plus extra leaves to garnish
1 medium egg, beaten

1 Heat a heavy-based pan over a high heat. Add the coriander and cumin seeds and shake them around for a few seconds until they darken slightly and start to smell aromatic. Tip into a spice grinder or mortar and grind to a fine powder, then mix with the turmeric, garam masala and cayenne pepper.
2 Heat the oil in a large saucepan. Add the onions and garlic and fry gently for 7–10 minutes, until lightly browned. Add the red chillies, spices and a little salt and pepper and cook gently for another 5 minutes. Put half the mixture into a mixing bowl and leave to cool. Meanwhile, add the ginger, tomato purée, stock, cinnamon, cloves, cardamom pods and coconut to the remaining mixture in the pan and bring up to a gentle simmer.
3 Put the lamb mince, chopped coriander, beaten egg and a little salt into the bowl with the fried onion mixture and, using your hands, mix together well. Shape into golf-sized balls and drop them into the simmering sauce. Partially cover and simmer gently for 30 minutes, stirring gently now and then once the meatballs have set. Cook until the sauce has reduced and thickened nicely. Spoon the meatballs into a sealable plastic container or 2, and leave to cool. Cover, label and freeze until needed. Freeze for up to 1 month.
4 The day before you want to eat, remove the kofta curry from the freezer and leave to thaw in the fridge overnight. The next day, transfer to a

delicious.**technique**
FRYING AND GRINDING SPICES

1. Heat a pan until quite hot. Add the spice. Lower the heat to moderately low and cook until the spices develop colour and become fragrant.

2. Place the spices in the mortar, and push down with the pestle. Use a circular motion to grind the spices, releasing their flavours.

saucepan, cover and leave to simmer gently for 15–20 minutes, stirring halfway, or until piping hot. Serve garnished with fresh coriander, steamed basmati rice topped with finely sliced shallot, if you like, and some poppadums.

Basic curry sauce

SAUCE FOR 3 CURRIES, EACH SERVING 4

TAKES **25 MINUTES TO MAKE**

3 large onions, roughly chopped
12 garlic cloves, roughly chopped
8cm piece fresh root ginger,
  peeled and roughly chopped
2 tsp cumin seeds
2 tsp fennel seeds
2 bay leaves
1 cinnamon stick
6 tbsp groundnut oil
1 tbsp ground coriander
1 tbsp ground turmeric
2 tbsp tomato purée
1 tsp salt

1 Place the chopped onions, garlic and ginger in a food processor and whizz until the vegetables and ginger have formed a paste.
2 Heat a large non-stick frying pan, add the cumin seeds, fennel seeds, bay leaves and cinnamon stick and let them sizzle for a minute (dry-frying the herbs releases richer flavours and aromas). Add the oil and, once hot, pour in the paste from the food processor and fry the spice mixture for 10–15 minutes until it has turned a rich golden brown.
3 Add the ground spices, tomato purée and salt and pour in 600ml water. Bring to a simmer for 10 minutes until thickened.
4 Leave to cool completely, then divide evenly between 3 freezer bags and freeze within rigid containers – once frozen solid, you can remove the containers and your sauces will be frozen into easily storable shapes. Label and freeze for up to 3 months. Defrost each portion as you need it; it can be used to make Chicken Korma (p.150) or Lamb Rogan Josh (see p.80).

Basic curry sauce

Keema lamb mince

Beef ragù

MAKES 3 MEALS, EACH SERVING 4
TAKES **1 HOUR 25 MINUTES TO MAKE**

1 tbsp olive oil
12 rashers smoked streaky bacon, chopped
3 large onions, chopped
4 celery sticks, chopped
6 garlic cloves, crushed
4 bay leaves
2kg lean beef steak mince
4 tbsp tomato purée
2 tsp dried mixed herbs
400ml red wine
600ml good beef stock, hot
800g chopped tomatoes

1 Divide the olive oil between 2 large pans and place both over a high heat. Add half the bacon to each pan and cook, stirring, for 3–4 minutes, until golden. Divide the onions, celery, garlic and bay leaves between the pans and cook over a medium heat for 5 minutes, stirring occasionally, until soft. Remove with a slotted spoon and set aside in a large bowl.
2 Return both pans to a high heat. When hot, add 1kg beef mince to each pan, breaking it up with a spoon. Cook, stirring occasionally, for 6–8 minutes until browned. Return the bacon and vegetables to the pans and mix together well.
3 Divide the tomato purée and herbs between the pans and cook, stirring, for 1 minute. Add half the red wine to each, and bubble until reduced by half. Divide the beef stock and chopped tomatoes between each pan. Season both and bring to the boil. Reduce the heat, partially cover and simmer gently, stirring occasionally, for 45 minutes or until thickened. Cool, then discard the bay leaves.
4 Divide the cooled ragù between 3 freezer bags. Label each and place inside plastic containers. Freeze until frozen, then remove the bags from the containers. Freeze again, for up to 3 months.
5 To defrost, remove from the freezer and thaw at room temperature for about 8 hours, or in the fridge for 24 hours. Use as a pasta sauce, or as a base for chilli, cottage pie or lasagne, or to make Nachos with Fresh Avocado Dressing (p.223).

Spiced beef and beet goulash soup

SERVES 6–8 TAKES **2 HOURS 20 MINUTES TO MAKE**

2 tbsp olive oil
1kg beef chuck steak,
  cut into small cubes
2 large onions, finely chopped
4 garlic cloves, finely chopped
2 tbsp hot paprika
2 tsp cumin seeds
500g potatoes, cut into small cubes
800g chopped tomatoes
1¹/₂ litres beef stock
4 medium beetroot,
  scrubbed and trimmed
2 tbsp chopped fresh dill
4 tbsp chopped fresh flatleaf parsley
Soured cream, toasted sourdough or
  rye bread and Jarlsberg cheese, to serve

1 Preheat the oven to 200°C/fan 180°C/gas 6. Heat the oil in a large flameproof casserole and brown the beef all over, cooking in 2 batches. Remove from the pan and set aside.
2 Add the chopped onions to the pan with the garlic and cook over a gentle heat for 3–4 minutes. Stir in the hot paprika and cumin seeds and cook for a further minute. Add the potatoes, toss well with the onions and spices, then tip in the beef, chopped tomatoes and beef stock. Season well, cover and cook over a very gentle heat for 1½ hours or until the beef is tender and the sauce has thickened and reduced.
3 Meanwhile, wrap the beetroot in foil and bake for 40 minutes or until very tender. Remove the foil, leave to cool, then peel the beetroot and cut it into 1cm pieces.
4 When the beef is cooked and tender, stir in the beetroot pieces and remove from the heat. Leave to cool completely, then ladle into sturdy freezer bags or rigid containers and freeze for up to 2 months.
5 Defrost in the fridge overnight and reheat thoroughly. Stir in the herbs and ladle into bowls with a dollop of soured cream. Serve with slices of toasted sourdough or rye bread with melted Jarlsberg cheese on top.

Beef ragù

3

occasion
cooking

- entertaining friends
- feasts for a crowd
- children's parties
- outdoor eating

entertaining friends

Moroccan spiced soup with jewelled couscous

SERVES 6 AS A **STARTER** TAKES **1 HOUR TO MAKE**

2 tbsp olive oil
450g beef rump or sirloin, trimmed of excess fat and cut into bite-size pieces
2 small onions, chopped
2 garlic cloves, crushed
1 carrot, cut into small dice
2 celery sticks, diced
1 heaped tbsp harissa paste, plus extra to serve
2 tsp plain flour
1.2 litres vegetable stock, hot
400g can chopped tomatoes
75g ready-to-eat dried apricots
900g butternut squash, deseeded, peeled and cut into small cubes

For the jewelled couscous
175g couscous
300ml vegetable stock, hot
2 tomatoes, deseeded and diced
2 tbsp chopped fresh mint

1 Heat the olive oil in a heavy-based pan over a medium-high heat. Add the beef and cook for 5 minutes or until browned all over. Remove with a slotted spoon and set aside.
2 Add the onions and garlic to the pan, reduce the heat slightly and cook for 5 minutes, until softened. Add the carrot and celery, cover and cook for 5 minutes, until the vegetables have softened slightly. Stir in the harissa paste and flour and cook for 2 minutes. Gradually whisk in the hot vegetable stock.
3 Stir in the tomatoes and apricots, then bring to the boil. Cover and simmer gently for 20 minutes. Season well with salt and pepper.
4 Add the butternut squash and return the beef to the pan. Cover and cook for about 25 minutes, stirring occasionally, until both the squash and beef are tender.
5 Meanwhile, make the jewelled couscous. Put the couscous into a large bowl. Pour over the hot stock, cover, and leave to stand for 5 minutes to absorb the liquid. Fluff up the grains with a fork, then stir in the tomatoes and mint. Season.
6 To serve, ladle the soup into warmed bowls. Pile a spoonful of couscous in the centre and serve with extra harissa on the side.

Twice-baked goat's cheese and chive soufflés

SERVES 6 AS A **STARTER** TAKES **50 MINUTES TO MAKE**

50g unsalted butter
40g plain flour
300ml milk
150g soft goat's cheese, crumbled
3 tbsp chopped fresh chives
3 large eggs, separated
50ml double cream
25g Parmesan, grated

1 Preheat the oven to 180°C/fan 160°C/gas 4. Melt the butter in a pan and brush a little inside 6 250ml ramekins. Add the flour to the remaining butter in the pan and cook for 2 minutes, stirring.
2 Gradually stir in the milk, bring to the boil and cook for 3–4 minutes until thick. Remove from the heat, and add the cheese, chives and egg yolks. Beat well and season.
3 Whisk the egg whites until stiff. Mix a spoonful into the cheese mixture, then gently fold in the rest. Fill the ramekins to the rim and run a finger around the edge to make a little "moat" (this helps the soufflés rise up straight). Place in a baking tray filled with boiling water to halfway up the ramekins. Bake for 15–20 minutes, remove and cool.

4 Preheat the oven to 220°C/fan 200°C/gas 7. Run a knife around the soufflés and turn out into an ovenproof dish. Drizzle each soufflé with cream, scatter with Parmesan and bake for 10 minutes. Serve immediately.
WINE NOTE Try a ripe, soft Sauvignon Blanc from California.

Hot Camembert pastry parcels

SERVES 4 AS A **STARTER** TAKES **30–35 MINUTES TO MAKE**

375g puff pastry sheet
1 round petit Camembert (150g)
4 tbsp roasted mixed peppers, cut into strips (see p.103, or use bottled ready-roasted peppers)
Black pepper
Sprig of fresh thyme leaves, chopped
1 egg yolk

1 Preheat the oven to 200°C/fan 180°C/gas 6, and pop in a baking sheet to heat up. Open out the pastry on a lightly floured surface and cut into 4 equally sized pieces.
2 Cut the round Camembert into quarters. Place 1 piece of cheese in the centre of each pastry rectangle, then top with a good tablespoonful of the peppers.
3 Season with freshly ground black pepper and sprinkle with thyme.
4 Beat the egg yolk with a little water. Brush the pastry edges with egg, then bring up the pastry around the cheese and peppers to form a parcel. Press the edges with a fork to seal, then brush each parcel with more egg. If you wish, scatter thyme over the top of each parcel to decorate.
5 Transfer to the hot baking sheet and bake for 15–20 minutes, until golden.

Cut though the crisp pastry to reveal warm, sensuously runny Camembert.

Moroccan spiced soup with jewelled couscous

Hot Camembert pastry parcels

Red onion tartes Tatin with Pecorino cream

Potted shrimps with pickled cucumber

Red onion tartes Tatin with Pecorino cream

SERVES 4 AS A **STARTER** TAKES **55 MINUTES TO MAKE**

2 medium red onions
75g caster sugar, plus extra for sprinkling
Knob of unsalted butter, plus extra for brushing
Plain flour, for dusting
250g puff pastry
Small handful fresh parsley, finely chopped

For the Pecorino cream
Knob of unsalted butter
4 spring onions, finely chopped
100ml double cream
100g Pecorino cheese, grated

1 For the Pecorino cream, melt the butter in a pan and gently sauté the spring onions for 2 minutes. Add the cream and bring to the boil. Take off the heat, add the Pecorino and stir until melted. When cool, add salt and pepper to taste.
2 Preheat the oven to 200°C/fan 180°C/gas 6. Peel the onions and cut in half. Add to a small pan of simmering salted water and cook for 10 minutes. Drain, then leave to cool.
3 Sprinkle the sugar over the base of a small non-stick pan, add the butter and melt over medium heat until lightly caramelised. Set the halved onions in the pan, cut-side down, and cook for about 2 minutes, until lightly caramelised.
4 Divide the pan juices between 4 individual 8cm x 2cm deep loose-bottomed tart cases and carefully lift and set an onion half in each, cut-side down. Leave to cool.
5 On a lightly floured surface, roll out the puff pastry and cut out 4 x 10cm circles, slightly larger than the tart cases. Cover the onions with the pastry circles, tucking the edges in around the sides. Prick the pastry a few times with a fork and brush with a little melted butter. Sprinkle with a little sugar and bake in the oven for 15 minutes or until the pastry is crisp and caramelised.
6 Reheat the Pecorino sauce, and spoon a little onto each plate. Invert a tart on each and sprinkle with the fresh parsley. Serve the rest of the sauce in a bowl on the side.

Potted shrimps with pickled cucumber
SERVES 6 AS A **STARTER** TAKES **2 HOURS TO MAKE**

500g salted butter
$1/2$ tsp cayenne pepper
Pinch of freshly grated nutmeg
Pinch of ground mace
600g peeled brown shrimps
Toast, to serve

For the pickled cucumber
1 cucumber
25g caster sugar
75ml rice vinegar or white wine vinegar
$1/2$ tsp fine table salt

1 Put 200g of the butter into a heavy-bottomed saucepan, and add the spices and plenty of black pepper. Melt the butter gently over a low heat, stir in the shrimps, take the pan off the heat and set aside for 10 minutes.
2 Meanwhile, clarify the rest of the butter by melting slowly in a small pan over a low heat. Set aside until the milky solids in the butter have sunk to the bottom, leaving a clear layer of melted butter at the top.
3 Divide the shrimp mixture between 6 x 150ml ramekins, pressing down firmly. Spoon over the clarified butter, spooning carefully from the top to avoid disturbing the deposits at the bottom, to cover the shrimps well. Discard the milky solids. Cover and chill for $1^1/2$ hours or until set.
4 Meanwhile, make the pickled cucumber. Put the sugar and vinegar into a small pan over a medium heat and stir until the sugar dissolves. Take off the heat and allow to cool.
5 Finely slice the cucumber (use a mandolin or food processor attachment, if you have one), then put it into a bowl and sprinkle with salt. Salting draws out some of the cucumber's bitter juices, making it sweeter and more tender. Leave for 10 minutes, rinse and drain well. Stir the cucumber into the vinegar mixture and set aside for 20 minutes. Bring the potted shrimps up to room temperature for serving.
6 Drain the cucumber and serve a spoonful with a pot of shrimps and some toast.

Hot-smoked trout and pea shoot salad
SERVES 2 AS A **STARTER** TAKES **40 MINUTES TO MAKE**

500g waxy new potatoes, diced
2 large eggs
$1/2$ tsp cumin seeds
$1/2$ tsp coriander seeds
$1/2$ tsp ground ginger
2 cloves
A very mean pinch of turmeric powder
  or saffron threads
2 whole hot-smoked trout
  or 4 medium-sized fillets
1 tbsp unsalted butter
1 tbsp mild salad oil (such as cold-pressed
  rapeseed oil)
100g (or 4 generous handfuls) pea shoots
Juice of 1 lemon, plus lemon wedges
  to garnish

1 Boil the potatoes in a pan of salted water until just tender, then drain, spread out on a dish to cool and set aside. Meanwhile, place the eggs in a pan of cold water over high heat and bring to the boil. Cook for 5 minutes, then drain, peel, halve, and set aside.
2 In a heavy-based frying pan, dry-fry the spices for a minute or so to bring out their flavours, being careful not to singe them, then grind with a pestle and mortar and set aside.
3 Take the trout off the bone and remove the skin, if necessary. Flake the fish into bite-size pieces, checking carefully to remove any fine bones, and set aside.
4 Heat the butter and oil in a wide-bottomed frying pan until it is fizzing. Then add the potatoes and spices, turn up the heat and fry for 7–8 minutes, or until the potatoes are a little crisp at the edges and smell good and spicy. Add the smoked fish and stir it around in the pan a couple of times to mix.
5 Remove the pan from the heat and toss the fish and potato mixture through the pea shoots and boiled eggs in a salad bowl. Squeeze the lemon juice over the salad. Check the seasoning and serve immediately, with extra lemon wedges to squeeze over.

Beef, onion, rosemary
and pine nut parcels

Hot-smoked salmon ravioli with dill butter sauce

SERVES 2 AS A **STARTER** TAKES **45 MINUTES TO MAKE**
PLUS **30 MINUTES CHILLING**

125g hot-smoked salmon fillets
150g ricotta or other soft cheese
2 tbsp snipped fresh chives
3 tbsp chopped fresh dill
Juice of 1 lemon
25g butter

For the pasta dough
150g "00" pasta flour (from large supermarkets
  and Italian delis), plus extra for dusting
1/4 tsp fine salt
1 large egg, plus 1 large egg yolk
1 tsp olive oil

1 Place the fish in a food processor with the ricotta
and whizz until combined. Transfer to a bowl and
stir in the chives, half the dill and half the lemon
juice. Season to taste with salt and black pepper.

2 To make the dough, sift the flour and salt on
a large, clean work surface. Make a well in the
centre. Beat together the egg, egg yolk and oil
and pour into the well. Using your fingertips,
gradually draw the flour into the egg mixture in
a circular motion to start creating a dough. Add
a dash of water if it's a little dry. Form into a firm
ball and knead for 5 minutes, until smooth. Wrap
in cling film and chill for 30 minutes.

3 Quarter the pasta dough, take 1 piece and set
the rest aside, covering with a tea towel to
prevent it from drying out. On a lightly floured
surface, roll out the dough quarter until you have
a long, very thin sheet, about 45cm long and
12cm wide. Set aside, dusted with flour. Divide
the remaining dough into three and roll out to
the same size.

4 Lay 2 of the sheets of pasta out on the work
surface. Spoon 4 heaped tablespoons of the
salmon filling, at intervals, down the middle of
1 of the sheets. Brush the edges of the pasta with
water and lay the second sheet on top, squeezing
out any air bubbles. Press together to seal. Using
a 10cm pastry cutter cut out 4 circles to create
large ravioli shapes. Repeat with the other
2 sheets of pasta and filling to make 8 ravioli.
(They can be made up to 1 day in advance and
chilled in the fridge until you are ready to serve.)

5 Depending on how hungry you are, either serve
2 or 4 ravioli each. If you're only eating 2 ravioli
each, freeze the rest for another day (see below).
To cook, bring a pan of water to a rapid boil. Drop
the ravioli into the water; when they rise to the
surface (after just 30 seconds) cook for 2 minutes
until tender but still al dente. Drain well.

6 Melt the butter in a small frying pan, squeeze
in the remaining lemon juice and the remaining
dill and whisk together well. Arrange the ravioli
on serving plates, spoon over the buttery sauce
and serve.

delicious.**tip**

FREEZING RAVIOLI
**Open-freeze uncooked ravioli until solid, then put in
a container and freeze for up to 3 months. Cook from
frozen in boiling water until piping hot and tender.**

Rosemary-seared scallops with pancetta, radicchio and toasted hazelnuts

SERVES 2 AS A **STARTER** TAKES **20 MINUTES TO MAKE**

6 large hand-dived scallops
6 thin pancetta slices
6 small fresh rosemary sprigs,
   all but the topmost leaves stripped
Knob of butter
1 small radicchio, finely sliced
2 tbsp extra-virgin olive oil
1 tbsp balsamic vinegar
3 tbsp toasted hazelnuts, chopped

1 Wrap each scallop in a slice of pancetta and secure in place with a sprig of rosemary, skewered through the scallop. (If making ahead, chill now until ready to cook.)
2 Melt the butter in a large frying pan over a high heat. Add the scallops and cook for 2 minutes each side until they are golden and the pancetta is crisp and cooked.
3 In a bowl, toss the radicchio with the oil, vinegar, hazelnuts and some seasoning. Spoon onto 2 serving plates, top with the scallops and spoon over any pan juices.

Figs and mozzarella wrapped in Parma ham

SERVES 6 AS A **STARTER** TAKES **25 MINUTES TO MAKE**

150g buffalo mozzarella
6 ripe fresh figs
6 slices Parma ham
3 plum tomatoes
6 tbsp extra-virgin olive oil
2 tbsp balsamic vinegar
Small bag of salad leaves
Vegetable oil, for brushing

1 Drain the mozzarella, pat dry on kitchen paper, and cut into 6 pieces. Cut each fig in half lengthways. Sandwich a piece of mozzarella between 2 fig halves. Sit on a slice of Parma ham and wrap the Parma ham up around the fig to completely encase it. Repeat to make 6 parcels.

2 Cut the tomatoes in half and scoop out the seeds. Cut the flesh into small dice and set aside. Whisk the olive oil and balsamic vinegar together and season well to make a dressing. Divide the salad leaves between 6 plates and scatter with the chopped tomatoes.
3 Brush the grill rack with a little oil. Grill the figs under a low heat for 8–10 minutes until the ham just starts to crisp underneath and the cheese begins to melt. Alternatively, cook them in the oven on a baking tray at 190°C/fan 170°C/gas 5 for 8–10 minutes.
4 Put a wrapped fig in the centre of each plate and drizzle with the balsamic dressing. Serve immediately, while the cheese is still warm.

Beef, onion, rosemary and pine nut parcels

SERVES 8 AS A **STARTER** TAKES **40 MINUTES TO MAKE**

150g beef mince
150g pork mince
1 onion, finely chopped
1 tbsp fennel seeds
1 garlic clove, crushed
1 tbsp finely chopped fresh oregano
2 x 375g packs ready-rolled puff pastry sheets
8 tsp onion marmalade
125g mozzarella ball, diced
25g fresh Parmesan cheese, grated
2 tbsp pine nuts, toasted
1 stem of rosemary, broken into
   small sprigs

1 Preheat the oven to 200°C/fan 180°C/gas 6. Put the beef, pork, onion, fennel, garlic, oregano and seasoning in a bowl and mix together well using your hands.
2 Cut each pastry sheet into 4 equal squares. Lay onto 2 baking sheets and spread each with a teaspoon of onion marmalade. Top with the mixture and fold in the corners to overlap the mixture. Bake for 15 minutes; top with the cheeses, pine nuts, and rosemary and bake for a further 10 minutes.
WINE NOTE Serve a lovely, ripe Tuscan Chianti Classico with this rich starter.

Prawns with crispy chorizo and braised baby leeks

SERVES 8 TAKES **50 MINUTES TO MAKE**

24 thin slices chorizo
24 very large raw prawns, heads and shells on
Handful of flatleaf parsley, finely chopped
Handful of basil, finely chopped

For the croûtes
1 brioche loaf, crusts removed
2 tbsp olive oil
2 tsp chilli oil

For the braised baby leeks
32 thin baby leeks, halved lengthways
2 garlic cloves, crushed
150ml extra-virgin olive oil
Grated zest and juice of 1 lemon

1 Preheat the oven to 190°C/ fan 170°C/gas 5. Make the croûtes. Cut the brioche into 8 thick squares, measuring 8cm x 3cm, and put on a baking sheet. Drizzle over both oils and season with a little salt. Bake for 12–15 minutes, turning occasionally, until golden. Allow to cool, then store in an airtight container until ready to serve.
2 Make the braised leeks. Cook the leeks in boiling, salted water for 2–3 minutes or until tender. Whisk the garlic, oil, lemon zest and juice and some seasoning together in a shallow, non-metallic dish. Drain the leeks and plunge them immediately in the dressing, turning to coat. Cover and set aside until cool, then chill until ready to serve.
3 Heat a large, heavy-based frying pan over a medium heat. Add the chorizo slices in 1 layer and fry for 2 minutes each side, until golden and crisp. Remove from the pan with a slotted spoon and drain on kitchen paper. Cool, then store in an airtight container until ready to serve.
4 Add the prawns to the chorizo oil left in the frying pan and cook for 2–3 minutes each side, until pink and cooked through. Remove from the pan and allow to cool, then add to the leeks and chill until ready to use.
5 To serve, bring everything up to room

temperature. Put a brioche croûte on each plate. Remove the leeks from the dressing and place on top of the croûtes. Layer the prawns and chorizo on top of the leeks, using a wooden skewer to secure. Whisk the herbs into the reserved dressing and spoon over the top, and serve.

Sri Lankan crab curry

SERVES 4 TAKES **1 HOUR TO MAKE**

2 whole large cooked brown crabs
  (ask your fishmonger to twist the body from the shell and show you the "dead men's fingers" – the bits to avoid)
3 cloves
1 cinnamon stick or $1/2$ tsp cinnamon powder
1 tsp cumin seeds
$1/2$ tsp coriander seeds
$1/2$ tsp fennel seeds
2 tbsp vegetable oil
3 garlic cloves, chopped
2 medium onions, chopped
2 red chillies, chopped
400ml can coconut milk
Juice of 1 lime,
  plus lime wedges to serve (optional)
$1/2$ tsp mustard powder
3–4 curry leaves or a bay leaf

1 Remove the crabs' claws. Leave them whole and set them aside. Pick out the rest of the meat from the shell, mixing white and brown together, and chill in the fridge until you need it. (You could reserve the crab remains to make Crab Bisque – see p.16.)
2 Heat a small frying pan or skillet and dry-roast the cloves, cinnamon, cumin, coriander and fennel seeds for a minute or so, until fragrant. Remove the spices from the heat and set aside.
3 In a pan or pot large enough for everything, heat the vegetable oil and fry the garlic, onions and chillies. If you don't like your food particularly hot (Sri Lankans do) remove the chilli seeds, or just use 1 chilli. Allow to cook quite briskly; it doesn't matter if the onions catch a little in the pan. Add the coconut milk to the curry, then fill

the can with water and add to the pan. Simmer for 10–15 minutes over a medium heat.
4 Combine the mixed crabmeat with the lime juice and mustard powder and add to the curry with the intact claws, spices and curry leaves or bay leaf. Heat through and stir gently. Check the seasoning and serve with a crab claw in each bowl, garnished with lime wedges, if you like.

Seared scallops with sauce vierge
SERVES 4 TAKES **55 MINUTES TO MAKE**

Olive oil, for searing
12 large prepared scallops with corals attached

For the sauce vierge
1 small red pepper
80ml extra-virgin olive oil
25ml lemon juice
50g vine-ripened tomatoes, skinned,
  deseeded and cut into small dice
8 fresh basil leaves, very finely shredded

1 Preheat the oven to 220°C/fan 200°C/gas 7. Make the sauce vierge. Roast the red pepper for 20–25 minutes, until the skin blackens, then seal in a plastic bag and cool. Tear the pepper in half, then remove and discard the stalk, seeds, and skin. Dice the flesh to the same size as the tomatoes. Put into a small, shallow pan with the oil, lemon juice and diced tomatoes, season and set aside.
2 Heat a large, non-stick, heavy-based frying pan until smoking hot. Lower the heat to medium-high, add a thin layer of oil, then add the scallops flat-side down. Sear for 4 minutes, seasoning as you cook, and turning halfway through. Press them down so they are nicely golden but still rare in the centre. Remove from the pan, cover and set aside.
3 Place the pan of sauce vierge over a low heat until warm, then stir in the basil. Spoon some sauce into the centre of 4 warmed plates and top with the scallops. Serve immediately.
WINE NOTE Pick up the Mediterranean theme with a Chardonnay or Viognier Vin de Pays d'Oc from the south of France.

Prawns with crispy chorizo and braised baby leeks

Sri Lankan crab curry

Mussels with tarragon and crème fraîche
SERVES 4 TAKES **20 MINUTES TO MAKE**

50g butter
4 large shallots, finely chopped
1 garlic clove, chopped
1.75kg live mussels, cleaned (see below)
50ml dry white wine
100ml crème fraîche
2 tbsp chopped fresh tarragon,
  plus a few tarragon leaves to garnish

1 Melt the butter in a very large pan over a medium heat. Add the shallots and garlic and cook, stirring gently, until soft but not browned. Turn up the heat, add the mussels and wine, and cover with a lid. Cook over a high heat, shaking the pan every now and then, for 3–4 minutes or until the mussels have all opened. Lift them out of the cooking liquor and divide between 4 large warmed serving bowls. Discard any mussels that haven't opened.
2 Return the pan to the hob, increase the heat and boil the cooking liquor to reduce by about half. Add the crème fraîche and tarragon, and season (taste before adding salt, as mussel liquor is salty). Spoon all but the last spoonful of the sauce back over the mussels (the bottom of the pan may be gritty). Garnish with tarragon; serve immediately with crusty French bread.

CLEANING LIVE MUSSELS

1. *Scrub the mussels thoroughly under cold running water, rinsing any grit and sand away. Discard any open or broken mussels.*

2. *To remove the "beard", pinch the dark stringy piece on the straighter side of the mussel between your fingers, tug it away, and discard.*

Grilled lobster thermidor
SERVES 6 TAKES **40 MINUTES TO MAKE**

3 cooked lobsters, each about 700g
25g butter
3 large shallots, finely chopped
400ml fresh fish stock
100ml dry white wine
100ml double cream
4 tbsp chopped mixed fresh herbs,
  such as parsley, chives and dill,
  plus extra sprigs to garnish
Pinch of cayenne pepper
30g fresh Parmesan cheese,
  finely grated

1 Prepare the lobsters. Remove the claws, then crack them by covering with a cloth and gently hitting with a rolling pin. Remove the meat in large pieces and put in a bowl. Remove and discard the legs.
2 Cut the lobsters in half lengthways; cut first through the head, between the eyes, then turn around and continue to cut through the tail. Remove the tail meat from each lobster half and cut into chunky pieces. Add to the bowl with the claw meat. Remove any red roe and add to the bowl – it has an excellent flavour. Gently mix.
3 Remove and discard the grit sacs and intestines – the long, thin, black line running the length of the body.
4 Transfer the empty shells to a baking tray. Divide the meat and roe equally between each shell cavity, then cover and chill until needed.
5 Make the sauce. Melt the butter in a frying pan and cook the shallots for 3–4 minutes, until beginning to soften. Add the fish stock and wine and boil until reduced by half. Stir in the cream and cook gently for a further 5 minutes, until the sauce has a good coating consistency. Take off the heat and stir in the chopped herbs and cayenne. Season to taste.
6 Preheat the grill to medium-high. Spoon the sauce over each lobster half and sprinkle with the Parmesan. Grill for 3–4 minutes, until golden and bubbling. Serve immediately, garnished with sprigs of herbs.

Monkfish in Parma ham
SERVES 4 TAKES **35 MINUTES TO MAKE**

2 tbsp sun-dried tomato paste
12 pitted black olives, chopped
4 monkfish fillets, about 200g each
8 slices of Parma ham
Salad leaves dressed with olive oil
  and white wine vinegar, to serve

1 Mix the tomato paste with the black olives. Season.
2 Spread over the top of the monkfish fillets, then wrap in slices of Parma ham.
3 Bake in a preheated oven at 220°C/fan 200°C/gas 7 for 25 minutes.
4 Slice the monkfish and serve with the dressed salad leaves.

Smoked haddock eggs Benedict
SERVES 2 TAKES **25 MINUTES TO MAKE**

250g undyed smoked haddock fillet
4 rashers smoked streaky bacon or pancetta
2 English muffins, split
4 eggs
300g carton fresh 4-cheese sauce
Green salad, to serve
Lemon wedges, to serve (optional)

1 Put the smoked haddock into a large, shallow pan and cover with cold water. (If the fish is too long to fit in the pan, you can cut it in half.) Bring the water to the boil, then remove the pan from the heat and set aside to poach for 10 minutes. Drain well, cool slightly, then discard the skin, flake the fish and discard any bones. Set aside, covered, to keep warm.
2 Meanwhile, preheat the grill to medium and put a large shallow pan with about a 5cm depth of water on to boil. Lay the bacon out on the grill pan and grill for 4–5 minutes, until crisp. Drain on kitchen paper and set aside.
3 Toast the muffins under the grill for a few minutes on both sides (or use the toaster) and set aside, keeping warm.

4 Break 1 egg into a teacup. Swirl the simmering water with a spoon to make a whirlpool and slide the egg into the centre to poach for 2½ minutes. Place on kitchen paper to drain, then keep warm while you cook the remaining eggs. (Confident cooks can cook all the eggs at the same time.)
5 Meanwhile, heat the cheese sauce in a small saucepan, or in the tub in the microwave, until it is piping hot.
6 Put 2 muffin halves on each plate and top each half with a quarter of the haddock, then place a poached egg and a slice of bacon on top of the haddock. Spoon over a generous amount of cheese sauce and season with plenty of black pepper. Serve with a green salad and lemon wedges to squeeze over, if you like.

delicious.tip

GOING EASY ON THE SALT
As haddock and bacon both contain salt there is no need to add extra salt for seasoning, but freshly ground black pepper adds a finishing touch.

Smoked haddock eggs Benedict

Smoked haddock, prawn and fennel fish pies

SERVES 6 TAKES **1 HOUR 20 MINUTES TO MAKE**

75g butter
1 large onion, finely chopped
1 fennel bulb, finely sliced
3 garlic cloves, finely chopped
25g plain flour
300ml fish stock
3 tbsp crème fraîche
450g haddock,
  skinned and cut into 2.5cm pieces
300g smoked haddock fillet,
  skinned and cut into 2.5cm pieces
250g medium-sized raw peeled prawns
1 tbsp capers, drained and rinsed
3 tbsp flatleaf parsley, finely chopped
Small bunch of fresh chives, snipped
1.25kg floury potatoes, such as maris piper, cubed
2 tbsp milk
50g Parmesan or Grana Padano cheese, grated

1 Heat 25g of the butter in a medium pan until melted and foaming. Add the onion, fennel and garlic and cook for 5–6 minutes, until beginning to soften. Add the flour and cook for 1 minute, until it begins to thicken. Gradually pour in the fish stock, stirring constantly with a wooden spoon. Remove from the heat and stir in the crème fraîche.
2 Season, then stir in the haddock, prawns, capers and herbs. Set aside.
3 Put the potatoes in a large pan and cover with water. Bring to the boil and cook for 15–20 minutes, until tender. Drain well and return to the pan with the remaining butter, milk, seasoning and half the cheese. Mash well until smooth.
4 Spoon the filling into six 350ml ovenproof dishes. Top with the potato and sprinkle over the remaining cheese.
5 Bake the pies for 35–40 minutes, until the topping is golden and the filling is cooked.
WINE NOTE The soft, vanilla flavour of oaky Chardonnay always works well with smoked fish – try an Australian Chardonnay-Semillon blend.

Smoked haddock, prawn and fennel fish pies

Black cod with
white miso and
pickled ginger

Black cod with white miso and pickled ginger

SERVES 4 TAKES **20 MINUTES TO MAKE** PLUS **OVERNIGHT MARINATING**

75g caster sugar
2 tbsp sake
250g sweet white miso
1 tbsp root ginger juice (the liquid from a jar
   or pack of pickled root ginger)
1 tbsp mirin
1 tbsp lemon juice
2 tsp grated lemon zest
$1/2$ green chilli,
   deseeded and finely chopped
$1/2$ red chilli, deseeded and finely chopped
1 tsp soy sauce
4 black cod fillets, about 150g each (also known
   as sablefish – use line-caught cod if you can't
   find black cod)
2 spring onions, shredded, to serve
Pickled root ginger, to serve

1 Put the sugar and sake in a pan over a low heat and cook, stirring, to dissolve the sugar – don't be tempted to hurry things up by increasing the heat, or it may burn. Put the sugary liquid into a large bowl, add all the remaining ingredients except the cod, and mix until smooth.
2 Add the cod and coat in the marinade. Cover and marinate for 24 hours, turning over halfway.
3 Preheat the grill to medium-high. Lift the cod from the marinade and transfer to a foil-lined grill pan. Pop it under the grill and cook, basting with the marinade a few times, for 3–5 minutes each side, until just cooked.
4 Serve immediately, garnished with the shredded spring onion and pickled ginger.

delicious.**tip**

BUYING JAPANESE INGREDIENTS

Most larger supermarkets stock sake, mirin and pickled ginger. For unusual ingredients, such as miso paste or black cod, visit Japanese food stores or health food stores.

Smart fish
and chips

Smart fish and chips
SERVES 4 TAKES **40 MINUTES TO MAKE**

6 large baking potatoes
Good splash of vegetable oil
Splash of olive oil
4 thick cod fillets, about 225g each
Plain flour, for dusting
2 handfuls of baby gherkins,
  drained and cut into quarters
2 handfuls of capers, drained
Juice of 2 lemons
2 handfuls of parsley, chopped
Large handful of chives, snipped
Mayonnaise, to serve

1 Preheat the oven to 220°C/fan 200°C/gas 7.
Cut the unpeeled potatoes into thick chips. Cook
in boiling water for 2–3 minutes. Drain and tip on
to kitchen paper. Put into a large roasting tray
and drizzle generously with vegetable oil. Toss the
chips well so they are coated all over. Pop into the
oven for 25–30 minutes, tossing once, until golden.

2 About 15 minutes before the chips are done,
heat a large, heavy-based pan with olive oil. Dust
the fish all over with flour and cook, skin side
down, for 4–5 minutes, then carefully turn over
and cook for a further 5–6 minutes until just
tender (put them into the oven for 5 minutes if
the fish is quite thick). Remove from the pan.
3 Add the gherkins and capers to the pan and fry
for 1 minute. Add the lemon juice and sizzle over
a high heat for about 30 seconds. Remove from
the heat and throw in the herbs. Put a spoonful of
mayonnaise on each piece of fish and spoon over
the gherkin sauce. Divide the chips between
plates and serve.

Grilled sea bass with fresh rosemary and parsley pesto
SERVES 2 TAKES **25 MINUTES TO MAKE**

2 x 300–350g sea bass, cleaned and trimmed
4 small sprigs of fresh rosemary
1 tsp olive oil

For the pesto
Leaves of 2 sprigs of fresh rosemary
Leaves of a small bunch of flatleaf parsley
1 garlic clove
1 tbsp finely grated fresh Parmesan
Grated zest and juice of 1/2 lemon
Small bunch of fresh chives, finely chopped
2–3 tbsp extra-virgin olive oil

1 Preheat the grill to medium. Make two or three
slashes through the skin of the fish on each side
and tuck rosemary sprigs into the gut cavities.
Brush each fish lightly with oil and sprinkle with
sea salt. Grill for 5–7 minutes on each side, until
the skin is crispy and the fish is cooked through.
2 Meanwhile, make the pesto. Put the rosemary,
parsley leaves and garlic in a mini-chopper or
food processor and whizz until finely chopped.
Add the cheese and lemon zest and whizz again.
Tip into a small serving bowl and stir in the lemon
juice, chives, olive oil and some salt and pepper.
3 Spoon the pesto over the fish. Serve with
buttery boiled new potatoes, if you like.

Grilled sea bass with fresh rosemary and parsley pesto

Teriyaki chicken with sesame vegetables
SERVES 4 TAKES **35 MINUTES TO MAKE**

4 chicken breasts
6 tbsp teriyaki sauce
3–4 tsp groundnut oil
600g stir-fry vegetables
Toasted sesame seeds

1 Remove any skin from the chicken breasts and cut into cubes. Place the pieces in a bowl, add the teriyaki sauce and mix together well, so that the chicken is well coated.
2 Thread the cubed chicken onto 8 skewers, arranging the pieces so that the meat will lie flat under the grill and cook evenly. Season and cook under a hot preheated grill for 6–8 minutes, until cooked through.
3 Heat the groundnut oil in a wok. Once it's hot, stir-fry the vegetables, adding a dash of teriyaki sauce as they cook.
4 Scatter the skewers and vegetables with toasted sesame seeds and serve.

Pan-fried chicken in a Grana Padano crust

Pan-fried chicken in a Grana Padano crust
SERVES 4 TAKES **20 MINUTES TO MAKE**

Pinch of saffron threads
4 chicken breasts
1 tbsp plain flour
1 large egg, beaten
4 tbsp olive oil
8 tbsp Grana Padano cheese,
  finely grated
1 tbsp thyme, chopped,
  plus a few extra sprigs to garnish
Lemon wedges, to serve

1 Put the saffron in a bowl, add a tablespoon of boiling water, and set aside for a few minutes for the flavour to infuse.
2 Meanwhile, remove any skin from the chicken breasts, then cut them in half lengthways to make 8 long, thin pieces. Dust the pieces very lightly in flour.
3 Crack the egg into the bowl of infused saffron water. Add a good grinding of black pepper to the mix and beat well.
4 Mix the grated cheese and thyme together on a plate. Heat half the oil in a large frying pan over a medium heat, and while it's heating, dip the chicken strips first in the egg mixture, then in the cheese and thyme.
5 Fry in 2 batches, adding the remaining oil with the second batch, until all of the chicken is crisp, golden and cooked through. It should take about 5 minutes each side, but don't be tempted to lift or turn the chicken too soon or the crust might stick to the bottom of the pan.
6 Serve 2 chicken pieces each, with lemon wedges to squeeze over. Garnish with thyme.
WINE NOTE Crack open a white wine that's got plenty of citrus flavour, such as a modern Sicilian Chardonnay.

delicious.tip
USING UP LEFTOVERS
Any leftovers from this meal make a great sandwich filling with just a touch of garlic mayonnaise and some baby salad leaves.

Chicken satay with Indonesian-style salad

SERVES 4 TAKES **25 MINUTES TO MAKE**

4 large, skinless chicken breasts
300g jar peanut cooking sauce
165ml coconut milk
1 lime
350g pack mixed stir-fry vegetables

1 Cut the chicken breasts widthways into strips about 1cm thick. Place them in a bowl with half a jar of the peanut cooking sauce and set aside to marinate for 10 minutes.
2 Meanwhile, soak 12 medium-length wooden skewers in hot water. Preheat the grill to high and line a baking tray with foil. Once the chicken has marinated, thread the chicken strips onto the drained skewers (2–3 strips on each) and lay them on the tray. Grill for 8–10 minutes, turning halfway, until the outside is lightly charred and they are cooked through.
3 While the chicken is grilling, put the remaining peanut cooking sauce in a saucepan with the coconut milk and the grated zest of ¹/₂ the lime. Place over a medium heat and simmer for 5 minutes. Stir in the juice of the zested ¹/₂ lime and set aside to cool and thicken slightly.
4 Divide the vegetable stir-fry, uncooked, between 4 small bowls and place on plates, along with the chicken satay. Cut the remaining ¹/₂ lime into 4 wedges and add one to each plate. Drizzle some warm peanut sauce over each salad, and serve the rest in bowls as a dip for the satay. Serve with cooked rice, if you like.

Chicken schnitzels

SERVES 4 TAKES **30 MINUTES TO MAKE**

4 chicken breasts
150g fresh breadcrumbs
75g feta, crumbled
2 tbsp thyme leaves
1 large egg
2–4 tbsp olive oil
Lemon wedges, to serve

Chicken satay with Indonesian-style salad

1 Flatten the chicken breasts between 2 sheets of cling film using a rolling pin.
2 Mix the breadcrumbs with the feta and thyme leaves in a bowl. Season well.
3 In a separate bowl, beat the egg. Dip each chicken breast in the beaten egg, turning to coat, then dredge in the breadcrumbs to coat and transfer to a plate.
4 Chill the schnitzels until you're ready to eat, then heat the olive oil in a frying pan and fry the schnitzels, 1 or 2 at a time, for 3–4 minutes each side, until golden. Serve with lemon wedges, and perhaps buttery new potatoes and stir-fried greens.

delicious.**tip**

RINGING THE CHANGES

Rather than flattening the chicken breasts, make a slit in them and stuff the pocket with a mixture of crumbled feta and thyme. Egg and breadcrumb them, pan-fry for 3–4 minutes each side, then finish off in an oven preheated to 190°C/fan 170°C/gas 5 for 15 minutes, until golden and crispy.

Pan-fried duck breasts with sour cranberry sauce

SERVES 4 TAKES **50 MINUTES TO MAKE** PLUS **OVERNIGHT SOAKING**

4 duck breasts, about 175-200g each

For the sour cranberry sauce
75g dried cranberries
300ml red wine, such as Cabernet Sauvignon
25g white sugar
1 tbsp red wine vinegar
$^3/_4$ tsp arrowroot

1 The day before, put the duck breasts on a plate and cover loosely with greaseproof paper (this helps to dry out the skin and make it extra crispy when cooked), then chill. Soak the dried cranberries in the red wine overnight.
2 The next day, put the sugar into a small pan with 1 tablespoon of cold water and put over a low heat until the sugar dissolves. Increase the heat

and boil vigorously until the syrup is an amber-coloured caramel. Take the pan off the heat, stand back (it will fizz) and add the vinegar.
3 Return the pan to the heat and add the cranberries and wine. Simmer for 20 minutes until it has a good sauce consistency. Mix the arrowroot with 2 tablespoons of water, add to the pan, stir, and simmer for 1 minute. Season and keep warm.
4 Lightly score the skin of each duck breast in a diamond pattern, taking care not to cut into the flesh. Season the meat with salt and pepper and the skin with salt. Put a dry, heavy-based frying pan over a high heat and add the duck, skin-side down. Lower the heat to medium and cook for 3–4 minutes until the skin is crisp and golden.
5 Turn the breasts over and cook for 5 minutes if you like them pink, or longer if you like them a little more cooked. Remove the breasts, place on a board and leave to rest for 5 minutes. Cut them diagonally to make long thin slices, lift onto warm plates and serve with the sauce, and with sautéed potatoes and baby spinach leaves, if you like.

Peppered duck with blackcurrant sauce

Peppered duck with blackcurrant sauce

SERVES 4 TAKES **25 MINUTES TO MAKE**

4 duck breasts
4 tbsp Szechuan peppercorns
6 tbsp port
4 tbsp red wine vinegar
8 tbsp blackcurrant conserve
400g tenderstem broccoli, to serve

1 Lightly score the skin of the duck breasts. Press Szechuan peppercorns into the skin and season with salt.
2 Pan-fry skin-side down over a high heat for 6 minutes, until crisp, then turn over and fry for 4 minutes more. Remove and set aside to rest. Pour the fat out of the pan.
3 Add the port, red wine vinegar and blackcurrant conserve to the pan. Bubble for 2 minutes until thickened, then season to taste.
4 Meanwhile, bring a small pan of salted water to the boil and cook the broccoli for 3 minutes, until

Plum duck
noodles with
pak choi

tender, then drain and set aside. Slice the duck breasts diagonally and arrange on warm plates, spoon over the sauce, and serve with the broccoli and some mashed potato, if you like.

Plum duck noodles with pak choi

SERVES 4 TAKES **15 MINUTES TO MAKE**

150g dried soba noodles
1 tsp vegetable oil
1 red chilli, deseeded and chopped
180g baby pak choi, halved
20g ginger root, grated
100ml plum and hoisin sauce
1 ready-cooked Chinese duck, shredded
  (discard the bones and excess fat)
200g frozen soy beans
4 spring onions, shredded

1 Cook the soba noodles in boiling water, according to pack instructions. Drain, refresh in cold water, drain again and set aside.

2 Heat the vegetable oil in a large wok over a medium heat and add the chilli. Fry, stirring, for 30 seconds, then add the pak choi and ginger along with 3 tablespoons of water.
3 Stir-fry for a minute before adding the plum and hoisin sauce, the Chinese duck, and the soy beans. When everything is bubbling, add the noodles and toss to mix.
4 Stir through most of the spring onions, setting a few aside. Divide the noodles between warmed bowls and top with the remaining spring onions.

Transform a
ready-cooked duck
into an Oriental
dish that's dressed
to impress.

Pot-roast guinea fowl with pistachio stuffing

SERVES 2 TAKES **2 HOURS TO MAKE**

1 guinea fowl with giblets, about 1kg
2 rashers dry-cured smoked streaky bacon
200g coarsely minced pork
Leaves of 1 sprig of fresh rosemary
2 garlic cloves
50g shelled pistachios
$1/2$ tsp salt
$1/2$ tsp finely ground black pepper
2 tbsp brandy
2 outer leaves of a savoy, round cabbage,
  or cavolo nero
1 tbsp butter, softened
2 tbsp olive oil
6 small shallots, peeled and left whole
1 celery stick, roughly sliced
2 carrots, thickly sliced
1 tbsp plain flour
100ml white wine
1 tbsp tomato purée

1 Remove the giblets from the guinea fowl, then chop the liver very finely with the bacon. Discard the rest of the giblets (or keep for stock to use in another recipe). Add the liver and bacon to a large bowl with the pork mince. Chop the rosemary and garlic with the pistachios and fold into the meat mixture. Season with the salt and ground black pepper and stir in the brandy. Chill until needed.
2 Blanch the cabbage leaves in boiling water for 2 minutes, then drain and plunge into a bowl of cold water. Drain again and pat dry with kitchen paper. Divide the stuffing mixture between the cabbage leaves, wrapping the soft leaves around the meat and shaping to make 2 neat, round packages.
3 Lightly season the cavity of the guinea fowl, then pop in the leaf-wrapped stuffing. Smear the butter over the outside of the bird and season with a little more salt.
4 Heat the olive oil in a casserole or large pot with a lid over a medium-high heat, and brown the guinea fowl all over. Transfer the bird to a plate, then add the shallots, sliced celery, and carrots to the casserole or pot and fry quite briskly for 10 minutes, allowing them to caramelise slightly. Add the flour, cook for 1 minute, then add the wine, tomato purée and 200ml water. Return the bird to the pot, breast-side up. Cover, reduce the heat to medium-low and simmer for about $1^{1}/4$ hours. To test whether the bird is cooked, pierce the leg to check the juices run clear. Allow the cooked bird to rest in the gravy for 10 minutes before slicing up. Serve with one stuffing parcel per person.

Pork schnitzels with apple and red cabbage sauerkraut

SERVES 4 TAKES **50 MINUTES TO MAKE**

4 pork escalopes, bashed out between cling film
  to about 75mm thickness
100g plain flour, seasoned
1 egg, lightly beaten
100g fresh breadcrumbs
Vegetable oil, for shallow frying

For the red cabbage sauerkraut
1 tbsp olive oil
1 onion, finely sliced
600g red cabbage, shredded
2 red apples, halved, cored and thinly sliced
4 tbsp white wine vinegar
2 tsp light muscovado sugar

1 Make the sauerkraut. Gently heat the oil in a large pan. Add the onion and cook for 6–8 minutes, until soft. Add the cabbage, apples, vinegar and sugar. Toss together with a good pinch of salt. Cover and simmer for 30–35 minutes, stirring occasionally.
2 Meanwhile, dust each escalope with the flour and dip into the egg, then press into the breadcrumbs to coat.
3 Add 2cm vegetable oil to a frying pan and put over a medium heat. When hot, cook the pork schnitzels for 2–3 minutes each side, until cooked through. Drain on kitchen paper and serve with the sauerkraut, with lemon wedges to squeeze over, if you like.

Maple syrup and mustard gammon with creamy gratin

SERVES 4 TAKES **1 HOUR 30 MINUTES TO MAKE**

1kg smoked gammon joint
2 tbsp maple syrup or runny honey
1 tbsp wholegrain mustard
1 tsp black peppercorns, coarsely crushed

For the creamy gratin
1kg potatoes, thinly sliced
1 onion, finely chopped
25g butter
50g plain flour
750ml semi-skimmed milk

1 Preheat the oven to 200°C/fan 180°C/gas 6. Start by making the creamy gratin. Put a quarter of the potatoes in a casserole dish, sprinkle with a third of the onion, dot with a third of the butter, then sprinkle with a third of the flour. Season well. Repeat to make 2 more layers, then finish with a layer of potato. Pour over the milk and cook for 1 hour 20 minutes, until the potatoes are tender and golden, and the sauce has thickened.
2 Meanwhile, put the gammon into a small roasting tin. Cover with foil and cook above the potatoes for 1 hour.
3 While the gammon and potatoes are cooking, mix the maple syrup or honey, mustard, and peppercorns. When the gammon has cooked for 1 hour, remove it from the oven and slice off any skin, leaving a layer of fat behind. Score the fat in a diamond pattern and spread with the syrupy mixture. Return to the oven for 20 minutes.
4 Leave the gammon and gratin to stand for 5 minutes, then serve slices of the gammon with the gratin and some green vegetables.

Salty-sweet gammon with creamy potato gratin – seriously tasty grub!

Pork schnitzels with apple and red cabbage sauerkraut

Maple syrup and mustard gammon with creamy gratin

Seared fillet of lamb with mint and chilli sauce

SERVES 4 TAKES **20 MINUTES TO MAKE**

Leaves from a bunch of fresh mint (about 12g),
  reserving the smallest to garnish
1 tsp sugar
2 tbsp red wine vinegar
1 tbsp capers, drained
1 tsp Dijon mustard
Good pinch of dried chilli flakes
4 tbsp mild olive oil, plus extra for frying
1 large garlic clove, peeled
4 lamb fillets or 8 trimmed lamb cutlets

1 Roughly chop the mint and put in a food processor with the sugar, wine vinegar, capers, mustard and chilli flakes, and whizz well. Add the oil and continue until very well blended and finely chopped. Season with freshly ground black pepper and put aside in a cool place (not the fridge) to let the flavours develop.
2 Rub the garlic clove all over the lamb fillets or cutlets. Heat a little oil in a large pan and cook the lamb for 2–3 minutes on each side until tender and still slightly pink in the middle. Fry for a few minutes longer on each side to cook through, if you prefer your lamb well-done.
3 Slice the lamb (if using fillets) and arrange on plates, with the mint and chilli sauce drizzled around. Garnish with a few baby mint leaves and serve immediately.

> Lamb and mint is a time-honoured partnership — try adding chilli for an exciting twist.

Herb-crusted rack of lamb with grilled vegetables

SERVES 4 TAKES **1 HOUR 15 MINUTES TO MAKE**

2 French-trimmed racks of lamb
1 tbsp olive oil
15g butter
100ml red wine
Sprig of fresh rosemary
2 tsp redcurrant jelly

For the olive herb crust
Handful of fresh parsley, roughly chopped
Leaves of 3 sprigs of fresh thyme
Leaves of 2 sprigs of fresh rosemary, chopped
50g fine white breadcrumbs
4 pitted black olives, roughly chopped
4 anchovies in oil, drained and chopped
1 tbsp Dijon mustard

For the grilled vegetables
2 courgettes, cut into medium-thick slices
1 aubergine, cut into medium-thick slices
1 red pepper, deseeded
1 yellow pepper, deseeded
4–5 tbsp olive oil
1 bay leaf
1 sprig of fresh rosemary
3 unpeeled garlic cloves, halved

1 Prepare the lamb. Cut away the thick layer of fat on the outside of each rack of lamb, taking with it the thin sinewy layer of meat underneath – this will leave you with a thick meaty fillet and a fatty layer that lies against the bones. Discard the fat but keep the meaty sinew for the sauce. Score the fat layer on each rack to help it crisp. Season well all over.
2 Heat the oil and butter in a large frying pan over a medium heat. When foaming, add the lamb and sear for 2 minutes on each side, until browned all over. Remove and set aside. Once cool, discard the fat in the pan and clean the pan with kitchen paper. Set aside.
3 Make the herb crust. Whizz the herbs in a food processor. Add the breadcrumbs, olives and anchovies and whizz to a fine, damp, vibrantly

Herb-crusted rack of lamb with grilled vegetables

green mixture. Season with freshly ground black pepper. Brush the meat on each lamb rack with the mustard, then coat with the breadcrumb mix, pressing it on firmly. Put the lamb in a large roasting tin and set aside.

4 For the vegetables, lightly score the flesh on 1 side of each courgette and aubergine slice. Peel the peppers with a potato peeler and cut into wide strips. Reserve any trimmings.

5 Put 1 tablespoon of olive oil into a griddle pan over a medium-high heat. When the oil is really hot and has just started smoking, add some of the vegetables, herbs, and garlic in a single layer, and fry for 1–2 minutes, turning, until charred on both sides and just tender. Place in an ovenproof dish and cover with cling film, so they continue to cook in the steam. Repeat with the remaining oil and vegetables, until they are all in the dish. Set aside, covered. Discard the garlic and herbs before serving.

6 Preheat the oven to 240°C/fan 220°C/gas 9, or as high as it will go, and then start to make a quick sauce. Heat the cleaned frying pan over

a medium heat. When hot, add the meaty sinew and vegetable trimmings. Cook for 5 minutes, stirring, until lightly browned. Add the wine and rosemary and simmer until reduced by half. Add 300ml boiling water and simmer rapidly for 5–6 minutes, removing any scum. Stir in the redcurrant jelly, bubble for a few minutes and season. Strain into a jug. It should be fairly thin but well-flavoured.

7 Meanwhile, cook the lamb – breadcrumbed side up – in the oven for 10–14 minutes, for pink to medium. Rest, covered loosely with foil, for 5 minutes. Cut between the bones into cutlets.

8 Divide the vegetables between 4 plates. Rest the lamb cutlets on top and drizzle with the sauce to serve.

delicious.**tip**

SAVING TIME ON THE DAY
You can cook the vegetables a day ahead, if you prefer. Simply cool, cover and chill them overnight. Reheat with the lamb for 5 minutes.

Spiced lamb
with apricots

Spiced lamb with apricots

SERVES 2 TAKES **25 MINUTES TO MAKE**

250g lamb neck fillet
1 small onion, chopped
1 tsp ground allspice
2 tbsp vegetable oil
200g can chopped tomatoes
150ml hot chicken stock
75g dried ready-to-eat apricots
2 tbsp toasted flaked almonds

1 Cut the lamb into chunks and put into a bowl.
Add the onion, ground allspice and vegetable oil.
Season and mix together.
2 Heat a large frying pan. When hot, add the lamb
mixture and cook for 5 minutes to brown the
meat and soften the onion. Stir in the chopped
tomatoes, hot chicken stock and dried apricots.
3 Bring to the boil, then simmer for 10 minutes,
until the lamb is cooked through and the sauce
has thickened. Season to taste, divide between
2 plates and scatter with toasted flaked almonds.

Seared fillet steak
with pizzaiola sauce

SERVES 4 TAKES **20 MINUTES TO MAKE**

4 fillet steaks, about 175g each,
  cut 4cm thick
3 tbsp olive oil,
  plus extra for brushing the steaks
2 garlic cloves, finely chopped
450g vine-ripened tomatoes, skinned,
  deseeded and coarsely chopped
Leaves from 3 sprigs of fresh oregano,
  finely chopped
1 tbsp capers, drained and rinsed
4 handfuls of wild rocket

1 Brush the steaks lightly with a little oil and
season. Heat a cast-iron griddle over a high heat.
Once smoking hot, add the steaks and reduce the
heat to medium-high. Cook for 2 minutes on each
side if you like your steak rare, or 2$^1/_2$ minutes on
each side for medium-rare. Rest the steaks
somewhere warm.
2 Meanwhile, put 3 tablespoons oil and the garlic
in a medium frying pan over a high heat. Once the
garlic sizzles, add the tomatoes and oregano and
cook for 2 minutes, shaking the pan every now
and then. Season.
3 Spoon the sauce onto warmed plates and
scatter with capers. Place the steaks on top
and garnish with the rocket to serve.

delicious.**technique**
CHAR-GRILLING STEAKS

1. While the griddle pan heats
up, brush the steaks – fillet,
rump or sirloin, as pictured –
with olive oil, then season with
salt and black pepper.

2. To achieve the classic criss-
cross pattern on the meat,
rotate each steak by 45°
halfway through the cooking
time on each side.

Steak tagliata with roasted vine tomatoes

SERVES 6 TAKES **20 MINUTES TO MAKE**

4 strings of cherry tomatoes on the vine
  (each with about 8 tomatoes)
8 tbsp extra-virgin olive oil
4 sirloin steaks, about 225–250g each
1 tsp Dijon mustard
4 tsp balsamic vinegar
175g rocket
75g Grana Padano cheese, cut into thin shavings

1 Preheat the oven to 180°C/fan 160°C/gas 4.
Put the cherry tomatoes into a small roasting tin,
drizzle with 3 tablespoons of the olive oil and
season. Roast in the oven for 12–15 minutes,
until the tomatoes are just tender.
2 Meanwhile, brush the steaks on both sides with
1 tablespoon of the oil and season to taste. Heat
a heavy-based griddle or frying pan over a high
heat until smoking. Add the steaks and cook for
2 minutes each side for rare, 3 minutes for
medium. Lift onto a board to rest.
3 While the steaks are cooking, whisk the
mustard and balsamic vinegar together in a
small bowl, then whisk in the remaining olive oil.
Season to taste with salt and freshly ground black
pepper, and set aside.
4 Divide the rocket between 4 plates, spreading
the leaves over the centre of each one. Slice the
steaks slightly on the diagonal, and lift onto the
rocket. Sprinkle over the balsamic dressing, then
scatter with the Grana Padano shavings. Serve
immediately with the roasted tomatoes.

Transform simple
grilled steaks
with these warm
Mediterranean
flavours.

Seared steaks with fresh salmoriglio and potato slices

SERVES 4 TAKES **25 MINUTES TO MAKE**

900g potatoes, such as maris piper
  or king edward, unpeeled
Vegetable oil
4 sirloin steaks, each about 225–300g

For the salmoriglio
5 tbsp oregano, thyme or marjoram,
  roughly chopped
1 plump garlic clove, roughly chopped
1 tsp sea salt
2 tbsp lemon juice
8 tbsp extra-virgin olive oil

1 Make the salmoriglio. Using a pestle and
mortar, pound your choice of herb with the garlic
clove and sea salt until you've formed a paste.
(Alternatively, use a mini processor to blend them
together.) Add the lemon juice, then slowly pour
in the olive oil, stirring well as you do so, until it
starts to look a little like pesto. Season well with
freshly ground black pepper. Set aside to allow
the flavours to develop.
2 Preheat the grill to medium. Cut the unpeeled
potatoes into slices about 1cm thick. Put into a
large bowl, drizzle with vegetable oil, and toss
until they are well coated in oil. Arrange the
potatoes on a grill pan and cook under the grill
for 10–14 minutes, turning once, until cooked
through. Set aside and keep warm.
3 Put the steaks under the grill and cook for 8–10
minutes (adding 1–2 minutes for well done steaks),
turning once. Arrange the steaks on a platter and
surround with potatoes. Spoon the salmoriglio
over the steaks. Serve with a green salad.

delicious.**tip**

GREAT OUTDOORS TOO!

This recipe works really well on a big barbecue.
You can cook the steaks and potatoes on a griddle
pan over the coals, following the same cooking
times. For a smaller barbecue, cook the potatoes
in batches and keep them warm in an oven.

Beef, caramelised onion and ale pie

Beef, caramelised onion and ale pie
SERVES 6 TAKES **2 HOURS 45 MINUTES TO MAKE**

25g plain flour
1kg braising steak, cut into bite-size chunks
5 tbsp sunflower oil
25g butter
225g small chestnut mushrooms, wiped clean
2 onions, halved and sliced
1 tbsp sugar
4 garlic cloves, crushed
300ml good-quality beef stock
300ml brown ale
1 tsp tomato purée
Leaves from 3 sprigs of thyme
3 tbsp Worcestershire sauce

For the mustard suet crust
350g self-raising flour, plus extra for dusting
1 tbsp English mustard powder
1 tsp salt
175g shredded beef suet
1 egg yolk, beaten

1 Make the suet pastry. Sift the flour, mustard powder and salt into a bowl and stir in the shredded suet. Stir in 250ml cold water to make a soft dough. Wrap in cling film and chill.
2 To make the pie filling, season the flour, put into a bowl with the beef and toss well until all the meat is coated. Shake off the excess flour and reserve. Heat 3 tablespoons of oil in a flameproof casserole, add half the beef and fry over a high heat until browned all over. Lift onto a plate and repeat with the rest of the beef. Set aside.
3 Add half the butter and all the mushrooms to the pan and fry briskly over a high heat for 2 minutes. Set aside with the beef.
4 Add the rest of the oil to the casserole with the onions and sugar, and cook over a medium-high heat for 20–30 minutes, stirring frequently, until caramelised. Add the rest of the butter and garlic and cook for 1 minute. Stir the reserved flour into the onions, followed by the stock, ale, tomato purée, thyme leaves and Worcestershire sauce. Bring to the boil, stirring, then return the beef and mushrooms to the pan. Season, then partially cover and simmer for 1^1/$_2$ hours, or until the beef is tender and the sauce has reduced and thickened.
5 Preheat the oven to 220°C/fan 200°C/gas 7. Spoon the mixture into a deep 2-litre oval pie dish. Push a pie funnel or piping nozzle into the centre of the dish.
6 Unwrap the pastry and roll it out on a lightly floured surface into a disc slightly larger than the top of the dish. Cut off a thin strip from the edge of the pastry, brush it with a little water, and press it onto the rim of the dish. Brush with more water (this helps the pastry layers stick together). Cut a small cross in the centre of the large piece of rolled pastry, then lay it over the dish so that the pie funnel or nozzle pokes through. Seal the pastry edges, trim away the overhanging pastry, then crimp the edges. Brush the entire pastry lid with the beaten egg yolk mixed with a little water. Bake for 30–35 minutes, until the pastry is crisp and golden brown.
WINE NOTE A good claret (red Bordeaux) is a traditional match for this recipe – pick a mature one. A glass of ale would also pair well.

Beef Wellington

SERVES 4–6 TAKES **1 HOUR 10 MINUTES TO MAKE**

3 tbsp mild olive oil
300g large black field mushrooms or portabella mushrooms, cleaned and finely diced
1 shallot, finely diced
1 beef fillet, 900g–1.2kg, cut from the middle and trimmed of any fat or sinew
2 x 375g packs ready-rolled puff pastry
Plain flour, for dusting
1 egg, beaten with 2 tbsp milk
175g smooth chicken liver pâté

1 Heat 1 tablespoon of the oil in a frying pan over a gentle heat, then add the mushrooms and shallot. Sauté very gently, until all the moisture from the mushrooms has evaporated (about 25 minutes, depending on the width of your pan).
2 Rub the fillet well with the rest of the oil, and season. Heat a cast-iron frying or griddle pan until it smokes. Sear the meat all over for 1 minute each side. If you want the finished beef cooked more than medium-rare, double the searing time. Transfer to a cooling rack and allow to go cold.
3 Preheat the oven to 200°C/fan 180°C/gas 6. Unroll both sheets of pastry on a lightly floured work surface and trim each so that they are about 2cm wider and longer than the fillet. Keep the trimmings handy.
4 Place 1 piece of pastry on a baking tray lined with baking paper. Egg-wash the pastry and place the fillet in the centre. Smear the top and sides of the fillet with pâté, then press the mushroom mixture onto the pâté. Drape the second piece of pastry over the top and crimp the edges.
5 Roll out the pastry trimmings and cut into strips to create a lattice over the top of the Wellington, like an old-fashioned pie, and then egg-wash the pastry.
6 Bake the Wellington for about 20 minutes, turning the tray halfway (no need to turn if you have a fan oven). It's ready when the pastry is golden and crisp – if not, it might need 5–10 minutes more in the oven. Allow the Wellington to rest for 10 minutes before carving.

Rare roast beef and winter coleslaw

SERVES 8 TAKES **1 HOUR 10 MINUTES TO MAKE**

1.5kg fillet of aged beef
150ml cold-pressed rapeseed or sunflower oil
1/2 small white cabbage
1 small celeriac
2 crisp pears
Juice of 2 small lemons
1 egg yolk
2 tbsp Dijon mustard

1 Preheat the oven to 190°C/fan 170°C/gas 5. Rub the beef with oil and season, then sear all over in a smoking-hot pan. Transfer to a roasting tin and cook for about 35 minutes. Set aside.
2 Core and shred the cabbage, and put into a very large bowl. Peel and core the celeriac and pears, slice into long thin strips, and add to the cabbage. Toss with the juice of 1 lemon. Set aside.
3 Beat the egg yolk and mustard, then slowly whisk in the oil. Thin with lemon juice, then season and toss with the cabbage. Serve with slices of beef.

Beef Wellington

feasts for a crowd

Spinach, Parmesan and sausage cannelloni

SERVES 8 TAKES **1 HOUR 15 MINUTES TO MAKE**

600g fresh spinach, washed
14 (about 700g) good Cumberland sausages
2 garlic cloves, crushed,
  plus 1 garlic clove, thinly sliced
Large handful fresh oregano,
  roughly chopped
Large handful fresh flatleaf parsley,
  roughly chopped
75g freshly grated Parmesan
100g fresh white breadcrumbs
1 large egg, lightly beaten
3 tbsp extra-virgin olive oil
700g jar tomato passata
400g can chopped tomatoes
32 cannelloni tubes
600ml crème fraîche
250g mozzarella, roughly torn

1 Preheat the oven to 180°C/fan 160°C/gas 4. Place the washed spinach in a large saucepan with just the water that clings to its leaves after washing, and heat until wilted. You may need to do this in 2 batches. Drain and set aside to cool. When cool, form into a ball and squeeze out any excess liquid between your hands, then roughly chop and set aside.
2 Remove the casings from the sausages and discard. Place the meat in a bowl with the crushed garlic, half the oregano, the parsley, 50g of the Parmesan, the breadcrumbs and seasoning. Add the egg and spinach, and mix well.

3 Heat the olive oil in a large saucepan and gently cook the sliced garlic for just 30 seconds. Add the passata and chopped tomatoes to the pan, then fill the can with water and add this to the tomatoes. Stir in the remaining oregano and season well to taste. Simmer for just 15 minutes, until you have a loose tomato sauce.
4 Meanwhile, fill the cannelloni tubes from both ends with the sausage stuffing mixture. Pour the tomato sauce into the bottom of a large roasting tin (so the cannelloni can sit in a single layer; use the largest tin you can find or 2 medium-size ovenproof dishes) and lay the filled cannelloni on top of the tomato sauce in one layer.
5 In a bowl, mix the crème fraîche with half of the remaining Parmesan and a little water to loosen, then spoon over the cannelloni. Scatter with the remaining Parmesan, the mozzarella and a good grinding of black pepper. Bake for 30–35 minutes, until golden and bubbling.

Chicken and chorizo paella

SERVES 8 TAKES **45 MINUTES TO MAKE**

220g cured chorizo, sliced
2 large Spanish onions, sliced
2 tbsp sweet smoked paprika
2 tsp hot paprika
6 chicken breasts, cut into large pieces
Large knob of butter
600g paella or risotto rice
2 litres hot chicken stock
2 red peppers, sliced
Handful of green beans, halved
20 cherry tomatoes, halved
Large handful of fresh flatleaf parsley,
  finely chopped

1 Heat a large pan over a medium heat and dry-fry the chorizo, sliced, until it is golden and the oil is released. Remove from the pan and set aside.
2 Add the onion to the pan and cook for 5 minutes, then stir in both types of paprika and cook for a further 2 minutes.
3 Add the chicken and cook for 7–8 minutes, then remove from the pan and set aside.

4 Heat the butter in the pan and stir in the rice, then add the hot chicken stock, stir well and cook for 15 minutes.
5 Return the chorizo, chicken and onion to the pan with the red pepper, green beans and tomatoes. Season and cook for a further 8-10 minutes, until the rice is tender.
6 Stir the chopped parsley into the paella and serve immediately.

Prawn and chorizo jambalaya
SERVES 8 TAKES **45 MINUTES TO MAKE**

300g piece chorizo, diced
1 each red and small pepper, deseeded and sliced
I large onion, finely sliced
4 celery sticks, finely sliced diagonally
4 garlic cloves, crushed
2 red chillis, finely chopped
Leaves from a few fresh thyme sprigs
400g long grain rice
454g canned chopped tomatoes
1.4 litres vegetable or chicken stock, hot
1 tsp Tabasco sauce, plus extra to serve
400g raw tiger prawns, peeled and deveined
8 spring onions, trimmed and finely sliced
Lime wedges, to serve

1 Cook the chorizo in a large frying pan over a medium-high heat, stirring occasionally, for 3–4 minutes. Remove and drain on kitchen paper.
2 Add the peppers, onion, celery, garlic and chilli to the pan and cook, stirring occasionally, for 8 minutes, until softened slightly. Stir in the thyme and rice, cook for 2 minutes, then add the tomatoes, stock and Tabasco and bring to the boil. Cover, reduce the heat to low and simmer very gently, stirring occasionally, for 18 minutes, until most of the liquid has evaporated. Season to taste.
3 Stir in the chorizo, prawns and spring onions and cook for 1 minute. Serve with lime wedges, to squeeze over.
WINE NOTE This is terrific with a glass of chilled, ripe rosé wine.

Prawn and chorizo jambalaya

Halibut, ratatouille and new potato tray bake

Lamb biryani

SERVES 6 TAKES **1 HOUR 30 MINUTES TO MAKE**
PLUS **OVERNIGHT MARINATING**

250ml natural yogurt
1 green chilli, deseeded and finely sliced
4 garlic cloves, crushed
50g piece fresh ginger, grated
$\frac{1}{4}$ tsp ground cloves
$\frac{1}{4}$ tsp ground cinnamon
2 tsp ground cumin
2 tsp ground coriander
750g lamb leg steaks, trimmed of excess fat
  and cut into bite-size pieces
350g basmati rice
100ml milk
1 tsp saffron threads
75g ghee (clarified butter), plus extra 1 tbsp
2 large onions, finely sliced
1 long cinnamon stick, broken into 3 pieces
12 cardamom pods, cracked
Chopped fresh coriander, to garnish

1 The day before serving, mix the yogurt, chilli, garlic, ginger, cinnamon, cloves, half the coriander and half the cumin in a bowl. Season well, then add the lamb and toss to coat. Cover, chill and marinate overnight.
2 The next day, bring the marinated lamb up to room temperature. Rinse and soak the rice in cold water for 30 minutes. Heat the milk until hot and stir in the saffron.
3 Preheat the oven to 150°C/fan 130°C/gas 2. Heat 75g ghee in a pan. Add the onions and cook gently for 15 minutes. Stir in the remaining cumin and coriander and cook for 1 minute. Set aside.
4 Put the cinnamon stick, cardamom pods and a good pinch of salt in a saucepan, half-fill with water and bring to the boil. Add the rice, stir and return to the boil. Cook for 2 minutes, drain and mix into the onions.
5 Melt the tablespoon of ghee in a flameproof casserole with a tight-fitting lid over a low heat. Spread a little rice in a thin layer on the bottom of the dish and top with half the lamb and marinade. Top with half the remaining rice, drizzle with half the saffron milk and sit the remaining lamb and marinade on top. Spread the last of the rice on top and drizzle with the remaining saffron milk. Cover tightly with foil, then the lid, and turn up the heat for 30 seconds to build up steam. Bake in the oven for 30–35 minutes, until the lamb and rice are tender – dig out a piece of lamb to check.
6 Sprinkle the biryani with chopped coriander, then spoon onto warm serving plates. Serve with extra yogurt, Indian pickles and naan bread.

Halibut, ratatouille and new potato tray bake

SERVES 8 TAKES **50 MINUTES TO MAKE**

1kg waxy new potatoes
4 tbsp olive oil, plus extra for drizzling
1.2kg Ratatouille, defrosted (see p.156)
4 tbsp baby capers, rinsed and drained
2 red chillis, chopped, or a pinch of chilli flakes
8 halibut steaks, about 200g each
2 lemons, finely sliced

1 Preheat the oven to 200°C/fan 180°C/gas 6. Thinly slice the new potatoes and place in a large bowl. Toss with the olive oil, plenty of black pepper, and a small pinch of salt. Arrange the potatoes in a single layer in 2 large baking trays or dishes and bake for 20–25 minutes or until turning golden.

2 Spoon the ratatouille on top of the potatoes and sprinkle with the capers and chilli.

3 Place the halibut over the ratatouille and layer the lemon slices over the fish. Drizzle with a little extra oil. Season well and bake for 15 minutes until the fish is cooked through.

Pancetta-wrapped salmon with saffron and herb rice
SERVES 8 TAKES **1 HOUR 25 MINUTES TO MAKE**

350ml fresh chicken stock
$1/2$ tsp saffron threads
25g butter
50g shallots, finely chopped
175g long grain rice
$1/4$ tsp salt
3 tbsp chopped fresh herbs,
  such as parsley, tarragon and chives
Finely grated zest of $1/2$ lemon
2 tsp lemon juice
2 x 550g thick pieces of skinned salmon fillet,
  taken from a large fish
16 slices thin smoked pancetta
4 fresh bay leaves
2 tbsp olive oil

1 Put the stock and saffron into a pan, bring to the boil and keep hot over a low heat. Melt the butter in a small pan, add the shallots and fry gently for a few minutes until soft. Stir in the rice, stock and salt and bring to the boil. Stir, cover, then reduce the heat to low and cook for 15 minutes. Remove from the heat and set aside for 5 minutes.

2 Uncover the rice and, using a fork, stir through the chopped fresh herbs, lemon zest and lemon juice. Add salt and freshly ground black pepper to taste and mix well.

3 Preheat the oven to 200°C/fan 180°C/gas 6 and put a large non-stick baking sheet into the oven to heat up. Trim the salmon fillets to the same size, then season on both sides with salt and freshly ground pepper. Spoon the rice mixture in an even layer over 1 salmon fillet and press down well. Cover with the other salmon fillet.

4 Place 2 pancetta slices on a board with the ends slightly overlapping to make 1 long strip. Arrange another 2 slices next to this, slightly overlapping as before. Repeat with the remaining slices. Lay the salmon down the centre of the pancetta sheet and bring up the slices to enclose the salmon, pressing down gently.

5 Arrange the bay leaves on top. Tie at intervals with 6–7 lengths of kitchen string to secure.

6 Carefully slide the salmon parcel onto the hot baking sheet. Drizzle with the olive oil and bake in the oven for 35–40 minutes for just-cooked salmon, or a little longer if you prefer.

7 Remove the salmon from the oven, cover and set aside to rest for 5–10 minutes. Slice thickly and serve with ready-made hollandaise sauce.

Pancetta-wrapped salmon with saffron and herb rice

Traditional roast turkey with sticky pancetta sausages

SERVES 8 TAKES **4 HOURS 35 MINUTES TO MAKE** PLUS **30–45 MINUTES RESTING**

2 tbsp runny honey
16 chipolata sausages
24 slices smoked pancetta
5.5kg oven-ready turkey (with giblets)
1 onion, quartered
3 small oranges, quartered
5 sprigs rosemary, halved
8 sprigs thyme
40g butter, at room temperature
Bay leaves, to garnish

1 Warm the honey and use a pastry brush to brush it over the sausages. Wrap each sausage in a pancetta slice, put into an ovenproof dish and chill until ready to cook.
2 Preheat the oven to 190°C/ fan 170°C/gas 5. Remove the giblets and set aside to make the gravy stock. Weigh the turkey and calculate the cooking time (see p.294); this 5.5kg turkey will need to cook for 3 hours 50 minutes. Rinse the turkey inside and out with cold water, and dry well. Season the body cavity, then push in the onion quarters, 5 of the orange quarters, and half of the herbs, alternating between the three ingredients. Put 3 orange quarters and the remaining herbs in the neck end of the turkey. Take a length of string and loop it round the

parson's nose (the tail hump) and drumstick ends and tie neatly in place. Put on a trivet sitting in a large roasting tin.
3 Spread the softened butter over the whole bird and season well. Place the remaining pancetta slices on top of the bird. Pour 450ml water into the roasting tin under the bird (see tip below) and cover the whole tray with a large sheet of foil. Put in the oven for 3 hours and 20 minutes (or whatever your calculated cooking time is for your turkey size, minus 30 minutes).
4 About 30 minutes before the turkey is fully cooked, uncover, baste with the juices in the tin, and return to the oven uncovered to cook for the remaining 30 minutes. To check the turkey is cooked, push a fine skewer into the thickest part of the thigh. If the juices run clear, it's cooked; if there are any traces of pink, cook for another 15 minutes or so and repeat the skewer test until the juices run clear.
5 Remove the cooked turkey from the oven, and increase the oven temperature to 200°C/fan 180°C/gas 6. Pop the sausages into the oven in their dish and cook for 30 minutes.
6 Carefully lift the turkey from the tin onto a board, letting as much juice drip back into the tin as possible. Set it aside in a warm place, covered in foil, to rest for 30–45 minutes to relax the meat, giving you a moist, tender turkey.
7 Strain the turkey's cooking juices from the tin into a jug. Allow to settle, then spoon off the excess fat from the surface, keeping what's left behind to add to the gravy (see page 205).
8 Present the roast turkey on a large serving platter and garnish with fresh bay leaves and the remaining orange wedges.Serve with sticky sausages, gravy and all the trimmings.

Flavours of oranges, onions and herbs and a crisp pancetta topping make this roast turkey something special.

delicious.**tip**

KEEPING IT SUCCULENT
Putting water in the bottom of the roasting dish as you cook the turkey is an excellent way to make sure it stays nice and moist during cooking. This is especially important for larger birds. It also gives you lots of lovely stock for the gravy.

Traditional roast turkey with sticky pancetta sausages

Lemon roast chicken with peppers
SERVES 8 TAKES **1 HOUR 20 MINUTES TO MAKE**

2 x 2kg chickens
4 tbsp olive oil
2 garlic bulbs, cloves separated but not peeled
2 red peppers, deseeded and sliced
2 yellow peppers, deseeded and sliced
Zest and juice of 2 lemons
4 rosemary sprigs, halved
Splash of white wine
200ml chicken stock

1 Joint each chicken into 8 pieces (see below). Alternatively, you can buy chicken pieces ready-cut, but jointing whole birds yourself is much more cost-effective than buying the pieces separately. If you choose to buy chicken pieces, make sure you have a mix of drumsticks, thighs and breasts.
2 Preheat the oven to 200°C/fan 180°C/gas 6. Put the chicken pieces into a large roasting tin along with the garlic and peppers, then drizzle with olive oil and the zest and juice of the lemons. Tuck the pieces of rosemary in amongst the chicken pieces and peppers.
3 Pour over a splash of white wine and the chicken stock, season with sea salt and freshly cracked pepper, and roast for 50–60 minutes, until cooked (so that the juices run clear).
4 Set aside to rest for 5–10 minutes, then serve with mash and steamed greens.
WINE NOTE A light, tart red wine will complement the sweet peppers here, such as a Chianti Classico. If you prefer white, try a German Riesling or a delicate Chardonnay.

JOINTING A CHICKEN

1. *Using a sharp knife, scrape the flesh away from the wishbone. Holding the flesh back with one hand, use the fingers of your other hand to twist and lift it free.*

2. *Place the bird breast-side up onto a cutting board. Using a sharp knife, cut down and through the thigh joint to separate the leg from the rest of the body.*

3. *Bend the leg back to dislodge the leg joint. When the ball is free from the socket, cut the leg away from the body. Repeat to remove the other leg.*

4. *Fully extend one wing, then use sharp poultry shears to cut off the winglet at the middle joint. Repeat on the other side to remove the second winglet.*

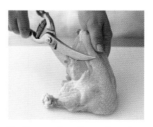

5. *Use your hands to grasp the backbone and break it from the breasts. Use poultry shears to cut the lower end of the backbone from the body.*

6. *Once the backbone is free, separate the breasts. Starting at the neck, use poultry shears to cut all the way through the breastbone.*

7. *Use poultry shears to cut each breast in half diagonally, producing one breast and one wing. Repeat to separate the other breast from the wing.*

8. *Cut each leg through the knee joint, above the drumstick that connects to the thigh, and cut through to separate. Repeat on the other leg.*

Maple-glazed roast chickens
SERVES 8 TAKES **2 HOURS TO MAKE**

2 x 2kg chickens
10 tbsp red wine vinegar
8 tbsp maple syrup
2 tsp ground cinnamon
2 tbsp sesame seeds

1 Preheat the oven to 200°C/fan 180°C/gas 6.
Season the chickens and pour 2 tablespoons of
vinegar into the body cavity of each one. Put in
1 large or two smaller roasting tins and roast for
1 hour 30 minutes.
2 Meanwhile, mix together the remaining vinegar
with the syrup, cinnamon, and sesame seeds.
Brush half the mixture over the chickens and
roast for a further 10 minutes.
3 Brush the chickens with the remaining glaze and
return to the oven for 10 minutes until golden and
shiny. Allow to rest for 5 minutes before carving.

Home-made chicken or turkey gravy
SERVES 8 TAKES **1 HOUR 30 MINUTES TO MAKE**

25g butter, softened
25g plain flour
1 tbsp sunflower oil
Giblets, plus any bones and cooking juices
4 large shallots, halved
1 large carrot, thickly sliced
2 celery sticks, thickly sliced
2 bay leaves
6 black peppercorns

1 Heat the oil in a large pan over a high heat. Add
the giblets and bones and fry for 3–4 minutes.
Add the vegetables and fry for 8 minutes.
2 Add the bay leaves, peppercorns, and 1.2 litres
of water, bring to the boil, then reduce the heat
and simmer, uncovered, for 1 hour. Strain through
a sieve and return the stock to the pan, discarding
the solids. You should have around 600ml. If not,
boil rapidly to reduce to this amount.
3 Mash the butter and flour together to a paste
(a *beurre manié*). Add the cooking juices from the

Lemon roast chicken with peppers

bird to the stock. Bring to the boil and simmer for
5 minutes. Gradually whisk in the beurre manié,
until the gravy is glossy and thickened. Simmer
for a further 5 minutes. Season to taste and serve.

Christmas ham with sweet-mustard crust
SERVES 8 TAKES **35 MINUTES TO MAKE**

2.5kg cooked ham joint
2 tbsp dark French mustard
1 egg yolk
2 tbsp English mustard powder
25g caster sugar
75g dried breadcrumbs
Handful of whole cloves

1 Preheat the oven to 200°C/fan 180°C/gas 6. Put
the ham in a roasting tin. Mix together the French
mustard and egg yolk, then spread over the ham.
2 Mix the mustard powder, sugar and dried
breadcrumbs and press onto the ham. Stud the
ham with the cloves. Bake for 20–25 minutes.

Sweet and herb stuffed roast pork

Sweet and herb stuffed roast pork
SERVES 6 TAKES **2 HOURS 15 MINUTES TO MAKE**

1 tbsp sage, chopped
1 tbsp thyme, chopped, plus thyme sprigs
   to garnish (optional)
3 garlic cloves, crushed
3 amaretti biscuits, crushed
1.4kg boned and rolled loin of pork or
   boned-out spare rib of pork, skin scored
3 tsp sea salt
Sunflower oil, for greasing
1 tsp plain flour
600ml pork or chicken stock, hot

For the stuffing
1 medium onion, finely chopped
25g butter, plus extra for brushing
75g fresh white breadcrumbs
25g amaretti biscuits, crushed
1 heaped tbsp sage, chopped
1 tbsp thyme, chopped
$^{1}/_{2}$ egg, beaten

1 Preheat the oven to 240°C/fan 220°C/gas 9, or as high as it will go. In a bowl, mix together the sage, thyme, garlic and biscuits, and season well. Unroll the pork, turn it skin-side down, and spread the herb mixture all over the meat side. Re-roll the joint and tie with string at 2cm intervals. Weigh to calculate the cooking time (see p.294; a 1.4kg joint with about 100g herb filling should take 1¾ hours), then rub 3 tsp salt into the skin, making sure it goes into the slits. Place in a lightly greased roasting tin, skin-side up, and roast for 20 minutes to crisp the crackling, then reduce the temperature to 180°C/fan 160°C/gas 4 and roast for the remainder of your calculated roasting time.

2 Meanwhile, make the separate dish of stuffing. Fry the onion gently in the butter until soft and lightly browned. Tip into a bowl and stir in the breadcrumbs, crushed biscuits, sage and thyme. Season. Stir in the egg, then spoon into a small, buttered ovenproof dish and rough up the surface with a fork. Cover and set aside.

3 Half an hour before the pork is ready, brush the top of the stuffing with a little melted butter and roast alongside the pork.

4 When the pork is cooked, remove from the oven and rest, uncovered, for 15 minutes. Turn the oven off. Lay a sheet of foil over the dish of stuffing and leave in the oven to keep warm.

5 To make the gravy, pour the excess fat from the tin and put it over a medium heat on the hob. Stir in the flour and gradually pour in the stock, stirring and scraping up all the juices from the base as you go. Bring to the boil, then simmer until reduced. Strain into a gravy boat. Take the pork to the table, garnished with thyme sprigs, if you like. Remove the string from the pork, slide a knife under the crackling and lift it off. Carve the meat and serve with the crackling, stuffing, and gravy.

delicious.tip
BUYING THE BEST CUT
Boned and rolled loin of pork is the ideal roasting joint because it has a thick layer of fat, which keeps the tender meat moist while roasting. Ask your butcher to bone the loin for you, if necessary.

Roast pork stuffed with orange and thyme

SERVES 8 TAKES **40–45 MINUTES TO MAKE**

8 thick slices white bread, crusts removed
Juice and finely grated zest of 2 oranges
12 fresh sprigs of thyme, leaves picked
4 pork tenderloin fillets, about 450g each,
  trimmed of any fat
4 tsp cornflour
600ml fresh vegetable or chicken stock, hot

1 Preheat the oven to 220°C/fan 200°C/gas 7. Whizz the bread in a food processor to make breadcrumbs. Tip into a bowl and mix in the orange zest and thyme. Season well.
2 Lay each fillet on a board and make a deep slit along the length – don't cut all the way through. Fill each with the breadcrumb mixture, packing it down as you go. Secure each fillet together with cocktail sticks, or string, then season. Put into 2 roasting tins and roast for 20–25 minutes, until cooked through. Transfer to a plate and cover.
3 Gradually mix the orange juice with the cornflour to a smooth paste. Scrape all the pork juices into one of the roasting tins. Put this tin on the hob over a high heat. Add the cornflour mixture, stirring to scrape any sticky juices from the base of the pan, then stir in the stock. Bring to the boil, stirring, and bubble for 3–4 minutes until thickened. Season to taste.
4 Remove the cocktail sticks or string from the fillets, then cut diagonally into slices and divide among 4 warm plates. Drizzle with the sauce. Serve with some sautéed potatoes and seasonal vegetables.

A roast to put on the table in just 45 minutes – what's not to like?

Lamb and date tagine with pomegranate couscous

SERVES 6–8 TAKES **3 HOURS 30 MINUTES TO MAKE**

2 tbsp olive oil
2 onions, chopped
1 large knob of fresh ginger, chopped
4 garlic cloves, crushed
1 cinnamon stick
1 tbsp coriander seeds, crushed
1 tsp cumin seeds, lightly crushed
1.5kg boned shoulder or leg of lamb,
  cut into cubes
200g medjool dates, pitted
400g can chopped tomatoes
400ml lamb or chicken stock, hot
1 lemon and 1 lime,
  cut into wedges, to serve

For the pomegranate couscous
500g couscous
1 tbsp olive oil
Grated zest and juice of 1 lemon
Handful of fresh mint, roughly chopped
Seeds of 1 pomegranate

1 Heat the oil in a large, heavy-based pan over a low heat and gently cook the onions, ginger and garlic for 10 minutes, until softened. Add the cinnamon stick, coriander seeds and cumin seeds and cook for 5 minutes, then add the lamb and cook for a further 10 minutes.
2 Add the dates and tomatoes and pour in the stock. Bring the mixture to the boil, then cover and simmer gently for 2½-3 hours, until the lamb is very tender.
3 Place the couscous, olive oil and the lemon zest and juice into a bowl and cover with 600ml boiling water. Cover and leave to cool completely, then use a fork to fluff up the couscous, separating the grains, and stir in the chopped mint and the pomegranate seeds.
4 Serve the couscous with the tagine and garnish with citrus wedges.
WINE NOTE With the sweet, spicy flavours here, find a red with ripe, smooth fruit and a peppery edge. Australian Shiraz is bang on.

Roast leg of lamb stuffed with spinach and gremolata

SERVES 6 TAKES **1 HOUR 50 MINUTES TO MAKE** PLUS **20 MINUTES RESTING**

4 tbsp extra-virgin olive oil
1 medium onion, finely chopped
125g spinach leaves, washed
1.75–2kg leg of lamb, shank bone left in and
  the hip bone removed (ask your butcher)

For the gremolata
Grated zest of 1 lemon
2 fat garlic cloves, finely chopped
15g fresh flatleaf parsley leaves, chopped

For the gravy
200ml white wine
400ml fresh chicken stock, hot
2 tsp butter, softened
2 tsp plain flour

1 Heat half the oil in a large pan over a medium-low heat. Gently sauté the onion for 7–8 minutes, until soft. Set aside in a bowl.
2 Add a tablespoon of the remaining oil to the same pan. Add the spinach and cook until just wilted. Tip into a colander and press out the excess liquid, then coarsely chop.
3 To make the gremolata, mix the lemon zest, garlic and parsley in a large bowl. Add the chopped spinach and onion. Stir and season well with salt and freshly ground black pepper. Where the hip bone has been removed, stuff the lamb with the gremolata mixture and seal the opening with fine metal trussing skewers or wooden cocktail sticks. Weigh the lamb and calculate the cooking time, allowing 16 minutes per 450g for pink lamb.
4 Preheat the oven to 230°C/ fan 210°C/gas 8. Rub the lamb with the remaining olive oil and season. Put in a roasting tin and roast for 15 minutes until it starts to brown. Lower the oven temperature to 200°C/ fan 180°C/gas 6 and leave to roast for the remainder of the calculated cooking time. When the lamb is done, remove from the oven and lift onto a platter. Cover tightly with foil and leave it to rest for 20 minutes, so the meat relaxes and becomes tender.
5 Meanwhile, make the gravy. Pour out and discard all but 2 tablespoons of fat from the roasting tin. Place the tin with the remaining fat over a medium-high heat and add the wine. Bring to the boil, scraping the meat juices from the bottom of the tin for additional flavour. Reduce the mixture to about 4 tablespoons. Add the stock and boil for about 4–5 minutes, until reduced to a well-flavoured gravy. Mix the butter and flour to a paste and whisk small lumps into the gravy. Simmer for 2-3 minutes, until thickened. Season to taste. Keep hot over a low heat.
6 Carve the lamb, removing the skewers or cocktail sticks as you go. Strain the gravy into a warmed jug. Divide the lamb between serving plates and serve with the gravy.

Roast sirloin

SERVES 6 TAKES **2 HOURS 30 MINUTES TO MAKE**

2kg piece boned and rolled sirloin beef
Beef dripping, softened
  (alternatively you can use olive oil)
1 tsp plain flour
600ml good beef stock

1 Preheat the oven to 240°C/fan 220°C/gas 9, or as high as it will go. Rub the outside of the joint with soft beef dripping or olive oil and season with salt and pepper. Place in a roasting tin and cook in the oven for 15 minutes until browned all over. Then reduce the temperature to 190°C/fan 170°C/gas 5 and cook for 12–13 minutes per 500g for rare; 17–18 minutes per 500g for medium; or 22–24 minutes per 500g for well done.
2 Remove the beef from the oven and turn the oven temperature back up to 220°C/fan 200°C/gas 7 if you are making Yorkshire puddings (see right). Lift the beef onto a carving board and loosely cover with a sheet of foil. Leave it somewhere warm (ideally on the top of the hob) to rest for 30 minutes.
3 Meanwhile, make the gravy. Pour away any excess fat from the roasting tin. Place the

roasting tin directly over a medium heat on the hob and sprinkle with the flour. Stir well with a small whisk, then add a little stock and stir again, scraping the base to release the juices. Add the rest of the stock and simmer until reduced to a well-flavoured gravy. Strain into a small saucepan, season, and keep hot.

4 Uncover the beef and add any juices from the carving tray to the gravy. Carve the beef as thinly as you can and serve with Yorkshire puddings, gravy, and vegetables of your choice.

Yorkshire puddings

MAKES 4–6 TAKES **40 MINUTES TO MAKE**

20g beef dripping or 2 tbsp vegetable oil
100ml full-fat milk
50ml sparkling water
115g plain flour
$1/4$ tsp salt
2 eggs, beaten

1 Preheat the oven to 220°C/fan 200°C/gas 7. Use the dripping or oil to grease the holes of either a 4-hole Yorkshire pudding tin or a deep, 6-hole muffin tin. Place the tin in the hot oven for 5 minutes or until the fat or oil is really hot and smoking.

2 Meanwhile, mix the milk and sparkling water together in a jug. Sift the flour and salt together into a large bowl. Crack the eggs into a bowl, beat and season well with freshly ground black pepper. Make a well in the centre of the flour, pour the beaten eggs into the well and whisk together, working from the inside out, drawing in the flour as you go. Gradually whisk in the milk and sparkling water, beating out the lumps until you have a smooth batter.

3 Transfer the batter to a jug. Remove the tin from the oven and pour the batter into the hot tin, filling each hole no more than three-quarters full. Return to the oven and cook, without opening the oven door, for 20–25 minutes or until the puddings have risen and are deep golden and crisp. Serve immediately.

Yorkshire puddings

children's parties

Baguette pizzas
SERVES 8 TAKES **45 MINUTES TO MAKE**

4 small part-baked baguettes
1 garlic clove, halved
8 tbsp tomato purée
16 tbsp tomato passata
Selection of toppings, such as: ham or
  Parma ham, salami, tuna, sweetcorn,
  sliced red and yellow peppers, sliced
  mushrooms, sliced cherry tomatoes,
  mozzarella, grated Parmesan, pesto

1 Preheat the oven to 220°C/fan 200°C/gas 7.
Bake the baguettes for 12–15 minutes or until
cooked. Halve each lengthways and put back into
the oven for a further 5 minutes to crisp up.
2 Rub each baguette half with the cut side of the
garlic. Spread with 1 tbsp purée and 2 tbsp passata.

delicious.technique
PREPARING PEPPERS

1. *Place the pepper on its side and cut off the ends. Stand the pepper on one of the cut ends and slice it in half lengthways. Discard the core and seeds.*

2. *Open each section and lay them flat on the cutting board. Using a sideways motion, remove the remaining pithy ribs, then slice as required.*

3 Let the children help themselves to the different
toppings to create their own combinations.
4 Put the pizzas on the baking tray and bake for
6–8 minutes, until the cheese is melted and golden.

Cherry tomato and pepperoni pizza
SERVES 8 TAKES **20 MINUTES TO MAKE**

4 plain naan breads
580g jar tomato and basil sauce
300g mozzarella, sliced
100g pepperoni, sliced
Handful of basil leaves

1 Preheat the oven to 200°C/fan 180°C/gas 6. Put
the naan breads on a large baking tray. Divide the
sauce between them, spreading evenly.
2 Top the sauce with mozzarella and pepperoni.
Season and pop in the oven for 10–12 minutes,
until piping hot and the cheese is turning golden.
3 Scatter with the basil leaves to serve.

Perfect home-made chips
SERVES 8 TAKES **30 MINUTES TO MAKE**

8 large floury potatoes, such as king edward
  or maris piper
Sunflower or corn oil, for deep-frying
Light mayonnaise, tomato ketchup,
  or malt vinegar to serve

1 Peel the potatoes, slice into 1cm rounds, then
cut each round into thin chips. Spread on a clean
tea towel, then pat as dry as possible. Line
2 baking trays with kitchen paper.
2 Take a large, deep saucepan and fill to no more
than one-third full with oil. Place over a medium
heat and heat until a cube of bread added to it
sizzles and browns in 1 minute. Carefully add a
couple of handfuls of chips to the pan. Cook for
4–5 minutes, stirring occasionally so they don't
stick together, until soft but not golden. Remove
with a slotted spoon to blot on the kitchen paper
on 1 of the baking trays. Repeat until all the
chips have been fried.

3 Add more oil to the pan if necessary. Return it to the heat and heat until a cube of bread added to the oil turns golden in 45 seconds. Fry the chips for the second time, in batches, for 2–3 minutes until golden and crisp. Remove with a slotted spoon, transfer to the other baking tray and keep warm. When all the chips are done, set the hot oil aside safely to cool completely.
4 Serve the hot chips immediately while still crisp and piping hot, with plenty of mayonnaise, tomato ketchup or vinegar.

Spicy potato wedges
SERVES 8 TAKES **35 MINUTES TO MAKE**

1kg large potatoes, scrubbed
8 tbsp olive oil
4 tbsp dried mixed seasoning (of choice)
284ml soured cream
4 spring onions, trimmed and chopped

1 Cut the potatoes in half, then put them flat-side down on a chopping board. Carefully cut each potato half into 6 wedges to make chunky, fairly even-sized chips.
2 Heat the olive oil in a large, heavy-based frying pan. Add the potatoes, sprinkle with the seasoning, and mix so that every wedge is coated evenly. Cook for 25 minutes over a medium heat, turning occasionally, until the wedges are golden on the outside but tender within.
3 Put the soured cream into a bowl and stir in the spring onions. Serve the potato wedges with the soured cream dip on the side and ketchup, relish or other favourite sauces.

Serve spicy potato wedges with a big pot of chilli for a Tex-Mex-style supper party.

Baguette pizzas

Spicy potato wedges

Salmon fishcakes

Salmon fishcakes
MAKES 8 TAKES **50 MINUTES TO MAKE**

1kg floury potatoes
50g butter
600ml milk
350g cod fillet, skin on
2 bay leaves
6 peppercorns
100g smoked salmon, chopped
Handful of chives, snipped
Handful of parsley, chopped
Flour, for dusting
2 eggs, beaten
100g fresh white breadcrumbs
Vegetable oil, for shallow frying
Lemon wedges, to serve

For the tartare sauce
25g gherkins, chopped
25g capers, chopped
Handful of parsley, chopped
Dash of lemon juice
4 heaped tbsp mayonnaise

1 Cut the potatoes into even-sized pieces and boil in salted water for 15–20 minutes until tender. Drain well, return to the saucepan and heat for 30 seconds to dry out. Add the butter and a splash of the milk, then mash well.
2 Meanwhile, put the cod in a shallow pan and pour over the milk to cover. Add a little water if the milk doesn't quite cover the fish. Add the bay leaves and peppercorns, then bring to the boil.
3 Reduce the heat and simmer for 5–6 minutes until tender. Remove from the heat. Flake the fish, discarding any bones and skin. Stir into the mash with the salmon, herbs and plenty of seasoning. Divide into 8 and shape each portion into a fishcake.
4 Put the flour, egg and breadcrumbs into 3 shallow dishes. Dip the fishcakes first in flour, then in egg, finally coat all over in breadcrumbs.
5 Mix all the tartare sauce ingredients together.
6 Heat the vegetable oil in a frying pan and fry the fishcakes for 5–6 minutes each side until golden and heated through. Serve with the sauce.

Lemon fish fingers
SERVES 6 TAKES **20 MINUTES TO MAKE**

6 tbsp plain flour
4 slices bread, whizzed to crumbs
Very finely grated zest of ½ lemon
1 egg
500g white fish, such as cod or haddock, skin removed

1 Put the flour on a plate and season. Mix the breadcrumbs with the lemon zest on another plate. Beat the egg in a bowl with 1 tbsp water.
2 Preheat the oven to 180°C/fan 160°C/gas 4. Remove any bones from the fish and cut into strips.
3 Dip each piece of fish into the flour and shake off any excess. Then dip into the egg, then into the breadcrumbs.
4 Brush a little oil over a baking tray. Put the fish onto the tray and bake for 5 minutes. Turn the fish over and cook for another 5 minutes. The fish should be golden on the outside and cooked through in the middle. Serve with lemon wedges.

Lemon fish
fingers

Witches' fingers
with blood sauce

Witches' fingers with blood sauce
MAKES 16 FINGERS TAKES **30 MINUTES TO MAKE**

Oil, for greasing
3 chicken breasts
Tomato ketchup
3 packets plain crisps

1 Preheat the oven to 190°C/fan 170°C/gas 5.
Rub a little oil over a baking tray.
2 Cut the chicken breasts into thin strips.
3 Put 3 tbsp tomato ketchup into a bowl, then add
the chicken, and mix to coat well.
4 Crush the crisps inside the bags until they are
broken into tiny pieces. Tip the crushed crisps
into a big bowl and dip the chicken strips into the
crisps to coat them.
5 Place the coated chicken pieces on to the oiled
baking tray. Roast for 10–12 minutes, until the
chicken is cooked through and the coating is
golden and perfectly crispy.
6 Serve the chicken fingers with tomato ketchup
"blood" for dipping.

Sticky chicken
MAKES 8 TAKES **20 MINUTES TO MAKE**

4 tbsp honey
4 tbsp sweet chilli sauce, plus extra to serve
A squeeze of lime
8 skinless, boneless chicken thighs
Steamed rice, to serve

1 Preheat the oven to 180°C/fan 160°C/gas 4. Mix
the honey and sweet chilli sauce in a small pan.
Add the lime juice and mix well. Place on the hob
and bubble over a medium heat until thickened.
2 Meanwhile, cook the chicken thighs in the hot
oven for 10 minutes.
3 Brush the sauce over the chicken and return to
the oven for a further 10 minutes, until gold and
sticky. Serve with steamed rice and chilli sauce.

Sage and onion sausage tart
SERVES 8 TAKES **55 MINUTES TO MAKE**

375g shortcrust pastry sheet,
  at room temperature
1 tbsp olive oil
2 onions, chopped
10 fresh sage leaves, chopped
600g good-quality pork sausages
100g fresh white breadcrumbs
1 egg, beaten
2 tbsp runny honey
1 tbsp sesame seeds

1 Preheat the oven to 180°C/ fan 160°C/gas 4 with
a baking sheet inside. Unroll the pastry and use it
to line a 20 x 30cm shallow, loose-bottomed,
fluted tart tin. Line with baking paper and baking
beans, transfer to the hot baking sheet and cook
for 5 minutes. Remove from the oven and take out
the paper and beans.
2 Meanwhile, heat the oil in a small frying pan
over a medium heat. Add the onions and cook for
8 minutes, stirring occasionally, until softened
and beginning to turn golden. Add the sage and
cook for 1 minute more, then tip the onions into
a large bowl.

3 Skin the sausages and add the meat to the bowl with the breadcrumbs, egg, and plenty of black pepper. Mix well.
4 Tip the sausage mixture into the pastry case and bake for 20 minutes. Brush with the honey, sprinkle with the sesame seeds, and bake for a further 5–10 minutes, until golden.
5 Cut into fingers and serve.

Sticky ribs with bean salsa and coleslaw
SERVES 8 TAKES **50 MINUTES TO MAKE**

1.2kg pork spare ribs (2 per child)
150ml Tomato & Worcestershire table sauce
1 red onion
410g can mixed pulses, drained and rinsed
2 ripe tomatoes, diced
Handful of flatleaf parsley, roughly chopped
$1/_2$ red cabbage, very thinly sliced
1 carrot, roughly grated
4 tbsp light mayonnaise
Juice of 1 small lemon

1 Preheat the oven to 200°C/fan 180°C/gas 6. Put the ribs into a roasting tin, pour over the table sauce, season, and toss together well. Roast for 40–45 minutes, turning halfway through cooking and rebasting with sauce. Cook until the ribs are sticky and lightly charred.
2 Meanwhile, make the salsa. Finely chop half the onion and mix with the pulses, tomato and parsley.
3 For the coleslaw, thinly slice the remaining onion half and add it to the cabbage and carrot in a serving bowl. Add the mayonnaise and lemon juice to taste, season, and toss together.
4 Serve the ribs with a spoonful of salsa and coleslaw, and plenty of paper napkins.

delicious.**tip**

BUYING RIBS FOR CHILDREN
Butchers and supermarkets often sell racks of baby pork ribs, easier for little fingers. Buy 2 racks and cook as you would spare ribs, then simply snip the ribs apart with scissors to serve.

Sticky chicken

Sage and onion sausage tart

Cheeseburgers in toasted sesame buns

Sticky sausages

MAKES 20 TAKES **40 MINUTES TO MAKE**

400g packet chipolatas
2 tbsp wholegrain mustard
2 tbsp runny honey
1 tbsp Worcestershire sauce
Leaves from 3 rosemary sprigs (optional)

1 Preheat the oven to 200°C/fan 180°C/gas 6. Pinch each chipolata in the middle, then twist and cut to make 2 mini sausages.
2 In a shallow ovenproof dish, mix the mustard, honey and Worcestershire sauce. Add the chipolatas and stir them through so they are thoroughly coated in the sticky glaze.
3 Roast for 15 minutes, then turn and sprinkle with the rosemary, if the children like it. Roast for a further 15 minutes until golden brown and nicely sticky but not burnt.
4 Serve skewered on cocktail sticks, topping each with a cherry tomato for a really colourful party touch.

Party sausage rolls

SERVES 8–10 TAKES **45 MINUTES TO MAKE**

8 large Cumberland sausages, skins removed
1 small onion, finely chopped
3 sun-dried tomatoes, finely chopped
3–4 sage leaves, finely chopped
3 tbsp chopped flatleaf parsley
500g fresh puff pastry
1 medium egg, lightly beaten
25g Parmesan, finely grated

1 Preheat the oven to 200°C/fan 180°C/gas 6. Place the sausagemeat in a bowl with the onion, tomatoes, herbs, a pinch of salt and a grinding of pepper. Mix together with a wooden spoon, or your hands, until very well combined.
2 Cut the pastry in half and roll out 1 piece to make a long oblong about 40cm x 17cm x 3mm thick. Form half the filling into a long log shape the length of the pastry. Place the sausage log about 5mm in from the long edge of the pastry rectangle. Brush the edge with the egg, then fold the pastry over the filling and press to seal the edges, either with your fingers or by pressing down with a fork. This seam will be hidden on the bottom of each sausage roll. Cut into 8 rolls. Prepare a second batch using the remaining pastry and filling.
3 Brush the tops of each sausage roll with beaten egg and sprinkle with the cheese. Place on a large baking tray lined with baking paper. Bake for 20–25 minutes in the hot oven, until golden, risen and flaky. Remove from the oven and cool slightly on a wire rack.

delicious.technique

ROLLING PASTRY

1. *A cool marble worktop is ideal. Roll directly on to a floured surface or a sheet of baking paper, to stop sticking. Rest your hands lightly at either end of the rolling pin and apply an even pressure to flatten and roll out the dough.*

Cheeseburgers in toasted sesame buns

SERVES 8 TAKES **30 MINUTES TO MAKE**
PLUS **30 MINUTES CHILLING**

Splash of olive oil
4 garlic cloves, crushed
1 onion, very finely chopped
1.3kg lean beef mince
Good splash of Worcestershire sauce
450g Cheddar, thinly sliced
8 sesame seed hamburger buns
   or crusty rolls, split
Lettuce, sliced tomato, sliced red onion,
   ketchup and mayonnaise, to serve

1 Heat the oil in a frying pan and cook the garlic and onion for 1–2 minutes until softened. Allow to cool slightly, then tip into a bowl with the mince and Worcestershire sauce, season and mix until well combined.
2 Divide the mixture into 8 and, using your hands, shape into burgers. Chill for 30 minutes to firm up. Meanwhile, preheat the grill to medium-hot.
3 Cook the burgers under the grill for 10–12 minutes, turning once. Top with cheese for the last 2–3 minutes of cooking time.
4 Toast the buns for 1–2 minutes. Put the burger in the bun, and let the children add their choice of lettuce, tomato, and onion before topping with the other bun half. Provide them with lots of ketchup and mayonnaise.

Lamb mince with chopped fresh mint or pork mince with grated apple also make tasty burgers.

Party sausage rolls

Cinnamon toffee apple wedges

Dead fly pies

Cinnamon toffee apple wedges

SERVES 4 TAKES **15 MINUTES TO MAKE**

100g butter
100g golden caster sugar
6 apples, cored and cut into wedges
$1/2$ tsp ground cinnamon
Handful of pecans, toasted and chopped

1 Heat the butter and sugar in a pan. As it turns golden brown, add the apples and cinnamon and cook for 5 minutes, turning to coat the apples.
2 Stir in the pecans. Serve immediately.

Butterscotch sponge cake

SERVES 8–10 TAKES **1 HOUR 15 MINUTES TO MAKE**

225g softened butter
125g light muscovado sugar
100g golden caster sugar
4 large eggs
225g self-raising flour
2 tsp vanilla extract
2 tbsp milk, if needed
400g full-fat cream cheese

For the butterscotch sauce
50g butter
75g light muscovado sugar
50g golden caster sugar
150g runny honey
120ml double cream
1 tsp vanilla extract

1 Preheat the oven to 190°C/fan 170°C/gas 5. Grease and line 2 x 20cm sandwich tins.
2 Make the sauce. Put the butter, both sugars and honey in a pan and stir over a low heat for 10-15 minutes until smooth. Stir in the cream and vanilla extract and cool.
3 Make the cake. Beat the butter and sugars until pale and fluffy. Beat in the eggs, one at a time, adding 1 tbsp flour with each egg. Beat in the vanilla. Fold in the remaining flour and a little milk so that the mixture drops reluctantly off the spoon.
4 Divide the mixture between the tins and bake for

about 25 minutes, until a skewer inserted into the centres comes away clean. Cool for 10 minutes, then turn out onto a wire rack and leave until cold.
5 Beat the cream cheese until smooth, then beat in 8 tbsp of the sauce. Place 1 cake on a serving plate and spread with frosting. Place the other cake on top and cover with the rest of the frosting. Decorate with birthday candles and extra sauce.

Dead fly pies
MAKES 12 TAKES **35 MINUTES TO MAKE**

Butter, for greasing
375g puff pastry sheet
Flour, for dusting
12 heaped tsp mincemeat
24 glacé cherries

1 Preheat the oven to 200°C/fan 180°C/gas 6. Lightly grease a 12-hole jam tart tin.
2 Unroll the pastry on a floured surface. Using a cutter that is slightly bigger than the holes in the tart tin, cut out 12 circles and press them into the tin. Prick the base of each tart with a fork.
3 Bake the pastry bases in the hot oven for 6 minutes, until the pastry is very pale golden.
4 Cut 12 small strips from the remaining pastry and cut into teeth shapes for the "mouths".
5 Take the tin out of the oven and add 1 heaped tsp mincemeat into each tart. Push 2 glacé cherries for "eyes" and add the pastry "teeth". Return the oven and bake for 8–10 minutes.
6 Leave to cool for a few minutes, then use a palette knife to gently prise the tarts out. Allow to cool completely on a wire rack.

Very easy fudge
MAKES 70–80 PIECES TAKES **2 HOURS TO MAKE**

450g icing sugar, plus extra for dusting
100g marshmallows
2 tbsp milk
100g unsalted butter
Few drops of vanilla extract

1 Sift the icing sugar into a large bowl. Make a well in the middle of the sugar with a spoon.
2 Put the marshmallows in a pan and add the milk, butter, and vanilla extract. Place the pan over a gentle heat and stir until melted.
3 Pour the mixture into the middle of the sugar and stir until smooth. Cool for 10 minutes, then form into a ball, cover with cling film and chill in the fridge for 1 hour.
4 Cut into 4 equal pieces, then roll to about 5mm thick. Cut into shapes and re-roll the trimmings; you should be able to make 70–80 shapes.
5 Put on baking paper and leave for 30 minutes to firm up. Store in an airtight container, with baking paper inbetween layers to prevent sticking. This fudge will keep in a cool place for up to 3 weeks.

delicious.**tip**
ROLLING FUDGE
When working with sticky sweets like fudge, sprinkle the work surface with icing sugar and rub a little icing sugar over your rolling pin to prevent sticking.

Very easy fudge

Coconut ice

Coconut ice

MAKES 40 PIECES TAKES **15 MINUTES TO MAKE**
PLUS **OVERNIGHT SETTING**

Butter, for greasing
397g can condensed milk
350g desiccated coconut
350g icing sugar
Few drops of vanilla extract
Pink or red food colouring

1 You will need a 23 x 20 x 4cm square cake tin.
Rub a little butter over the inside of the tin, then
line with baking paper, allowing it to run up and
over 2 sides of the tin.
2 Pour the condensed milk into a big bowl. Add
the coconut, icing sugar and vanilla extract and
mix well. Spoon half the mixture into the tin then
press it flat with damp fingers.
3 Add a few drops of pink or red food colouring to
the mixture left in the bowl and mix evenly. Spoon
the coloured mixture over the top of the white
layer and use damp fingers to smooth the top.

4 Loosely cover with cling film and put in a cool
place overnight to set and dry out – don't be
tempted to eat it yet, as it needs 12 hours to set
(you may need to hide it!). Use the overhanging
baking paper to lift the coconut ice from the tin,
then cut into about 40 pieces. Stored in an airtight
tin, it will keep in a cool place for up to 3 weeks.

Marshmallow and honeycomb sandwiches

MAKES 8 TAKES **1 HOUR 20 MINUTES TO MAKE**

150g raspberries
50g icing sugar
4 tbsp blackcurrant cordial
250g mascarpone
142ml pot double cream
100g pink marshmallows, snipped into pieces
  with wet scissors
50g chocolate honeycomb bars, broken into bits
16 rectangular ice cream wafers

1 Empty the raspberries into a bowl and sift over
the icing sugar. Pour over the blackcurrant
cordial and mash with a fork until pulpy. Stir in
the mascarpone.
2 In a separate bowl, whisk the cream to soft
peaks. Fold the cream into the raspberry mixture,
adding the marshmallows and chocolate pieces.
Cover with cling film and chill for 1 hour.
3 Place a spoonful of the chilled mixture between
two wafers, gently squashing each one to flatten
the raspberry and marshmallow filling. Eat the
wafer sandwiches straightaway or, for ice cream,
wrap each in baking paper and freeze for a few
hours until firm – the wafers will soften as a
result of freezing but the texture of the ice cream
is worth the sacrifice.

delicious.**tip**

ADDING A DECORATIVE FLOURISH
Try crumbling a bar of flaky chocolate (or toasted
desiccated coconut or chopped nuts) on to a plate
then dipping the 4 sides of the sandwich into the
mix so it sticks to the filling and acts as decoration.

Marshmallow and
honeycomb sandwiches

Outdoor eating

for 1 minute each side, until marked with golden griddle marks, then transfer to a serving plate. Drizzle with the infused olive oil, sprinkle with a little sea salt and plenty of black pepper, and serve with the tomato bread, ham and olives.
WINE NOTE There's nothing better with mezze than a crisp, fruity, young rosé. Choose one from the Mediterranean, perhaps Provence.

Mezze platter
SERVES 8 TAKES **35 MINUTES TO MAKE**

16 slices Serrano or Parma ham
150g tub mixed olives

For the tomato bread
1 loaf crusty sourdough bread or ciabatta
4 tbsp extra-virgin olive oil
1 large garlic clove, peeled
6 ripe tomatoes, roughly chopped

For the lemon and oregano haloumi
3 tbsp extra-virgin olive oil
Juice of 1 small lemon
2 tbsp chopped fresh oregano
500g haloumi

1 For the haloumi, mix the olive oil with the lemon juice and oregano in a bowl and set aside to infuse.
2 For the tomato bread, heat a griddle pan until hot. Cut the bread into thin slices, brush with a little of the olive oil and griddle for a few minutes each side until charred and golden. Rub the garlic clove over 1 side of each slice of bread and arrange on a serving platter.
3 Place the chopped tomatoes in a bowl and toss with 2 tablespoons of olive oil, a pinch of salt and plenty of ground black pepper. Spoon over the griddled bread slices and drizzle with the remaining olive oil.
4 Slice the haloumi into lengths and place on the hot griddle pan you used to cook the bread. Cook

Quick falafel with harissa dressing
SERVES 2 TAKES **20 MINUTES TO MAKE**

410g can chickpeas, drained
4 spring onions, chopped
$1/2$ tsp ground cumin
2 tbsp harissa paste
1 lemon
3 tbsp olive oil

1 Tip the chickpeas into a food processor. Add three-quarters of the spring onion, the cumin and 1 tablespoon harissa paste. Cut the lemon in half. Juice one half – add 1 tablespoon of juice to the chickpeas, and set the rest aside. Cut the other half into wedges to serve. Season and whizz everything in the processor until the mixture comes together. Shape into 6 small, firm patties.
2 Heat 1 tablespoon of oil in a frying pan over a medium heat. Add the patties and fry for 3–4 minutes each side until golden.
3 Meanwhile, mix the remaining harissa and olive oil with some lemon juice, to taste. Season and stir in the remaining spring onion. Divide the falafels between 2 plates and drizzle with some dressing. Serve with the lemon wedges, and some rocket and toasted ciabatta, if you like.

The salty flavour of haloumi is exquisite bathed in a sweet-sharp dressing.

Nachos with fresh avocado salsa

SERVES 2 TAKES **20 MINUTES TO MAKE**

300g Beef Ragù, defrosted (see p.168)
150g tortilla chips
60g mature Cheddar, grated

For the salsa
1 ripe avocado
Juice of 1 small lime, plus lime wedges to serve
1 tomato, roughly chopped
1 red chilli, deseeded and finely chopped
Small handful of fresh coriander,
  roughly chopped

1 Preheat the grill to medium-high. Put the ragù into a small pan and heat for 5 minutes or until piping hot.
2 Arrange the tortilla chips on 2 heatproof plates or in 2 dishes, piling them up in interwoven layers. Spoon the hot beef ragù on top, evenly distributing it around the tortilla chips and then sprinkle over the cheese. Grill for 2–3 minutes until the grated cheese has melted and turned golden.
3 Meanwhile, halve, stone (see below) and peel the avocado, then cut it into cubes. Mix the cubed avocado with the other salsa ingredients and season. Scatter the avocado salsa over the nachos and serve immediately, with some lime wedges to squeeze over.

delicious.**technique**

STONING AN AVOCADO

1. Use a chef's knife to slice into the avocado, cutting around the stone. Gently twist the halves in opposite directions and separate.

2. Strike the cutting edge of your knife into the stone. Lift the knife (wiggling it slightly if necessary) to remove the stone from the avocado.

Quick falafel with harissa dressing

Nachos with fresh avocado salsa

Barbecued
corn on the cob

Barbecued corn on the cob

SERVES 4 TAKES **25 MINUTES TO MAKE**

4 cobs of corn
125g softened butter
1 red chilli
Handful of fresh coriander, chopped

1 Put 4 cobs of corn into a large bowl of cold water to soak for 30 minutes.
2 Deseed the red chilli and chop finely. Beat together the butter, chilli and coriander. Shake off the excess water from the corn and put each onto a sheet of foil. Divide the butter between them and wrap up in the foil.
3 Cook on the barbecue over a low to medium heat for 25–30 minutes, turning occasionally. Open carefully, keeping all the flavoured butter.

Red pepper, aubergine and coriander dip

SERVES 8 TAKES **55 MINUTES TO MAKE**

4 aubergines
4 red peppers
Oil, for brushing
4 plump garlic cloves, crushed
$1/2$ tsp ground cumin
$1/2$ tsp paprika
Juice of 1 lemon
300ml Greek yogurt
Good handful of fresh coriander, chopped
8 pitta breads, to serve

1 Light the barbecue. Lightly brush the aubergines and peppers with oil. Place over a direct medium heat, close the lid and barbecue for 20–25 minutes, turning once, until blackened and tender (or cook under a hot grill). Remove and set the aubergines aside to cool slightly. Put the peppers in a plastic food bag, seal and cool for 15 minutes.
2 When the aubergines are cool enough to handle, halve lengthways and scoop the flesh into a food processor. Discard the skins. Halve, deseed, de-stalk and peel the peppers, then add to the food processor with the garlic, cumin, paprika, lemon juice and seasoning. Whizz to a

Quick houmous

purée. Add the yogurt and coriander and whizz again briefly. Check the seasoning.
3 Sear the pittas on the barbecue for 1–2 minutes (or warm under the grill). Serve warm with the dip.

Tapenade
SERVES 4 TAKES **15 MINUTES TO MAKE**

100g black olives, pitted
2 tbsp capers, drained and rinsed
1 plump garlic clove, crushed
85ml extra-virgin olive oil, plus extra to store

1 Put the olives, capers and garlic into a food processor and blend until smooth. With the motor running, pour in the oil in a slow, steady stream.
2 Season well, and transfer to a small bowl or jar and top with a film of oil.

Quick houmous
SERVES 12 TAKES **30 MINUTES TO MAKE**

150g dried chickpeas
Zest and juice of 1 lemon
3 tbsp tahini
2 large garlic cloves, crushed
120–140ml olive oil

1 Soak the chickpeas overnight in water. Drain and boil in a pan of fresh water for 45–55 minutes until very tender. Drain and cool.
2 Place in a food processor with the lemon zest and juice, tahini and garlic cloves. Whizz, gradually adding the olive oil. Season well.

Quick summer pickle with mustard seeds
MAKES 1 LARGE JAR TAKES **45 MINUTES TO MAKE**

$1/2$ cucumber
1 red onion, cut into thin half-moon slices
1 bunch of baby carrots, trimmed
1 bunch of small radishes
1 red or yellow pepper,
 deseeded and cut into strips
1 fennel bulb, trimmed and cut into strips
 (keep the feathery tops)
2 tsp brown mustard seeds
1 tsp coriander seeds, lightly crushed
1 tsp fennel seeds
250ml cider, white wine or rice vinegar
1 tbsp sugar
2–3 small red chillies, halved
2–3 bay leaves
2–3 sprigs fresh thyme
2–3 garlic cloves, halved

1 Halve the cucumber lengthways and scoop out the seeds. Cut into 5cm batons or thin half-moon slices and place in a colander. Toss with 1 teaspoon of sea salt and leave for 30 minutes to remove some moisture. Rinse and drain.
2 Meanwhile, separate the onion slices into layers. Cut the washed but unpeeled baby carrots into halves or quarters, depending on how thick they are. Wash, trim and slice or halve the radishes.
3 Toss all the vegetables, apart from the cucumber, in a large non-metallic bowl. Cover with boiling water, drain immediately and refresh under cold running water. Drain thoroughly, then return to the bowl and add the cucumber and any fennel tops, chopped.
4 Place the mustard, coriander and fennel seeds in a medium pan over a low heat and warm until the mustard seeds start to "pop". Add the vinegar, sugar, $1/2$ teaspoon of salt, chilli, bay leaves, thyme and garlic. Simmer for a few minutes. Pour the hot vinegar over the vegetables and allow to cool, tossing to mix from time to time.
5 Arrange the vegetables and herbs in a large, scrupulously clean jar. Taste the vinegar for sweetness and add a little more sugar to taste, then pour back over the vegetables, making sure they are covered. Seal. Store in the fridge.

delicious.**tip**
IMPROVING WITH AGE
You can eat this pickle after a few hours, but it will keep in the fridge for a couple of weeks. As it stands, the vegetables will lose a little colour and crispness, but the flavour will deepen and mellow.

Antipasti pizza

MAKES 4 TAKES **1 HOUR 25 MINUTES TO MAKE**

2 tbsp extra-virgin olive oil
1 fat garlic clove, finely chopped
750ml jar tomato passata
1 tbsp chopped fresh oregano or thyme
$\frac{1}{2}$ tsp sugar
250g chargrilled artichoke hearts in oil,
  drained and halved
200g roasted red peppers in oil or brine, drained
80g sun-dried tomatoes in oil, drained
250g mini mozzarella balls (about 10), drained
  and halved, or a 250g ball mozzarella, torn
50g pitted black olives
50g Cheddar, coarsely grated

For the dough
350g strong plain flour, plus extra for dusting
2 tsp dried fast-action yeast
1 tsp salt
Olive oil, plus extra for oiling and brushing

1 Make the pizza dough. Sift the flour, yeast and salt into a mixing bowl, add 225ml hand-hot water and mix to a soft dough. Turn the dough out onto a floured work surface and knead for 5 minutes until smooth and elastic. Place in a lightly oiled bowl, cover with cling film and leave somewhere warm for 1 hour or until doubled in size.
2 If using a charcoal barbecue, light it about 30 minutes before you want to cook. If using a gas barbecue, preheat 10 minutes beforehand.
3 Meanwhile, make the topping. Heat the olive oil and garlic in a medium pan for 1–2 minutes until the garlic sizzles. Add the passata, oregano or thyme and sugar and simmer quite vigorously, stirring now and then, for 30 minutes, until reduced to a thick sauce. Season and set aside.
4 Punch the risen dough to knock out the air, turn out onto a floured work surface and knead briefly. Halve, then roll each piece to about a 25cm circle. Transfer to 2 baking sheets and brush with oil.
5 Lift the pizza bases, oil-side down, onto the barbecue bars and cook over direct medium heat for 2–3 minutes, until marked by the barbecue

Antipasti
pizza

bars. Flip over and cook for a further 2 minutes.
6 Slide the pizza bases back onto the baking
sheets and spread with the tomato sauce. Cut the
peppers and tomato into strips. Scatter over the
artichokes, peppers, tomatoes, mozzarella, pitted
olives and grated Cheddar. Brush the bars of the
barbecue with oil, slide the pizzas back onto the
bars, cover with a lid and cook for 4–5 minutes.
Lift the pizzas onto a chopping board, cut into
wedges and serve with a mixed salad.

Tomato, mozzarella and basil tarts
MAKES 4 TAKES **55 MINUTES TO MAKE**

600g shortcrust pastry
4 tsp green pesto
8 slices mozzarella
1 beef tomato, sliced
2 cloves garlic, finely sliced
Handful of small basil leaves
3 tsp olive oil

1 On a sheet of baking paper, roll out the pastry
until it is 3mm thick. Put a 12cm wide x 1cm deep
tartlet tin on top and cut out a circle of pastry
about 3cm wider than the tin. Repeat 3 times.
2 Put the pastry rounds into the four tins, gently
pressing the pastry into the edges. Roll a rolling
pin over the top of each tartlet tin to neaten and
trim off the edges, then prick the base with a fork
to stop air bubbles forming during baking.
3 Ensure the pastry cases stay crisp by blind
baking them. Put a square of baking paper on
top of each piece of pastry, and cover with baking
beans, dried chickpeas or dry rice. Put the tartlet
tins in the fridge to chill for 15 minutes (this will
make sure the pastry doesn't shrink as it cooks).
Preheat the oven to 220°C/fan200°C/gas 7.
4 Bake the tarts for 10–15 minutes until pale-
golden. Remove the paper and beans, and set
the tartlet cases aside to cool. Leave the oven on.
5 Spread some pesto into the tartlet cases, then
arrange 2 slices of mozzarella and 2 or 3 slices
of tomato on top. Add a few slices of garlic, and
some salt and freshly ground black pepper. Finish
with 2–3 basil leaves and a drizzle of olive oil.

6 Return the tartlet cases to the baking tray and
bake for 10 minutes, until the cheese is bubbling.
Lift the tarts from the tins onto a serving plate.
Serve with a green salad, if you like.

Griddled vegetables and feta couscous
MAKES 4 TAKES **30 MINUTES TO MAKE**

250g wholegrain couscous
1 courgette, cut lengthways into thin slices
1 aubergine, cut lengthways into narrow slices
2 red peppers, deseeded and cut into strips
3 tbsp olive oil
1 tbsp cumin seeds
1 tbsp fennel seeds
Juice of 1 large lemon
1 large red chilli, finely chopped
50g pine nuts, toasted
50g dried sour cherries
150g feta, crumbled into pieces
Handful of fresh coriander, chopped
Fresh houmous, to serve

1 Place the couscous in a large bowl and pour
over boiling water until just covered. Cover with
a clean tea towel and leave for 5 minutes or until
the couscous has absorbed the water. Fluff up
the grains with a fork.
2 Heat a griddle pan until hot. Place the courgette,
aubergine and peppers in a large bowl and toss
with 2 tablespoons of the olive oil, the cumin and
fennel seeds. Place the vegetables on the griddle
pan, a few at a time, and griddle for 2 minutes
each side, until charred and softened.
3 Stir the vegetables into the couscous with the
remaining olive oil, lemon juice, chilli, pine nuts
and sour cherries. Fold in the feta and coriander
and season well. Serve with the houmous.

delicious.**tip**
CHOOSING COUSCOUS
Look out for wholegrain couscous as it has a
wonderful nutty taste and texture and holds its
shape better in salads. It's readily available in
major supermarkets.

Grilled sardines with panzanella
SERVES 4 TAKES **1 HOUR TO MAKE**

12 fresh sardines, about 100g each
2 small yellow peppers
2 small red peppers
3 tbsp extra-virgin olive oil
2 tbsp red wine vinegar
200g ripe small plum tomatoes, halved
1 small red onion, thinly sliced
1 tbsp capers, rinsed
125g stale Italian bread, such as ciabatta
  or focaccia, cut into bite-size pieces
Good handful of fresh basil leaves

1 Hold the sardines under cold running water and use your fingers to push off the scales and gut them (or ask your fishmonger to do this). Pat them thoroughly dry with kitchen paper and scatter them with sea salt. Set aside while you make the panzanella.
2 If you are grilling the peppers, halve them and place under a hot grill until the skins have blistered and blackened. Leave to cool in a bowl covered with cling film – the steam helps to loosen the blackened skin. Once cooled, remove the skin, stalk and seeds and cut the flesh into slices. Return the peppers to the bowl, keeping the juices that have collected. If you don't want to cook the peppers, simply remove the stalk and seeds and slice them for a crunchier texture.
3 Make the dressing. Combine the extra-virgin olive oil with the red wine vinegar in a large bowl and season to taste. Add the tomatoes, onion, capers and bread to the bowl of peppers, drizzle with the dressing and gently toss everything together. Set the panzanella aside for 20 minutes, so the bread can soak up the dressing.
4 Heat a ridged griddle pan over a high heat (or preheat a barbecue). When it is smoking hot, cook the sardines – in batches as necessary – for just 4 minutes, turning halfway. Don't add any oil, as sardines are best when dry-fried. Remove from the heat and allow to rest for 2 minutes, so that they become extra sweet and tender.
5 Fold the basil leaves into the panzanella, divide between plates and serve alongside the sardines.

Chilli crab and prawn tarts
SERVES 4 TAKES **45 MINUTES TO MAKE**

375g pack ready-rolled shortcrust pastry,
  at room temperature
25g butter
Bunch of spring onions,
  trimmed and finely sliced
1 large red chilli,
  deseeded and finely chopped
250g raw peeled prawns
170g canned or fresh white crab meat
200ml single cream
3 large egg yolks
Bunch of fresh coriander, chopped
Grated zest of 1 lime

1 Preheat the oven to 180°C/fan 160°C/gas 4. Cut the pastry into 4 squares and use to line 4 fluted tart tins, about 10cm wide and 2cm deep. Trim the excess pastry and prick the bases with a fork. Line each with baking paper and fill with baking beans or rice. Bake for 15 minutes.
2 Meanwhile, melt the butter in a frying pan and gently cook the spring onions and chilli for 2–3 minutes. Add the prawns and cook for 2 minutes, until pink. Remove from the heat and stir in the crab and some seasoning.
3 Mix together the cream, egg yolks, coriander and lime zest in a jug. Remove the paper and beans from the pastry cases. Spoon in the crab mixture, then pour in the egg mixture. Bake for a further 15 minutes, until set but still with a slight wobble. Stand for 10 minutes before serving.
WINE NOTE This mix of flavours calls for a dry New Zealand Riesling.

Fish has a clean, light quality that perfectly suits a hot sunny day.

Chilli crab and
prawn tarts

Barbecue-style chicken 'n' coleslaw

SERVES 4 TAKES **45 MINUTES TO MAKE**
PLUS **OVERNIGHT MARINATING**

330ml cola
200g tomato passata
15g fresh ginger, grated
1 large garlic clove, crushed
2 tbsp Worcestershire sauce
1 tbsp dark soy sauce
1$^1/_2$ tbsp cider vinegar
1 tbsp light muscovado sugar
4 skinless chicken breasts,
  cut into 3cm chunks
2 red peppers,
  cut into 3cm chunks
Lime wedges, to serve

For the coleslaw
100g fat-free yogurt
1 tsp caster sugar
1 tsp Dijon mustard
1 tbsp cider vinegar

1 large carrot, grated
100g radishes, coarsely grated
4 spring onions, thinly sliced on the diagonal
3 celery sticks, thinly sliced on the diagonal

1 Soak 12 wooden skewers in water. Meanwhile, put the cola, passata, ginger, Worcestershire sauce, garlic, soy sauce, vinegar and sugar in a large, non-stick saucepan. Bring to the boil and cook for 15–20 minutes, until the sauce has thickened. Season and cool. When cool, add the chicken, coat in the sauce and marinate overnight.
2 The next day, make the coleslaw. Whisk together the yogurt, sugar, mustard and vinegar in a large bowl. Add the carrot, radishes, spring onions and celery. Mix together and season well.
3 Preheat the barbecue or grill to medium.
4 Thread the chicken and pepper pieces alternately onto the skewers. Season and barbecue or grill for 10 minutes, turning halfway, until the chicken is cooked through.
5 Serve the chicken skewers with the coleslaw and lime wedges to squeeze over.

Barbecue-style
chicken 'n' coleslaw

Buffalo chicken wings

SERVES 4–6 TAKES **40 MINUTES TO MAKE**
PLUS **1–6 HOURS MARINATING**

24 large chicken wings
4 tsp Tabasco sauce
Olive oil, for brushing
100g unsalted butter
4 tsp cider vinegar
2 tsp sweet chilli sauce

For the blue cheese dressing
50g creamy blue cheese, such as Danish Blue
1 small garlic clove, crushed
4 tbsp mayonnaise
2 tsp lemon juice
4 tbsp soured cream,
  or wholemilk natural yogurt
1 large shallot, finely chopped
1 tbsp chopped fresh parsley leaves
1 tbsp milk (optional)

1 Cut off and discard the pointy tip from each chicken wing, then make a shallow slash through the skin. Put in a bowl, drizzle over 1 teaspoon of Tabasco and massage into the slashes. Cover and marinate in the fridge for 1–6 hours.
2 If you're using a charcoal barbecue, light it about 30 minutes before you want to cook. For a gas barbecue, preheat 10 minutes beforehand.
3 Make the dressing. Crumble the cheese into a bowl, add 2 tablespoons of mayonnaise and the garlic, then cream together until smooth but with a few small lumps. Stir in the lemon juice, soured cream or yogurt, shallot, parsley and the remaining mayonnaise, loosened with milk if necessary. Spoon into 4 small pots, cover and chill until serving.
4 Brush the chicken wings with a little oil, season and barbecue directly over a medium heat for about 8 minutes each side, or until golden and cooked through.
5 Just before the wings are ready, melt the butter in a large, deep frying pan on the barbecue. Stir in the remaining Tabasco, the vinegar and the sweet chilli sauce and season with salt to taste. Using tongs, transfer the chicken to the pan and

toss well in the sauce. Take to the table and serve with the pots of blue cheese dressing, for dunking. These wings are also good with celery, iceberg lettuce and crusty bread.

Crispy skin chicken legs

SERVES 6 TAKES **1 HOUR 20 MINUTES TO MAKE**

2 tbsp Dijon mustard
Grated zest and juice of 1 lemon
2 tbsp chopped fresh tarragon
6 whole chicken legs

1 Mix the mustard, zest, tarragon, and some salt and black pepper together in a bowl. Loosen the chicken skin and spread a little of the mixture under the skin, pushing right down to the drumstick. Repeat with the other chicken legs.
2 Put in a dish, pour over the lemon juice and season. Marinate at room temperature for 30 minutes. Barbecue for 40 minutes, turning once, until cooked and crispy.

Crispy skin
chicken legs

Pork and chorizo
kebabs

Pork and chorizo kebabs

SERVES 6 TAKES **1 HOUR TO MAKE**

2 pork tenderloins, about 350–450g each
2 thick slices granary bread, cut into 24 cubes
200g thin chorizo, cut into 24 slices
6 tbsp olive oil
$1/2$ tsp paprika
1 tbsp chopped fresh sage
Vegetable oil, for brushing

1 If using wooden or bamboo skewers to hold the kebabs, soak 6 in cold water for at least 30 minutes. Preheat the barbecue.
2 Meanwhile, trim the pork of any excess fat, then cut into bite-sized cubes, giving 24 pieces in all. Thread 4 pork pieces, 4 bread pieces and 4 chorizo slices alternately onto each soaked skewer. Mix the olive oil with the paprika, sage and some seasoning, and brush over the skewers, making sure you soak the bread well.
3 Brush the cooking grate with a little oil. Barbecue the skewers directly over a medium heat for 10–12 minutes – turning halfway and brushing with any remaining paprika oil – until cooked through. Serve with couscous, grilled tomatoes and rocket, if you like.

Jerk pork fillet with spicy pineapple relish

SERVES 4 TAKES **30 MINUTES TO MAKE** PLUS **MARINATING**

432g can pineapple in natural juice
150ml jerk barbecue sauce
2.5cm piece fresh ginger, grated
1 tbsp vegetable oil
2 pork tenderloins, about 300g each,
   trimmed of excess fat and halved
2 spring onions, finely sliced

1 Preheat the barbecue. Drain the pineapple, reserving the juice. Set aside. In a flat dish, mix all but 1 tablespoon of the barbecue sauce with the ginger, 2 tablespoons reserved pineapple juice and the oil. Add the pork and toss to coat. Set aside for at least 30 minutes, or overnight.

2 Lift the pork from the marinade, discarding any excess. Cook on the hot barbecue, covered, for 20 minutes or until just cooked through, turning halfway. Set aside to rest for 5 minutes.

3 Meanwhile, chop the pineapple and heat in a pan with a little of the pineapple juice and the remaining barbecue sauce. Cook until softened, then stir in the onions. Remove from the heat and season. Cut the pork into thick slices. Serve with the pineapple relish and jacket sweet potatoes.

Barbecued leg of lamb with tomato and mint salsa

SERVES 6 TAKES **50 MINUTES TO MAKE** PLUS **MARINATING OVERNIGHT**

1.3–1.5kg leg of lamb, boned and butterflied
3 garlic cloves, sliced
3 shallots, halved
Few sprigs of fresh rosemary
3 bay leaves
Few sprigs of fresh oregano
375ml red wine
Vegetable oil, for brushing

For the tomato and mint salsa
6 ripe plum or vine tomatoes, halved and seeded
Small bunch of fresh mint, chopped
Good pinch of caster sugar

Bunch of spring onions, thinly sliced
2 garlic cloves, crushed
1 tbsp extra-virgin olive oil
2 tsp balsamic vinegar

1 Put the lamb into a large freezer bag, then add the garlic, shallots and herbs. Holding the bag carefully, pour in the wine, then seal and put into a container in the fridge. Leave to marinate for 24 hours.

2 A few hours before you want to eat, make the salsa. Roughly dice the tomato flesh and put it into a bowl with the mint. Sprinkle with the sugar, then add the spring onions, crushed garlic, olive oil and balsamic vinegar. Toss well, then set aside.

3 Take the lamb out of the marinade and discard the marinade. Brush the cooking grate with oil. Barbecue the lamb over a direct medium heat, turning once. Cook for 20–30 minutes for medium-cooked meat, or 15–25 minutes if you like it pinker. Leave to rest for 5 minutes before slicing. Serve with the salsa.

Barbecued leg of lamb with tomato and mint salsa

delicious.**technique**

BUTTERFLYING A LEG OF LAMB

1. *Locate the wide pelvis, and cut around it to expose the leg bone. Cut down from the pelvis, using short strokes, to free the leg bone. Cut it away from the end joint and shank.*

2. *All 3 bones – pelvis, thigh and shank – should come away together. Make short downward cuts through the thick areas of meat to open out the flesh completely.*

Tandoori lamb burgers

1 Mix all the ingredients for the burgers in a large bowl. Season with salt and pepper then, using wet hands, shape the mixture into 10 burgers. Cover and chill for 1 hour.

2 Heat a griddle pan or barbecue to hot (if you have a charcoal barbecue, light it 30 minutes before you're ready to cook). Brush both sides of the burgers with oil and cook for 3–4 minutes each side or until cooked through.

3 Meanwhile, use a vegetable peeler to cut ribbons of cucumber. Place in a bowl with the red onion, lemon juice, and a pinch of sugar and salt, and leave to stand for about 10 minutes. Toast the naan breads.

4 Top each naan bread with some onion and cucumber. Add the burgers and a dollop of mint raita. Sprinkle with mint leaves, if you like.

Spicy lamb kofta kebabs with houmous dressing

SERVES 4 TAKES **25 MINUTES TO MAKE**

500g lamb mince
1 tbsp Moroccan spice mix
1 spring onion, finely chopped
2 tbsp chopped fresh coriander,
  plus extra for the salad
4 tbsp apricot jam, warmed
3 tbsp houmous
150g natural yogurt
Warm pittas, to serve
Green salad and sliced red onion, to serve

1 Preheat the grill or barbecue to medium-hot. Soak 8 wooden skewers in water.

2 Meanwhile, in a bowl, mix the lamb mince, spice mix, spring onion and coriander. Season well. Shape the mix into 32 balls and thread 4 onto each skewer. Grill or barbecue for 10–15 minutes, turning, until cooked. Just before they are ready, brush with the jam.

3 Mix together the houmous and yogurt. Season with salt and freshly ground black pepper. Serve the kebabs accompanied with warm pittas, green salad, sliced red onion sprinkled with coriander, and the houmous dressing.

Tandoori lamb burgers

SERVES 10 TAKES **45 MINUTES TO MAKE**

1kg good-quality lamb mince
1 small onion, finely chopped
2 garlic cloves, crushed
1 tbsp mango chutney
2.5cm piece fresh ginger, finely grated
1 tsp ground coriander
1 tsp ground cumin
$\frac{1}{2}$ tsp garam masala
$\frac{1}{4}$ tsp ground turmeric
Pinch of cayenne pepper

To serve
1 tbsp sunflower oil
1 cucumber
1 red onion, sliced into rings
Juice of 1 lemon
10 mini naan breads
Mint raita
Fresh mint leaves, to garnish

Spicy lamb kofta
kebabs with
houmous dressing

Honey- and soy-glazed steaks with mango and chilli salsa

SERVES 4 TAKES **1 HOUR TO MAKE**

6 tbsp clear honey
4 tbsp dark soy sauce
Large pinch of five-spice powder
4 good rib-eye or sirloin steaks,
  about 225–300g each in weight, 2.5cm thick
Oil, for brushing

For the mango and chilli salsa
1 large ripe mango, peeled, pitted and diced
1 red chilli, deseeded and finely sliced
3 spring onions, thinly sliced on the diagonal
1 tbsp lime juice

1 Mix the honey, soy sauce and five-spice powder with plenty of freshly ground black pepper. Add the steaks and massage the mixture well into both sides. Cover and set aside for 30 minutes.
2 If using a charcoal barbecue, light it about 30 minutes before you want to cook. Season the steaks with a little salt. Brush the cooking grate with oil, add the steaks and barbecue directly for 3 minutes each side for rare; 4–5 minutes for medium; or 6–7 minutes for well-done. Set aside, covered with foil, to rest for 5 minutes.
3 Meanwhile, mix the salsa ingredients together with a pinch of salt and serve with the steaks.

delicious.**technique**

STONING AND DICING A MANGO

1. *Stand the mango on its side and cut down through it on either side of its flat stone. Place the halves cut-side up on the chopping board.*

2. *Cut into strips across the length and width, not cutting through the skin. Invert the skin and run your knife along it to remove the segments.*

The ultimate beef and cheese burger

The ultimate beef and cheese burger

SERVES 4 TAKES **25 MINUTES TO MAKE**

1 large red onion
500g beef steak mince
2 tbsp Worcestershire sauce
Handful of fresh parsley, chopped
80g piece mature Cheddar,
  cut into 4 equal cubes
Olive oil, for brushing
4 ciabatta rolls, split in two
1 little gem lettuce, leaves separated
2 ripe tomatoes, sliced
Tomato or other relish, to serve

1 Preheat the barbecue (if you have a charcoal barbecue, light it 30 minutes before you're ready to cook). Cut half the onion into rings and set aside. Finely chop the remainder and put into a large bowl, along with the mince, Worcestershire sauce and parsley. Season and mix well with your hands.
2 Shape into 4 burgers, push a cube of Cheddar into the centre of each, then re-shape to fully enclose the cheese. Brush the burgers with a little oil and cook on the hot barbecue for 10 minutes, turning halfway, until just cooked through and charred. Set aside to rest for a few minutes, covered in foil.
3 Meanwhile, brush the cut side of each ciabatta roll with oil. Barbecue, cut-side down, until lightly toasted.
4 Put some onion rings, lettuce and tomato onto the base of each roll. Top with a burger, spoon over some relish and top with the remaining ciabatta halves. Serve with extra relish on the side and some oven chips, if you like.

Juicy barbecued burgers are a real treat on a warm summer's evening.

Barbecue pepper steak sandwiches

SERVES 4 TAKES **35 MINUTES TO MAKE**

3 red peppers, pricked with a fork
2 sirloin steaks, about 300g each,
 trimmed of excess fat
2 tbsp olive oil
1 red onion, sliced into rings
4 small baguettes, bread rolls
 or an unsliced crusty loaf
Handful of salad leaves
1 ripe avocado, halved and pitted
4 tbsp good-quality tomato chutney
 (buy from a local farm shop or deli)

1 Light the barbecue and get the coals to medium heat (if you have a charcoal barbecue, light it 30 minutes before you're ready to cook). Cook the peppers whole for 20 minutes, turning occasionally, until the skins are blackened and they feel quite soft when prodded with tongs. Put in a bowl, cover with cling film and set aside to cool.
2 Meanwhile, lay the steaks out on a board and cover each with cling film. Using a rolling pin or the end of a wooden spoon, flatten out the steaks until 1cm thick. Brush the steaks on both sides with half the olive oil and place on a plate. Sprinkle with ground black pepper.
3 Add the steaks to the barbecue and cook for 1–2 minutes each side for medium-rare (or cook for longer if you like). Set them aside to rest for 5 minutes, then halve each one. While the steaks are cooking and resting, brush the red onion rings with the remaining oil. Cook on the barbecue for 3–4 minutes, turning halfway or until softened.
4 Peel off and discard the blackened skin from the peppers, then halve, deseed and cut them into strips. Split or slice the bread and grill on the barbecue for 1 minute each side, until toasted.
5 Top each bread base with a handful of salad leaves. Using a spoon, scoop the avocado out of its skin and press on top of the salad. Add a steak half and some grilled pepper strips, a dollop of tomato chutney and the onion rings. Top with the remaining bread to serve.

Barbecue pepper
steak sandwiches

desserts,
cakes
and bakes

- everyday desserts
- indulgent desserts
- cakes
- breads, buns and biscuits

everyday desserts

French toast with fruit and ice cream
SERVES 6 TAKES **10 MINUTES TO MAKE**

6 thick slices of brioche or panettone
2 large eggs
2 tbsp milk
3 tbsp sweet sherry or vanilla extract
1 tbsp caster sugar
Canned or fresh fruit and ice cream, to serve

1 Whisk the egg, milk and sweet sherry or vanilla extract in a shallow bowl.
2 Soak the brioche or panettone in the mixture, remove, dust each side with sugar, then pan-fry in a knob of butter until golden and caramelised. Serve with fruit and ice cream.

Plum and apple crumble
SERVES 6 TAKES **1 HOUR TO MAKE**

550g plums, quartered and pitted
3 bramley apples, peeled and cut into chunks
125g caster sugar
75g butter
170g plain flour
30g oat flakes

1 Preheat the oven to 180°C/fan 160°C/gas 4. Put the plums and apples in a 1.2-litre pie dish and sprinkle with 50g of the caster sugar.
2 Make the crumble. Rub the butter into the flour and oats just until the mixture resembles coarse breadcrumbs (don't rub it in too much or the

topping won't be crunchy), then mix in the remaining sugar.
3 Sprinkle the crumble mixture over the fruit and bake for 30–45 minutes until cooked and golden. Serve warm with whipped cream or vanilla ice cream.

Fruity oat cinnamon crumble
SERVES 6 TAKES **35 MINUTES TO MAKE**

500g pears
Juice of $1/2$ lemon
200g golden caster sugar
1 tsp cinnamon
500g frozen forest fruits
100g butter, chilled
200g plain or wholemeal flour
150g porridge oats

1 Preheat the oven to 200°C/fan 180°C/gas 6. Peel, quarter, core and slice the pears, then put into a 1.6-litre ovenproof dish and squeeze over the lemon juice. Add the cinnamon and 100g of the sugar, then gently stir in the forest fruits.
2 Cut the butter into pieces. Put the butter and remaining sugar in a bowl (or food processor) and add the butter. Rub in (see below) or whizz in the processor until the mixture resembles fine breadcrumbs. Add the oats, mix together, then sprinkle on top of the fruit. Bake for 20 minutes until it is pale golden. Serve with fromage frais.

delicious.technique
MAKING CRUMBLE TOPPING

1. *Sift the flour into a bowl, then add the chilled butter, cut into cubes.*

2. *Using your fingers, rub the mix together until it resembles breadcrumbs. Mix in the sugar.*

Old-fashioned cherry pie
SERVES 8–10 TAKES **2 HOURS TO MAKE**

1kg fresh cherries
Lemon juice, to taste
2 tbsp cornflour
100g caster sugar,
  plus extra for dusting
1/2 vanilla pod, split lengthways
1 tbsp kirsch or cherry brandy
  (optional)

For the pastry
350g plain flour,
  plus extra for dusting
150g cold unsalted butter, diced
100g caster sugar
50g ground almonds
2 large egg yolks
Few splashes of cold milk

1 Make the pastry. You can either rub together the flour and butter using your hands, or whizz them together in a food processor, if you prefer. Once the flour and butter has the texture of breadcrumbs, add the sugar, almonds and egg yolks. Work into a dough, either by hand-kneading or pulsing in the processor. You might need a dash of cold milk to bind the dough together. Wrap in cling film and chill in the fridge for at least 30 minutes.
2 Meanwhile, pit the cherries. Toss with a squeeze of lemon juice and set aside. In a small bowl, mix the cornflour with 2 tablespoons of water to form a paste and set aside.
3 Use the tip of a sharp knife to slit down the side of the vanilla pod and scrape out the seeds (see p.256). Put the sugar in a wide pan, and add the vanilla seeds. Over a low heat, dissolve the sugar, then increase the heat and cook, without stirring, until you have a dark caramel.
4 Lower the heat and add the cherries and liqueur, if using. At first the mixture will seem unpromising, but as the cherries cook their juices will start to run. Once you have a juicy, dark compote, add the cornflour mix and stir until thick enough to coat the back of a spoon. Set aside to cool.

5 Preheat the oven to 200°C/fan 180°C/gas 6 and pop in a baking sheet. On a lightly floured surface, roll out two-thirds of the pastry and use it to line a 20 x 4cm deep pie dish or fluted tart tin. Fill with the compote.
6 Roll out the rest of the pastry to make a lid, then brush the edge of the base with water. Lay the lid on top of the pie and crimp the edges to seal. Brush with a little cold milk.
7 Transfer the pie to the hot baking sheet and bake for 30–35 minutes or until golden and bubbling. Rest for 10 minutes. Dust with caster sugar and serve hot or cold with vanilla ice cream.

Everyone loves a scrumptious, old-fashioned fruit pie or crumble.

Old-fashioned cherry pie

241

Lemon tart

floured surface and use to line a 23cm fluted flan tin. Chill for 30 minutes. Preheat the oven to 190°C/fan 170°C/gas 5.
2 Line the pastry case with greaseproof paper, fill with baking beans and bake for 10 minutes. Lift out the paper, return to the oven and bake for a further 5 minutes until the pastry is dry. Brush the pastry case with egg white and return to the oven for 5 minutes until the egg white has dried and the pastry is shiny – this will prevent the pastry going soggy once the filling is poured in. Lower the oven to 150°C/fan 130°C/gas 2.
3 For the filling, whisk the caster sugar and eggs until foamy. Beat in the cream, then the lemon zest and juice. Pour into the tart case and return to the oven for 40–50 minutes until just set – don't worry if it's slightly wobbly in the centre, as it will set as it cools. Cool, slip out of the tin onto a serving platter, and dust with extra icing sugar just before serving.

Lemon tart
SERVES 8–10 TAKES **1 HOUR 15 MINUTES TO MAKE**

200g plain flour
50g ground almonds
1/2 tsp salt
2 tbsp icing sugar, plus extra to dust
125g chilled butter, diced
2 egg yolks
1 egg white, beaten

For the filling
200g golden caster sugar
4 eggs
142ml double cream
Finely grated zest and juice of 2 lemons

1 Put the flour, ground almonds, salt, icing sugar and butter in a food processor and whizz to make fine crumbs. Add the yolks and 2–3 tablespoons of cold water and pulse until the mixture comes together to make a firm but moist dough. Lightly shape the pastry into a ball, then roll out on a

Treacle tart
SERVES 6 TAKES **1 HOUR 20 MINUTES TO MAKE**

250g golden syrup
175g fresh white breadcrumbs
Finely grated zest and juice of 1 lemon
Flour, for dusting

For the pastry
200g plain flour
100g butter, chilled and cut into small cubes
2 egg yolks

1 Make the pastry. Sieve the flour into a bowl and add a pinch of salt. Add the butter to the flour, rubbing everything together with your fingertips until the mixture resembles breadcrumbs (see p.240). Add the egg yolk and 1 teaspoon of cold water. Mix with your hands, squeezing the crumbs together with your fingers. The dough should be soft but not sticky.
2 Turn the dough onto a sheet of baking paper and shape it into a ball. Wrap the pastry in cling film and chill it for 20 minutes. This makes the shortcrust pastry light and less likely to shrink.

3 Preheat the oven to 200°C/fan 180°C/gas 6. Put a baking tray into the oven to heat up. Roll out the pastry and use it to line a 20 x 2.5cm round, fluted, loose-bottomed tart tin. Reserve the trimmings to decorate. Chill for 20 minutes.

4 Meanwhile, heat the golden syrup in a saucepan over a low heat until warm and runny. Remove from the heat and stir in the breadcrumbs, lemon zest and juice. Tip into the pastry case and spread evenly.

5 On a lightly floured surface, roll out the reserved pastry trimmings and cut into 10–12 long, narrow strips. Carefully twist each strip until spiral-shaped, then lay half of them, spaced apart, across the pie filling. Arrange the remaining strips at right angles to the first strips, to form a lattice. Press the edges of the strips around the rim of the pastry case, trimming off any excess.

6 Place the tart on the hot baking sheet and bake for 10 minutes. Reduce the oven temperature to 180°C/fan 160°C/gas 4 and bake for a further 20 minutes or until the filling is lightly set and the pastry golden. Cool in the tin for 10 minutes, then carefully remove and transfer to a board. Cut into slices and serve with ice cream, custard or cream.

No-bake sticky toffee apple tart

SERVES 6 TAKES **30 MINUTES TO MAKE**

Juice of ¹/₂ lemon
8 eating apples, peeled, cored and sliced
100g butter
175g golden caster sugar
4 tbsp single cream, plus extra to serve
50g butter
12 digestive biscuits

1 Put the lemon juice into a large bowl. Add the apples and toss in the juice – the acid in the lemon juice prevents the apples from going brown. Melt the butter in a 25cm non-stick frying pan over a low heat. Add the sugar and cream, and cook for a few minutes, stirring, until the sugar has dissolved. Add the apples and

lemon juice to the pan and cook for 15 minutes, stirring from time to time, until the apples are tender and browned. Set aside.

2 Make the biscuit base. Put the biscuits into a plastic bag and crush with a wooden spoon, then put into a bowl. Melt the butter in a pan, pour onto the biscuit and mix to combine. Sprinkle on top of the apples in the pan and press down with the wooden spoon. Leave to firm up for about 10 minutes. Serve straight from the pan, inverting each portion so the fruit sits on top. Serve drizzled with cream.

This squidgy concoction will become a real family favourite.

Treacle tart

Marmalade bread and butter pudding

SERVES 6–8 TAKES **1 HOUR TO MAKE**

50g butter, softened
7 slices white bread, crusts removed
9 tbsp thick-cut marmalade
100g sultanas
225ml double cream,
  plus extra whipped cream to serve
225ml full-fat milk
3 eggs
50g caster sugar
1 vanilla pod, split lengthways
Icing sugar, for dusting

1 Preheat the oven to 190°C/fan 170°C/gas 5. Spread the butter on 1 side of each slice of bread, then spread the marmalade thickly on top. Arrange about half of the bread in a single layer in the base of a 1.5-litre shallow ovenproof dish. Sprinkle the sultanas over, then cut the remaining bread into triangles and arrange on top.
2 Lightly whisk the double cream, milk, eggs and sugar in a bowl and pass through a sieve. Scrape the vanilla seeds from the pod into the mixture. Discard the pod. Pour over the bread and leave to soak for 5 minutes.
3 Put the dish in a deep roasting tin and pour in enough hot water to come halfway up the sides of the dish. Bake for 30 minutes until the top is golden and the custard has lightly set but still has a good wobble. Take the dish out of the roasting tin and leave to cool for about 10 minutes.
4 Preheat the grill to high. Dust the pudding with icing sugar and pop under the grill for about 1 minute until golden – watch it carefully, as it can brown very fast. Serve warm with whipped cream.

Syrupy marmalade steamed pudding

SERVES 4–6 TAKES **1 HOUR 50 MINUTES TO MAKE**

100g softened butter,
  plus extra for greasing
125ml golden syrup
Finely grated zest and juice (about 100ml)
  of 2 oranges
100g caster sugar
2 large eggs
2 tbsp orange marmalade
100g self-raising flour
50ml milk

1 Grease a 1-litre pudding basin with butter. Put 2 tablespoons of the golden syrup and 2 teaspoons orange zest in the bottom of the pudding basin.
2 In a bowl, beat the butter and sugar together until creamy and light. Add the eggs, 1 at a time, mixing well after each addition. Beat in the marmalade. Sift over half the flour and gently fold into the mixture. Add a little milk to loosen, then sift in the rest of the flour and fold into the mixture with the remaining milk until you have a soft dropping consistency.
3 Spoon into the prepared basin and cover with a disc of buttered baking paper (butter-side-down). Cover with a piece of foil pleated in the centre to allow room for the pudding to expand. Tie with string to secure.
4 Put an inverted saucer in the base of a large pan and place the pudding basin on top. This stops the pudding being too near the heat source. Pour in enough boiling water to come three-quarters of the way up the side of the basin. Bring to the boil and cover with a tight-fitting lid. Reduce the heat and simmer gently for 1½ hours, adding more hot water to the pan to prevent it boiling dry, if necessary.
5 Meanwhile, to make the sticky marmalade sauce, put the remaining golden syrup, orange zest and juice in a small saucepan and bring to the boil. Simmer over a very gentle heat for 5-6 minutes, until thick and syrupy.
6 Remove the pudding from the pan, turn it out onto a serving plate and pour over the sauce to serve.

delicious.tip

PREVENTING CURDLING
Make sure the eggs and butter are at room temperature before using as this will prevent them curdling as you beat the mixture.

Syrupy marmalade
steamed pudding

Chocolate
sponge pudding

Bake for 35–40 minutes, then test by inserting a skewer into the middle. It might not come out quite clean – expect some stickiness. Cool for a good 20–30 minutes before cutting into squares and serving with unsweetened cream.

Self-saucing lemon sponge
SERVES 6 TAKES **1 HOUR TO MAKE**

75g butter, plus extra for greasing
190g golden caster sugar
Finely grated zest and juice of 3 lemons
3 eggs, separated
75g self-raising flour
200ml milk
Whipped cream, to serve (optional)

1 Lightly grease a 1.5-litre ovenproof dish with a little butter. Preheat the oven to 180°C/fan 160°C/gas 4.
2 Using an electric hand whisk, beat together the butter, sugar and lemon zest until softened. Beat in the egg yolks, one at a time, then mix in the flour. Gradually stir in the milk and lemon juice. The mixture will look slightly curdled, but don't panic – this is meant to happen.
3 In a clean, absolutely grease-free bowl, whisk the egg whites until they form soft peaks. Using a large metal spoon, fold them into the lemon mixture. Pour the mixture into the prepared dish and bake in the oven for 40 minutes, until the sponge layer is firm and golden on top.
4 Divide the pudding between bowls and serve immediately, with a spoonful of whipped cream, if you like.

Chocolate sponge pudding
SERVES 6–8 TAKES **1 HOUR TO MAKE**

225g unsalted butter, plus extra for greasing
100g plain, bitter chocolate (70% cocoa)
2 large eggs
250g soft dark brown sugar
200g plain flour
1 tsp baking powder
1 tbsp strong coffee (instant coffee is fine)

1 Preheat the oven to 180°C/fan 160°C/ gas 4. Dice the butter and chocolate. Put in a bowl over a pan of simmering water, without letting the water touch the base of the bowl, and gently melt. Don't stir as it is easy to overwork bitter chocolate.
2 In a bowl, beat the eggs and sugar until pale(ish) and smooth. Fold in the chocolate mix, then the flour and baking powder and beat until smooth. Finally, beat in the coffee and 250ml boiling water. You now have a smooth batter.
3 Line an 18cm square tin with butter and baking paper and pour in the chocolate and coffee batter.

Dense, sticky puddings are great with cream, custard or ice cream.

White chocolate and raspberry trifle
SERVES 6–8 TAKES **40 MINUTES TO MAKE**

· ·

115g caster sugar
115g softened butter
2 large eggs
115g self-raising flour
200g white chocolate, chopped
450g fresh or frozen raspberries,
  plus extra for decorating
3 tbsp icing sugar
250ml double cream
300g mascarpone
100ml amaretto liqueur
500ml thick, ready-made custard

· ·

1 Preheat the oven to 190°C/fan 170°C/gas 5.
Cream together the caster sugar and butter
until light and creamy. Add the eggs, 1 at a time,
mixing well after each addition. Sift over the flour
and fold in gently. Stir two-thirds of the white
chocolate into the batter along with a quarter
of the raspberries. Place 12 fairy cake cases in
a bun tin and half-fill each with the batter.
Bake for 12–15 minutes, until golden brown.
2 Lightly crush half the remaining raspberries
with 1 tbsp icing sugar in a bowl and set aside.
In a bowl, briefly whisk the cream, mascarpone
and the remaining icing sugar together until just
combined and smooth.
3 Discard the fairy cake cases, halve the cakes
horizontally and use to cover the bottom of a
large glass dish, pressing each cake against the
side so that there are no gaps. Pour the amaretto
over the cakes and top with crushed and whole
remaining raspberries and white chocolate. Top
with custard, then spoon over the mascarpone
cream. Decorate with the extra raspberries.

delicious.**tip**
SAVING TIME
This dessert can be made a day ahead and chilled in
the fridge overnight. If you are really short of time,
you could substitute trifle sponges or amaretti
biscuits for the white chocolate cupcakes.

White chocolate and
raspberry trifle

Cheesecake cups with fresh raspberry sauce

4 tablespoons of icing sugar in a bowl and whisk by hand until smooth – don't use an electric whisk. Add the cream and continue to whisk, gradually adding 2 tablespoons of the orange juice, until soft peaks form. Divide between the cases and chill for 1 hour.
4 Meanwhile, put the raspberries in a pan with the remaining icing sugar and orange juice. Place over a medium heat, stirring to dissolve the icing sugar, then simmer for 2–3 minutes. Pass through a fine sieve and discard the pips. Set aside to cool and thicken slightly.
5 Top each cup with fresh raspberries and spoon over the raspberry sauce to serve.

Chocolate mousse
SERVES 4 TAKES **25 MINUTES TO MAKE**

3 very fresh eggs, separated
250g plain chocolate, chopped
2 tbsp brandy or rum
300ml double cream

1 In a small bowl, lightly whip the egg yolks. Melt 200g of the chocolate with the brandy or rum in a heatproof bowl set over a pan of simmering water. Don't allow the water to touch the base of the bowl. Stir occasionally until smooth.
2 Remove from the heat and gradually add the beaten yolks to the chocolate. Fold in the cream.
3 In a large, clean bowl, whisk the egg whites with an electric hand whisk until soft peaks form, then fold into the chocolate mixture. Pour evenly into glasses or cups, cover with cling film and chill for at least 3 hours or until firm.
4 Grate the remaining chocolate into small shards and sprinkle over the top before serving.

delicious.tip
USING RAW EGGS
Raw meat and eggs may contain salmonella bacteria, which can cause food poisoning. Eggs are normally protected by their shells, but minimize risk by washing eggs before cracking them and only using high-quality, farm-fresh eggs.

Cheesecake cups with raspberry sauce
MAKES 9 TAKES **2 HOURS TO MAKE**

100g plain chocolate (70% cocoa solids),
  broken up
40g unsalted butter
250g digestive biscuits
300g cream cheese
6 tbsp icing sugar
142ml double cream
Juice of 1 orange
250g raspberries, plus extra to decorate

1 Line a muffin tin with 9 paper muffin cases. Crush the digestive biscuits (whizz them in the food processor or put them in a freezer bag and crush them with a rolling pin). Put the chocolate and butter into a medium pan over a low heat. Stir occasionally until melted. Remove from the heat and stir in the biscuits.
2 Spread the mixture across the base and up the sides of each paper case. Chill for 15 minutes.
3 For the filling, put the cream cheese and

Rhubarb with Greek yogurt and short biscuits

SERVES 4 TAKES **1 HOUR TO MAKE**

Juice of 2 oranges
2 tbsp caster sugar
3 slices fresh ginger
1kg forced rhubarb, cut into strips
1 tub Greek yogurt

For the biscuits
250g butter, chilled
400g plain flour
125g caster sugar
Zest of 1 orange

1 Make the biscuits. A food processor is great for this: just pulse all the ingredients together until the butter has disappeared into the flour, leaving you with a rough powder. Otherwise, rub the butter into the flour and sugar by hand as if you were making a crumble topping (see p.240). Then add the orange juice and knead the mixture together into a rough ball. This sometimes looks unlikely, but have faith – it will happen!
2 Roll the dough into a cigar shape (approx 5cm in diameter) and wrap it in clingfilm. Chill in the fridge for at least half an hour. It must rest and be cold before you start to slice it.
3 Preheat the oven to 180°C/fan 160°C/gas 4. Unwrap the biscuit mixture. Using a sharp knife, slice the mixture into discs about 0.5cm thick, then lay them on a baking tray about 2cm apart. For beautifully pale-yellow biscuits cook for about 15–20 minutes, or until they have spread a little and look slightly "fractured" on the surface. Lift from the tray only when completely cool.
4 Meanwhile, squeeze the orange juice into a large pan and add the sugar, ginger and rhubarb. Toss everything together and gently bring to a simmer. Cover and remove from the heat. You can serve the rhubarb mixture warm after about 10 minutes, or leave it to cool further. Serve with the biscuits and Greek yogurt. In the unlikely event that you have biscuits left over, they can be stored in an airtight tin or box.

Rhubarb with Greek yogurt and short biscuits

Bramley apple pancakes with toffee sauce and yogurt
SERVES 4–6 TAKES **30 MINUTES TO MAKE**

50g butter
225g self-raising flour
2 tsp baking powder
50g caster sugar
175ml buttermilk
2 eggs
175ml full-cream milk
2 bramley cooking apples (about 500g in weight)
1 tsp vanilla extract
Greek-style natural yogurt, to serve

For the toffee sauce
50g unsalted butter
50g light muscovado sugar
2 tbsp golden syrup
2 tbsp double cream

1 Make the toffee sauce. Put the butter, sugar and golden syrup into a small saucepan and bring slowly to the boil, stirring. Reduce the heat and simmer for 3 minutes or until thick. Stir in the cream, then remove from the heat and set aside to cool.
2 Make clarified butter by melting the butter in a pan. Remove from the heat and stand for a few minutes. Pour off the clear butter into a bowl and reserve. Discard the milky-white solids at the bottom of the pan.
3 Sift the flour, baking powder and sugar into a bowl. Make a well in the centre, then add the buttermilk, eggs and milk. Whisk, working from the centre outwards, until the batter is smooth and thick.
4 Peel, core and coarsely grate the apples and measure out 300g. Stir the grated apple into the batter with the vanilla.
5 Heat a large, non-stick frying pan over a medium heat. Brush the base with a little of the clarified butter. Add 4 large spoonfuls of the batter, spaced well apart, and cook for 2 minutes or until bubbles appear on top of the pancakes and they are golden brown underneath. Flip and cook for another minute. Transfer to a plate and

keep warm while you cook the rest – you should be able to make about 16 pancakes in all.
6 Pile the pancakes onto warmed plates, top with a large spoonful of yogurt and drizzle with the toffee sauce. Serve immediately.

Apple crumble ice cream
SERVES 8 TAKES **3 HOURS 30 MINUTES TO MAKE**
PLUS **OVERNIGHT CHILLING**

5 large egg yolks
120g golden caster sugar
300ml full-cream milk
284ml double cream
2 tsp vanilla extract
2 bramley cooking apples (about 500g in weight)
25g unsalted butter
50g golden granulated sugar, or to taste

For the crumble
75g plain flour
50g butter, chilled and cubed
50g golden caster sugar

1 Whisk the egg yolks and caster sugar together in a bowl until pale and creamy. Pour the milk and cream into a small pan and bring just to the boil. Gradually stir the hot milk into the yolk mixture. Return to the pan over a gentle heat and cook, stirring, until thick enough to lightly coat the back of a wooden spoon. Stir in the vanilla extract, then set aside to cool. Chill overnight.
2 The next day, core and peel the apples and cut them into 1cm cubes. Melt the butter in a large, heavy-based frying pan, add the sugar and cook over a medium heat until it resembles a toffee-coloured sauce. Add the chopped apples and cook for 5–7 minutes or until the fruit is tender but not falling apart. Check the sweetness – add more sugar if it is too sour. Set aside to cool.
3 Preheat the oven to 190°C/fan 170°C/gas 5. Make the crumble. Sift the plain flour and a pinch of salt into a bowl, add the chilled butter and rub in until it resembles crumbs (see Making a Crumble Topping, p.240). Add the sugar and work the mixture between your fingers until it

Vanilla ice cream

starts to clump together. Spread over a large baking tray and bake for 10 minutes until the crumble is biscuit-coloured. Set aside to cool.
4 To make the ice cream, churn the custard in an ice cream maker, or churn by hand (see below). Add the cooked apple mixture and baked crumble pieces, churn to lightly mix through, then serve.

Vanilla ice cream

SERVES 8–10 TAKES **7 HOURS TO MAKE**

568ml double cream
568ml full-fat milk
2 vanilla pods, split lengthways
5 large egg yolks
225g golden caster sugar

1 Heat the cream, milk and vanilla pods in a large, heavy-based saucepan until almost boiling, then remove from the heat and leave to infuse for 20 minutes. Remove the vanilla pods, scrape out the seeds and mix into the cream.

2 Put the yolks, sugar and a pinch of salt in a bowl and beat for 3 minutes until thick and pale, leaving a ribbon trail. Gradually beat in the cream mix, then pour into a clean pan.
3 Cook over a very low heat, stirring constantly, for about 10 minutes until thickened. The custard should coat the back of the spoon. Pour into a bowl and cover with cling film. Cool for 1 hour, then chill for at least 2 hours.
4 Churn the custard in an ice-cream maker or by hand (see below), until thick but still soft enough to be spoonable. Transfer to a plastic, lidded, 2-litre container and put in the freezer for at least 3 hours or until firm enough to scoop.

delicious.**tip**
CHURNING ICE CREAM BY HAND
To make ice cream by hand, pour the mixture into a large freezer-proof dish and put it in the freezer. After 45 minutes, remove and whisk vigorously, then return to the freezer. Whisk every 30 minutes as the mixture freezes over 2–3 hours.

indulgent desserts

After dinner minty chocolate mousse
SERVES 6 TAKES **1 HOUR 40 MINUTES TO MAKE**

75g caster sugar
Handful of fresh mint leaves (about 10g),
  plus extra to decorate
100g plain chocolate
  (minimum 70% cocoa solids)
2 tbsp strong espresso coffee
142ml double cream
2 large egg whites

1 Pound the caster sugar and mint leaves using a mortar and pestle until you have green-coloured sugar. Set aside. Break up the chocolate and put into a heatproof bowl with the coffee. Sit the bowl over a pan of barely simmering water (making sure the bowl doesn't touch the water) until just melted. Stir, remove from the heat and cool.
2 Whip the cream with about one-third of the mint sugar until soft peaks form. In a clean, grease-free bowl, whip the egg whites until these form soft peaks. Add the remaining mint sugar a little at a time, until the mixture becomes soft and glossy.
3 When the chocolate has completely cooled, fold in the stiff egg whites until smooth. Then fold in the mint cream until smooth and no traces of white are left. Spoon into 6 glasses and chill for at least 1 hour until set. Decorate each with a mint leaf.
WINE NOTE This goes well with the lightest, freshest sweet wines, such as a sweet German Riesling – or a good strong coffee!

Chocolate fudge pots with blueberries in cassis
SERVES 6 TAKES **1 HOUR 20 MINUTES TO MAKE**

200g plain chocolate (up to 50% cocoa solids),
  broken into pieces
100g unsalted butter, cut into 6 pieces
4 eggs, separated
150g blueberries
150ml cassis (blackcurrant) liqueur
6 tbsp Greek yogurt, crème fraîche
  or fromage frais, to serve

1 Put the chocolate and butter in a heatproof bowl. Melt in a microwave on medium for 30-second bursts, until melted. Stir well to combine.
2 Whisk the egg whites to soft peaks. Add the yolks to the chocolate mixture and mix together until smooth and glossy, then gently fold in the whisked egg whites. Carefully spoon the mixture into pots and chill for at least 1 hour.
3 Put the blueberries into a pan with the cassis liqueur. Bring just to the boil, to soften, then remove the fruit with a slotted spoon and put in a bowl. Boil the cassis for 2–3 minutes, until reduced and syrupy. Pour over the blueberries and cool. To serve, top each chocolate fudge pot with a generous tablespoon of Greek yogurt, crème fraîche or fromage frais. Crown with blueberries and cassis syrup.
WINE NOTE Choose a wine that can hold up against the acidity of the blueberries. Hungarian Tokaji has enough acidity and goes well with chocolate.

Sweet, plump blueberries and sumptuous rich chocolate combine – truly divine!

Chocolate fudge pots
with blueberries
in cassis

Chilled lemon soufflé

and the chestnuts to this mix and stir to combine. Pour into the loaf or cake tin. Chill in the fridge overnight. To serve the torte, invert onto a plate, remove the cling film and dust with icing sugar and cocoa. To cut the torte, dip the knife into hot water between slices.

WINE NOTE Try a luxurious, toffee-scented sweet wine from Australia, such as a liqueur muscat from Rutherglen.

Chilled lemon soufflé

SERVES 8 TAKES **5 HOURS TO MAKE**

4 gelatine leaves
Finely grated zest and juice of 3 unwaxed lemons
6 eggs, separated
300g golden caster sugar
425ml whipping cream

1 Take a 24cm length of baking paper and fold it into 3, then tie it around a 1-litre straight-sided soufflé dish, so that the paper extends 2–4cm above the top. Set aside. Immerse the gelatine leaves in plenty of cold water and set aside.
2 Put the lemon juice and zest into a large heatproof bowl with the egg yolks and sugar. Bring a saucepan of water to the boil, then turn off the heat. Place the bowl over the pan of hot water, making sure the bottom of the bowl is not touching the water. Using an electric hand whisk, whisk the lemon mixture for about 5 minutes, until thickened and pale in colour.
3 Heat 2–3 tablespoons of water in a small pan. When hot, take the soaked gelatine and squeeze out any excess water, drop the leaves into the pan and immediately remove the pan from the heat. Stir until dissolved, then whisk into the thickened lemon mixture. Remove the bowl from the pan and set aside to cool completely.
4 In a clean, grease-free bowl, whisk the egg whites to soft peaks. In another clean bowl, whisk the whipping cream until softly thickened (be careful not to beat the cream to stiff peaks or it will be too thick to fold into the soufflé). Fold the whipped cream into the lemon mixture until no traces of white are left. Then fold in the egg white,

Chestnut and chocolate torte

SERVES 10–12 TAKES **30 MINUTES TO MAKE**
PLUS **OVERNIGHT CHILLING**

300g ready-cooked chestnuts
300g bitter dark chocolate
  (at least 70% cocoa solids)
250g unsalted butter, softened
200g icing sugar, plus extra to dust
Cocoa powder, to dust

1 Put the chestnuts into a food processor and whizz to grind finely. Set aside. Lightly wet a 900g loaf tin or 20cm round cake tin with a little water, then line with cling film, smoothing out any creases.
2 Melt the chocolate in a bowl set over a pan of simmering water – don't let the water touch the base of the bowl. Stir it as little as possible, as it is easy to overwork very dark chocolate. Remove from the heat and set aside.
3 In a separate bowl, beat the butter and sugar until pale and fluffy. Add the melted chocolate

again until no traces of white are left. Pour into the prepared dish and chill for at least 4 hours or until set. To serve, carefully remove the string and paper collar from around the soufflé (slide a wet knife between the paper and soufflé to make this easier). Serve immediately.

Summer fruit gateau

SERVES 12 TAKES **1 HOUR 30 MINUTES TO MAKE** PLUS **OVERNIGHT COOLING (OPTIONAL)**

Butter, for greasing
Flour, for dusting
150g caster sugar
6 eggs
25g cornflour
125g plain flour
2 ripe peaches
250g strawberries
250g raspberries
2 tbsp icing sugar
75g flaked almonds, toasted, to decorate
25g blueberries, to decorate

For the custard cream
250ml milk
1 vanilla pod, deseeded and seeds reserved
  (see p.256)
1 egg
50g caster sugar
25g plain flour
568ml double cream

1 For the best results, make the sponge the day before you make the gateau: this isn't essential but will make the sponge easier to slice into layers. Preheat the oven to 190°C/fan 170°C/gas 5. Grease a 23cm round, deep, loose-bottomed cake tin. Cut a disc of baking paper to fit the base of the tin and put it in. Dust the inside of the tin with flour. Put the sugar and eggs into the bowl of an electric mixer. Whisk for 10 minutes until pale and doubled in volume. Sift over the cornflour and flour and carefully fold in with a large metal spoon until just mixed. Pour into the tin and bake for 35–40 minutes until risen and pale golden.

Cool for 10 minutes, then turn out to cool completely. Store in an airtight container overnight.
2 The next day, stone and slice the peaches and set aside 12 slices for decorating. Cut 3 of the strawberries into quarters and chop the remainder. Reserve 6 raspberries, put the rest in a liquidizer with the icing sugar, and purée. Chill.
3 Make the custard cream. Put the milk, split vanilla pod and seeds in a pan and bring to the boil. Set aside for 15 minutes. Mix the egg and sugar in a bowl until creamy. Stir in the flour, then whisk in the hot milk. Return to the pan and cook, stirring, over a medium heat for 2–3 minutes until thick. Discard the vanilla pod. Tip into a bowl, cover the surface with cling film to prevent a skin forming, and allow to cool.
4 In a separate bowl, whisk the cream to soft peaks. Mix half the cream into the cooled custard.
5 Cut the cake horizontally into 3 thin discs. Spread the bottom disc with a third of the purée and a third of the custard cream. Push in half the peach slices and half the chopped strawberries, and top with half the remaining purée and another cake disc. Spread with half the remaining custard cream, the remaining peach slices and chopped strawberries and the rest of the purée. Finish with the top cake disc. Smooth the rest of the custard over the sides of the cake.
6 Push the almonds into the custard cream around the sides of the cake. Spread a little of the remaining double cream on top of the cake, and put the remainder in a piping bag fitted with a star-shaped nozzle. Pipe a cream swirl around the edge. Pipe a rosette in the centre, and arrange the reserved peach slices and strawberry quarters around it so they stand up. Arrange the reserved raspberries and blueberries on top. Chill and serve within 24 hours.

> delicious.**tip**
>
> **MIXING BY HAND**
> If you don't have an electric mixer, whisk the sugar and eggs (step 1) in a bowl over a saucepan of simmering water (don't let the water touch the bottom of the bowl) for about 15 minutes. Cool before adding the cornflour and flour.

Italian baked almond cheesecake

SERVES 8 TAKES **2 HOURS TO MAKE**

200g amaretti biscuits, crushed
50g unsalted butter, melted
Seeds from1 vanilla pod (see below)
500g ricotta
125g golden caster sugar
250g tub mascarpone
100g ground almonds
2 tbsp cornflour
3 large eggs
Grated zest of 1 lemon
Handful of flaked almonds
Icing sugar, for dusting

1 Preheat the oven to 180°C/fan 160°C/gas 4. Put the crushed biscuits into a large bowl, pour over the melted butter and mix well. Pour the mixture into the base of a 20cm non-stick springform cake tin, pressing down firmly with the back of a spoon. Chill in the fridge for 5–10 minutes.
2 Meanwhile, put the vanilla seeds into a large mixing bowl. Add the ricotta, sugar, mascarpone, almonds, cornflour, eggs and lemon zest and beat until smooth. Pour the mixture into the prepared tin and scatter with the flaked almonds.
3 Place on a baking sheet and bake in the oven for 45 minutes until golden. Turn off the oven, open the door and leave the cheesecake inside until completely cool. Chill for a further hour, then dust with icing sugar and serve with fresh cream.

delicious.technique
DESEEDING A VANILLA POD

1. *Hold the vanilla pod on the board. Use the tip of a sharp knife to slice it lengthways.*

2. *Using a teaspoon, scrape down firmly along the pod to release the sticky seeds.*

Basic Swiss meringue

MAKES 6 LARGE MERINGUES
TAKES **1 HOUR 30 MINUTES TO MAKE** PLUS **COOLING**

3 large egg whites
175g white caster sugar
1/2 tsp vanilla extract

1 Preheat the oven to 140°C/fan 120°C/gas 1. In a large, grease-free mixing bowl, whisk the egg whites to form soft peaks. While continuously whisking, slowly add the sugar – 1 tablespoon at a time – until you have a stiff, glossy white meringue mixture. Whisk in the vanilla extract until combined.
2 Line a baking tray with baking paper, fixing it in place with a tiny dot of meringue in each corner. Using a metal spoon, place 6 craggy heaps of meringue on the baking paper, well spaced apart.
3 Bake for 1¼ hours for mallowy centres, or 1½ hours if you prefer crisper meringues. Peel off the baking paper, then transfer mallowy meringues to a wire rack to cool. Leave crisper ones in the turned-off oven for at least 4 hours to cool slowly, then transfer to a wire rack.

Summer fruit Eton Mess

SERVES 6 TAKES **35 MINUTES TO MAKE**

3 large meringues (see recipe above)
150g raspberries
150g blueberries
250g strawberries
4 tbsp cassis (blackcurrant) liqueur
500g Greek yogurt
Sprigs of fresh mint

1 Hull and chop the strawberries. Put them in a bowl with the raspberries and blueberries. Add the cassis, gently toss and set aside for 15 minutes until juicy.
2 Put the yogurt in a large bowl and fold in three-quarters of the berries, leaving the juice behind. Roughly crumble in 3 large cooked meringues and briefly mix. Spoon into 6 glasses, top with the remaining berries and garnish with fresh mint.

Fig and Marsala trifle with toasted meringue

SERVES 6 TAKES **35 MINUTES TO MAKE**

100g high-quality white chocolate
150g Madeira sponge
6 tbsp Marsala
3 fresh figs
1 pomegranate
500g fresh egg custard
125g granulated sugar
2 egg whites

1 Break up the chocolate and melt it in a heatproof bowl over a pan of simmering water. Remove from the heat and stir until just smooth. Cool slightly.
2 Cut the Madeira sponge into small cubes and divide between 6 serving glasses. Drizzle each pile of sponge with 1 tablespoon Marsala. Cut the fresh figs into eighths and arrange 4 pieces on top of the sponge in each glass.
3 Peel the pomegranate and extract the seeds. Divide the seeds between the 6 glasses.
4 Gradually stir the fresh egg custard into the melted chocolate, until thickened. Spoon into glasses. Cover and chill until needed.
5 Put the granulated sugar and 2 tablespoons of water into a heavy saucepan. Bring slowly to the boil and simmer gently for 15 minutes.
6 Meanwhile, whisk 2 egg whites in a clean, grease-free bowl until they form stiff peaks. Using an electric mixer, pour the hot syrup onto the egg whites in a steady stream while whisking, until it is stiff and shiny. Cover with cling film.
7 Just before serving, spoon the meringue onto the custard. Toast the tips of the meringue under a very hot grill for 30 seconds (or use a blow torch). Serve sprinkled with silver balls.

White chocolate and meringue is a combination made in heaven.

Fig and Marsala trifle with toasted meringue

Italian baked almond cheesecake

Baked honeycomb Alaska
SERVES 10–12 TAKES **50 MINUTES TO MAKE** PLUS **COOLING**

115g butter, softened, plus extra for greasing
115g caster sugar
2 large eggs
85g self-raising flour
25g cocoa powder
1–2 tbsp milk

For the Alaska topping
4 large egg whites
170g caster sugar
75ml Amaretto liqueur
225g raspberries
500ml vanilla ice cream
1 Crunchie bar (34g), crushed

1 Preheat the oven to 190°C/fan 170°C/gas 5. Grease a 20cm, round cake tin and line the base with a disc of baking paper. Using a mixer or electric hand whisk, cream the butter and sugar until light and fluffy. Add the eggs, 1 at a time, whisking after each is added. Sift in the flour and cocoa and mix gently, adding enough milk to make a soft dropping consistency. Spoon evenly into the tin and bake for 20 minutes or until a skewer inserted into the centre comes out clean. Cool the cake completely.
2 Shortly before serving, preheat the oven to a very hot setting – 240°C/fan 220°C/gas 9. In a clean, grease-free bowl, use an electric hand whisk to beat the egg whites to stiff peaks. Slowly pour in the caster sugar, whisking all the time, until the meringue forms glossy white peaks.
3 Place the chocolate cake in the centre of a shallow ovenproof dish, and prick it all over with a thin skewer. Drizzle over the Amaretto and scatter over half the raspberries. Cut the ice cream into 4 and pile it on top of the raspberries. Top with the remaining berries and sprinkle over the Crunchie crumbs.
4 Using a spatula, cover with the meringue, ensuring that the filling and cake are completely covered, leaving no gaps. Smooth the meringue into swirled peaks and bake for 3–4 minutes, until lightly golden. Serve immediately.

Stem ginger and dark muscovado puddings
SERVES 6 TAKES **1 HOUR TO MAKE**

150g softened butter, plus extra for greasing
240g stem ginger from a jar, plus 4 tbsp of the syrup
175g dark muscovado sugar
315ml double cream
175g plain flour
$1/2$ tsp ground ginger
$1/2$ tsp baking powder
$1/2$ rounded tsp bicarbonate of soda
2 eggs, beaten
2 tbsp molasses sugar

1 Preheat the oven to 200°C/fan 180°C/gas 4 and put a baking tray on the middle shelf. Lightly grease 6 medium (120ml) non-stick pudding moulds with a little butter.
2 Put the stem ginger and its syrup into a food processor and whizz until finely chopped but not completely smooth. Spoon half of this into a small pan and add 75g muscovado sugar, half the butter and 200ml of double cream. Set aside.
3 Sift the flour, ground ginger, baking powder and bicarbonate of soda into a mixing bowl. Add the eggs, and the remaining butter and muscovado sugar. Mix the molasses sugar with 1 tablespoon of the cream and add to the bowl. Whisk together until smooth. Whisk in 150ml warm water and the remaining whizzed ginger.
4 Spoon the pudding mixture evenly into the prepared moulds, put on the hot baking tray and cook for 20 minutes. Meanwhile, stir the ginger sauce over a low heat until heated. Turn out the puddings onto 6 warmed plates, pour over the sauce and serve with the remaining cream.

Soft and syrupy, steamed puddings are a taste of nostalgia.

Baked honeycomb Alaska

Rice pudding with marinated strawberries

until smooth, then beat the mascarpone into the egg and sugar mixture, along with the vanilla extract.

3 Whisk the egg whites in a clean, grease-free bowl until they are just beginning to show signs of stiffening, then gradually whisk in the reserved caster sugar to form a soft meringue. Don't let the mixture become too stiff – the tips of the peaks should fall over, not stand upright. Gently fold into the mascarpone mixture.

4 Briefly dip half the sponge fingers, one at a time, into the coffee mixture and then lay them side by side on a flat, rectangular serving plate. Spoon over half of the mascarpone mixture and spread out evenly. Cover with another layer of coffee-soaked sponge fingers and the rest of the mascarpone mixture. Chill in the fridge for 1¹/₂ hours.

5 Mix the remaining molasses sugar with the dark muscovado sugar, using your fingers to rub and separate the grains, as you would when making pastry. This helps to remove any lumps. Sprinkle the sugar mix over the top of the dessert and chill for another 15–20 minutes to allow time for the sugar to dissolve before serving.

Coffee and rum tiramisu with molasses topping

SERVES 6–8 TAKES **2 HOURS 30 MINUTES TO MAKE**

150ml freshly made strong dark coffee
4 tbsp dark rum
5 tsp molasses sugar
40g golden caster sugar
2 eggs, separated
250g tub mascarpone
Few drops of vanilla extract
20 sponge finger biscuits
1 tbsp dark muscovado sugar

1 Mix the coffee with the rum and 2 teaspoons of the molasses sugar. Stir until the sugar has dissolved, then pour the liquid into a small, shallow dish.

2 Set aside 2 tablespoons of the caster sugar. Beat the egg yolks and the remaining caster sugar together in a bowl for about 4 minutes, or until pale and as thick as a mousse. Beat the mascarpone cheese in another bowl

Rice pudding with marinated strawberries

SERVES 4 TAKES **50 MINUTES TO MAKE**

125g caster sugar
1 egg, plus 3 egg yolks
400ml milk
142ml double cream
1 vanilla pod, deseeded and seeds reserved (see p.256)
125g pudding rice
Vanilla ice cream, to serve
Strawberry coulis, to serve

For the marinated strawberries
250g small strawberries, hulled and halved, plus 4 whole strawberries to serve
25g icing sugar, sifted
Juice of 1 small lemon
1 tbsp chopped fresh basil

1 Whisk 50g of the sugar with the egg and egg yolks in a bowl until fluffy. Put 100ml milk and all of the cream in a saucepan over a medium heat. Add half the vanilla pod and seeds and bring to the boil, stirring. Slowly stir into the egg mixture. Pass through a sieve into a jug (discarding the solids), mix and set aside to cool.

2 Meanwhile, boil the rice in a medium, non-stick pan for 2–3 minutes. Drain and refresh. Return to the pan and stir in the remaining sugar, milk, vanilla pod and seeds. Bring to the boil, reduce the heat and simmer for 15–20 minutes, stirring frequently. Drain well.

3 Preheat the oven to 140°C/fan 120°C/gas 1. Wrap a double layer of foil tightly around the bottom half of 4 round, deep, metal rings (8cm each), to seal well. Place on a baking tray.

4 Transfer the drained rice to a bowl and stir in the cooled cream. Divide between the rings. Bake for 25–30 minutes in the oven.

5 Meanwhile, put the halved strawberries, icing sugar, lemon juice, ½ teaspoon of ground black pepper and basil in a large bowl, mix well and leave to macerate for at least 15 minutes. Transfer each rice pudding to a serving plate, and remove the foil and ring.

6 Spoon over the strawberries. Top with a scoop of vanilla ice cream and decorate each plate with some coulis and a whole strawberry.

Orange and date sticky toffee pudding
SERVES 6 TAKES **20 MINUTES TO MAKE**

1 large, plain Madeira cake
6 Medjool dates, sliced
170g jar of toffee sauce
Zest of 1 orange

1 Preheat the oven to 160°C/fan 140°C/gas 3. Slice the cake and layer it vertically (as shown below) with the dates in a 1-litre baking dish.

2 Pour over the toffee sauce and scatter with the zest of 1 orange. Cover with foil and bake for 15 minutes. Serve piping hot with clotted cream or ice cream.

Orange and date sticky toffee pudding

Crêpes suzette

Crêpes suzette

SERVES 4 TAKES **30 MINUTES TO MAKE**

125g plain flour
1 egg, beaten
275–300ml semi-skimmed milk
1 teaspoon icing sugar
Grated zest of $1/2$ orange
Vegetable or sunflower oil, for frying

For the sauce
40g caster sugar
40g butter
Juice of 2 small oranges
2 tbsp Cointreau
2 tbsp brandy
Few strips of orange zest
Icing sugar, for dusting

1 Make a pancake batter mix (see Perfect Pancakes, p.37), adding 1 teaspoon of icing sugar and the grated zest of $1/2$ orange to the batter. Rest and cook as before (see also right).

2 Fold the pancakes into eighths or quarters, depending on their size, and then set aside somewhere warm.
3 Make the sauce. Slowly heat the caster sugar in a heavy-based frying pan, stirring as it gently dissolves. Increase the heat and cook until golden. Add the butter and orange juice and cook until the sauce is simmering. Stir in 2 tablespoons of Cointreau and allow the sauce to bubble lightly.
4 Return the folded pancakes to the pan and pour over 2 tablespoons of brandy. Flambé the sauce by igniting it with a long taper or match, standing back slightly from the pan.
5 Remove from the heat while the flames die down. Divide the hot pancakes and sauce between 4 plates. Scatter with thin strips of orange zest, dust lightly with icing sugar and serve with crème fraîche, if you like.

delicious.**technique**
MAKING CRÊPES

1. Heat a little oil and swirl it around to coat the pan, then pour off any excess. Holding the pan at an angle, pour in a ladleful of batter.

2. As you finish pouring the batter, tilt and whirl the pan so the batter spreads out, coating the whole of the base thinly and evenly.

3. When the crêpe has cooked to a pale gold underneath, use a long spatula to loosen the crêpe, then flip it over and back into the pan.

4. Cook until the second side is golden. Place on baking paper, putting a layer between each finished crêpe as you cook the rest of the batter.

Christmas
pudding

Christmas pudding

MAKES 2 1-LITRE PUDDINGS/10 MINI PUDDINGS
TAKES **6/3 HOURS TO MAKE** PLUS **OVERNIGHT SOAKING**

250g raisins
250g sultanas
75g blanched almonds, chopped
100g glacé cherries, halved
75g mixed peel
Zest of 1 lemon, finely grated
Zest of 1 orange, finely grated
100ml orange juice
75g fresh white breadcrumbs
1 tsp mixed spice
100g molasses sugar
100ml Grand Marnier
100ml milk
100g self-raising flour
1 large bramley cooking apple, grated
250g vegetable suet
4 eggs
Butter, for greasing

1 Put all the dried fruit, nuts, cherries and mixed peel into a large bowl. Add the zests, orange juice, breadcrumbs, spice, sugar, Grand Marnier and milk. Mix well, cover and leave overnight.
2 The next day, mix in the flour, apple, suet and eggs. Butter either 2 large (1-litre) pudding basins or 10 small (175ml) pudding basins. Fill a good three-quarters full with the mixture. Cover with a double layer of buttered, pleated, greaseproof paper, tied on with string.
3 For the large puddings: put an upturned saucer inside a large saucepan and sit 1 pudding on top. Repeat for the other pudding. Pour boiling water into each pan, reaching halfway up the basins. Cover and bring to the boil. Reduce to a simmer for 5 hours, topping up with boiling water if necessary, until a skewer comes out clean. For the mini puddings: preheat the oven to 180°C/fan 160°C/gas 4. Place in a deep roasting tin filled with boiling water to halfway up the pudding sides. Cover the tin with foil and bake for 2 hours.
4 Decorate with holly and dust with icing sugar if you like, and serve with brandy butter.

cakes

Lemon and rosemary cakes
MAKES 10 TAKES **1 HOUR TO MAKE**

100g spreadable butter
100g golden caster sugar
2 eggs
100g self-raising flour
1 tsp chopped fresh rosemary leaves,
  plus rosemary blossom, to decorate
Grated zest of 1 lemon
1 tbsp milk
100g icing sugar
Pink, blue and yellow food colourings
50g coloured sugar eggs

1 Preheat the oven to 180°C/fan 160°C/gas 4.
Line a bun tin with 10 paper cake cases.
2 Put the butter, sugar, eggs, self-raising flour,
chopped rosemary, lemon zest and milk in a large
bowl and beat with a wooden spoon or electric
whisk until smooth. Divide the mixture between
the paper cake cases, until each is about three-
quarters full.
3 Bake in the oven for 15–20 minutes, until risen,
golden and just firm to the touch. Remove from
the heat and allow to cool.
4 Mix the icing sugar with about 1 tablespoon of
cold water until smooth. Divide the icing between
3 bowls and add a drop of food colouring to each.
Drizzle a teaspoonful of the coloured icings onto
the cakes – one colour per cake, to make a pretty
collection. Put a sprig of rosemary blossom and
a sugar egg onto each one. The cakes can be kept
in a cake tin for up to 3 days.

Little raspberry muffins
MAKES 12 TAKES **25 MINUTES TO MAKE**

125g plain flour
1$^1/_2$ tsp baking powder
$^1/_2$ tsp bicarbonate of soda
1 tsp ground cinnamon
150g low-fat natural yogurt
100g light muscovado sugar
1 large egg
2 tbsp sunflower oil
1 tsp vanilla extract
125g fresh or frozen (and thawed) raspberries
1 tbsp raw or demerara sugar

1 Preheat the oven to 180°C/ fan 160°C/gas 4.
Line a 12-hole bun tray with 12 paper fairy
cake cases.
2 Sieve the flour, baking powder, bicarbonate
of soda and cinnamon into a bowl, then make
a well in the centre.
3 Put the yogurt, sugar, egg, sunflower oil and
vanilla extract into a jug and whisk with a fork,
then pour into the well in the flour. Mix together,
working from the centre, blending the flour into
the egg mixture a little at a time. Add the
raspberries and briefly fold in – don't overmix
or the raspberries will completely disintegrate.
4 Spoon a generous tablespoonful of the muffin
mixture into each paper case. Sprinkle each
muffin with the raw or demerara sugar. Bake
in the oven for 15 minutes, or until risen and
springy. To check if they're cooked, push a
cocktail stick into the centre of a muffin –
they're ready if the cocktail stick comes out
clean. Cool in the tin on a wire rack.

It's the delicacy of
these little muffins
that makes them
so appealing.

Mini Victoria sponge cakes
MAKES 8 TAKES **1 HOUR 10 MINUTES TO MAKE**

170g unsalted butter, softened,
  plus extra for greasing
170g caster sugar
3 eggs
1 tsp vanilla extract
170g self-raising flour
284ml whipping cream
Icing sugar, for dusting

For the strawberry jam
450g strawberries, hulled
500g preserving sugar
Juice of 1 lemon

1 First make the jam. Put 2 saucers in the freezer. Put the strawberries, sugar and lemon juice in a wide, deep pan over a medium-low heat, stirring until the sugar has dissolved. Bring to the boil for 6 minutes. Remove from the heat. Put a spoonful onto one of the chilled saucers and push against it – if it wrinkles, it's ready. If not, boil for another 2 minutes and repeat. Discard any scum from the surface and stand for 15 minutes. Spoon into sterilized jars. Cool and cover with waxed discs (the jam can be stored for up to 3 months).
2 Preheat the oven to 180°C/fan 160°C/gas 4. Grease 2 Yorkshire pudding trays (those with 4 straight-sided holes of about 8cm each), and cut discs of baking paper to sit in the bottom of each of the holes.
3 Put the butter and sugar in a large bowl and beat until fluffy. Lightly beat the eggs with the vanilla, then gradually beat into the creamed mixture, adding a little of the flour. Sift over the remaining flour and gently fold in until combined.
4 Divide evenly between the holes. Bake for 20 minutes until risen and golden. Cool in the tins, then turn out onto a wire rack and cool. Peel off the baking paper.
5 Lightly whip the cream to soft peaks. Spread onto 4 sponge bases, top with some of the jam and sandwich with the remaining sponge discs. Dust each with icing sugar to serve.

Little raspberry muffins

Mini Victoria sponge cakes

Snowflake
carrot cupcakes

Snowflake carrot cupcakes
MAKES 28 TAKES **2 HOURS 15 MINUTES TO MAKE**

250ml vegetable oil,
  plus extra for greasing
3 large carrots, about 350g, grated
75g macadamia nuts, chopped
75g pecan halves, chopped
170g mixed dried berries
  and cherries
100g ready-to-eat dried figs,
  apricots or prunes, roughly chopped
300g golden granulated sugar
300g self-raising flour
1 tsp mixed spice
1 tsp freshly grated nutmeg
2 tsp baking powder
4 large eggs, beaten

For the vanilla butter cream
125g salted butter, at room temperature
250g icing sugar, sifted
1 tsp vanilla extract

For the chocolate frosting
200g plain chocolate, roughly chopped
4 tbsp milk
100g unsalted butter
150g icing sugar

To decorate
500g white sugar paste
Red colouring paste
Icing sugar, for dusting
5g clear edible glitter flakes

1 Preheat the oven to 180°C/fan 160°C/gas 4.
Line 2 12-hole muffin tins with paper muffin cases.
In a large bowl, combine the vegetable oil, nuts,
carrots, dried fruit and sugar. Sift the flour, spices
and baking powder over the mixture and mix
thoroughly. Add the eggs and mix until combined.
2 Divide most of the mixture between the paper
cases, filling them about three-quarters full.
Bake for 22–25 minutes, until risen and golden.
Remove from the tin and place on a wire rack to
cool. Line 4 holes of one of the muffin tins with

muffin cases and fill these with the remaining mixture. Bake and cool as before.

3 Make the butter cream. Beat the butter until soft and creamy, then gradually add the icing sugar. Beat in the vanilla extract for about 1 minute, until light and fluffy.

4 Make the chocolate frosting. Put the chocolate, milk and butter in a small saucepan and heat gently until the chocolate and butter have melted. Take off the heat and stir in the icing sugar until smooth.

5 Pour the chocolate frosting over half the cupcakes and allow to set slightly before decorating. Spread the butter cream over the remaining cupcakes, using a small palette knife.

6 For the snowflake decorations, colour 250g of the white sugar paste to a rich red with the red colouring paste – knead until evenly coloured. Roll out to 3mm thick on a surface dusted with icing sugar, rotating it to stop it sticking. Using cutters, cut out a variety of snowflakes and place on a tray lined with baking paper. Repeat with the rest of the sugar paste. You will need 28 snowflakes in each colour. Set aside to dry and firm up.

7 Using a pastry brush, brush the snowflakes lightly with water. Sprinkle liberally with edible glitter and arrange on top of the cupcakes.

Apple, pecan and raisin muffins
MAKES 12 TAKES **45 MINUTES TO MAKE**

75g butter, melted, plus extra for greasing
300ml skimmed milk
125g oat bran
2 eggs
75g light muscovado sugar
$^1/_2$ tsp vanilla extract
60g wholemeal flour
125g self-raising flour
$^1/_2$ tsp salt
2 tsp baking powder
2 apples, peeled, cored and chopped
2 tbsp raisins soaked in 2 tbsp rum
  or orange juice
25g pecan nuts, toasted and chopped

1 Preheat the oven to 190°C/fan170°C/gas 5. Grease a 12-hole muffin tray with a little butter. Put the milk and oat bran in a bowl and set aside.

2 In a small bowl, beat the eggs, butter, sugar and vanilla. In a larger bowl, sift together the flours, salt and baking powder, then stir in the apple.

3 Mix the bran into the egg mixture, then briefly stir this into the dry ingredients. Divide the mixture into two. Briefly stir the raisins into one half, and the pecans into the other.

4 Put a heaped dessertspoonful of each mixture into the muffin holes so you have 6 of each flavour. Bake in the oven for 25–30 minutes, or until risen and golden. Cool in the tin for 10 minutes, then turn out onto a wire rack. Serve warm.

These muffins are low-fat and packed with fruit and fibre.

Apple, pecan and raisin muffins

Swiss roll

it evenly into the corners. Bake in the centre of the oven for 10–12 minutes, until golden, risen and just firm to the touch. Meanwhile, put the jam in a bowl and stir well to loosen.

4 Lay out a damp clean cloth on the work surface. Lay a piece of greaseproof paper (larger than the sponge) on top, dusted with caster sugar. Run a knife around the edge of the warm sponge and turn it out on to the sugar-dusted paper. Peel the paper off the base of the sponge. Trim off the edges of the sponge. Spoon the jam onto the sponge and spread out, leaving a little border of clean sponge all around. Make an incision about 1cm in from the short edge near you, being careful not to cut through the cake: this makes it easier to roll up.

5 Start rolling, using the incision to help you make the first turn. Use the paper to help you roll the sponge tightly. Sit it seam-side down until cold.

Swiss roll

SERVES 8–10 TAKES **40 MINUTES TO MAKE**

125g golden caster sugar, plus extra for dusting
125g plain flour, plus extra for dusting
$1/2$ jar of strawberry or raspberry jam
3 large eggs
Vegetable oil, for greasing

1 Preheat the oven to 200°C/fan 180°C/gas 6. Brush the base of a 33 x 23cm Swiss roll tin with vegetable oil. Cut a sheet of greaseproof paper to fit the base of the tin. Brush the paper with a little more oil, then dust with sugar and flour.
2 Whisk the sugar and eggs with an electric hand whisk for 10 minutes, until the mixture is pale and thick enough to leave a trail.
3 Sift half the flour into the mixture and fold in very carefully until no traces of flour are left. Repeat with the remaining flour. It's important to take your time and do it very gently. Fold in 1 tablespoon lukewarm water. Pour the mixture into the prepared tin and use a spatula to smooth

delicious.**technique**

ROLLING A SWISS ROLL

1. *Make sure the sheet of baking paper fits the tin. Brushing with oil and dusting with sugar and flour will help you keep the sponge intact.*

2. *Very gentle folding until all traces of dry flour have disappeared will give you a sponge mixture less likely to break up once cooked.*

3. *Once the sponge is cooked and spread with jam, make a cut across 1cm from the short edge nearest you, without cutting through the cake.*

4. *The cut will help you make the first turn of the sponge, then lift the paper with one hand to help you complete a neat, even roll.*

Carrot cake

MAKES 12 SQUARES TAKES **1 HOUR TO MAKE**

250ml sunflower oil, plus extra for greasing
225g golden caster sugar
3 large eggs
225g self-raising flour
250g carrots, peeled

For the cream cheese icing
25g olive oil spread
300g half-fat cream cheese
25g unrefined golden icing sugar
1 orange

1 Preheat the oven to 180°C/fan 160°C/gas 4. Using a pastry brush, grease a rectangular cake tin measuring about 18 x 28cm and 2.5cm deep. Line the tin with baking paper.
2 Pour the oil into a large bowl. Add the sugar and mix with a large whisk for a few minutes.
3 Crack 1 egg into the sugar. Whisk until the egg disappears, then repeat with the other 2 eggs.

4 Sieve the flour into the bowl and fold into the egg.
5 Cut the ends off the carrots, then coarsely grate them. Fold the carrots into the mixture, then pour it all into the prepared tin and spread evenly.
6 Bake in the oven for 40 minutes, until well risen and golden. Push a skewer into the centre to check if it's cooked – if so, it will come out clean. If not, cook for 2–3 minutes then check again. Set aside to cool in the tin.
7 Meanwhile, put the olive oil spread and cream cheese into a bowl. Mix until soft and smooth. Sieve the icing sugar into the bowl. Finely grate the zest from the orange and add three-quarters of it to the bowl. Mix well together, then spread the icing over the cooled cake. Sprinkle the rest of the zest over the cake and cut it into 12 squares.

delicious.**tip**

STORING A CREAM CHEESE CAKE
Cakes with cream cheese icing should be stored in the fridge, where they will keep for about 4 days if stored in a tight-lidded container.

Carrot cake

Spiced apple sauce cake

SERVES 12–16 TAKES **1 HOUR 30 MINUTES TO MAKE**

1kg cooking apples, such as bramleys
1 tbsp fresh lemon juice
50ml sunflower oil, plus extra for greasing
100g plain flour
100g wholemeal flour
1 tbsp cornflour
2 tsp bicarbonate of soda
$1/2$ tsp each ground cinnamon, cloves,
  ginger and nutmeg
225g golden caster sugar
100g raisins
50g walnut pieces

For the frosting
250g quark (virtually fat-free soft cheese)
25g caster sugar
2 tsp vanilla extract
$1/2$ tsp ground cinnamon, plus extra for dusting
12 walnut halves (optional)

1 Peel, core and slice the apples and put in a non-stick saucepan. Add the lemon juice and 2 tablespoons of water. Cover and cook over a low heat until broken down into a purée. Uncover, increase the heat slightly and cook for 5 minutes or so, stirring, to cook off the excess moisture. Set aside to cool.
2 Preheat the oven to 160°C/fan 140°C/gas 3. Grease a non-stick 20cm springform tin and line the base with baking paper. Sift the flours, bicarbonate of soda, spices and sugar into a mixing bowl, plus any bran left in the sieve. Stir in the raisins and walnuts. Weigh out 550g apple purée and stir into the dry ingredients with the oil.
3 Spoon the mixture into the tin, level the top and bake on the middle shelf for 55–60 minutes, until a skewer pushed into the centre comes out clean.
4 Meanwhile, put the frosting ingredients – except the walnuts – in a bowl and beat until smooth. Cover and chill. Take out the cake and cool in the tin for 10 minutes, then turn out onto a wire rack to cool. Spread over the frosting, sprinkle with more cinnamon and decorate with walnuts.

Spiced apple
sauce cake

Butterscotch sponge cake with cream cheese frosting
SERVES 8–10 TAKES **1 HOUR 15 MINUTES TO MAKE**

225g softened butter, plus extra for greasing
125g light muscovado sugar
100g golden caster sugar
4 large eggs
225g self-raising flour
2 tsp vanilla extract
2 tbsp milk, if needed
400g full-fat cream cheese

For the butterscotch sauce
50g butter
75g light muscovado sugar
50g golden granulated sugar
150g runny honey
120ml double cream
1 tsp vanilla extract

1 Preheat the oven to 190°C/fan 170°C/gas 5. Grease 2 sandwich tins (20cm diameter) and line the bases with non-stick baking paper.
2 Make the butterscotch sauce. Put the butter, both sugars and the honey in a pan and stir over a low heat for 10–15 minutes until smooth. Stir in the cream and vanilla extract and cool.
3 Meanwhile, make the cake. Beat the butter with a wooden spoon until soft. Add the sugars and beat together until pale and fluffy. Beat in the eggs, one at a time, adding a dessertspoonful of flour with each egg. Beat in the vanilla. Fold in the remaining flour and a little milk, if necessary, to give a mixture that reluctantly drops off the spoon.
4 Divide the mixture between the tins and bake for about 25 minutes, until they start to shrink from the sides and a skewer inserted into the centres comes away clean. Sit the tins on a wire rack for 10 minutes, then turn the cakes out onto the rack and leave until completely cold.
5 Beat the cream cheese in a bowl until smooth, then beat in 8 tablespoons of the butterscotch sauce. Place 1 cake on a serving plate and spread with half the mixture. Place the other cake on top and cover with the rest. Drizzle another 2–3 tablespoons of the sauce over the top of the cake.

Rose petal chocolate cake
SERVES 10–12 TAKES **2 HOURS TO MAKE**

125g softened butter, plus extra for greasing
250ml milk
1 tbsp white wine vinegar
125g plain chocolate (50% cocoa solids), broken up
350g self-raising flour, sifted
15g cocoa, sifted
1 tsp bicarbonate of soda
250g golden caster sugar
2 eggs, beaten

For the filling and decoration
4 tbsp sweet sherry or Marsala (optional)
185g plain chocolate (50% cocoa solids), broken up
100g butter, diced
100ml double cream
1 large pink rose, to decorate

1 Preheat the oven to 160°C/fan 140°C/gas 3. Grease a 20cm round, deep cake tin and line the base with baking paper. Put the milk in a jug and add the vinegar – it will curdle. Melt 125g chocolate in a large bowl set over a pan of simmering water, making sure the bottom of the bowl doesn't touch the water. Stir until smooth.
2 Add the butter and remaining cake ingredients plus the vinegar and milk mixture to the melted chocolate. Beat until smooth, then tip into the tin. Bake for 1¼–1½ hours or until a skewer inserted into the centre comes out clean. Cool in the tin for 10 minutes, then turn out onto a wire rack and cool completely.
3 Using a bread knife, halve the cake horizontally into two discs. Sprinkle the cut sides with sherry or Marsala, if using.
4 Make the filling. Melt the chocolate and butter in a pan over a low heat. Stir until smooth, then remove from the heat. Cool for a few minutes, then beat in the cream. Set aside to thicken slightly. Use a quarter of the icing to sandwich the 2 cake halves together, then spread the remaining icing over the top and sides of the cake. Decorate with rose petals to serve.

Gluten-free rich fruit cake

SERVES 10 TAKES **4 HOURS TO MAKE**
PLUS **SOAKING OVERNIGHT**

450g currants
170g sultanas
170g raisins
50g mixed candied peel
50g glacé cherries, rinsed and halved
2 tsp mixed spice
Grated zest of 1 orange
Grated zest of 1 lemon
4 tbsp brandy or rum,
  plus extra for "feeding" the cake
2 tbsp black treacle
50g blanched almonds, chopped
100g ground almonds
50g rice flour
50g cornflour
$1/2$ tsp salt
225g softened butter or dairy-free margarine,
  plus extra for greasing
225g soft dark brown sugar

6 large eggs, beaten
4 tbsp apricot jam
Mixed whole dried fruits and nuts – such as figs,
  apricots, almonds, glacé cherries, walnuts,
  blanched almonds and orange and lemon slices

1 The day before making the cake, put the dried
fruit, mixed spice and citrus zests in a bowl. Stir
in the spirits, cover and leave to soak overnight.
2 The following day, preheat the oven to 150°C/
fan 130°C/gas 2. Stir the treacle and almonds
into the fruit mixture. Grease a 20cm round,
deep cake tin and line both the base and sides
with baking paper.
3 Mix the ground almonds, flours and salt in a
small bowl. In a separate, large bowl, beat the
butter and sugar together until pale and fluffy,
then beat in the eggs, 1 tablespoon at a time.
If it starts to curdle, add a spoonful of flour and
almonds. Fold the flour mixture into the eggs
and butter, and gently fold in the fruit. Spoon
into the tin and level the top.
4 Wrap a double layer of brown paper around

Gluten-free
rich fruit cake

the outside of the tin so that it stands 5cm above the rim, and secure carefully with kitchen string. Cover the top of the cake with 2 pieces of baking paper cut to the size of the tin, and then cut a small hole in the centre to allow steam to escape. Bake for 3 hours on the middle shelf of the oven.

5 Remove the baking paper and return the cake to the oven to bake for another 30 minutes, until it is browned on top and a skewer inserted into the middle comes out clean.

6 Turn out and cool in the paper on a wire rack. Once cold, make a few holes in the top with a skewer, drilling down about 2.5cm into the cake. Drizzle over 2 tbsp brandy or rum.

7 To store, leave the cake in the baking paper and wrap it tightly in cling film, then in foil. Place in an airtight container and keep in a cool dry place. Once a month, unwrap and "feed" the cake with 1–2 tablespoons of brandy or rum. When ready to decorate, heat the apricot jam in a small saucepan until melted, then brush over the cake. Decorate with the mixed dried fruits and nuts, then brush with more jam.

The delicious. Christmas cake

SERVES 16 TAKES **4 HOURS TO MAKE** PLUS **OVERNIGHT SOAKING**

175g raisins
175g sultanas
175g ready-to-eat prunes,
  roughly chopped
150g natural glacé cherries, halved
50g dried blueberries
50g dried cranberries
50g crystallized stem ginger
Grated zest of 1 large orange
250ml brandy (or use whisky
  or Madeira)
175g unsalted butter, softened
175g dark muscovado sugar
4 eggs, beaten
200g self-raising flour
1 tbsp golden syrup
1 tbsp vanilla extract

For the brandy butter icing
450g golden icing sugar, sieved
3 tbsp glucose syrup
50g unsalted butter, softened
4 tbsp brandy

1 The day before making the cake, put the raisins, sultanas, prunes, cherries, blueberries, cranberries, stem ginger and orange zest into a large bowl. Pour over the brandy, cover and leave to soak for at least 24 hours, stirring occasionally until most of the brandy has been absorbed.

2 The next day, grease the base and sides of a 20cm round cake tin and line with baking paper. Using a slotted spoon, drain and weigh out 450g of the soaked fruit and put into a food processor. Blend to a thick, dark purée.

3 Preheat the oven to 150°C/fan 130°C/gas 2. In a clean bowl, beat the butter and sugar until light and fluffy. Beat in the eggs a little at a time, adding touches of flour if it starts to curdle.

4 Add the fruit purée, the remaining soaked fruit and flour, together with the brandy, golden syrup and vanilla. Fold everything together until well combined. Spoon into the prepared tin and smooth with the back of the spoon. Bake for 2$\frac{1}{2}$–3 hours or until a skewer inserted into the middle comes out clean. Cool in the tin for a few hours, then turn the cake out and allow to cool completely on a wire rack.

5 For the brandy butter icing, put the sieved icing sugar, glucose, butter and brandy into a large bowl and beat until soft and smooth. Swirl the icing decoratively over the top of the cake, then tie a wide ribbon and bow around the side of the cake. Store the cake in an airtight container and keep in a cool place or the fridge. Eat within two weeks.

delicious.**tip**
DECORATING WITH CARAMEL
It's simple to decorate with caramelised decorations. Dissolve 225g granulated sugar over a gentle heat until it turns a pale caramel colour. Remove from the heat and slowly drizzle onto a lightly oiled tray in the shape of a star or a word. Add to the cake once set.

Mocha and hazelnut cake

Mocha and hazelnut cake

SERVES 8 TAKES **1 HOUR 30 MINUTES TO MAKE**

120g whole blanched hazelnuts,
 plus extra to decorate (optional)
200g unsalted butter, plus extra for greasing
200g golden caster sugar
3 large eggs
200g self-raising flour
1 tsp baking powder
1 tbsp cold made-up espresso or Camp coffee

For the butter icing
100g unsalted butter
200g icing sugar
1 tsp cocoa powder

1 Preheat the oven to 180°C/fan 160°C/gas 4. Lay the hazelnuts in a single layer on a large baking tray and roast for 15–20 minutes until toasted. Cool. Finely chop or pulse in a food processor and set aside. Leave the oven on.
2 Make the sponges. Use an electric hand whisk to beat the butter and caster sugar in a large bowl for a few minutes until light and fluffy. Beat in the eggs 1 at a time. Sift in the flour and baking powder, then fold through gently with a large metal spoon until just combined – you want it light and airy. Fold in the coffee and half the toasted nuts. Divide between the 2 sponge tins, gently level the surfaces and then bake for 30–35 minutes, until firm and risen. Remove and allow to cool in the tins on a wire rack for 20 minutes. Carefully turn out the sponges and allow to cool completely.
3 Meanwhile, make the butter icing. In a large bowl, beat the butter and sugar until pale and fluffy. Sift in the cocoa powder and fold in, along with the remaining chopped nuts.
4 When the sponges are cold, place 1 upside-down on a serving plate. Cover with half of the butter icing. Top with the other sponge and spread the remaining butter icing over the top. For a more decorative finish, stud the cake with whole blanched hazelnuts around the top and/or shavings of plain chocolate.

Exotic fruit and spice cake

SERVES 16–20 TAKES **4 HOURS 30 MINUTES TO MAKE**
PLUS **2 OVERNIGHT PROCESSES (SOAKING AND DRYING OUT)**

75g soft dried apricots
75g soft dried figs
75g soft dried pitted Agen prunes
75g soft dried pitted dates
75g soft dried mixed candied peel
425g can pineapple in natural juice
75g raisins
75g currants
75g natural-coloured glacé cherries
Zest of 1 small orange, finely grated
Zest of 1 lemon, finely grated
$1/4$ tsp ground cinnamon
$1/4$ tsp grated fresh nutmeg
1 tsp vanilla extract
125g brazil nuts, coarsely chopped
100g dark muscovado sugar
185ml dark rum
175g softened butter
75g molasses sugar
3 eggs
175g plain flour
175g self-raising flour

For the marzipan
225g golden caster sugar
225g golden icing sugar, sifted
450g ground almonds
2 eggs
2 tsp dark rum
6 tbsp marmalade, warmed and sieved

To decorate
2 large egg whites
500g golden icing sugar, sifted,
  plus extra for dusting
2 tsp liquid glucose
Whole glacé fruits, cut into pieces
Fresh bay leaves

1 The day before making the cake, drain the pineapple, reserving the juice. Cut the apricots, figs, prunes, dates, peel and pineapple into pieces the same size as the raisins. Put in a saucepan with the raisins, currants, cherries, zest, cinnamon, nutmeg, vanilla, nuts, 1 tablespoon of muscovado sugar, the rum and the reserved pineapple juice. Heat, then simmer very gently, uncovered, for 15 minutes, stirring once or twice. Transfer to a bowl, cool, then cover with cling film and leave to soak in the fridge overnight.

2 Preheat the oven to 180°C/fan 160°C/gas 4. Grease and double-line a deep 20cm round cake tin with baking paper. Beat the butter until very soft. Gradually beat in the rest of the sugars and the eggs, 1 at a time, adding a dessertspoonful of the plain flour with the last egg. Sift the remaining plain flour with the self-raising flour and fold in, along with the soaked fruits.

3 Spoon the mixture into the prepared tin. Bake for 30 minutes. Reduce the oven temperature to 150°C/fan 130°C/gas 2 and bake for a further $2^{1}/_{2}$–3 hours, or until firm to the touch. Cool in the tin, then remove, wrap in a double thickness of foil, put in an airtight tin and leave for up to 1 week before icing. You can freeze the cake at this point, if you like.

4 Make the marzipan. Mix together the sugars and almonds. Lightly whisk the eggs and rum in a separate bowl, then add to the dry ingredients. Mix to form a paste and knead until smooth.

5 Brush the cake all over with the marmalade. Roll out the marzipan on an icing sugar-dusted surface to a circle large enough to cover the top and sides of the cake. Lift onto the cake and smooth the top and sides. Trim the edges neatly. Leave overnight to dry out.

6 For the icing, lightly beat the egg whites in a large bowl. Add the icing sugar a little at a time, stirring continuously, until you have a stiff icing that stands in peaks. Beat in the glucose. Use a palette knife to spread the icing all over the cake, giving a slightly swirled finish. Arrange the glacé fruit and bay leaves on top. Decorate with a ribbon.

delicious.**tip**

FROSTING LEAVES
You can give the bay leaves a delicate frosted white finish by dipping their tips in egg white then sugar. You can also sugar-frost flowers in this way.

Chocolate yule log

Chocolate yule log

SERVES 8 TAKES **50 MINUTES TO MAKE**
PLUS **2 HOURS OR OVERNIGHT CHILLING**

300g dark chocolate, broken up
6 large eggs, separated
175g golden caster sugar
Icing sugar, to dust

For the filling
4 tbsp Nutella spread
250g mascarpone
2 tbsp brandy

1 Preheat the oven to 180°C/fan 160°C/gas 4. Grease and line a 28 x 38cm Swiss roll tin with baking paper. Put 175g of the chocolate into a bowl over a pan of simmering water – the water should not touch the bottom of the bowl – and heat gently until melted. Remove from the heat and stir until smooth.
2 Put the egg yolks and sugar into a large bowl. Using an electric hand whisk, whisk until

mousse-like, then whisk in the melted chocolate.
3 In a dry, grease-free bowl, whisk the egg whites until they form soft peaks. Stir a little egg white into the chocolate mixture, then carefully fold in the rest with a metal spoon. Pour into the tin and bake for 20–25 minutes, until spongy to the touch. Cool for 10 minutes, then cover the tin with a clean damp tea towel. When cool, chill for at least 2 hours or overnight.
4 While the roulade is chilling, make the filling. Mix the Nutella and mascarpone together until smooth. Gradually mix in the brandy. Cover and chill until needed.
5 Carefully turn out the roulade onto a sheet of baking paper. (At this stage, you can wrap it in cling film and freeze for up to one month. When ready to use, thaw at room temperature, then fill and roll.)
6 Make the chocolate "bark" for the yule log. Melt the remaining chocolate (as for step 1) then allow it to cool for 10 minutes. Pour onto a baking tray lined with baking paper and thinly spread out with a spatula. Chill for 8–10 minutes, until the chocolate is firm but still pliable. Tear the chocolate into small jagged pieces. Put in a single layer on a large lined baking sheet. Chill for 15 minutes until crisp.
7 Spread half the filling over the roulade. Holding the baking paper, lift up the nearest short edge to you and carefully roll up the roulade (see Rolling a Swiss Roll, p.268) – but don't worry if it cracks. Transfer to a plate. Spread the rest of the filling over the top of the roulade, then arrange the chocolate on top, overlapping. Chill for 1 hour. Dust with icing sugar to serve.

A chocolate yule
log is a tempting
alternative for those
who don't like fruit
cake at Christmas.

Chocolate ice cream cake

SERVES 12 TAKES **20 MINUTES TO MAKE**
PLUS **OVERNIGHT FREEZING**

3 x 500ml tubs chocolate fudge brownie ice cream,
  just softened
1 500ml tub strawberry cheesecake ice cream,
  just softened
200g milk chocolate

1 Start preparing the day before you want to eat the ice cream cake. Stand a 23cm springform tin on a sheet of baking paper, draw around the tin, then cut out the circle of baking paper and lay it in the base of the springform tin.
2 Tip two-thirds of the chocolate fudge brownie ice cream into the lined tin and spread around evenly using a palette knife (or spatula).
3 Spread the strawberry cheesecake ice cream in a layer over the chocolate ice cream, then top with the remaining chocolate ice cream. Cover and place on a flat surface in the freezer overnight, or for up to 3 days.

4 Prepare the chocolate curls on the same day as the ice cream. Put a sheet of baking paper onto a baking tray. Hold the milk chocolate over the tray and pull a vegetable peeler along the long thin edge of the chocolate to make curly strips, letting the strips fall onto the tray. Put the tray of chocolate curls in the fridge to firm up overnight.
5 About 15 minutes before serving, take the ice cream cake out of the freezer. Run a hot knife around the edges of the tin. Unclip the tin sides. Ease a palette knife under the base, then slide the cake onto a serving dish. Scatter the curls of chocolate onto the cake. Use a hot knife to cut the cake into slices.

delicious.**tip**

WORKING WITH ICE CREAM
If you make this as soon as you bring the food shopping home, the ice cream will be soft enough to spread easily. Otherwise, you'll need to take it out of the freezer for about 20 minutes to soften. Don't be tempted to freeze any leftovers.

Chocolate ice
cream cake

breads, buns and biscuits

Garlic focaccia

SERVES 4 TAKES **1 HOUR 10 MINUTES TO MAKE**

250g strong plain white flour,
  plus extra for dusting
1 tsp salt
7g fast-action dried yeast
Olive oil
2 garlic cloves, thinly sliced
2 tsp sea salt

1 Put the flour into a bowl with the salt, yeast and
1 tablespoon olive oil. Add 150ml warm water, stir
with a wooden spoon, then use your hands to mix
it all into a ball.
2 Sprinkle flour over a clean work surface and tip
out the dough. Work the dough for 10 minutes to
stretch and make smooth.
3 Pour 1 tablespoon of olive oil onto the work
surface. Sit the dough on top and roll out to a
round about 30cm across with a rolling pin.
Grease a pizza tray or large baking tray, line
with baking paper and put the dough on it.
4 Scatter the garlic over the dough, then
sprinkle with the salt. Cover loosely with
greased cling film (the dough needs room to
expand) and leave to rise in a warm place for
30 minutes to 1 hour. It will become quite puffy
– almost doubled in size.
5 Preheat the oven to 220°C/fan 200°C/gas 7.
Discard the cling film and press your finger into
the dough about 16 times. Pour over a little more
olive oil. Bake for 15 minutes until golden brown.
Cool for 5 minutes, then tear into pieces to serve.

Basic white rustic loaf

MAKES A 750G LOAF TAKES **1 HOUR 15 MINUTES TO MAKE**

500g strong white bread flour,
  plus extra for dusting
1 tsp fine salt
7g fast-action dried yeast
1 tbsp olive oil, plus extra for greasing

1 Sift the flour and salt into a large bowl. Stir in
the yeast. Make a well in the centre and gradually
mix in 300ml warm water and the oil until the
dough comes together – add a dash more water
if it seems a little dry.
2 Tip out onto a lightly floured surface, put a
little oil on your hands and knead the dough for
5–10 minutes until smooth and elastic. If you
pause for a minute now and then while kneading,
you'll achieve a better textured dough. Shape the

delicious.technique

KNEADING DOUGH

1. *Rub your hands with a little oil. Form the dough into a flat patty shape, then bring the far edge up over the top towards you and fold it over.*

2. *Use the thumb of one hand to hold the dough in place; use the heel of your other hand to press down and away from the centre of the dough.*

3. *Lift and rotate the dough a quarter-turn, then fold it (step 1) and press it (step 2) again. Repeat this sequence of folding, pressing and rotating.*

4. *Knead for 5–10 minutes. As you knead, the dough will change from a slightly lumpen piece of dough to one with a more silken and elastic feel.*

Garlic focaccia

dough so that it resembles a flattened rugby ball and put onto an oiled, large baking sheet. Set aside in a warm place for 40 minutes or until doubled in size. This is known as proving or rising.

3 Preheat the oven to 220°C/fan 200°C/gas 7. Using a sharp knife, make 4–5 deep slashes across the top of the dough and dust with flour. Put into the hot oven and bake for 20–25 minutes, until risen, golden and cooked. To test if it's ready, tap the base of the loaf with your knuckles – the bread will sound hollow when cooked. Cool on a wire rack and slice to serve.

Cheddar and bacon loaf

MAKES A 450G LOAF (10 SLICES) TAKES **40 MINUTES**

Butter, for greasing
4 rashers streaky bacon
275g plain flour
1 level tbsp baking powder
1 tsp salt
Pinch of English mustard powder
50g mature Cheddar, cut into 1cm cubes
1 large egg
225ml milk, plus 1 tbsp
2–3 tbsp chopped fresh parsley

1 Preheat the oven to 200°C/fan 180°C/gas 6. Grease the base and sides of a 450g loaf tin and line the base with baking paper.
2 Snip the bacon into strips and dry-fry in a pan until crisp, then cool.
3 Meanwhile, put the flour, baking powder, salt and mustard powder into a bowl and stir. Add the cheese, bacon, egg, 225ml milk and parsley. Stir well with a wooden spoon until it has a soft dropping consistency – add extra milk, if needed.
4 Spread in the tin and bake for 25 minutes, until risen, golden brown and just firm to the touch. Serve warm or cold, with butter and cheese.

Basic white rustic loaf

Hot bread straight from the oven – impossible to resist!

Sunflower and honey rolls

MAKES 12 ROLLS TAKES **1 HOUR 10 MINUTES**

400g granary malted brown bread flour
400g strong white bread flour,
  plus extra for dusting
2 tsp salt
25g butter, cubed, plus extra for greasing
7g fast-action dried yeast
3 tbsp clear honey, plus 1 tsp extra
2 tbsp milk
4 tbsp sunflower seeds

1 Put all the flour in a large bowl with the salt. Add the butter, then rub it in between your thumb and fingers until the butter breaks into tiny pieces.
2 Stir in the yeast and use a measuring spoon to add 3 tablespoons of clear honey. Measure out 560ml of warm water – it should be pleasantly warm. Pour it into the bowl and stir with a wooden spoon, then use your hand to mix all the flour into a dough that leaves the sides of the bowl clean. Add a little more flour if it's too sticky.
3 Sprinkle some flour onto a clean, dry work surface, tip out the dough and cut it in half. Knead each half of the dough separately, pulling and stretching it for 10 minutes until springy and smooth (see Kneading Dough, p.278).
4 Shape each piece of dough into a ball. Cut each ball into 6 equal pieces (to make 12 in total). Roll each piece into a smooth round. Grease 2 baking trays (or line them with baking paper), then space the rounds well apart on them.
5 Put the extra 1 teaspoon of honey in a small bowl and microwave on medium for 10 seconds (or heat in a pan) to warm through. Add the milk and mix. Brush a little honeyed milk onto each roll and sprinkle over a few sunflower seeds. Rub some butter on 1 side of 2 large pieces of cling film and place greased side down over the baking trays. Put in a warm place for 30 minutes, or until the rolls have doubled in size.
6 Preheat the oven to 220°C/fan 200°C/gas 7. Remove and discard the cling film. Bake for 15 minutes, until golden brown and the bases are firm when tapped. Cool for at least 15 minutes before eating.

Cream tea scones

MAKES 8 TAKES **30 MINUTES**

225g self-raising flour,
  plus a little more for dusting
50g butter, at room temperature
1¹/₂ tbsp caster sugar
100ml milk

1 Preheat the oven to 220°C/fan 200°C/gas 7. Place the flour in a large bowl and rub in the butter to form a crumbly mixture.
2 Using a table knife, stir in the sugar, a pinch of salt, then the milk. You're aiming to make a soft dough – if it feels slightly dry, add a touch more milk. Lightly dust a rolling surface with a little flour, then roll out the dough. This needs to be at least 2cm thick.
3 Using a 5cm plain cutter, firmly stamp out the scone rounds. Try not to twist the cutter as this makes the scones rise unevenly. Re-roll the trimmings and stamp out more rounds until all the dough has been used.
4 Transfer the dough rounds to a non–stick baking sheet, dust with a little more flour and bake for 12 minutes or until they are well risen and golden.
5 Cool on a rack and serve just warm or at room temperature with clotted cream and strawberry jam. These scones are best eaten on the day that you bake them.

ROLLING AND CUTTING SCONES

1. *Roll out the scone dough on a lightly floured surface until around 2cm deep. Keep an even pressure on both ends of the rolling pin.*

2. *Use a round cutter (about 6cm) to stamp out dough circles. Press down firmly to cut through to the rolling surface without twisting.*

Cream tea
scones

Strawberry buns

Strawberry buns

MAKES 12 TAKES **50 MINUTES TO MAKE**

150g plain flour
3/4 tsp salt
100g butter, cut into cubes
4 large eggs

For the filling
500g mascarpone
200g Greek yogurt
300g ready-made custard
100g golden caster sugar
1 tsp vanilla extract
500g strawberries
2 tbsp unrefined golden icing sugar, for dusting

1 Preheat the oven to 200°C/fan 180°C/gas 6. Sieve the flour onto a large sheet of baking or greaseproof paper.
2 Make the choux buns. Put 250ml cold water into a pan with the salt and butter, and start to heat gently. As soon as the butter is melted and the liquid is bubbling, lift up the flour on the paper and tip it into the pan. Stir it together until the mixture forms a ball and comes away from the sides of the pan. Turn off the heat, tip the mixture into a large bowl and set aside to cool for 5 minutes.
3 Place a sheet of baking paper over a large baking sheet. Beat the eggs lightly in a jug with a fork. Pour some of the egg into the butter and flour mixture – at first it will look like scrambled eggs but don't worry, just beat well with a wooden spoon. Tip in some more egg and beat again. Continue until all the egg is added, and the mixture is shiny and smooth.
4 Place 12 tablespoonfuls of the mixture onto the lined baking sheet, well spaced apart. Bake for 20 minutes (don't open the door or the buns will sink). Turn off the oven and leave them in the oven for a further 15 minutes.
5 Take each of the buns out of the oven in turn, piercing the base of each bun with a skewer to help the steam escape. Put the buns back into the warm oven (without turning it on), and leave them there for 15 minutes to dry out.
6 Remove the buns from the oven and place on a wire rack to cool. Using a serrated knife, carefully cut each bun in half, then put the bases into paper muffin cases. The buns can be eaten immediately or stored in an airtight tin for a few days until ready to use.
7 Make the filling. Put the mascarpone in a large bowl and mix until smooth. Stir in the Greek yogurt, custard, sugar and vanilla. Remove any leaves from the strawberries and cut each of the fruits in half.
8 Put a spoonful of filling in each bun and arrange a few strawberries on top. Sandwich together with the bun lid. Repeat to fill all the buns. Hold a tea strainer over each bun and dust with a little icing sugar.

Choux buns are a handful of pastry magic.

Sticky hot cross buns

MAKES 12 TAKES **2 HOURS TO MAKE**

500g plain flour
7g easy-blend yeast
50g golden caster sugar,
  plus 2 tbsp extra for the glaze
1 tsp salt
1 tsp ground mixed spice
50g dried cranberries
  and/or blueberries
50g sultanas
Grated zest of 1 lemon
200ml milk
1 egg, beaten
50g butter

1 In a large bowl, mix together the flour, yeast, sugar, salt, spice, fruit and lemon zest.
2 Warm the milk in a pan (or for 10 seconds in the microwave) and melt the butter. Make a well in the centre of the bowl and add the warm milk, beaten egg and melted butter. Stir together to make a soft dough. Knead (see Kneading Dough, p.278) on a surface for 5 minutes until smooth. Return to the bowl, cover with a clean tea towel and leave for 1 hour until risen.
3 Line a 12-hole muffin tin with circles of greaseproof paper or muffin cases. Briefly knead the dough and roll out into 12 balls, putting one in each case. Cut a cross in the top of each ball, cover again and leave to rise for 30 minutes.
4 Preheat the oven to 200°C/fan 180°C/gas 6. Bake the buns for 15–20 minutes until golden. Mix together the remaining sugar with 2 tablespoons of water. Brush the buns with the sugar water as soon as they come out of the oven. Leave to cool a little before eating.

delicious.**tip**

USING UP LEFTOVERS

There are lots of tempting ways to use any leftover hot cross buns, especially in place of bread. They can be used to make delicious French toast (see p.240) or bread and butter pudding (see p.244).

Sticky hot
cross buns

Cardamom-scented Chelsea buns
MAKES 9 TAKES **3 HOURS TO MAKE**

....

50g unsalted butter, diced,
   plus extra for greasing
450g strong white bread flour,
   plus extra for dusting
$^1/_2$ tsp salt
7g sachet fast-action dried yeast
25g golden caster sugar
1 egg
225ml warm milk
2 tsp clear honey
2 tbsp shelled pistachios, roughly chopped

For the filling
50g butter, softened
1 tsp roughly crushed cardamom seeds
50g sultanas
50g currants
50g light muscovado sugar

....

1 Grease a deep, 23cm square tin with butter. Sift the flour and salt into a large bowl. Rub in the butter (see Making Crumble Topping, p.240), then stir in the dried yeast.
2 In another bowl, whisk the sugar and egg together. Add to the dry ingredients with all but 2 tablespoons of the milk. Mix to a soft dough, adding the remaining milk, if needed.
3 Turn out onto a lightly floured surface and knead the dough (see Kneading Dough, p.278) for at least 15 minutes, until it feels smooth and elastic. Put in a lightly greased bowl, cover with cling film and leave in a warm place to rise for about 1 hour or until doubled in size.
4 Punch the dough in the bowl to "knock it back", taking the air out of it. Tip it back out onto the floured surface and, using a rolling pin, roll out into a rectangle about 25cm x 35cm.
5 Make the filling. Spread the butter over the dough, then scatter over the cardamom, fruit and sugar. Roll up like a Swiss roll (see Making a Swiss Roll, p.000) from the long end, then cut into 9 rounds. Arrange in the tin, cut-side down, 3 to a row. Cover with lightly greased cling film and put in a warm place for 45 minutes until well risen.

6 Preheat the oven to 200°C/fan 180°C/gas 6. Bake the buns for 25–30 minutes or until golden. Remove from the oven and brush with the honey and sprinkle with the pistachios. Cool in the tin for about 10 minutes, then eat warm or transfer to a wire rack to cool completely.

Peanut butter and cranberry cookies
MAKES 30 TAKES **40 MINUTES TO MAKE**

....

100g butter, softened,
   plus extra for greasing (optional)
250g crunchy peanut butter
250g light soft brown sugar
1 large egg
Few drops of vanilla extract
125g oats
90g dried cranberries
125g plain flour
1 tsp bicarbonate of soda

....

1 Preheat the oven to 160°C/fan 140°C/ gas 3. Cut baking paper to fit 3 baking trays or rub a little butter over the trays. If you don't have 3 trays, just cook 1 tray at a time.
2 Beat the softened butter and peanut butter in a bowl with a wooden spoon. Add the sugar and beat again until well mixed.
3 Crack the egg into a bowl and whisk with a fork. Add the vanilla extract and egg to the peanut butter mixture and beat again with the wooden spoon.
4 Add the oats and cranberries to the mixture, sift over the flour and bicarbonate of soda and mix well.
5 Put large spoonfuls of the mixture onto the trays, spacing slightly apart, and bake for 18–20 minutes until light golden. Remove from the oven. Leave to firm up on their trays for a few minutes, then transfer using a fish slice onto wire racks to cool completely.
6 When they are cool, eat or store in an airtight container in a cool place for up to 3 days. These cookies make fun gifts for children and adults – just make a little stack of the biscuits, wrap them in cellophane and tie with a pretty ribbon.

Cardamom-scented
Chelsea buns

Macaroons

then remove from the oven. Leave on the baking sheets for 2 minutes, then transfer to a wire rack to cool. Eat immediately or store in an airtight container for up to 5 days.

Macaroons
MAKES 20 TAKES **40 MINUTES TO MAKE**

125g ground almonds
250g icing sugar
3 egg whites
8g dried egg white powder
30g caster sugar
Few drops of pink food colouring

For the filling
100g plain chocolate, broken up
50g butter
142ml double cream

1 Line 2–3 large baking trays with baking paper. Preheat the oven to 190°C/fan 170°C/gas 5. Mix the ground almonds and icing sugar together in a bowl. In another bowl, whisk the egg whites and egg powder together to stiff peaks. Gradually whisk the caster sugar into the egg mixture until thick and glossy.
2 Using a slotted spoon, fold the almond and icing sugar mixture and the food colouring into the egg white, until combined and evenly coloured.
3 Put the mixture into a disposable piping bag and snip off the end so that you have a hole about 1cm wide. Pipe small rounds, about 4cm in diameter, onto the baking sheets, spaced apart (you should get about 40). Set aside for 10 minutes to allow a crust to form on each.
4 Bake the macaroons for 5 minutes or until the underside is set. Carefully turn each macaroon over and bake for a further 5 minutes. Set aside to cool completely.
5 Meanwhile, put the chocolate and butter in a small pan over a low heat. Gently melt, then stir until smooth. Set aside to cool slightly. In a bowl, whisk the cream to soft peaks. Fold into the melted chocolate and butter. Lift the macaroons from the paper and spread half of

Chocolate chip cookies
MAKES 15 TAKES **25 MINUTES TO MAKE**

115g unsalted butter, softened
50g granulated sugar
70g light muscovado sugar
$^1/_2$ tsp vanilla extract
1 large egg, lightly beaten
160g plain flour
$^1/_4$ tsp bicarbonate of soda
100g milk or dark chocolate, cut into chunks

1 Preheat the oven to 180°C/fan 160°C/gas 4. Lightly grease 2–3 non-stick baking sheets. Put the butter and sugars into a large bowl and cream together using an electric hand whisk until pale and fluffy. Gradually beat in the vanilla and egg.
2 In a small bowl, mix the flour, bicarbonate of soda and a good pinch of salt, then add to the creamed mixture, along with the chocolate chunks. Mix until combined to a soft dough.
3 Put tablespoonfuls of the dough onto the baking sheets, spaced well apart. Bake for 8–10 minutes,

them with the chocolate mixture. Sandwich together with the remaining macaroons to make about 20. Allow to firm up for 1 hour before serving, and eat within 2–3 hours.

Florentines
MAKES 24 TAKES **1 HOUR 10 MINUTES TO MAKE**

50g unsalted butter
50g golden caster sugar
2 tsp runny honey
50g plain flour
40g chopped mixed candied peel
40g mixed glacé cherries, chopped
50g toasted flaked almonds, lightly crushed
150g milk chocolate, broken up

1 Preheat the oven to 180°C/fan 160°C/gas 4. Line 2 large baking trays with non-stick baking paper.
2 Melt the butter, sugar and honey in a pan over a medium-low heat, stirring to dissolve the sugar. Remove from the heat and cool to room temperature. Stir in the flour, candied peel, cherries and almonds. Using your hands, shape the mixture into small mounds, then place 9 on each baking tray, spaced apart. Press down each mound slightly. Bake for 7-8 minutes. Leave for 5 minutes to firm up, then transfer to a wire rack to cool. Bake 6 more with the remaining mixture.
3 Melt the chocolate in a heatproof bowl set over a pan of simmering water – don't let the bowl touch the water. Remove from the heat and stir until smooth. Using a palette knife, spread the flat side of each biscuit with the chocolate and allow to set. Spread another layer of chocolate over the first and use a fork to mark wavy lines. Allow to set again, then eat or store.

delicious.**tip**
STORING FLORENTINES
Store florentines in airtight containers, layered, with baking paper between each layer. Keep them somewhere cool or the chocolate will melt. Florentines can be frozen for up to 1 month.

Florentines

5

reference

- glossary
- useful information

glossary

Al dente Italian term, literally "to the tooth". Pasta, rice and vegetables may be cooked until al dente: just tender yet still offering a slight resistance when you bite into them.

Amaretti biscuits Small almond biscuits from Italy, which are made using Amaretto liqueur.

Arborio rice Absorbent, short-grained Italian rice used for making risotto.

Baharat Arabic spice mix, often including cinnamon, nutmeg, cumin, cloves, cardamom and coriander.

Baking beans Used to weigh down pastry while "baking blind" – baking a tart case without its filling, to set it while preventing it from puffing up. Ceramic baking beans can be bought, or you can use dried haricot beans.

Baste To spoon fat over food as it cooks to stop it drying out.

Béchamel White sauce.

Beurre manié "Kneaded butter", a paste of butter and flour, added at the end of cooking to thicken a sauce.

Blanch To immerse in boiling water for a very short time. Blanching is done to set colour (vegetables); to eliminate strong flavours (some vegetables, sweetbreads); and to loosen skins before peeling (tomatoes, stone fruit).

Braise To cook using both dry and moist heat; the food is first browned, then cooked in a covered pot or pan in liquid. Braised meat and poultry may also be referred to as pot-roasted.

Browning Cooking food quickly so it colours all over and the juices are sealed. Meat and poultry may be browned prior to oven-cooking.

Bulgur Also burghul and bulgar, wheat grains that are boiled until they crack. Bulgur is a staple in the Middle East and is used to make kibbeh and tabbouleh.

Butterfly To bone and open out flat a piece of meat.

Buttermilk Originally a by-product of butter making, today it is made by adding bacteria to milk to thicken and sour it.

Caramel Sugar syrup heated above 156ºC until it contains very little water and takes on a dark colour.

Caramelise To heat savoury or sweet foods until the surface sugars break down and turn brown.

Chipotle Type of chilli with a distinctive smoky flavour.

Compôte Fruits poached gently in a sugar syrup so they hold their shape.

Confit Meat or poultry cooked in its own fat to preserve it.

Cornichons The French name for gherkins.

Cornmeal Fine or coarse meal from dried corn, used in America to make cornbread and in Italy to make polenta.

Couscous A mixture of fine and coarse semolina, in which the finer flour binds itself around the coarser grains to form granules. Traditionally takes a long time to cook, but instant couscous is precooked and just needs rehydrating.

Crème anglaise A thin, vanilla-flavoured English custard.

Crème fraîche A fermented, thickened tangy cream.

Croûtons Small cubes of bread fried until crisp.

Deglaze To use the caramelised juices released by roasted or fried meat or vegetables to make a sauce or gravy. A pan is deglazed by adding stock, water or wine and scraping it to loosen the juices that stick to the bottom.

Emulsion A suspension of droplets of fat, such as oil or melted butter, in liquids such as water, vinegar or lemon juice, produced by whisking. Mayonnaise and hollandaise are emulsified sauces.

En croûte Literally "in a crust", this term refers to food cooked encased in pastry, such as Beef Wellington.

Escalope A thin cut of chicken, pork or veal flattened to tenderise it and to help the meat cook evenly.

Fold To incorporate a light, airy mixture (such as beaten egg white) into a heavier mixture using gentle "slicing" strokes so as not to knock the air out.

Gelatin A setting agent available in leaf or powder form, gelatin must be soaked in cold water before being dissolved in a warm liquid.

Gnocchi Bite-size potato dumplings.

Gratin A dish (typically sliced potatoes in a cream sauce) cooked in such a way that a crust forms, often by sprinkling with cheese or breadcrumbs and grilling.

Griddle A flat pan, like a frying pan with thick ridges running across the cooking surface.

Haloumi A salty, rubbery Greek cheese.

Harissa A potent North African chilli paste perfumed with caraway seeds, garlic and coriander.

Julienne To cut vegetables such as carrots and leeks into matchstick-sized pieces, about 5cm long.

Jus French term for a light sauce produced by reducing a well-flavoured stock.

Lardons Cubes of bacon, smoked or unsmoked.

Lemon grass A thick grass often used in Thai cooking.

Mascarpone A rich Italian soft cheese made from cow's cream, typically used in desserts such as tiramisu.

Mezze An array of Middle Eastern appetizers that might include olives, dips, meatballs or stuffed vine leaves.

Nam pla (Thai fish sauce) A very concentrated, salty flavouring and dipping sauce made from fermented fish.

Pancetta Italian cured pork belly, similar to bacon but not smoked. It can be bought as cubes or very thin rashers.

Parboil To partially cook in boiling water.

Preserved lemons Lemons pickled in salt and lemon juice, typically used in North African dishes. The pickling softens the skins, which can be eaten.

Pulses Also known as legumes, pulses include beans, peas and lentils. The term usually refers to the dried seeds, which are a valuable source of protein.

Ras-el-hanout Moroccan spice mix, typically including cumin, coriander, turmeric, ginger, chilli and nutmeg, often with cloves, cinnamon and allspice.

Reduce To boil rapidly in order to evaporate excess liquid. Reducing intensifies flavour and thickens sauces.

Refresh To cool down in ice water. This is a way of quickly stopping the cooking process for vegetables that have been blanched or boiled, preventing overcooking.

Rehydrate To add water to a food that has been dried, such as mushrooms, to reconstitute it.

Rest To rest meat after roasting allows the muscle to relax so that the juices are retained within the meat, improving its taste and texture and making carving easier. Pastry is also rested, chilled, so it can relax and soften. A batter is rested so the flour particles can expand in the liquid.

Roux A cooked mixture of butter and flour used to thicken white sauces such as béchamel.

Saffron threads The dried red stigmas of the saffron crocus are one of the most expensive spices in the world. They add colour and a warm, musky flavour to dishes.

Shiitake Brown cap mushrooms that can be bought fresh or dried and are often used in Asian cooking.

Skim To remove fats and other impurities from a sauce or liquid using a perforated skimmer.

Suet The hard white fat that surrounds sheep or beef kidneys and may be used in cooking to make pastries or puddings. Vegetarian suet is available.

Tagine North African slow-cooked stew named after the conical-lidded terracotta pot in which it is made.

Tahini A paste made from sesame seeds and oil.

Tomato passata Sieved, smooth tomato pulp that can be bought in bottles or cartons.

Vanilla sugar Caster sugar that has been flavoured with vanilla extract or by leaving a vanilla pod in it.

Verjuice Acidic juice made from pressing unripe grapes.

Zest The coloured, outer rind of a citrus fruit, and the action of removing it, usually with a fine grater. Avoid zesting the bitter white pith.

useful information

Conversion tables

Precise quantities and cooking temperatures are all part of the chemistry that creates a perfect plate of food. Use these charts to help you achieve perfection.

Oven temperature equivalents

Celsius	Fan°C	Fahrenheit	Gas	Description
110	90	225	¼	Very cool
120	100	250	½	Very cool
140	120	275	1	Cool
150	130	300	2	Cool
160	140	325	3	Warm
180	160	350	4	Moderate
190	170	375	5	Moderately hot
200	180	400	6	Fairly hot
220	200	425	7	Hot
230	210	450	8	Very hot
240	220	475	8	Very hot

Weight equivalents

Metric	Imperial	Metric	Imperial
7g	¼oz	350g	12oz
15g	½oz	375g	13oz
20g	¾oz	400g	14oz
25g	1oz	425g	15oz
40g	1½oz	450g	1lb
50g	2oz	500g	1lb 2oz
60g	2½oz	550g	1¼lb
75g	3oz	600g	1lb 5oz
100g	3½oz	650g	1lb 7oz
125g	4oz	675g	1½lb
140g	4½oz	700g	1lb 9oz
150g	5oz	750g	1lb 11oz
165g	5½oz	800g	1¾lb
175g	6oz	900g	2lb
200g	7oz	1kg	2¼lb
225g	8oz	1.5kg	3lb 6oz
250g	9oz	2kg	4½lb
275g	10oz	2.5kg	5½lb
300g	11oz	2.75kg	6lb

Volume equivalents

Metric	Imperial	US
25ml	1fl oz	
50ml	2fl oz	¼ cup
75ml	3fl oz	
100ml	3½fl oz	
120ml	4fl oz	½ cup
150ml	5fl oz	
175ml	6fl oz	¾ cup
200ml	7fl oz	
250ml	8fl oz	1 cup
300ml	½ pint	1¼ cups
360ml	12fl oz	1½ cups
400ml	14fl oz	
450ml	15fl oz	2 cups/1 pint
600ml	1 pint	2½ cups
750ml	1¼ pints	
900ml	1½ pints	
1 litre	1¾ pints	1 quart
1.2 litres	2 pints	
1.4 litres	2½ pints	
1.5 litres	2¾ pints	
1.7 litres	3 pints	
2 litres	3½ pints	
3 litres	5¼ pints	

Fridge and freezer storage guidelines

We suggest below recommended maximum storage times in the fridge and freezer for a variety of different raw and cooked foods. In the fridge, never allow raw and cooked meat to touch (ideally, keep them on separate shelves), and never store raw meat on a shelf above cooked meat or other ready-to-eat foods, as blood may drip down and contaminate them.

Remember, also, that to store food safely, non-frostfree freezers and fridge-freezer compartments need to be regularly defrosted. Check your freezer temperature – it should be around -18°C (-4°F).

Fridge and freezer storage guide

Food	Fridge	Freezer
Raw poultry, fish, and meat (small pieces)	2–3 days	3–6 months
Raw minced beef and poultry	1–2 days	3 months
Cooked whole roasts or whole poultry	2–3 days	9 months
Cooked poultry pieces	1–2 days	1 month (6 months in stock or gravy)
Bread		3 months
Ice cream		1–2 months
Soups and stews	2–3 days	1–3 months
Casseroles	2–3 days	2–4 weeks
Biscuits		6–8 months

Best cuts for fast cooking

Quick techniques and recipes are great when you're pushed for time, but in order to make the meat taste really good, you'll need to buy the right cuts. Choose any of the cuts given below to ensure the meat is tender and delicious no matter how quickly you cook it.

Beef

Sirloin Often sold as slices of meat, this cut is a large piece of meat taken from the middle of the animal's back, next to the fillet. A good piece of sirloin should have a visible marbling of fat, to give good flavour, and be almost as tender as a piece of fillet.

Rump A good value steak that has much more flavour than a fillet or sirloin as the muscle that it comes from works harder in the animal. This also means that it can be chewier, particularly if the meat has not been matured properly.

Fillet The most prized and expensive piece of meat on the animal. It is very tender as it is the least used muscle, but it doesn't have as much flavour as some other cuts, so be careful not to overcook it.

Rib eye A very popular steak in America. This is the trimmed fillet or eye of a forerib of beef, which is a classic roasting joint. It has lots of marbling, which gives it fantastic depth of flavour.

Lamb

Leg steaks These are slices of boned leg of lamb, ideal for frying and grilling.

Loin chops From the centre of a loin of lamb, these have a good layer of fat, making tender, tasty chops. The bone can make them a bit fiddly to eat.

Cutlets From the best end of lamb, otherwise known as a rack of lamb, the cutlets can be cut from the rack and pan-fried individually.

Pork

Chump chops Further down a whole loin of pork comes the chump end. Chops from here are the most generous as they are boneless and nice and lean.

Escalope The eye of a loin, trimmed, then sliced into rounds for quick frying.

Cubed loin Rather than a whole chop, the loin can be trimmed and diced for cooking in stir-fries and quick dishes.

Best cuts for slow cooking

Slow cooking is becoming more popular because the method is a convenient way of cooking less expensive cuts of meat to create dishes that offer superb depth of flavour. Here's a breakdown of which cuts are best.

Beef

Shn and leg Inexpensive cuts with bags of flavour, made up of very lean muscle.

Chuck and blade The best-known type of braising steak, and what most recipes mean when they call for this. A very tasty cut of beef that can be sliced or diced.

Middle ribs When boned and rolled, this is a beautiful joint for pot-roasting. It can also be sliced or diced for use in casseroles.

Brisket Because this comes from the belly of the animal this can sometimes be fatty, but this is what adds to the flavour of the stock during cooking. A cylindrical joint that gives nice neat slices when carved.

Short ribs Traditionally an American cut that is often called "oven-busters" over here, short ribs are becoming quite trendy. Slowly braised in wine or beer with vegetables and lots of aromatics, they become very tender and almost velvety in texture, with a fantastic flavour.

Minced neck and flank Mince made from the tougher cuts of meat is best used in dishes requiring slow cooking. Mince from a prime cut, such as tail of the fillet, is usually reserved for serving raw in dishes such as steak tartare.

Skirt Usually reserved for slow cooking in either steak and kidney pudding or Cornish pasties.

Silverside Neat, cylindrical joint, ideally suited to braising or pot-roasting.

Oxtail Tough off-cut of beef that requires long, slow cooking to become tender. Because it is a cut of meat still on the bone – and also comes with quite a lot of fat, cartilage and marrow – it contains a staggering amount of flavour. The cut to use for osso bucco.

Lamb

Scrag end This cut is tough and has less meat, but has bags of flavour. Excellent slow-cooked in soups and stews, either on or off the bone.

Middle neck or neck Can be cut into 2.5cm slices, and is traditionally used for slow-cooking on the bone in dishes such as Lancashire hot pot.

Neck fillets Although these are ideal for all methods of fast cooking, these also produce beautifully tender meat when slow-cooked.It also takes a lot less time to cook them in a stew – no more than 45 minutes.

Boned and diced shoulder or leg Both of these are perfect in stews or casseroles. Meat from the shoulder needs to be trimmed of excess fat first. The leg will give neater, leaner pieces of meat, but both are meltingly tender and packed with fantastic flavour.

Leg and shoulder joints Both great slow-roasted in a covered pan for hours, until the meat is literally falling off the bone.

Lamb shanks Lean, gelatinous, well-flavoured meat that is ideal for slow cooking, and produces melt-in-the-mouth results.

Chump Solid, lean, well-flavoured meat, that is great for dicing and long, slow cooking.

Breast Despite being quite a fatty cut, it can still be slow-cooked very successfully, and becomes wonderfully tender. Skim off any excess fat before serving

Pork

Spare rib and hand Both of these joints can be successfully braised. Brown them first to give some colour, then place on a bed of vegetables together with a little liquid, and cook in a covered casserole in the oven. Slow cooking will make the meat meltingly tender meat. Or dice for casseroles.

Loin As above. This method of cooking can also help keep what can be a slightly drier cut of meat nicely moist. This joint will also give much neater slices.

Chump end When diced, this is ideal for stews, curries and casseroles and tends to be more tender than leg.

Belly Although this is quite a fatty cut, it can still be very successfully slow-cooked. During cooking, the excess fat melts and rises to the surface, where it can be skimmed away before serving.

Tenderloin and leg Both of these cuts are commonly diced and used in casseroles and stews, as they provide lean, well-textured meat which retains its shape during cooking.

Roasting meat

Different cuts of meat require different temperatures and timings, so those specified below are intended only as a general guide. When calculating timings, add an extra 450g of weight to your joint if it weighs less than 1.35kg. Always preheat the oven before cooking your meat, and use a meat thermometer (inserted into the thickest part of the cut, away from any bones) for an accurate internal temperature. Allow the meat to rest for 15–30 minutes before carving to improve its texture.

| Heading | | | | |
Meat		Oven temperature	Cooking time	Internal temperature
Beef	Rare	180°C (350°F/ Gas 4)	15 mins per 450g	60°C (140°F)
	Medium	180°C (350°F/ Gas 4)	20 mins per 450g	70°C (160°F)
Veal	Well-done	180°C (350°F/ Gas 4)	25 mins per 450g	80°C (175°F)
Lamb	Well-done	180°C (350°F/ Gas 4)	25 mins per 450g	80°C (175°F)
	Medium	180°C (350°F/ Gas 4)	20 mins per 450g	70°C (160°F)
	Well-done	180°C (350°F/ Gas 4)	25 mins per 450g	85°C (175°F)

Roasting poultry

Use these times as a guide, bearing in mind the size and weight of each bird varies within the weights specified here. Preheat the oven before cooking your bird(s), and always check that the bird is fully cooked before serving.

| Heading | | | |
Meat		Oven temperature	Cooking time
Poussin		190°C (375°F/ Gas 5)	12 mins per 450g plus 12 mins
Chicken		200°C (400°F/ Gas 6)	20 mins per 450g plus 20 mins
Duck		180°C (350°F/ Gas 4)	20 mins per 450g plus 20 mins
Goose		180°C (350°F/ Gas 4)	20 mins per 450g plus 20 mins
Pheasant		200°C (400°F/ Gas 6)	50 mins total cooking
Turkey	3.5–4.5kg	190°C (375°F/ Gas 5)	2½–3 hrs total cooking
	5–6kg	190°C (375°F/ Gas 5)	3½–4 hrs total cooking
	6.5–8.5kg	190°C (375°F/ Gas 5)	4½–5 hrs total cooking

Boiling and steaming vegetables

This chart suggests times for boiling and steaming vegetables. Some people like vegetables to be fully done while others prefer some to be cooked al dente, so a range of timings is given. The range also covers differences that may result from the vegetable's age, size or variety. Whether you start in cold or boiling water, lower the heat when it reaches or returns to the boil. Then cover the pan if indicated. For perfect results, test doneness with the point of a sharp knife.

Delay the washing, peeling and cutting of vegetables until just before cooking, if you can, as exposure to air and moisture causes vegetables to deteriorate and lose their vitamins. If you have to prepare ahead, discoloration can be minimized by immersing cut vegetables in water to which lemon juice or vinegar has been added.

| Boiling and steaming vegetables | | | | |
| Vegetable | Boiling | | | Steaming |
	Time (in mins)	Cold/ boiling start	Cook covered?	Time (in mins)
Artickoke bottoms	20–30	Cold	No	15–20
Artichokes, whole	20–24	Cold	No	25–35
Artichokes, baby	15–18	Cold	No	15–20
Asparagus	3–4	Boiling	No	4–10
Beans, green	2–8	Boiling	No	5–12
Beetroot, whole	30–60	Cold	Yes	30–60
Broccoli florets	2–3	Boiling	No	5–10
Brussels sprouts	5–12	Boiling	No	10–15
Cabbage, quartered	5–15	Boiling	No	6–15
Cabbage, shredded	3–5	Boiling	No	5–10
Carrots, baby	3–4	Boiling	Yes	10
Carrots, sliced/ diced	5–10	Boiling	Yes	8–10
Cauliflower florets	2–3	Boiling	No	5–8
Cauliflower, whole	1—15	Boiling	No	15–20
Celeraiac, cubed/ wedges	8–10	Cold	No	8–10
Corn-on-the-cob	3–4	Boiling	No	6–10
Greens, heart, sliced	5–7	Boiling	No	10–12
Leeks, whole/halved	1—15	Boiling	No	12–15
Mangetouts	2–3	Boiling	No	5–10
Peas, fresh	3–5	Boiling	No	5–10
Potatoes, boiling/new	10–25	Cold	No	15–35
Potatoes, floury, cubed	15–20	Cold	No	15–35
Spinach	1–2	Boiling	No	3–4
Squashes, summer, sliced	5–8	Boiling	No	5–10
Squashes, winter, pieces	12–15	Boiling	Yes	15–30
Swede, thickly sliced	8–12	Cold	Yes	10–15
Sweet potatoes, cubed	15–35	Cold	Yes	30–45
Turnip, thickly sliced/ cubed sliced/cubed	8–12	Cold	Yes	10–15

Cooking and preparation methods for rice

There are more than 2,000 varieties of rice grown in over 110 countres around the world. Cooking and preparation methods vary; the main techniques are given below.

Boiling Boil the rice in 5–6 times its own volume in water at a rolling boil. Do not stir the rice as it boils because the cells in the grains will rupture, making the rice sticky.

Using the absorption method In this method, which is common in Asia, the rice can be cooked in a pan on the stovetop or in the oven. It depends on accurate propotions of rice and water (or stock) so careful measurement is a must. For long-grain white rice, the proportions are 450g rice to 600ml of water, but check the packet for instructions.
1. Put both rice and water into a large saucepan. Bring to the boil, stir once, then simmer for 10–12 minutes or until all the liquid is absorbed.
2. Cover the pan with a tea towel and a very tight fitting lid. Return to a very low heat and leave for 10 minutes.
3. Remove from the heat and leave undisturbed for a futher 5 minutes before serving.

Steaming This involves cooking the rice in a specialized steamer that has a lower compartment for the water and an upper compartment for the rice. Timing is important; overcooked steamed rice can be tasteless.

Making risotto and paella See pp.46 and 198.

Using a rice cooker This electric appliance is ideal for glutinous rice and requires a precise ratio of water to rice. Buy a good quality model and follow the manufacturer's instructions.

Washing Asian rice should be washed several times in cold water before cooking to help keep the grains separate. Western packaged rice will already have been washed thoroughly.

Soaking Most rice, with the exception of basmati and some wild rice, needs no soaking before cooking. Follow the instructions on the packet.

Toasting Some varieties of rice can be lightly toasted in oil or butter for 1–2 minutes before boiling, to enhance the flavour.

Preparation and cooking times for rice

Type of rice	Best for	Special preparation	Best cooking methods and approximate cooking times
Long-grain			
White and brown	Pilaffs, salads, stuffings, stir fries	Can be toasted	Absorption: 20 mins (white), 30–40 mins (brown); steam: 20 mins (white), 30–35 mins (brown)
Basmati (white and brown)	Indian pilaus, spicy Indian dishes	Soak for 30 mins; can be toasted	Absorption: 20–35 mins; boil: 20 mins (white), 40 mins (brown)
Short-grain			
Risotto (arborio, carnaroli, vialone nano)	Classic risottos	Can be toasted	Risotto method: 20–25 mins
Paella (Valencia, calaspara, granza)	Paella, other Spanish rice dishes	Can be toasted	Paella method: 20–25 mins
Pudding	Rice pudding, sweet dishes		Absorption (oven): 1–1¼ hours
Oriental			
Chinese black	Sweet and savoury dishes, rice dumplings	Soak overnight	Boil: 30–40 mins
Glutinous (sticky)	Sweet and savoury dishes, rice dumplings	Soak for 4 hours minimum	Absorption (rice cooker): 20 mins; steam: 15–20 mins
Jasmine (Thai fragrant)	Spicy Thai dishes, congees, stir-fries	Wash	Absorption (rice cooker): 25 mins; boil: 20–25 mins
Sushi	Sushi, sweet dishes	Wash	Absorption (rice cooker): 20 mins; boil: 20–25 mins
Specialist			
Red or Carmargue, Himalayan red	Stuffings, salads, pilaffs, stir fries	Soak for 1 hour; can be toasted	Boil: 40–60 mins
Wild	Stuffings, salads, pilaffs, stir fries		Boil: 40–60 mins

index

acknowledgements

Publisher's acknowledgements

DK would like to thank everyone at delicious., especially Matthew Drennan and Tanya Grossman. Thanks also to Jimmy Topham, Ross Hilton, Lucy Bannell and Alastair Laing for editorial work, Laura Mingozzi for design work, and Hilary Bird for the index.

Picture credits

(b) = bottom, (c) = centre, (l) = left, (r) =right, (t) = top.

2 Steve Baxter. 4–5 Janine Hosegood. 6 Steve Baxter (bl) (bc); Jonathan Gregson (br). 7 Steve Baxter (bl); Jean Cazals (bc); Kate Whitaker (br). 8–9 Craig Robertson. 10 Steve Baxter (tr). 11 Kate Whitaker (br). 13 Andrew Montgomery (c). 15 Craig Robertson (br). 17 Craig Robertson (tr) (br). 18 Claire Richardson (tl). 19 Steve Baxter (tr) (br). 21 Steve Baxter (tr); Claire Richardson (br). 22 Michael Paul (tl). 23 Richard Jung (c). 24 Steve Baxter (tl). 25 Craig Robertson (bc). 26 Steve Baxter (bc). 27 Craig Robertson (tr). 29 Lucinda Symons (tc). 30 Janine Hosegood (tl). 31 Craig Robertson (c). 33 Lucinda Symons (tr) (br). 35 Richard Jung (tr); Claire Richardson (br). 36 Steve Baxter (bc). 37 Rob White (tc). 38 Clive Streeter (tl); Lis Parsons (bl). 41 Steve Baxter (c). 43 Stuart West (tr); Craig Robertson (br). 44–45 Craig Robertson. 47 Rob White (tr); Philip Webb (br). 48 Peter Cassidy (bl). 49 Janine Hosegood (tr). 51 Lucinda Symons (c). 52 Stuart West (bc). 53 Gareth Morgans (tr). 54 Stuart West (tl). 55 Kate Whitaker (tr); Steve Baxter (br). 56 Clive Streeter (bl). 57 Lis Parsons (tc). 58 Steve Baxter (tl). 59 Craig Robertson (bc). 60 Stuart West (bl). 61 Stuart West (c). 63 Steve Baxter (tr); Lucinda Symons (br). 64 Claire Richardson (tl); Rob White (bl). 65 Philip Webb (br). 66 Maja Smend (bl). 67 Richard Jung (tc). 68 Peter Thiedeke (tl). 69 Steve Baxter (c). 70 Clive Streeter (tc). 73 Lis Parsons (c). 74 Craig Robertson (tc). 75 Richard Jung (bc). 76 Stuart West (tl) (bl). 78 Janine Hosegood (bl). 79 Rob White (tc). 80 Craig Robertson (tl); Lis Parsons (bl). 81 Emma Lee (bc). 82 Gareth Morgans (tl). 83 Steve Baxter (tc). 85 Stuart West (c). 86 Craig Robertson (tc). 87 Steve Baxter (tr); Stuart West (br). 88 Lucinda Symons (bl). 89 Philip Webb (tc). 90 Stuart West (tl); Lucinda Symons (bl). 93 Tara Fisher (c). 95 David Loftus (tc). 97 Steve Baxter (c). 98 Craig Robertson (bc). 99 Claire Richardson (tr). 101 Stuart West (c). 102 Peter Cassidy (tc). 104 Craig Robertson (tc). 105 Gareth Morgans (bc). 106 Craig Robertson (tl); Lis Parsons (bl). 109 Kate Whitaker (c). 110 Jonathan Gregson (tl). 111 Will Heap (tr); Steve Baxter (br). 112 Jonathan Gregson (bc). 113 Craig Robertson (tr). 114 Jonathan Gregson (bc). 115 Lis Parsons (tc). 117 Steve Baxter (c). 118 Steve Baxter (tl). 119 Steve Baxter (bc). 121 Craig Robertson (tr); Steve Baxter (br). 122 Craig Robertson (tc). 123 Craig Robertson (tc). 124 Emma Lee (tl); Jean Cazals (bl). 126 Lis Parsons (bl). 127 Karen Thomas (tr). 128 Rob White (c). 130 Michael Paul (bc). 131 Richard Jung (tr). 133 Lis Parsons (tr). 134 Peter Thiedeke (tc). 135 Steve Baxter (bc). 136 Tara Fisher (tl); Claire Richardson (bl). 139 Peter Thiedeke (c). 140 Gareth Morgans (tl). 141 Richard Jung (bc).

142 Craig Robertson (tc). 143 Lis Parsons (bc). 145 Gareth Morgans (c). 146 Lis Parsons (bc). 147 Craig Robertson (tr); Tara Fisher (br). 148 Steve Baxter (tc). 149 Gareth Morgans (bc). 150 Gareth Morgans (bl). 151 Lis Parsons (c). 152 Stuart West (tl); Steve Baxter (bl). 153 Lis Parsons (bc). 154 Kate Whitaker (tc). 155 Tara Fisher (tr); Will Heap (br). 157 Tara Fisher (c). 158 Jonathan Gregson (bc). 159 David Loftus (tr). 161 Steve Baxter (br). 162 Steve Baxter (tc). 163 Peter Cassidy/ Ewen Francis (bc). 164 Peter Cassidy/Ewen Francis (bc). 165 Peter Cassidy/Ewen Francis (tr). 167 Lis Parsons (tr); Jean Cazals (br). 169 Craig Robertson (c). 170–171 Lis Parsons. 173 Steve Baxter (tr); Peter Thiedeke (br). 174 Craig Robertson (tl); David Loftus (bl). 176 Kate Whitaker (tl). 179 Craig Robertson (tr); Jean Cazals (br). 181 Lucinda Symons (br). 182 Craig Robertson (bc). 183 Kate Whitaker (tc). 184 Lucinda Symons (tl). 185 Jonathan Gregson (c). 186 Jonathan Gregson (bl). 187 Lis Parsons (tr). 188 Craig Robertson (tr). 189 Craig Robertson (tc). 191 Craig Robertson (tr); Lucinda Symons (br). 193 Lucinda Symons (tr). 194 Peter Thiedeke (tl). 196 Steve Baxter (tl). 197 Malou Burger (br). 199 Jonathan Gregson (bc). 200 Tara Fisher (tl). 201 Lis Parsons (br). 203 Lucinda Symons (c). 205 Steve Baxter (tr). 206 Lis Parsons (tl). 209 Rob White (bc). 211 Tara Fisher (tr); Claire Richardson (br). 212 Tara Fisher (tl). 213 Tara Fisher (c). 214 Tara Fisher (tl). 215 Craig Robertson (tr) (br). 216 Steve Baxter (tl). 217 Craig Robertson (bc). 218 Gus Filgate (tl); Tara Fisher (bl). 219 Tara Fisher (br). 220 Tara Fisher (tl). 221 Steve Baxter (c). 223 Gareth Morgans (tr); Lis Parsons (br). 224 Lucinda Symons (tl); Stuart West (bl). 226 Emma Lee (bc). 229 Philip Webb (c). 230 Tara Fisher (bc). 231 Lis Parsons (br). 232 Steve Baxter (tl). 233 Steve Baxter (br). 234 Craig Robertson (tl). 235 Gareth Morgans (tc). 236 Lis Parsons (tc). 237 Craig Robertson (bc). 238–239 Rob White. 241 Lis Parsons (br). 242 Steve Lee (tl). 243 Steve Baxter (br). 245 Richard Jung (c). 246 Jonathan Gregson (tr). 247 Craig Robertson (bc). 248 Michael Paul (tl). 249 Deidre Rooney (bc). 251 Jean Cazals (tc). 253 Steve Baxter (c). 254 Lucinda Symons (tl). 257 Craig Robertson (tr); Peter Cassidy (br). 259 Kate Whitaker (c). 260 Craig Robertson (tc). 261 Yuki Sugiura (bc). 262 Rob White (tl). 263 Richard Jung (tc). 265 Claire Richardson (tr); Michael Paul (br). 266 Richard Jung (tc). 267 Steve Baxter (br). 268 Lucinda Symons (tl) (c) (cr) (bc). 269 Claire Richardson (bc). 270 Kate Whitaker (bc). 272 Nato Weltom (bc). 274 Jonathan Gregson (tc). 276 Jean Cazals (tl). 277 Claire Richardson (bc). 279 Claire Richardson (tr); Rob White (br). 281 Steve Lee (c). 282 Claire Richardson (tl). 283 Steve Baxter (bc). 285 Brett Stevens (c). 286 Michael Paul (tl). 287 Lucinda Symons (bc). 288–289 Stuart West.

Jacket images: Kate Whitaker (front), Steve Baxter (spine), Lis Parsons (back, left and second left), Craig Robertson (back, second right), Steve Lee (back right).

All other images © Dorling Kindersley. For further information visit www.dkimages.com